Mastering Akka

M000206063

Master the art of creating scalable, concurrent, and reactive applications using Akka

Christian Baxter

BIRMINGHAM - MUMBAI

Mastering Akka

First published: October 2016

Production reference: 1141016

Published by Packt Publishing Ltd.
Livery Place
35 Livery Street
Birmingham
B3 2PB, UK.
ISBN 978-1-78646-502-3

www.packtpub.com

Credits

Author

Christian Baxter

Reviewer

Dennis Vriend

Commissioning Editor

Kunal Parikh

Acquisition Editor

Dharmesh Parmar

Content Development Editor

Anish Sukumaran

Technical Editor

Sunith Shetty

Copy Editor

Zainab Bootwala

Project Coordinator

Suzanne Coutinho

Proofreader

Safis Editing

Indexer

Tejal Daruwale Soni

Graphics

Jason Monteiro

Production Coordinator

Melwyn Dsa

About the Author

Christian Baxter, from an early age, has always had an interest in understanding how things worked. Growing up, he loved challenges and liked to tinker with and fix things. This inquisitive nature was the driving force that eventually led him into computer programming. While his primary focus in college was life sciences, he always set aside time to study computers and to explore all aspects of computer programming. When he graduated from college during the height of the Internet boom, he taught himself the necessary skills to get a job as a programmer. He's been happily programming ever since, working across diverse industries such as insurance, travel, recruiting, and advertising. He loves building out high-performance distributed systems using Scala on the Akka platform.

Christian was a long time Java programmer before making the switch over to Scala in 2010. He was looking for new technologies to build out high throughput and asynchronous systems and loved what he saw from Scala and Akka. Since then, he's been a major advocate for Akka, getting multiple ad tech companies he's worked for to adopt it as a means of building out reactive applications. He's also been an occasional contributor to the Akka codebase, identifying and helping to fix issues. When he's not hacking away on Scala and Akka, you can usually find him answering questions on Stackoverflow as *cmbaxter*.

Acknowledgments

A lot went into the writing of this book, and not just from me. As such, I'd like to thank a few people, starting with the two special women in my life.

To my beautiful wife, Laurie. Thank you for being so patient throughout the writing of this book, and with me, in general. All this time, you've somehow been able to put up with all my quirks, which is a feat in and of itself. You've always believed in me, even if, at times, I didn't believe in myself. Thank you for always challenging me and never letting me be complacent. Without you, this book would have never been possible.

To my amazing mother, you taught me how to be a good person by instilling in me the values one needs to be successful in life. Your strength of character and resilience to life's challenges have served as inspirations to me. You've always been there for me, no matter how hard the times got. For this, I am eternally grateful.

Lastly, I'd like to thank my very first mentor, Dan Gallagher. I learned so much from you during our time together. Who knows how my career would have ended up if you weren't there in the beginning to screw my head on straight. I appreciate the enormous amount of patience that must have gone into dealing with me way back then. Thank you so much for starting my career down the right path to where I am today.

About the Reviewer

Dennis Vriend is a professional with more than 10 years of experience in programming for the Java Virtual Machine. Over the last 4 years, Dennis has been developing and designing fault tolerant, scalable, distributed, and highly performant systems using Scala, Akka, and Spark, and maintaining them across multiple servers. Dennis is active in the open source community and maintains two very successful Akka plugins—the akka-persistence-jdbc plugin and the akka-persistence-inmemory plugin—both useful to design and test state of the art business components leveraging domain-driven design and event sourcing in a distributed environment. Dennis is currently working as a software development engineer for Trivento in the Netherlands.

www.PacktPub.com

For support files and downloads related to your book, please visit www.PacktPub.com.

Did you know that Packt offers eBook versions of every book published, with PDF and ePub files available? You can upgrade to the eBook version at www.PacktPub.com and as a print book customer, you are entitled to a discount on the eBook copy. Get in touch with us at service@packtpub.com for more details.

At www.PacktPub.com, you can also read a collection of free technical articles, sign up for a range of free newsletters and receive exclusive discounts and offers on Packt books and eBooks.

https://www.packtpub.com/mapt

Get the most in-demand software skills with Mapt. Mapt gives you full access to all Packt books and video courses, as well as industry-leading tools to help you plan your personal development and advance your career.

Why subscribe?

- Fully searchable across every book published by Packt
- Copy and paste, print, and bookmark content
- On demand and accessible via a web browser

Table of Contents

Preface

The Akka library is well known in the Scala world for providing a means to build reactive applications. Akka's core building block is the Actor, which is a simple concurrency unit that allows you to build asynchronous, event driven, fault tolerant, and potentially distributed components on top of. Actors are an excellent starting point to build your reactive applications and services on top of, but there's a lot more within the entire Akka platform that you should be considering as well.

This book will provide the reader with a purpose-built tour through some of the additional modules within the Akka platform. The tour will be conducted by progressively refactoring an initial Akka application from an inflexible monolith all the way to a set of loosely coupled microservices. Along the way, you will learn how to apply new features, such as event sourcing via Akka Persistence, to the application in an effort to help it scale better. When the journey is complete, you will have a much better understanding of these additional offerings within the Akka platform and how they can help you build your applications and services.

Throughout the refactoring process, new concepts and libraries within Akka will be introduced to the reader on a chapter by chapter basis. Within those chapters, I will detail what each new feature is, and how that feature fits into breaking down a monolith into a set of loosely coupled services. Each chapter will also involve coding homework for the reader, giving them an active role in the progressive refactoring process. This hands-on experience will give the reader an immersive understanding of how to use these newer Akka features in the real-world code, which is the main goal of this book.

What this book covers

Chapter 1, *Building a Better Reactive App*, introduces you to the initial sample application and how it will be improved over the course of this book.

Chapter 2, *Simplifying Concurrent Programming with Actors*, is a refresher on Actors with some refactoring work using Akka's FSM.

Chapter 3, *Curing Anemic Models with Domain-Driven Design*, introduces you to domain-driven design (DDD) and how it helps in modeling and building software.

Chapter 4, *Making History with Event Sourcing*, presents Akka Persistence as a means to build event-sourced entities.

Chapter 5, *Separating Concerns with CQRS*, teaches you how to separate read and write models using the CQRS pattern.

Chapter 6, *Going with the Flow with Akka Streams*, explains how Akka Streams can be used to build back-pressure aware, stream-based processing components.

Chapter 7, *REST Easy with Akka HTTP*, shows you how to leverage Akka HTTP to build and consume RESTful interfaces.

Chapter 8, *Scaling Out with Akka Remoting/Clustering*, demonstrates how to use remoting and clustering to gain horizontal scalability and high availability.

Chapter 9, *Managing Deployments with ConductR*, illustrates building, deploying, and locating your microservices with ConductR.

Chapter 10, *Troubleshooting and Best Practices*, presents a few final tips and best practices for using Akka.

What you need for this book

You will need a computer (Windows or Mac OS X) with Java 8 installed on it. You will need to have Simple Build Tool (sbt) installed on that computer as well. This book also leverages Docker, with the installation of Docker being covered in more detail in Chapter 1, *Building a Better Reactive App*.

Who this book is for

If you want to use the Lightbend platform to create highly-performant reactive applications, then this book is for you. If you are a Scala developer looking for techniques to use all features of the new Akka release and want to incorporate these solutions in your current or new projects, then this book is for you. Expert Java developers who want to build scalable, concurrent, and reactive application will find this book helpful.

Conventions

In this book, you will find a number of text styles that distinguish between different kinds of information. Here are some examples of these styles and an explanation of their meaning.

Code words in text, database table names, folder names, filenames, file extensions, pathnames, dummy URLs, user input, and Twitter handles are shown as follows: "If you want to stop a Docker container, use the `docker stop` command, supplying the name of the container you want to stop."

A block of code is set as follows:

```
{
    "firstName": "Chris",
    "lastName": "Baxter",
    "email": "chris@masteringakka.com"
}
```

Any command-line input or output is written as follows:

```
docker-build.sh
```

New terms and **important words** are shown in bold. Words that you see on the screen, for example, in menus or dialog boxes, appear in the text like this: "Click the Docker whale icon in your system tray and select **Preferences** in the context menu that pops up."

> Warnings or important notes appear in a box like this.

> Tips and tricks appear like this.

Reader feedback

Feedback from our readers is always welcome. Let us know what you think about this book-what you liked or disliked. Reader feedback is important for us as it helps us develop titles that you will really get the most out of. To send us general feedback, simply e-mail feedback@packtpub.com, and mention the book's title in the subject of your message. If there is a topic that you have expertise in and you are interested in either writing or contributing to a book, see our author guide at www.packtpub.com/authors.

Customer support

Now that you are the proud owner of a Packt book, we have a number of things to help you to get the most from your purchase.

Downloading the example code

You can download the example code files for this book from your account at `http://www.packtpub.com`. If you purchased this book elsewhere, you can visit `http://www.packtpub.com/support` and register to have the files e-mailed directly to you.

You can download the code files by following these steps:

1. Log in or register to our website using your e-mail address and password.
2. Hover the mouse pointer on the **SUPPORT** tab at the top.
3. Click on **Code Downloads & Errata**.
4. Enter the name of the book in the **Search** box.
5. Select the book for which you're looking to download the code files.
6. Choose from the drop-down menu where you purchased this book from.
7. Click on **Code Download**.

Once the file is downloaded, please make sure that you unzip or extract the folder using the latest version of:

- WinRAR / 7-Zip for Windows
- Zipeg / iZip / UnRarX for Mac
- 7-Zip / PeaZip for Linux

The code bundle for the book is also hosted on GitHub at `https://github.com/PacktPublishing/Mastering-Akka`. We also have other code bundles from our rich catalog of books and videos available at `https://github.com/PacktPublishing/`. Check them out!

Downloading the color images of this book

We also provide you with a PDF file that has color images of the screenshots/diagrams used in this book. The color images will help you better understand the changes in the output. You can download this file from `https://www.packtpub.com/sites/default/files/downloads/MasteringAkka_ColorImages.pdf`.

Errata

Although we have taken every care to ensure the accuracy of our content, mistakes do happen. If you find a mistake in one of our books-maybe a mistake in the text or the code-we would be grateful if you could report this to us. By doing so, you can save other readers from frustration and help us improve subsequent versions of this book. If you find any errata, please report them by visiting http://www.packtpub.com/submit-errata, selecting your book, clicking on the **Errata Submission Form** link, and entering the details of your errata. Once your errata are verified, your submission will be accepted and the errata will be uploaded to our website or added to any list of existing errata under the Errata section of that title.

To view the previously submitted errata, go to https://www.packtpub.com/books/content/support and enter the name of the book in the search field. The required information will appear under the **Errata** section.

Piracy

Piracy of copyrighted material on the Internet is an ongoing problem across all media. At Packt, we take the protection of our copyright and licenses very seriously. If you come across any illegal copies of our works in any form on the Internet, please provide us with the location address or website name immediately so that we can pursue a remedy.

Please contact us at copyright@packtpub.com with a link to the suspected pirated material.

We appreciate your help in protecting our authors and our ability to bring you valuable content.

Questions

If you have a problem with any aspect of this book, you can contact us at questions@packtpub.com, and we will do our best to address the problem.

1

Building a Better Reactive App

This book is meant to be geared towards the more experienced Scala and Akka developers looking to build reactive applications on top of the Akka platform.

This book is written for an engineer who has already leveraged Akka in the 2.3.x series and below to build reactive applications. You have a firm understanding of the actor model and how the Akka framework leverages actors to build highly scalable, concurrent, asynchronous, event-driven, and fault-tolerant applications. You've seen the new changes rolled out in Akka 2.4.2 and are curious about how some of these new features such as Akka Streams and Akka HTTP can be leveraged within your reactive applications.

This book will serve as a guide for an engineer who wants to take a functional but flawed reactive application and, through a series of refactors, make improvements to it. It will help you understand what some of the common pitfalls are when building Akka applications. Throughout the various chapters in the book, you will learn how to use Akka and some of the newer features to address the following shortcomings:

- Building a more domain-centric model using domain-driven design
- Using event sourcing and Akka Persistence for high throughput persistence
- Understanding reactive streams and how Akka makes use of them in Akka Streams and Akka HTTP
- Decomposing a monolith into a set of fully decoupled and independent services

Understanding the initial example app

Imagine you woke up one morning and decided that you were going to take down the mighty Amazon.com. They've spread themselves too thin in trying to sell anything and everything the world has to offer. You see an opportunity back in their original space of online book selling and have started a company to challenge them in that area.

Over the past few months, you and your team of engineers have built out a simple **Minimum Viable Product (MVP)** reactive bookstore application build on top of the Akka 2.3.x series. As this is an MVP, it's pretty basic, but it has served its purpose of getting something to the market quickly to establish a user base and get good feedback to iterate on. The current application covers the following subdomains within the overall domain of a bookstore application:

- User management
- Book (inventory) management
- Credit card processing
- Sales order processing

The code that represents the initial application can be found in the `initial-example-app` folder within the code distribution for this book. The application is an sbt multi-project build with the following individual projects:

- **common**: Common utilities and a shared domain model
- **user-services**: User management related services
- **book-services**: Book management related services
- **credit-services**: Credit card processing services
- **sales-services**: Sales order processing services
- **server**: A single project that aggregates the individual service projects and contains a main method to launch the server

If you were to look at the different projects from a dependency view, they would look like this:

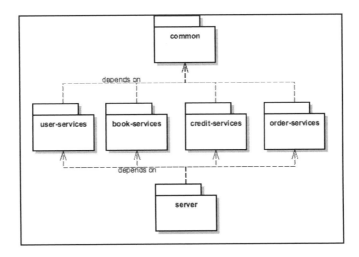

The individual services subprojects were set up to avoid any direct code dependencies to each other. If services in different modules need to communicate with each other, then they use the shared domain model (entities and messages) from the common project as the protocol. The initial intention was to allow each module to eventually be built and deployed independent of each other, even though currently it's built together and deployed as a monolith.

Each service module is made up of HTTP endpoint classes, services, and, in some cases, **Data Access Objects** (**DAOs**). The endpoint classes are built on top of the Unfiltered library and allow inbound, REST-oriented HTTP requests to be serviced asynchronously, using Netty under the hood. The service business logic is modeled using the actor model and implemented with Akka actors that are called from the endpoints. Service actors that need to talk to the relational Postgres db do so via DAOs that reside within the same `.scala` files as the services that use them. The DAOs use Lightbend's Slick library with the Plain SQL approach to talk to Postgres.

The way the application is currently structured, an inbound request that talks to the db would be handled as follows:

1. The HTTP request comes in and is handled by Netty's NIO channel handling code on top of its own thread pool.
2. Netty passes the code off to the Unfiltered framework for handling, still using Netty's thread pool.

3. Unfiltered looks up a service actor via actor selection and uses the ask pattern to send it a message, returning a Future that will hold the result of the service call.
4. The service actor that receives the message is running on the actor system's main Fork/Join thread pool.
5. The actor talks to the Postgres db via the Slick DAO. The SQL itself runs within Slick's `AsycExecutor` system, on top of another separate thread pool.
6. The actor sends a response back to the sender (the Future from the endpoint) using the pipe pattern.
7. The Future in the endpoint, which runs on the actor system's dispatcher, is completed, which results in a response being communicated through Unfiltered and Netty and then back into the wire.

As you can see from the preceding steps, there are a few different thread pools involved in the servicing of the request, but it's done completely asynchronously. The only real blocking done in this flow is the JDBC calls done via Slick (sadly, JDBC has yet to incorporate async calls into the API). Thankfully though, those blocking calls are isolated behind Slick's own thread pool.

If you've played with Akka long enough, you know it's taboo to block in the actor system's main Fork/Join pool. Akka is built around the concept of using very few threads to do a lot of work. If you start blocking the dispatcher threads themselves, then your actors can suffer from thread starvation and fall behind in the processing of their mailboxes. This will lead to higher latency in call times, upsetting end users, and nobody wins when that happens. We avoided such problems with this app, so we can pat ourselves on the back for that.

You should take a little time in going through the example code to understand how everything is wired together. Understanding this example app is critical as this serves as the foundation for our progressive refactoring. Spending a little time upfront getting familiar with things will help as different sections are discussed in the upcoming chapters.

The app itself is not perfect. It has intentional shortcomings to give us something to refactor. It was certainly beyond the scope of this book to have me build out a fully functioning, coherent, and production-ready storefront application. The code is just a medium in which to communicate some of the flawed ways in which an Akka reactive application could be put together. It was purposely built as a lead-in to discover some of the newer features in the Akka toolkit as a way to solve some common shortcomings. View it as such, with an open mind, and you will have already taken the first step in our refactoring journey.

Detailed steps to download the code bundle are mentioned in the Preface of this book. Please have a look. The code bundle for the book is also hosted on GitHub at `https://github.com/PacktPublishing/Mastering-Akka`. We also have other code bundles from our rich catalog of books and videos available at `https://github.com/PacktPublishing/`. Check them out!

Working with the example application

Now that you have an understanding of the initial code, we can build it and then get it up and running. It's assumed that you already have Scala and sbt installed. Assuming you have those two initial requirements installed, we can get started on getting the example app functional.

Setting up Docker

Throughout this book, we will be using Docker to handle setting up any additional applications (such as Postgres) and for running the bookstore application itself (within a container). For those unfamiliar with Docker, it is a containerization platform that will let you package and run your applications, ensuring that they run and behave the same no matter what the environment is that they are running on. This means that when you are testing things locally, on your Mac or Windows computer, the components will run and behave the same as when they eventually get deployed to whatever production environment you run (say some Linux distribution on Amazon's Elastic Compute Cloud). You package up all of the application components and their dependencies into a neat little container that can then be run anywhere Docker itself is running.

The decision to use Docker here should make set up simpler (as Docker will handle the majority of it). Also, you won't clutter up your computer with these applications as they will only run as Docker containers instead of being directly installed. When it comes to your Docker installation, you have two possible options:

- Install Docker Toolbox, which will install the docker engine, docker-machine and docker-compose, which are necessary for running the bookstore application.
- Install one of the native Docker apps (Docker for Windows or Docker for Mac), both of which will also work for running the bookstore application.

The biggest difference between these two options will be what local host address Docker uses when binding applications to ports. When using Docker Toolbox, docker-machine is used, which will by default bind applications to the local address of `192.168.99.100`. When using one of the native Docker apps, the loopback address of `127.0.0.1` (localhost) will be used instead.

If you already have Docker installed, then you can use that pre-existing installation. If you don't have Docker installed, and you are on a Mac, then please read through the link from below to help you decide between Docker for Mac and Docker Toolbox: `https://docs.docker.com/docker-for-mac/docker-toolbox/`.

For Windows users, you should check out the following link, reading through the section titled *What to know before you install*, to see if your computer can support the requirements of Docker for Windows. If so, then go ahead and install that flavor. If not, then callback to using Docker Toolbox: `https://docs.docker.com/docker-for-windows/`.

Adding the boot2docker hosts entry

Because we gave you a choice in which Docker flavor to run, and because each different flavor will bind to different local addresses, we need a consistent way to refer to the host address that is being used by Docker. The easiest way to do this is to add an entry to your hosts file, setting up an alias for a host called `boot2docker`. We can then use that alias going forward to when referring to the local Docker bind address, both in the scripts provided in the code content for this book and in any examples in the book content.

The entry we need to add to this file will be the same regardless of if you are on Windows or a Mac. This is the format of the entry that you will need to add to that file:

```
<docker_ip>        boot2docker
```

You will need to replace the `<docker_ip>` portion of that line with whatever local host your Docker install is using. So for example, if you installed the native Docker app, then the line would look like this:

```
127.0.0.1        boot2docker
```

And if you installed Docker Toolkit and are thus using docker-machine, then the line would look like this:

```
192.168.99.100   boot2docker
```

The location of that file will be different depending on if you are running Windows or are on a Mac. If you are on Windows, then the file an be found at the following location: `C:\Windows\System32\Drivers\etc\hosts`.

If you are running in a Mac, then the file can be found here: `/etc/hosts`.

Understanding the bookstore Postgres schema

The initial example app uses Postgres for its persistence needs. It's a good choice for a relational database as it's lightweight and fast (for a relational database at least). It also has fantastic support for JSON fields, so much so that people have been using it for a document store too.

We will use Docker to handle setting up Postgres locally for us, so no need to go out and install it yourself. There are also setup scripts provided as part of the code for this chapter that will handle setting up the schema and database tables that the bookstore application needs. I've included an ERD diagram of that schema below for reference as I feel it's important in understanding the table relationships between the entities for the initial version of the bookstore app.

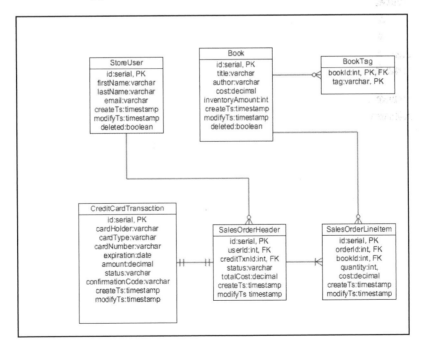

If you are interested in the script that was used to create the tables from this diagram, then you can find it in the `sql` directory under the `intial-example-app` root folder from the code distribution, in a file called `example-app.sql`.

Running bash scripts on Windows

If you are using a Mac, you can skip reading this section. It only pertains to running the `.sh` scripts used to start up the app on Windows.

As part of the code content for each chapter, there are some bash scripts that handle building and running the bookstore application. As bash is not native to the Windows operating system, you will have to decide how you want to build and start the bookstore application, choosing from one of the the following possibilities:

1. If you are using Git for Windows, then you have Git BASH installed locally and you should be able to use that tool to run these fairly simple scripts.
2. If you are on Windows 10, then you can use the new Windows Subsystem for Linux and install a bash shell. Check out this link for instructions: `http://www.howtogeek.com/249966/how-to-install-and-use-the-linux-bash-shell-on-windows-1`.
3. You can install cygwin.
4. As a last resort, if none of the above options work then you can look at the .sh files referenced and just run the commands (which are a mix of sbt and Docker commands) individually yourself. There's not a lot of them per file, so this is not a bad last resort.

Starting up the example application

Now that the database is up and running, we can get the Scala code built and then packaged into a Docker container (along with Java8 and Postgres, via docker-compose) so we can run and play with it locally. First, make sure that you have Docker up and running locally. If you are running one of the native Docker apps, then look for the whale in your system tray. If it's not there, then go and start it up and make sure it shows there before continuing. If you are running Docker Toolbox, then fire up the Docker Quickstart Terminal, which will start up a local docker-machine session within a terminal window with a whale as ASCII art at the top of it. Stay in that window for the remainder of the rest of the following commands as that's the only window where you can run Docker-related commands.

From a terminal window within the root of the `initial-example-app` folder run the following command to get the app all packaged up into a Docker container:

```
docker-build.sh
```

This script will instruct sbt to build and package the application. The script will then build a docker image, tag it and store it in the local docker repository. This script could take a while to run initially, as it will need to download a bunch of Docker-related dependencies, so be patient. Once that completes, you can then run the following command in that same terminal window:

```
launch.sh
```

This command will also take a while initially as it pulls down all of the components of our container, including Postgres. Once this command completes, you will have the bookstore initial example application container up and running locally, which you can verify by running the following command:

```
docker ps
```

That will print out a process list for the containers running under Docker. You should see two rows in that list, one for the bookstore and one for Postgres. If you want to log into Postgres via the **psql** client, to maybe look at the db before and after interacting with the app, then you can do so by executing the following command:

```
docker run -it --rm --network initialexampleapp_default postgres psql -h
postgres -U docker
```

When prompted for the password, enter `docker`. Once in the database, you can switch to the schema used by the example app by running the following command from within psql:

```
\c akkaexampleapp
```

From there, you can interact with any of the tables described in the ERD diagram shown earlier.

 If you want to stop a Docker container, use the `docker stop` command, supplying the name of the container you want to stop. Then, use the `docker rm` command to remove the stopped container or `docker restart` if you want to start it up again.

Interacting with the example application endpoints

Once the app is up and running, we can start interacting with its REST-like API in an effort to see what it can do. The interactions will be broken down by subdomain within the app (represented by the -services projects), detailing the capabilities of the endpoint(s) within that subdomain. We will use the `httpie` utility to execute our HTTP requests. Here are the installation instructions for each platform.

Installing httpie on Mac OS X

You can install `httpie` on your Mac via homebrew. The command to install is as follows:

```
$ brew install httpie
```

Installing httpie on Windows

The installation on Windows is going to be a bit more complicated as you will need Python, curl, and pip. The full instructions are too long to include directly in this book and can be found
at: http://jaspreetchahal.org/setting-up-httpie-and-curl-on-windows-environment/.

Interacting with the user endpoint

The first thing we can do when playing with the app's endpoints is to create a new `BookstoreUser` entity that will be stored in the `StoreUser` Postgres table. If you `cd` into the `json` folder under the `initial-example-app` root, there will be a `user.json` file that contains the following json object:

```
{
  "firstName": "Chris",
  "lastName": "Baxter",
  "email": "chris@masteringakka.com"
}
```

In order to create a user with these fields, you can execute the following `httpie` command when in the `json` folder:

```
http -v POST boot2docker:8080/api/user   < user.json
```

Here, you can see that we are making use of the hosts file alias we created in section *Adding the boot2docker hosts entry*. This let us make HTTP calls to the bookstore app container that is running in Docker regardless of what local address it is bound to.

The `-v` option supplied in that command will allow you to see the entire request that was sent (headers, body, path, and params), which can be helpful if it becomes necessary to debug issues. We won't supply this param on the remainder of the example requests, but you can if you feel you want to see the full request and response. The < symbol implies that we want to send the contents of the `user.json` file as the `POST` body. The resulting `user.json` will look like the following:

```
{
  "meta": {
    "statusCode": 200
  },
  "response": {
    "createTs": "2016-04-13T00:00:00.000Z",
    "deleted:":false,
    "email": "chris@masteringakka.com",
    "firstName": "Chris",
    "id": 1,
    "lastName": "Baxter",
    "modifyTs": "2016-04-13T00:00:00.000Z"
  }
}
```

This response structure is going to be the standard for endpoint responses. The `"meta"` section mirrors the HTTP status code and can optionally contain error information if the request was not successful. The `"response"` section will be there if the request was successful and can contain either a single object as JSON or an array of objects. Notice that the ID of the new user is also returned in case you want to look that user up later.

You should add a few more JSON files of your own to that directory representing more users to create and run the same command referenced earlier (albeit with a different file name) to create the additional users. If you happen to try and create a user with the same e-mail as an existing user, you will get an error.

If you want to view a user that you have created, as long as you know the ID, you can run the following command to do so, using user ID 1 as the example:

```
http boot2docker:8080/api/user/1
```

Notice on this request that we don't include an explicit HTTP request verb. That's because `httpie` assumes a `GET` request if you do not include a verb.

You can also look up a user by e-mail address with the following request:

```
http boot2docker:8080/api/user email==chris@masteringakka.com
```

The `httpie` client uses the `param==value convention` to supply query params for requests. In this example, the query string would be: `?email=chris%40masteringakka.com`.

You can make changes to a user's basic info (`firstName`, `lastName`, `email`) by executing the following command:

```
http PUT boot2docker:8080/api/user/1 < user-edit.json
```

The included `user-edit.json` file contains a set of request json to change the initially created user's e-mail address. As with the creation, if you pick an e-mail here that is already in use by another user, you will get an error.

If at any time you decide you want to delete a user, you can do so with the following request, using user ID 1 as the example:

```
http DELETE boot2docker:8080/api/user/1
```

This will perform a soft delete against the database, so the record will still exist but it won't come back on lookups anymore.

Interacting with the Book endpoint

The Book endpoint is for taking actions against the `Book` entity. Books are what are added to sales orders, so in order to test sales orders, we will need to create a few books first. To create a Book, you can run the following command:

```
http POST boot2docker:8080/api/book < book.json
```

As with the `BookstoreUser` entity, you should create a few more `book.json` files of your own and run the command to create those books too. Once you are satisfied, you can view a book that you have created by running the following command (using book ID 1 as the example):

```
http boot2docker:8080/api/book/1
```

Books support the concept of **tags**. These tags represent categories that the book is associated with. For example, the `20000 Leagues Under the Sea book` that is represented in the `book.json` file is initially tagged as `fiction` and `sci-fi`. The Book endpoint allows you to add additional tags to the book, and it also allows you to remove a tag. Adding the tag `ocean` to book ID 1 can be done with the following command:

```
http PUT boot2docker:8080/api/book/1/tag/ocean
```

If you decide that you would like to remove that tag, then you can execute the following command to do so:

```
http DELETE boot2docker:8080/api/book/1/tag/ocean
```

If you want to look up books that match a set of input tags, you can run the following command:

```
http boot2docker:8080/api/book tag==fiction
```

This endpoint request supports supplying the tag param multiple times. The query on the backend uses an AND condition across all of the tags supplied, so if you supply multiple tags, then the books that match must have each of the tags supplied. An example of supplying multiple tags would be as follows:

```
http boot2docker:8080/api/book tag==fiction tag==scifi
```

You can also look up a book by author by executing a request like this:

```
http boot2docker:8080/api/book author==Verne
```

This request supports partial matching on the author, so you don't have to supply the complete author name to get matches.

The last concept that we can test out related to book management is allocating inventory to the book once it's been created. Books get created initially with a inventory amount. If a book does not have any available inventory, it can not be included on any sale orders. Since not being able to sell books would be bad for business, we need the ability to allocate available inventory for a book in the system.

To indicate that we have five copies of book ID 1 in stock, the request would be as follows:

```
http PUT boot2docker:8080/api/book/1/inventory/5
```

Like the `BookstoreUser` entity, you can also perform a soft delete for a book. You can do so by executing the following request, using book ID 1 as the example:

```
http DELETE boot2docker:8080/api/book/1
```

Now that we have users and books created and we have a book with inventory, we can move on to pushing sales orders through the system.

Interacting with the Order endpoint

If you want to run a profitable business, at some point, you need to start taking in money. For our bookstore app, this is done by accepting sales orders for the books that we are keeping in inventory. All of the playing with the user and book-related endpoints was done so that we could create SalesOrder entities in the system. A SalesOrder is tied to a BookstoreUser (by user ID) and has *1-n* line items, each for a book (by book ID).

The request to create a SalesOrder also contains the credit card info so that we can first charge that card, which is where our money will come from. In the OrderManager code, before moving forward with creating the order, we first call over to the CreditCardTransactionHandler service to charge the card and keep a persistent record of the transaction. As we don't actually own the logic for charging the card ourselves, we call out over HTTP to a fake third-party service (implemented in PretentCreditCardService in the server project) to simulate this interaction.

Within the JSON directory, there is an order.json file that has the valid JSON in it for creating a new SalesOrder within the system. This file assumes that we have already created a BookstoreUser with ID of 1 and a book with an ID of 1, and we have added inventory to that book, which we did in the previous two sections. To create the new order, execute the following command:

```
http POST :8080/api/order < order.json
```

As long as the userId supplied and bookId supplied exist and that Book has inventory available, then the order should be successfully created. Each SalesOrderLineItem will draw down inventory (atomically) for the book that item is for in the amount tied to the quantity input for that line item. If you run that same command enough times, you should eventually exhaust all of the available inventory on that book, and you should start getting errors on the creation. This can be fixed by adding more inventory back on the book.

If you want to view a previously created SalesOrder, as long as you know the ID (which is returned in the create response JSON), then you can make the following request (using order ID 1 as the example):

```
http boot2docker:8080/api/order/1
```

If you want to lookup all of the orders for a particular user ID, then you can execute the following request:

```
http boot2docker:8080/api/order userId==1
```

The `Order` endpoint also supports looking up `SalesOrders` that contains a line item for a particular book by its ID value. Using book ID 1 as the example, that request looks like this:

```
http boot2docker:8080/api/order bookId==1
```

Lastly, you can also look up `SalesOrders` that have line items for books with a particular tag. That kind of request, using `fiction` as the tag, would be as follows:

```
http boot2docker:8080/api/order bookTag==fiction
```

Unlike the search books by tag functionality, this request only supports supplying a single `bookTag` param.

So what's wrong with this application?

By this point, you've had some time to interact with the example app to see what it can do. You've also looked at the code enough to see how everything is coded. In fact, maybe you've coded something similar to this yourself when building reactive apps on top of Akka. So now, the million dollar question is, "What's actually wrong with this app?"

The short answer is probably nothing. Wrong is a very black and white word, and when it comes to coding and application design, you're dealing more with shades of gray. This app may suit some needs perfectly well. For example, if high scalability is not a concern, you have a small development team and/or if the app's functionality doesn't need to expand much more.

This wouldn't be much of a book if we left it at that though. The long answer is that while nothing is absolutely wrong, there is a lot that we can improve upon to help our app and team continue to grow and scale. I'll break down some of the areas that I think can be made better in the following sections. This will help serve as a primer for some of the refactors that we will do in the upcoming chapters.

Understanding the meanings of scalability

To me, scalability is a nebulous term. I think a lot of people, when they hear scalability, immediately begin to think of things such as performance, throughput, queries per second, and the likes. These types of areas address the runtime characteristics of whatever application you have deployed. This is certainly a big aspect of the scalability umbrella and very important to your app's growth, but it's not the only thing you should be thinking of.

Another key area of scalability, that I think of when discussing the topic, is how well your application codebase will scale to the growth of both in-app functionality and to the growth of the development team. When your team is small (like me as the single developer of this example app) and the feature set of the application is minimal (again, like this example app), then codebase scalability is probably not the first thing on your mind. However, if you expect your company to be successful and grow, then your codebase needs to grow along with it; or else you run the risk of becoming impediment to the business as opposed to an enabler of the business. Therefore, there are some decisions that you can make earlier on in the growth process to help enable the codebase to scale with the growth of the business and development team.

There's a lot to discuss related to these two areas of application scalability, and we will break them down in more detail in the subsequent sections.

The scalability cube

If you haven't encountered Martin L. Abbot and Michael T. Fisher's excellent book, *The Art of Scalability*, then you should give it a look some time. This book covers all aspects of scaling a business and the technology that goes along with it. In many a meeting, I've referenced materials from this book when discussing how to architect software components. There's a ton of valuable lessons in here for beginners all the way up to the more seasoned technologists.

In the book, the authors discuss the concept of the the *Three Dimensions of Scalability* for a running application. Those dimensions are represented in the following diagram of the cube:

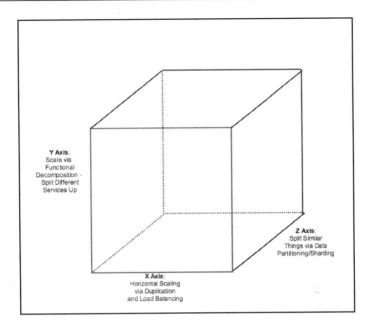

X axis scaling

The X axis scaling is the one that most people are familiar with. You run multiple copies of the application code on different servers and put a load balancer in front to partition inbound traffic. This kind of scaling gives you high availability, in that, if one server dies, the app can still serve traffic as the load balancer will redirect that traffic to the other nodes. This technique also gives your better per-node throughput as each node is only handling a percentage of the traffic. If you see your nodes are struggling to handle the current traffic rate, simply add another node to ease the burden a little on the existing nodes.

This is the kind of scaling that a monolith, like the example app, is most likely to use. It's pretty simple to keep scaling out by just adding more application nodes, but it seems a little inefficient in terms of resource usage. For example, if in your monolith, it's really only one of the services that is receiving the bulk of the additional load, you still need to deploy every other service into the new server even though they do not need the additional headroom.

In this kind of deployment, your services can't really have their own individual scaling profile. They are all scaling out together because they are co-deployed in a monolith. When you are sizing out the new instance node to deploy into in terms of CPU and RAM, you are stuck with a more generic profile as this node will handle traffic for all of the services. If certain services were more CPU heavy and others were more RAM heavy, you end up having to pick a node that has both a lot of RAM and a high number of CPUs as opposed to being able to choose between either one. These kinds of decisions can be cost prohibitive in the cloud-based world where changes in either of those two areas cost more money and more do when they need to be coupled together.

Microservices and Y axis scaling

The Y axis scaling approach addresses this exact kind of problem. With y axis scaling, you break up the application around functional boundaries and then deploy these different functional areas separately and independent of one another. This way, if functional area A needs high CPU and functional area B needs high RAM, you can select individual node instances that are the best suited to those needs. In addition, if functional area A receives the bulk of the traffic, then you can increase the number of nodes that handle that area without having to do the same thing for functional areas that receive less traffic.

If you've heard of the Microservices approach to building software (and it would be hard not to have, given how much technical literature on the Web is dedicated to it), then you are familiar with an example of using Y axis scaling to build software. This kind of approach achieves the goal of small independent services that can scale independent of each other, but it comes with additional complexity around the deployment and management of those components. In a simple monolithic, X axis style deployment, you know that every component is on every node, so the load balancer can send traffic to any of the available nodes.

In a Microservice deployment, you need to know where in the node set service A lives (and it should be in multiple nodes to give high availability) so that you can route traffic accordingly. This service location concern complicates these kinds of deployments and can involve bringing in another moving part (software component) to handle it, which further increases the complexity. Many times though, the benefits gained from decoupled, independent services outweigh these additional complexities enough to make this kind of approach worth pursuing.

Z axis scaling

In Z axis scaling, you take the same component and duplicate it across an entire set of nodes, but you make each node responsible for only a subset of the requests or data. This is commonly referred to as sharding, and it is quite often seen in database-related technologies. If you are running in-memory caching on the nodes, then this kind of approach eliminates duplicate cached data in each node (which can occur with X axis scaling). Only the node responsible for each data set (defined by your partitioning scheme) will receive traffic for that data.

When using Akka Cluster Sharding, you can be sure only one actor instance is receiving requests for a particular entity or piece of data, and this is an example of z axis scaling.

Monolith versus microservices

Our initial example app is a monolith, and even though that approach now carries negative connotations, it's not necessarily a bad thing. When starting out on a new application, a **monolith-first** kind of approach may actually be the right choice. It's simpler to code, build, deploy, and deal with when it's in production as opposed to a more sophisticated (but complicated) microservices deployment. Sometimes, trying to start out with something like microservices can lead to the team and application collapsing under the weight of the additional complexity of that pattern.

Within an Agile development approach, getting the software in the hands of users quickly so you can get feedback and iterate further is going to be way more important then having a fancy, new fangled architecture. The product team is not going to want to hear that they have deployment impediments, because you still can't figure out how to get all of your decoupled services to communicate together. At the end of the day, as an engineer, you're there to build and deploy a product. If your initial architecture prevents doing this easily, then it will be hard for you and your business to be successful.

In the beginning stages of a new business, it's important to be able to iterate and change features easily in response to feedback. Take too long (due to a complicated initial architecture) and you risk being passed by a competitor, or dropped by those very users who provided that valuable feedback. That's why it's not necessarily bad to start out with something like a monolith. It's simple to deploy and scale initially with an Xx axis style approach, and that can suit most needs just fine in the beginning.

Scale issues with our monolith

In the case of our bookstore application, we followed the more simple monolith-first approach, but now, the rubber is finally hitting the road. We have traction with users. Our product feature set is growing and so is the team and the complexity of the application. Our monolith is starting to become an impediment to our agility and that's going to be a problem. Because of this, we are going to embrace the microservices style of small, independent, decoupled services. The subsections to follow will detail how we arrived at this decision.

Issues with the size of deployments

Currently, we need to build and deploy the entire codebase even if we are touching a single line within a single service. The less code you have to deploy, the less risky the deployment is. Also, as the monolith continues to grow, so does the build and test cycle associated with it. If all you have to do is change a single line buried deep down within a service, but the ensuing build and test cycle takes 30 minutes because it's rebuilding everything, this will eventually become a problem. If you have an issue in production and need to get a hotfix out as soon as possible, you don't want this monolith-side effect to get in the way of that. This is where a microservices-like approach will help alleviate that problem.

Supporting different runtime characteristics of services

Now that our app has been in production for a while, we are starting to better understand the runtime usage patterns of our different sets of services. We know which services are being hit the most in the normal app flows, and we would like to be able to have more instances of these critical services available compared to other less important services. Our current monolith does not support us in doing this, but switching to a microservices-like system will enable it.

The pain of a shared domain model

The shared domain model in the app (in the common project) is going to be an issue when it comes to isolating the deployments. Changes to this shared model will necessitate full deployments, and that will prevent our goal of smaller isolated deployments. When we initially designed the example app structure, we thought we were being forward looking in separating services into different projects and then allowing them to communicate via the shared domain model. We eventually wanted to package and deploy these projects separately, but now, in hindsight, the shared domain model is actually going to make this harder as opposed to enabling it to happen.

If we do end up packaging and separating the services fully for deployments, each one will have to have a copy of the shared domain library code available to it at runtime in order to run. If we change the domain model and then only deploy one of the services, you run the risk of having issues when that service communicates with another service that was not rebuilt and redeployed after the model change.

If we had decided to use Akka remoting to handle remote communication between actor services, then we could run into issues with Java serialization when deserializing the messages and result types exchanged by the services.

We could work around this by using a different serialization scheme (such as **protobuf**), but this is certainly more work, and there are more flexible ways to communicate between our services.

We should try and decouple our components and modules as much as possible. We need an approach that allows them to communicate indirectly, outside of the normal request/response cycle of a user interaction with the application. This most likely means some form of event based interaction between our modules, with schemas and versioning for those events, so that other modules can consume them safely even as the model continues to evolve.

We can fall back on direct communication over HTTP (with versioning of endpoints), if necessary to support some interactions. We should only use that as a last resort though if an indirect approach just won't fit a certain situation well enough. Direct communications like this create the kind of coupling that we are trying to avoid, so they should used sparingly.

Issues with our relational database usage

When we built out our bookstore application, the team decided to use a relational database to store data, selecting Postgres as one to use. As far as relational databases go, Postgres is a solid choice. As I mentioned earlier, it's fast and has a lot of great additional features such as JSON column type support. But now that we are moving towards a microservices approach, is it going to still be the right choice for our application? I see the following shortcomings with our current usage of Postgres that will likely lead to us moving away from it as we evolve our application.

Sharing the same schema across all services

The Microservices approach promotes the shared nothing model of software development. This means that each microservice should not share any of its code models or database schemas with any other component in the system. Sharing creates coupling and we are trying to decouple or components as much as possible. If you try and have fully decoupled services, but they end up sharing a single database and schema underneath them, then you're going to end up in trouble pretty quickly. If you make a change to the schema, it's highly possible that change is going to ripple through multiple services, causing you to have to recode and redeploy more than you intended. When this happens, you're right back to where you were with your monolith and don't actually have service independence.

A traditional relational database model is designed around having a highly related and normalized model that will span all subdomains within your business. You will more than likely have database entities from one subdomain related (via foreign key) to an entity from another subdomain. We see it in the example app's schema where we have foreign keys from `SalesOrderHeader` to `StoreUser` and from `SalesOrderLineItem` to `Book`. These cross-subdomain relationships will end up causing problems if we are trying to do a share nothing microservices type model. If we are going to go down this path, then we will need to consider alternatives to a relational model.

Fixing a single point of failure

When building out complex systems, you are only ever as strong as your weakest link. In our current application, that weak link is our Postgres database because it's not highly available; in fact, it's a single point of failure.

With our current deployment model, the app itself is highly available because we have duplicated it across a set of nodes and put a load balancer in front (X axis scaling). We can survive the failure of a node because we have others that can pick up the slack for it until we get it back online. Unfortunately, we cannot say the same for Postgres. Currently, we are only rolling out a single Postgres instance, and so, if that goes down, it's game over for our application.

Postgres certainly supports techniques to eliminate it being a single point of failure. You can start by setting it up with a node as a hot standby using log shipping. In the case of a failure in the master, you can cut over to the secondary node with only minimal data loss. You can't write to that secondary node (it's master/slave, not master/master). However, if you put a little work into your application layer, you could leverage that secondary for reads and ease the burden on the master node a little as long as you can deal with potential replication lag (stale data) when performing reads.

This kind of model is better than the single point of failure we had before, but it still seems prone to the database itself having to deal with a lot of activity as our user base grows, especially the master node. We need to make sure we size that instance correctly (vertically scaled) to allow it to handle the load we expect to happen as our user base grows.

We could try and ease this burden by sharding (Zz axis scaling) the data in Postgres, but as this is not natively supported, we would need to roll out our own solution. If we distribute the data to a bunch of Postgres instances, we can no longer rely on the auto-generated keys in the tables to be globally unique across all of the database nodes. Because of this, we would have to do something like generating the keys in the application layer (as GUIDs perhaps) as opposed to letting the database generate them. We would then have to write our own shard-routing logic in the application layer to consistently hash the key to determine which node to store it or retrieve it from. In addition, for queries that look up more than one record, we would have to write out our own logic to distribute that query across all shards (a global query) as the matching records will likely be in multiple shards.

A custom sharding solution like this could certainly work, but this seems like a lot more complexity being put on our code base. If we don't get this shard routing logic right, then the consequences are pretty bad as we could miss data, and the app will act as if it didn't exist even though it might. There must be something we can more easily do to give us high availability and avoid having all of the data stored in one single location.

Avoiding cross-domain transactions

Another potential problem that has crept up with our usage of a relational database is that we are performing a database transaction that crosses service-domain boundaries. You can see this transaction within the `OrderManager` service when it's creating a new `SalesOrder`. If you look at the code in the DAO class, you can see these three steps being executed in a single transaction:

1. Insert the `SalesOrderHeader` record.
2. Insert each `SalesOrderLineItem` record for the order.
3. For each book (on each line item), decrement the inventory for that book.

We coded this using a transaction because we felt it was required to have strong consistency between the number of sales for a book and the remaining inventory for that book. The code does check to make sure that the inventory is available before attempting to write to the database, but that inventory could be sold out from underneath us after we checked it and before we commit it.

The statement to decrement inventory uses an optimistic concurrency-checking technique to ensure this does not happen. That statement looks like this:

```
update Book set inventoryAmount = inventoryAmount - $ {item.quantity}
where id = ${item.bookId} and inventoryAmount >=  ${item.quantity}
```

The key there is the `where` clause, where we are checking to make sure that the row we are about to apply our atomic decrement to still has at least the quantity we plan on deducting from it. If it doesn't, then our code fails the transaction explicitly by applying a filter on the result, making sure the number of rows updated is 1 and not 0. The code that handles that responsibility is as follows:

```
insert.
andThen(decrementInv).
filter(_ == 1)
```

This is all coded soundly and works as expected, but is this the best way that we can be handling the requirement of keeping inventory aligned with sales quantities?

I think the main issue here is the fact that we are executing a transaction that really spans two separate subdomains within our application; sales order processing and inventory management. We did this because we thought that the strong consistency gained from an **atomicity, consistency, isolation, and durability (ACID)** transaction was the only way to make this work properly. The problem with this approach though is that it's not going to scale, both from a performance perspective and from a code design and deployment perspective.

These kinds of ACID transactions are heavy weight for the database and can start to cripple it if they are happening at a high frequency. We obviously expect and want sales to be happening at a very high frequency, so there's a clear conflict of interest here. Also, currently, we are sort of benefitting from the fact that there is a shared single database under the app. What if we decided to keep using a relational database, but separated it out so that each service had its own schema or db instance? How would we make something like this multitable, cross-domain transaction work then?

If we were faced with such a problem, we'd probably need to look into getting distributed transactions (XA transactions) working across the different databases, and that's not a good direction to be forced into. While it would allow us to keep our strong consistency guarantees and ACID compliance, XA transactions can be initially difficult to set up and get working correctly in your code. In addition, they are a big performance drain, as the two-phase commit involves longer lock durations than the same transaction would in a local only mode, also increasing the possibility of deadlocks. Distributed transactions are also tied to the availability of multiple systems (databases in our case), so if either of those systems is not available, you cannot proceed with your transaction.

So, we need to be able to support high throughput handling of sales orders while at the same time be able to properly keep inventory in sync with the sales of our books. Also, we want to avoid crossing over into another domain's responsibility when processing that sales order. There must be a technique that will allow us to do this and fit well into our proposed microservices model for developing our services.

Understanding the CAP theorem

When designing the way sales orders were handled, we were sure that ACID level consistency was the proper way to handle things. Now that we are faced with the issues discussed in the previous section, that decision is starting to look more like a problem than a solution. We do want some level of consistency in the data, but strong consistency is not the only game in town, and there is another model that can help us avoid being burned by ACID.

We also have realized that our current Postgres deployment sets the db up as a single point of failure. Ideally, we need to embrace a model where the data is distributed across a set of nodes (with replication) so that we can get both high availability and be able to deal with the temporary loss of a node within that cluster.

The CAP theorem, also known as Brewer's theorem after the University of California Berkley computer scientist Eric Brewer, is a way to think about consistency guarantees within a distributed system. The theorem states that it's not possible for a distributed system to supply all three of the following simultaneously:

- **Consistency**: Do all my nodes see (on a read) the same exact data after a write has occurred?
- **Availability**: Do all my requests get a response?
- **Partition tolerance**: Will my system continue to operate in the face of arbitrary loss of parts of the system?

We all want a system that is consistent, highly available, and has partition failure tolerance, but this theorem states that the best you can do is two out of the three. There are a few databases out there now that can give us high availability and partition tolerance, sacrificing strong consistence for an eventually consistent model instead. These kinds of databases do not support the atomic, consistent, isolated, and durable guarantees that an ACID compliant database will give you. Instead, these databases give you guarantees of basically available, soft state, eventually consistent, or BASE.

It's a bit of a mental shift to embrace this new model of eventual consistency, but the tradeoff of a highly available system with partition failure tolerance can mitigate that change. We need to find a database that fits in this space as that will best support our shift to a share nothing microservices like model.

Cassandra to the rescue

Apache's Cassandra is a distributed key/value document store that also supports queries of that data using secondary indexes. From the CAP theorem, Cassandra's model gives you both high availability and partition tolerance. Cassandra achieves this by having a cluster of nodes where a specific range of keys is assigned to multiple nodes in the cluster. This way, if you need to look up a key, there will be multiple possible nodes that the request could be serviced by. If one of the nodes goes down, then you will still be able to have that request serviced by another cluster member that also handles that range of keys.

The thing to be careful of in Cassandra is that the data in the cluster is only eventually consistent. If nodes A, D, and F in my cluster house the key **foo**, and I update that key in node A, and then I read it again, and the read goes to node D, it's not guaranteed yet that my update has been received by that node D, which can lead to a stale read. Cassandra offers the ability to tune the consistency model to make it more consistent, but this comes at the price of latency, so be careful if you decide to go this route.

So, how can we apply Cassandra and its model to our initial cross-domain transaction problem? Well, we could use Akka Persistence (which works with Cassandra) to first write the `SalesOrder` into the system in an event-sourced manner, with an initial status of pending as it's awaiting inventory allocation. The `Book` subsystem could be listening on the event stream for `SalesOrder` activity, and when it sees a new one, it can see what books and quantities are on it and reserve inventory for it (if available), resulting in a new `InventoryReserved` event for that `SalesOrder` ID. The `Order` subsystem is in turn listening on the event stream for inventory-related activity and will update its status to approved and start the process of packing and shipping the order once it sees that inventory is available.

So, using Cassandra here, we get a database that is very fast in writing `SalesOrder` into the system. It's also a database that is highly available and can handle node failure, which are guarantees that our current Postgres database can't make. Then, leveraging Akka Persistence and using an event-sourced model on top of Cassandra, we can use an eventually consistent approach to get the `SalesOrder` and book inventory systems working together.

This approach eliminates direct interaction between those services and also does away with that nasty cross-domain transaction. It allows us to better scale the runtime performance of the app and the codebase itself, which are both big wins for the future health of our app.

Assessing the application's domain model

If you have looked at the example app's code, you have probably seen the following structure related to entities and services:

- Entities (such as `Book`, `BookstoreUser`, and `SalesOrder`) are modeled as very simple case classes without any business logic
- Services (ending with the `*Manager` suffix) are set up to handle the business logic for those entities

This is a common paradigm seen in software development, so it's not like we were going off the rails with this approach. It's pretty simple to develop and understand, and can be a good approach to use when your problem domain and codebase are small and simple. The only problem is that its modeling of our problem domain is not entirely representative of how things work in the real world of book sales. In fact, models like this have been referred to as being anemic, in that, they only weakly resemble the problem domain they are trying to represent.

The **domain-driven design** (**DDD**) is a newer approach to software modeling that aims to have a more representative modeling of software components. The term was coined by Eric Evans in his book of the same name. The goal of a DDD approach is to model the software components after representations within the domain. These domain representations will encapsulate the business logic and functions of those business entities entirely. In doing so, you have the business entities in your system that are much richer representations of their real-life counterparts.

In our current example app, this means something such as `Book`, which is a very simple case class, becomes an actor that accepts messages that allow you to do things to that book as part of the user interactions with our app. The DDD approach has its own set of building blocks, such as aggregates and bounded contexts, that we can use to remodel our current app into something that better represents the business domain.

This kind of approach is a bit more complex than the simpler model the app currently uses. Its true benefit is realized within complex business domains as the one-to-one relationship between the software and the domain concepts eases the development burden of that complex domain. This is a bit of a stretch for the relatively simple mode in our example app, but we're going to give it a shot anyway as part of one of our refactors. At the very least, we can explore a different way of modeling software, one that might really benefit our app if it starts to get more complex in what it's doing.

Recognizing poorly written actors

If you happened to look at the logic within the `SalesOrderManager` actor, you will notice a fairly complicated actor, at least in terms of the other actors in this app. This actor needs to work with a bunch of the other services in the app to first gather some data (to perform validations) before it talks to the database to create the order. The bulk of the work is laid out in the `createOrder` method and is as follows:

```
val bookMgrFut = lookup(BookMgrName)
val userMgrFut = lookup(UserManagerName)
val creditMgrFut = lookup(CreditHandlerName)
for{
  bookMgr <- bookMgrFut
  userMgr <- userMgrFut
  creditMgr <- creditMgrFut
  (user, lineItems) <- loadUser(request, userMgr).
  zip(buildLineItems(request, bookMgr))
  total = lineItems.map(_.cost).sum
  creditTxn <- chargeCreditCard(request, total, creditMgr)
  order = SalesOrder(0, user.id, creditTxn.id,
  SalesOrderStatus.InProgress, total,
  lineItems, new Date, new Date)
  daoResult <- dao.createSalesOrder(order)
} yield daoResult
```

This all looks nice and neat, and the code is pretty well organized. Readability is enhanced by delegating a lot of the work into separate methods instead of directly in the body of the `for` comprehension. So what's wrong with an approach like this?

Mixing actors and Futures is a topic that has received much chatter out there on the Internet. A lot of people call it anti-pattern, and I agree mostly. I think a little Future usage, like how the other actors use the DAO and then pipe the result back to the sender, is okay, but this clearly crosses the line.

One of the biggest concerns with mixing Futures and actors is the fear that you might accidentally close over mutable scope (variables) and access them in an unsafe way. Once the actor code execution hits the first Future callback, you are done processing that message and the actor moves on to the next one in the mailbox. If you close over something that is mutable (`sender()` being the classic example), you run the risk of you trying to access it while another thread (the one processing the next message in the mailbox) is also accessing it. This basically eliminates one of the biggest benefits of actors, in that, you get serialized mailbox handling and thus don't have to worry about concurrent modifications to internal state. This particular actor doesn't have issues with mishandling of mutable state, but that alone doesn't mean it's a good use of actors. So, much work is being done outside of the context of message handling via the mailbox, that coded as is, it's not really worth using an actor.

On top of that, there is a fair amount of using the ask pattern here (the ? operator). This pattern involved making a request/response semantic out of what is normally a one way messaging pattern with tell (!). The Akka team pushes you to try and limit as it leads more into mixing Futures with your actors, which can lead to undesired behavior. In addition, a short-lived actor instance is created behind the Future so that the receiver has an actual `sender() ActorRef` to send a response back to. This creation of short-lived instance is inefficient, especially when you consider the total number of times it's happening within the servicing of a `CreateOrder` request.

We need to clean up this actor so that we don't use it to set a precedent for Future actors that also have complex workflows. For me, when faced with a rather involved flow like this one, I use a pattern of an actor per request in combination with using Akka's **finite-state machine (FSM)**. Using FSM, we can design all of the different aspects of the flow as states and then progress through them as we react to the different data we're loading and processing.

An approach like this makes the code more intuitive as you just need to understand the different states and what triggers are allowing you to move between them, eventually reaching a termination point. As a side effect, this approach also allows me to get rid of ask and focus completely on tell when communicating with other actors. Having cleaner, more intuitive, and idiomatic actor code is a big win, and we will jump right into this refactor in `Chapter 2`, *Simplifying Concurrent Programming with Actors*.

Replacing our HTTP libraries

Within the example app, we have the need for both inbound and outbound HTTP handling. These two needs are met by unfiltered and dispatch, respectively. These two **sister** libraries have personally accomplished a lot for me in my Scala development projects. Unfortunately, neither is as actively maintained as we would like and that can be a problem moving forward. For instance, if you suddenly needed a new feature within this app, such as HTTP/2 support, you might be stuck waiting a while to get it. If you are going all in on using a third-party library, it's always a good practice to use one that is very actively maintained and with a lot of people using it. This means that things such as bugs will be fixed early and often, and there is also a lot of community information out there to help you if and when you get stuck.

Fortunately, starting with release version 2.4.2, Akka now includes full support for both inbound and outbound non-blocking HTTP handling. The HTTP support is based on the excellent **spray** library and is fully integrated with Akka's Reactive Streams project. These modules (Akka Streams and Akka HTTP) had been available separately before, with their own versioning scheme, but now they are available and versioned along with the other core Akka projects. Also, before being folded into the core Akka repo, these modules had been tagged as experimental. Now these modules are no longer tagged as experimental, with `akka-http` being the only exception as of the writing of this book.

Being an Akka library, and thus built on top of actors, Akka HTTP will be a much better fit with our current use of actors then either the Unfiltered or Dispatch libraries were. We can eliminate some extra thread pools that unfiltered and dispatch were using, using the actor system's dispatcher(s) instead, which should lead to better use of our CPU (less total threads to deal with).

As with all Akka libraries, the HTTP module is very actively maintained, and there is great community support out there. As we are all in on Akka already with this app, getting rid of two third-party libraries and replacing them with something from Akka can also be considered a big win. Depending on too many third-party libraries from many different sources can be an impediment to upgrading Scala (due to binary incompatibility) when that need arises, and that's not a boat we want to be in.

All in all, this seems like a great decision and will be part of our ongoing refactor process in the upcoming chapters.

Summary

Hopefully, at this point, you have a good understanding of what the example is. This includes knowing how the code is structured and works as well as how to interact with it using its endpoints. You also know the big shortcomings with the app and how we plan to go about fixing them. Armed with that knowledge, you are officially ready to start our progressive refactor to building a better reactive application.

Over the next set of chapters, we will take a tour through Akka's different feature offerings above and beyond just actors. We will incorporate these features into the example app one by one in an effort to resolve the shortcomings called out in this chapter. At the end of our journey, the hope is that you will have a much deeper understanding of these newer features and be well on your way to mastering Akka.

2
Simplifying Concurrent Programming with Actors

Before we get started on our refactoring journey (which I promise will start in earnest in Chapter 3, *Curing Anemic Models with Domain-Driven Design*), it makes sense to refresh ourselves on the actor model and Akka's implementation of it. We will tear down the walls and reframe our house with new programming techniques, but Akka's actors will always be the foundation to that house. Even though some of the newer aspects of Akka (such as Streams and HTTP) abstract up one level from directly using actors, the actor is still a core building block of those frameworks. As such, we should have a solid understanding of what an actor is and how they fit into the world of concurrent programming. We'll even do a little bit of refactoring work in this chapter as we have some bad actor debt (the SalesOrderManager) to clean up first. Here are the things you can expect to learn in this chapter:

- The origins of the actor model and how Akka originated from it
- What concurrency and parallelism are, and how you can use Akka actors to achieve them
- The different types of Dispatchers and Mailboxes in Akka and what use cases each one is good for
- How to employ Akka's FSM feature to simplify the coding of complex workflows
- The different types of automated testing within the testing pyramid
- How to test your Akka actors

Understanding the actor model's origin

If you had never bumped into the actor model concept before using it within Akka, it would be easy to think that the Akka team created this programming paradigm themselves, but that's not at all true. In fact, the origins of the actor model idea itself can be traced back to a 1973 publication by Carl Hewitt, Peter Bishop, and Richard Steiger titled *A Universal Modular Actor Formalism for Artificial Intelligence*.

After that publication, things were a bit quiet on the actor model front until Erlang came onto the scene in 1986. The Erlang language was developed by a team within Ericsson, a Swedish telecom company, as the software backbone of their telecommunication network. The language was designed to be highly scalable, with distributed programming and concurrency as the enablers of that scalability. Erlang adopted the actor model as the foundation for both concurrent programming and distributed programming (via message passing) within the language.

The team at Ericsson furthered the ideas of the actor model, adding the concept of supervision to handle failures and perform restarting of components. This provided them with the fault tolerance that they needed to run their telecommunication networks.

In 2006, an initial actor model implementation by Phillip Haller was included as part of Scala 2.1.7. Later, in 2009, Jones Bonèr created the Akka framework as an Erlang-inspired Scala implementation of the actor model. As this implementation was deemed more mature and more feature rich than the one included in the main Scala distribution, it eventually supplanted that native implementation, starting in Scala 2.10. Now, when you think of actors and Scala, Akka is the defacto framework that comes to mind.

Differentiating concurrency and parallelism

Concurrency and parallelism are two terms that you hear a lot about now when it comes to programming for multiprocessor machines. While the terms themselves and techniques behind the two are distinctly different, sometimes people will confuse one for the other. Because of this, I think it's important to quickly clear the air on these two terms before moving forward, as I will reference them in various places throughout the rest of the book.

Defining concurrency in computing

If you go and look up the word concurrent in the dictionary, you will see that it's a term that applies some form of competition. I think that's a good place to start when trying to understand how concurrency relates to computing and computer programming.

Back in the old days, when computers only had one CPU, that processor had to be smart about how it scheduled and executed the work that was being requested of it. Imagine you were on your old, single CPU computer and were typing out a document and then decided to also download a file from the Internet. Your single CPU can only do one thing at once. So, if it decided to pessimistically schedule that work serially, then your download would not start until you have completely finished using and closed your word-processor application.

In a model like that, there is no concurrency at all. Each task runs to completion sequentially, one after the other. There is no point at all when progress has been made on multiple tasks. This would be an extremely frustrating end user experience, so thankfully, the people who built your CPU designed it to be able to properly schedule and handle multiple concurrently executing tasks. When you are not actively typing in your word processor, the CPU can switch over and start to make progress on your download request. If you start typing again, it can switch control back to the word-processor application and stop making progress on the download.

This type of back and forth handling of two different tasks by the CPU is referred to as time slicing. The execution of either task never overlaps, but progress is still made on both tasks (back and forth) as opposed to completely finishing one before starting the other (which would be serial). This concurrent execution process can be seen visually in the following diagram:

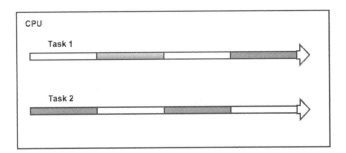

In the preceding diagram, the white/non-shaded line pieces represent the time where that task is not being executed by the CPU. Then, the colored/shaded line pieces are times when that task is being executed by the CPU. You can see that there is no point at all across the two tasks where the white and green lines overlap. Another way to refer to those tasks would be as threads of execution within the CPU. This is a good way to think of things moving forward as you probably already are familiar with threads and multi-threaded programming within Scala/Java and in the JVM.

Defining parallelism

In defining concurrency, I used a dictionary definition to set the baseline understanding that concurrency is about competition. We can use the same approach here when defining parallelism.

If you look up parallel in the dictionary, it's basically defined as two independent lines that do not meet or intersect with each other. If the concurrent model of task execution never involves two tasks overlapping in execution, then parallelism is the opposite, in that, the tasks entirely overlap. Parallelism is not something that can be leveraged in a single CPU machine. You need multiple CPUs to each run the tasks that are overlapping in their execution.

The main goal of parallelism in programming is to get stuff done faster by breaking sequential steps up into tasks that can run in parallel. Say, you have a task A, and in order for A to complete, it must complete subtasks 1, 2, and 3, each taking one second to complete. The naive approach would be to execute these three subtasks serially, back to back to back, similar to the following diagram:

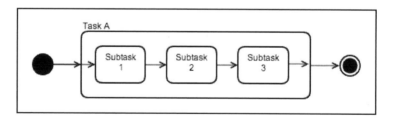

If we took this serial approach to task A's execution, then it would take three total seconds to complete. If we instead decided to execute the subtasks in parallel, then the picture should change to look like the following diagram:

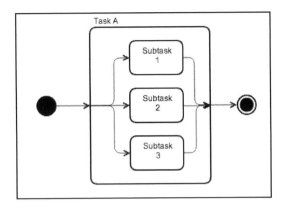

If we decided to follow this parallel model for subtask execution, then the total execution time for `Task A` would be one second, as we are running all of the subtasks at the exact same time. Even though each subtask takes one second to execute, because we are running them all at the same time (as opposed to sequentially), then the total time to execute is still only one second.

If you compare the two pictures, you can think of the length dimension of task A bubble as representing execution time and the height as representing processor or thread needs. If you want to get things done more quickly, in parallel, you need to have more CPUs available to run those tasks at the same time.

The dangers of concurrent programming

When defining concurrency, I gave a pretty low-level description. So how does this description relate to the code that you write on the JVM? Well, if the code you write is ever running inside of a JVM where there is more than one Java thread running, then you need to be aware of and think of concurrency and concurrent access to the state on your class instances. In a multi-threaded JVM, the CPU will start time slicing back and forth between those multiple threads, increasing the likelihood that these threads could get in each other's way and create inconsistent states within your in-memory data.

When you add in multi-core CPUs to the mix and their ability to run more than one thread at once, it increases the likelihood that multiple threads will be competing to access the same data. The multi-core CPU world really ups the ante when it comes to writing safe, concurrency-aware code. As machines get more powerful with more and more CPUs, it quickly becomes clear that concurrency is something programmers need to be aware of and keep an account for when writing their code.

Because of the threat of concurrent access to things such as state, programmers have to protect their code by synchronizing access to that state. Doing so ensures that only one thread at a time is in certain blocks within your code. Unfortunately, this really slows things down as threads are constantly competing for locks instead of executing their program code. Also, writing good, safe synchronized code can be difficult and error prone, sometimes leading to the dreaded deadlock. Thankfully, safe concurrent code is what Akka actors are all about, and we will demonstrate that in the next section.

Using Akka actors for safe concurrency

In the previous section, we talked about writing concurrent code in the JVM and how it can be both error prone and also inefficient due to the overhead of obtaining instance locks. Since multi-threaded apps and multi-core machines are a way of life, we can't really ignore concurrency in the apps that we write on the JVM. Thankfully, Akka actors take the pain out of writing concurrency-aware components. In fact, it's so simple and consistent that I often forget how complicated the underlying concept used to be without Akka.

A lot of that simplicity stems from the way actor components communicate with each other via message passing. If component A (an actor) needs to use some functionality represented by component B (another actor), then component A will send component B a message, and if necessary, asynchronously react to a response that B can route back to it.

This model of message passing is different than life in the synchronous world. In a synchronous model, component B would expose a public method that A would invoke, creating a potentially deep call stack that represents everything that was done in the servicing of that request. In fact, actors don't expose any public methods at all to the outside world. They are represented within an ActorSystem (a container for actor instances) by an ActorRef, which is a location transparent proxy that communicates with the underlying actor instance, hiding all internal implementation details.

When a message is sent to an actor (via its ActorRef), the following sequence of events occurs:

1. A component uses an ActorRef to send a message to its underlying actor instance.
2. The ActorRef asynchronously delivers the message to the mailbox for the actor instance it represents.
3. The dispatcher for that actor instance is notified of the receipt of a new mailbox message.

4. The dispatcher schedules that actor instance for execution, assigning a thread to run its handling of that message via the receive `PartialFunction`.

5. While the instance is handling this message, any other incoming messages are queued in the mailbox and are not handled until this message is done.

6. When the actor instance is done, it can opt to send a response back to the sending `ActorRef` or it can choose to do nothing.

7. At this point, if there are other messages in the mailbox, steps 4-7 can be executed again for each message.

There are a couple of truths from the preceding steps that ensure that an actor is safe for concurrent programming. First, you can only affect the internal state of an actor by sending it a message. There's no way to see or interact with any of that state any other way because the actor instance is only ever represented by an `ActorRef`. Second, only one thread can be executing logic in the actor instance's receive functionality at one time. The combination of the mailbox and the dispatcher will ensure this for you.

Knowing those two simple truths, you can safely and easily write state-management code that can handle concurrent access. The underlying `ActorSystem` as well as the dispatcher and the mailbox do the majority of the heavy lifting for you with regards to thread management and queueing of messages. By taking these complicated burdens away from the developer, they can spend more time working on the functionality and logic of the code they are writing and stop worrying about protecting their code from concurrent access issues.

To me, that's the biggest benefit to using Akka's actor-model implementation. Once you fully understand the rules of the system, you can code wonderfully simple things that can be used in complex ways in a multi-threaded, multi-core, concurrent runtime environment. It's this very simplicity and consistency that keeps me coming back to Akka for my application development needs.

Concurrent programming with actors

Now that we understand how Akka's actors can handle safe concurrency, let's do a quick code example to show that power in action. Our code example will center around a queue implemented as an actor, as well as producer and consumer actors to access that queue. This will help demonstrate some of the rules of how actors handle concurrency in a safe and simple way.

Let's first start with the definition of the queue actor class's companion object:

```
object ActorQueue{
  case class Enqueue(item:Int)
  case object Dequeue
  def props = Props[ActorQueue]
}
```

We're using the companion here to define the messages that our actor can handle, which is always a good practice. It scopes the definition of these message classes to the owning class that uses them instead of leaving them free floating on their own at the package level. We also define the props method on the companion which is used to setup the properties for creation of the actor. This is also a good practice.

Now that we have the companion defined, let's take a look at just the declaration of the Actor and its receive PartialFunction:

```
class ActorQueue extends Actor with Stash{
  import ActorQueue._
  def receive = emptyReceive
    . . .
}
```

Here, we defined a new class and extended it from Akka's Actor trait. We also added a mixin here for the Stash trait. The Stash trait allows us to defer message handling for a set of messages until a certain condition has been met. We will use it to handle a request to dequeue when there is nothing in the queue, which was handled in our SafeQueue class with a call to wait.

All actor classes need the receive PartialFunction defined, which is where the message-handling functionality lives. We define receive as PartialFunction[Any, Unit], which means that the incoming message is of type Any and we don't need to return anything as part of the handling process (because it's defined as Unit). Here, we set up our receive to reference another defined method of type Receive (which is a shorthand type defined as PartialFunction[Any, Unit]) called emptyReceive, which is defined as follows:

```
def emptyReceive:Receive = {
  case Enqueue(item) =>
  context.become(nonEmptyReceive(List(item)))
  unstashAll

  case Dequeue =>
  stash
}
```

We modeled this actor class to have two possible states: queue empty and queue non-empty. The message handling behavior is different depending on which of those two states we are in as one will hold dequeue requests until we have items and one won't. This message-handling method represents the state where the queue is empty, which it will be upon initialization. Hence, this will be our default state.

This state handles two possible request messages: Enqueue and Dequeue. They were defined on our companion object. In this state, if we receive a request to enqueue a new item, we create a new list with that item at the head and then switch our message handling over to the non-empty state for handling of subsequent messages, passing in the single item list as the current queue to that state. Lastly, we call unstashAll() (from the Stash mixin) to put any previous dequeue requests back into the mailbox as we can now support them as we have an item in the queue.

The other request that is handled while in the empty queue state is a request to dequeue an item and return it to the caller. If we have no items in the queue, then we cannot handle that request. We need to defer it until we have items, and we do that by calling stash(). This removes that message from the mailbox, putting it off to the side for a while, until we can handle it. When we can handle it, we call unstashAll() (as seen in the handling of Enqueue) to put those deferred messages back into the mailbox for re-handling.

In the handling of Enqueue, we used a technique called hot-swapping to change the message-handling functionality to a different set of logic. This is accomplished via a call to context.become. In this example, we are switching to a new Receive called nonEmptyReceive, which is defined as follows:

```
def nonEmptyReceive(items:List[Int]):Receive = {
  case Enqueue(item) =>
  context.become(nonEmptyReceive(items :+ item))

  case Dequeue =>
  val item = items.head
  sender() ! item
  val newReceive = items.tail match{
    case Nil => emptyReceive
    case nonNil => nonEmptyReceive(nonNil)
  }
  context.become(newReceive)
}
```

One of the first things to look at here is the usage of a param to the method that returns the new `Receive`. This param is essentially the current state of the queue and is scoped only to this `Receive` as opposed to being global to the entire class. This is purely a style thing and not a requirement for implementing an actor-based solution to the queue problem. I personally think it's a best practice to scope your variables within actors as small as possible, hence this approach. You could very easily define a `var items:List[Int]` as a class-level field and then have no args for the `nonEmptyReceive` method. I like to avoid using `var` as class-level fields, but that's just a personal preference.

The handling of the `Enqueue` request is pretty simple in this state. We just reset the message-handling functionality back to `nonEmptyReceive`, passing in the current list plus the new item to add to the end.

The `Dequeue` functionality is a little more meaty when in this state. The first thing to do is to take the head off the queue and route it back to the actor that sent us the request. This is accomplished by using the tell functionality (represented by the `!` symbol) and referencing the `sender()` method of that message as the destination to route the response to.

> Keep in mind that `sender()` here is a method (not a field) and that it refers to the mutable state on your actor instance. Avoid closing over it if you mix Futures with your actors.

We don't need to check whether the list is empty here because that fact is indicated by the current state (message handling) the actor is in. Once the response is sent, we need to determine which state to be in for the processing of the next message in the mailbox. If the tail of the list is empty, then we transition back into the `emptyReceive` state. If there are still items, then we stay in this current message-handling state, passing in the list minus the first item as the new list to work with.

Now that we have the queue actor fully defined, we need to code a producer and a consumer to communicate with it, which each of those components being actors too. The new producer for our queue will be as follows:

```
object ProducerActor{
  def props(queue:ActorRef) = Props(classOf[ProducerActor], queue)
}
class ProducerActor(queue:ActorRef) extends Actor{
  def receive = {
    case "start" =>
    for(i <- 1 to 1000) queue ! ActorQueue.Enqueue(i)
  }
}
```

Here, we have both the `Actor` class and its companion. The companion supports a props method that takes the shared queue `ActorRef` that the producer will communicate with. This ref will be passed into the constructor for the `ProducerActor`. The functionality of the producer is simple. It just sends 1000 requests to put an `Int` into the queue. Since enqueuing does not send a response, this actor does not need to handle any other message except the request to start.

The consumer has a bit more code to it as it needs to wait for a response from each request to dequeue an item before sending the next request. The consumer code is:

```
class ConsumerActor(queue:ActorRef) extends Actor
  with ActorLogging{
  def receive = consumerReceive(1000)

  def consumerReceive(remaining:Int):Receive = {
    case "start" =>
    queue ! ActorQueue.Dequeue

    case i:Int =>
    val newRemaining = remaining - 1
    if (newRemaining == 0){
      log.info("Consumer {} is done consuming", self.path)
      context.stop(self)
    }
    else{
      queue ! ActorQueue.Dequeue
      context.become(consumerReceive(newRemaining))
    }
  }
}
```

This actor starts out in a custom `receive` block that has an `Int` representing the remaining number of `Dequeue` response messages it must receive before it has completed all of its work (initially set to `1000`). It handles two possible messages, with the first being a request to start the dequeueing process. Upon receiving this request, it will send the first `Dequeue` request to the queue actor.

The consumer also handles the items coming back from the dequeue request (in the line starting with `case i:Int =>`). Inside that message-handling block, the logic subtracts 1 from the `remaining` responses to receive. If the `remaining` responses hit 0, then a message is printed signaling completion and the actor stops itself. If we are not yet at 0, then another request to dequeue an item is sent to the queue actor before resetting the receive handling with the new remaining number.

Now that we have the producer and consumer redefined, we need a little bit of code to start up the whole process of interacting with our queue actor. This code is as follows:

```
object ActorQueueExample extends App{
  val system = ActorSystem()
  val queue = system.actorOf(ActorQueue.props)
  val pairs =
  for(i <- 1 to 10) yield {
    val producer = system.actorOf(ProducerActor.props(queue))
    val consumer = system.actorOf(ConsumerActor.props(queue))
    (consumer, producer)
  }

  val reaper = system.actorOf(ShutdownReaper.props)
  pairs.foreach{
    case (consumer, producer) =>
    reaper ! consumer
    consumer ! "start"
    producer ! "start"
  }
}
```

Here, we start out by creating an `ActorSystem` to house the different actors participating in our process. Next, the queue actor is created as we need to share this instance across the multiple producers and consumers we create. Then, 10 instances of `ProducerActor` and 10 instances of `ConsumerActor` are created. Then, we loop through the pairs of producer and consumer and instruct them to start using the queue.

I am using another actor here called `ShutdownReaper` to get the JVM to properly exit once all the consumers are done. This is so that when you run the program via `sbt`, it properly terminates the JVM. Akka will start up non-daemon threads as part of the default dispatcher, and these threads will halt full shutdown of the JVM unless the `ActorSystem` itself is properly terminated. This code is not critical to the reworked queue logic, so it's not included inline here. It is available in the full code sample for the actor-based queue, which can be found under the `chapter2` root folder at the following path: `chapter2/samples/src/main/scala/code/ActorQueue.scala`.

If you want to run this code example, you can do so by first entering into the `sbt` shell and then running the following command:

```
> runMain code.ActorQueueExample
```

Achieving parallelism with Akka actors and routers

In the previous section, we saw how you can write safe concurrent code with Akka's actors. The example presented there was about protecting yourself (and your state) from concurrent access when running in a multi-threaded and multi-core system. But what if we wanted to exploit the fact that we had multiple processors in our CPU, in an effort to get more work done faster? Can we write parallel code with Akka and actors?

The answer, of course, is yes, indeed we can leverage parallelism when using Akka. Under the hood of an actor system in Akka, we have a dispatcher. This component (which we will discuss in more detail later in this chapter) essentially fronts for a thread pool and uses those threads to handle the work that the actors instances themselves need to do. If we have a lot of work to do and we have multiple CPUs to truly do that work in parallel, then all we should need to do is ramp up the number of actor instances doing that work, and we should be able to get that work done faster.

Now, not all work can be done faster by leveraging more CPU cores. It all depends on the nature of the work being done. CPU-heavy tasks lend themselves really well to being parallelized across the multiple cores on your machine. If you try the same trick with I/O-heavy tasks, where the machine's I/O throughput capabilities become a limiting factor instead of the CPU horsepower, you won't get the additional speed you desire.

For this example of using Akka for parallelism, I have crafted up a master/worker situation where the workers are doing CPU-bound work. It's a very contrived example, but it shows that having additional workers gets the work done faster (provided you are running on a multi-core machine). The first component to look at is the WorkMaster actor's companion:

```
object WorkMaster{
  case object StartProcessing
  case object DoWorkerWork
  case class IterationCount(count:Long)
  def props(workerCount:Int) =
  Props(classOf[WordCountMaster], workerCount)
}
```

Here, we set up some messages that will be exchanged between our actors. We also defined a props method for creating the actor and specifying the number of child workers. The code for the master actor definition is as follows:

```
class WordCountMaster(workerCount:Int) extends Actor{
  import WorkMaster._

  val workers = context.actorOf(
```

```
      ParallelismWorker.props.withRouter(
        RoundRobinPool(workerCount)), "workerRouter")
    def receive = waitingForRequest
    . . .
  }
```

The important thing to note here is that we are creating a round-robin pool of child worker actors and a router to manage and distribute work to that pool. The number of workers in the pool will vary based on the `workerCount` constructor argument supplied. This worker pool and router will allow us to parallelize our work, using multiple actor instances to do the work (which will correlate to multiple threads under the hood).

The router itself is a very lightweight mechanism to distribute work to child actors based on some selected work-distribution algorithm. Here, we select a simple round-robin work distribution algorithm for the router, but there are other algorithms available, some tailored to very specific use cases. If you haven't encountered and used routers yet in your Akka code, you should take a look at them in the Akka documentation. They are one of the ways that you can achieve parallelism in Akka.

The master actor uses a custom receive-handling method called `waitingForRequest` that is defined as follows:

```
  def waitingForRequest:Receive = {
    case StartProcessing =>
    val requestCount = 50000
    for(i <- 1 to requestCount){
      workers ! DoWorkerWork
    }
    context.become(collectingResults(requestCount, sender()))
  }
```

In this receive-handling method, we will pick some arbitrary amount of work to get done, represented here by `requestCount`, which we set to `50000`. This equates to number of `DoWorkerWork` requests that we will pass on to our worker actors via the round-robin pool. After we send all of those requests, we switch to a new set of message-handling logic returned from the call to `collectingResults`. The code passes in the number of responses to expect (based on the number of requests sent), which we will use to count down to completion.

Another thing to pay attention to is the fact that we pass in the original sender reference to our new message-handling logic so that we can respond to that original sender. If we don't do this, and use a call to `sender()` later on when we have received all of our responses from the workers, then we will have the wrong sender to respond to. Each time you receive a message in your actor instance, a mutable sender variable will be set to the `ActorRef` that sent you that message. In this case, when we are done with the work, the sender will be the last worker that sent me a response. Because of this, we need to capture the sender of the original request up front and hang on to it for the final response. You need to remember to do this when you are farming off work to other actors and then need to respond to the original caller.

The second receive block defined in this actor handles the responses from the workers and looks like this:

```
def collectingResults(remaining:Int,
caller:ActorRef, iterations:Long = 0):Receive = {
  case IterationCount(count) =>
  val newRemaining = remaining - 1
  val newIterations = count + iterations
  if (newRemaining == 0){
    caller ! IterationCount(newIterations)
    context.stop(self)
    context.system.terminate
  }
  else{
    context.become(
    collectingResults(newRemaining, caller, newIterations)
    )
  }
}
```

The `iterations` input here is used to track the total number of loop iterations that the workers are doing for their CPU-intensive work. We keep resetting to this receive functionality until we get the last response from the workers. When that happens, a response is sent back to the sender that sent the original `StartProcessing` message and then the actor stops itself.

Now that we've seen what the master is doing, let's take a look at the worker actor. The code for both the companion and the worker actor itself is as follows:

```
object ParallelismWorker{
  def props() = Props[ParallelismWorker]
}

class ParallelismWorker extends Actor {
```

```
import WorkMaster._
def receive = {
  case DoWorkerWork =>
  var totalIterations = 0L
  var count = 10000000
  while(count > 0){
    totalIterations += 1
    count -= 1
  }
  sender() ! IterationCount(totalIterations)
}
}
```

When the worker receives a message, it will do a fixed number of loop iterations to simulate some CPU-intensive piece of work being done. It then responds to the sender with the total number of loop iterations that were executed.

It may seem silly to be explicitly counting the loop iterations when it's always going to match the initial value of count, but this was done intentionally. The JVM has a habit of optimizing code to remove things that it thinks are not being used. If we didn't do something inside the loop and then use that something outside the loop, we run the risk of the loop itself being removed at runtime. This would kill the effectiveness of the demonstration, so I set things up this way to explicitly avoid that happening.

Lastly, we need some code to kick off the master and get the work started. That code looks like this:

```
object ParallelismExample extends App{
  implicit val timeout = Timeout(60 seconds)
  val workerCount = args.headOption.getOrElse("8").toInt
  println(s"Using $workerCount worker instances")

  val system = ActorSystem("parallelism")
  import system.dispatcher
  sys.addShutdownHook(system.terminate)

  val master = system.actorOf(WorkMaster.props(workerCount), "master")
  val start = System.currentTimeMillis()
  (master ? WorkMaster.StartProcessing).
  mapTo[WorkMaster.IterationCount].
  flatMap { iterations =>
    val time = System.currentTimeMillis() - start
    println(s"total time was: $time ms")
    println(s"total iterations was: ${iterations.count}")
    system.terminate()
  }.
  recover {
```

```
    case t: Throwable ⇒
    t.printStackTrace()
    system.terminate()
  }
}
```

Here, we start up an `ActorSystem` and then create the master actor within it. A message is sent to it to start up the work, using ask. This returns a `Future` that will eventually hold the result of the completed work. An `onComplete` callback is added to the `Future` so that we can track the total time taken for all of the work done.

The full code for this example can be found in the samples project in the `chapter2` code distribution under this path:
`chapter2/samples/src/main/scala/Parallelism.scala`.

To run this code example, open up a terminal window and get into the root samples directory within the `chapter2` code distribution. Open up the sbt shell and run the following command:

> **runMain code.ParallelismExample**

When run without any input argument, the code will use the default of eight workers. When running this on my MacBook, I can see all eight cores light up quickly during the test, signaling that my CPU is being fully utilized to run this code. Running with eight workers takes around three or so seconds on average.

Once you try that a few times, try running the example with the following command:

> **runMain code.ParallelismExample 1**

When you run the code like this (with an explicit worker count input), the system only uses one worker actor. Running with only one worker will take significantly more time to do that large amount of work compared to properly parallelizing the work out across all of your available CPU cores. For me, running with a single worker took about 12 seconds on average. That amounts to around a four-fold increase in processing time when doing the work in parallel. Again, this is a rather contrived example, but it's a simple one that shows the potential of doing work in parallel with Akka actors.

There's one last thing to call out here before moving on. This code example not only involved parallelism, it's also highly concurrent, with the master representing that safe concurrency handling. All of the workers will be sending their responses back to the master to indicate they finished a set of work. The master needs to keep track of the number of responses received, and if it doesn't do this safely, it may miss counting a response and thus never finish. Parallelism and concurrency are often used together within Akka, and this code is an example of just how simple leveraging both can be with actors.

A word on dispatchers in Akka

Throughout some of the previous sections, I've mentioned the dispatcher within Akka. This is an extremely important component within Akka's actor system. In Akka's docs, they refer to it as the engine that makes the actor system tick, which I think is a very apt description. Since this component is so important, I want to touch on what it does a bit and also describe the different types and why you might use them.

Dispatchers and executors

The dispatcher in your actor system is responsible for assigning a thread to an actor instance so that it can do work. When an actor instance has no messages to process, it just sits there idle, not taking up any threads. This is why it's okay to have so many actor instances within your system at once (as long as they are not all trying to do work all the time). They don't take any resources, aside from a small amount of heap memory, unless they are processing a message.

Akka is an event-driven system. Work is only done in response to an event being received. The event in this case is a message being received in the mailbox of an actor instance. When the dispatcher sees this, a thread is allocated, and the work of processing that message can begin. When there are no messages to process, the threads sit idle until something happens and there is work to be done.

So where does the dispatcher get those threads from? A dispatcher will always be paired up with an executor, which will define what kind of thread pool model is used to support the actors. In fact, `MessageDispatcher` in Akka inherits from `ExecutionContext`. This means that any place where you need `ExecutionContext`, like when using Futures in your actors, you can use that actor's dispatcher to satisfy that requirement. You may have noticed me doing this in a few places in the various code samples in this chapter.

Dispatcher types in Akka

Akka offers a total of three different dispatcher types, with an additional fourth one that is only really used for testing. Each of these has its own purpose and sweet spot within Akka. I'll try and describe that briefly here. If you want a more detailed explanation, check out the Akka docs on dispatchers.

Dispatcher

This is the default type for any actor instance where an explicit dispatcher is not specified. It is completely all purpose, in that, it can be used as the main dispatcher for the actor system as well as firewalling (or bulkheading) off actors that may block or cause problems for the main dispatcher. It can be used with any mailbox type and works with both a Fork/Join pool executor or a basic thread pool executor for its thread handling.

PinnedDispatcher

This dispatcher is unique, in that, each and every actor instance created under it will get assigned its own single thread for executing it. This is a specialist dispatcher that can be used to firewall off (protect against) actors that block as part of their execution. It can also be used for actors whose execution might have a negative effect on the main dispatcher, perhaps hogging threads from that dispatcher.

BalancingDispatcher

This dispatcher is unique, in that, every actor instance created under it will share a single mailbox. This is to support redistribution of work from instances that are busy to instances that are idle. If you find that you have a use case where you have a pool of the same actors and they get a lot of work and each piece may take a variable amount of time, this may be a good dispatcher to try. If this dispatcher is able to better redistribute work in that situation, then you may find that your work will be done more quickly.

CallingThreadDispatcher

This is the dispatcher that should only be used in testing situations. Using this dispatcher (which automatically happens if you wrap an actor with `TestActorRef`) will ensure that all execution within your test will be synchronous instead of the default asynchronous behavior.

This makes testing your actor code a lot easier as requests to your actors (via tell) will return control to the calling thread (hence, the name) only after all of the code in receive has executed. Having this guarantee makes performing test assertions more consistent.

Configuring a dispatcher for your actors

When you need to use a dispatcher for an actor other than the default one, then you first have to configure that dispatcher. Here, I'm going to configure a new thread pool-based dispatcher to section off some blocking I/O work that a particular actor has to do:

```
thread-pool-dispatcher {
  type = Dispatcher
  executor = "thread-pool-executor"
  thread-pool-executor {
    core-pool-size-min = 2
    core-pool-size-factor = 2.0
    core-pool-size-max = 10
  }
  throughput = 100
}
```

Here, I have configured that new dispatcher, with a type of `Dispatcher`, which is the normal event-based dispatcher. It's set up to use a thread pool as its executor, with the min and max size of the pool set to 2 and 10 respectively. The `throughput` setting here means that the dispatcher will process up to 100 messages on any given actor instance before context switching the thread over to another actor instance.

Once you have that config defined, then you can apply it to an actor instance. The first possible way to do this is via the deployment config for that actor instance, which is shown below:

```
akka.actor.deployment{
  /foo-actor{
    dispatcher = thread-pool-dispatcher
  }
}
```

With config like that in place, I can then simply spin up an actor instance like this and get it to use my custom dispatcher:

```
Val fooRef = system.actorOf(Props[FooActor], "foo-actor")
```

If you don't want to go the route of using deployment config to set the dispatcher for your actor instance, then you can manually set it at time of creation via the `Props` for that actor, like so:

```
val fooRef =
  context.actorOf(
    Props[FooActor].
      withDispatcher("thread-pool-dispatcher"), "myactor1"
  )
```

These two approaches are semantically the same, so just choose which of the two suits your style better.

One thing to note when specifying dispatchers that way; the config path that you are referencing to the mailbox config section must be fully qualified within the context of your complete config tree. If you are nesting that custom dispatcher config section under some other parent sections, then you must fully qualify the path to the dispatcher config when referencing it or it will not be applied to your actor instance.

Mailbox types in Akka

Like dispatchers, mailboxes are central to the functionality within Akka's actor system. Every actor instance has a mailbox (be it isolated or shared) that acts as a queue, feeding the work that the actor does. The mailbox always processes one message at a time, serially, which is a guarantee that enables the safe concurrent programming with actors. Since there are a few different flavors of mailboxes, it makes sense to discuss them briefly here so that you can understand at a high level which ones to use for what situations. There are two major of categories of mailbox types that will be discussed here: unbounded and bounded.

Unbounded mailboxes

As their name implies, these mailboxes are not bound by any size limit. You can stuff as many messages into them as possible as long as you have enough heap memory to handle those messages. All of these mailboxes are non-blocking, so they will all provide good performance. The default implementation is called `UnboundedMailbox` and is a good choice for most work as it's non-blocking and fast, being backed by `ConcurrentLinkedQueue`.

If you want something even faster, you can consider trying the `SingleConsumerOnlyUnboundedMailbox`. It cannot be used in a sharing dispatcher (such as the `BalancingDispatcher`), but it may be able to provide even better performance compared to the default `UnboundedMailbox`.

If you need priority ordering of the messages the actor receives (regardless of their arrival into the queue), then you can look at using `UnboundedControlAwareMailbox`. This implementation ensures that any message that extends from `akka.dispatch.ControlMessage` will be treated with a higher priority and thus handled before regular messages in the mailbox. As the name implies, this is a good choice if you need to get control type messages (things that might change internal behavior in the actor) handled before other messages in the mailbox.

If you need more fine-grained control over the ordering, you can consider using `UnboundedPriorityMailbox`. As long as the messages you send to it implement Java's comparable interface, then they will be ordered according to the rules defined by your custom `compareTo` implementation. One thing to consider is that the ordering for items of equal priority is undefined with this mailbox. If you need to have FIFO order enforced for items of equal priority, then you can use the similar `UnboundedStablePriorityMailbox` instead.

Bounded mailboxes

If you build with actors long enough, you may end up with situations that will require you to have a limit on the total number of messages that an actor can have in its mailbox. This could include situations where you are concerned with the memory buildup of a mailbox that gets too big. This could also cover a scenario where you treat a growing mailbox as a sign of trouble for an actor and use bounding to slow or limit the damage from that trouble.

The most efficient bounded mailbox is the `NonBlockingBoundedMailbox`. As the name implies, this bounded mailbox does not come at the cost of blocking whoever is trying to put the message into it. That non-blocking nature comes with a negative thought, in that, if you try to put a message into the mailbox and it's at its upper bound, that message will never be delivered and becomes a dead letter.

If you want to mitigate the risk of losing messages when the mailbox is full, then you can consider using a regular `BoundedMailbox`. With this kind of mailbox, you can choose to block the sender for a specified amount of time if the mailbox is full, waiting for it to go below its capacity before unblocking. This behavior is controlled by the mailbox-push-timeout-time setting that you configure for your mailbox.

Set this to anything other then 0 and you will incur blocking for up to that amount of time, waiting for the mailbox to go below capacity. If that does not happen, then the sender will get unblocked after that time, and the message becomes a dead letter. If you set this to 0, then no blocking will happen, and messages above capacity immediately become dead letters.

Like in the unbounded family of mailboxes, the bounded family has three variants to handle priority-based queueing: `BoundedControlAwareMailbox`, `BoundedPriorityMailbox` and `BoundedStablePriorityMailbox`. These three variants have the same priority-handling behavior as their unbounded counterparts. They also adhere to the same blocking and non-blocking behavior that the regular `BoundedMailbox` does, being governed by how you decide to set the mailbox-push-timeout-time setting.

Configuring mailboxes for your actors

If you decide that you want to use a mailbox for your actors other than the default, then you first need to decide on the scope of this mailbox change. If you want to use this mailbox for all actor instances created in the system, then simply set the default mailbox setting in your config like so:

```
akka.actor.default-mailbox{
    mailbox-type = "fully qualified class name"
}
```

In that example, you need to replace `fully qualified class name` with the class name of the mailbox that you want to use by default.

You can also change the mailbox just for an individual dispatcher, by setting the `mailbox-requirement` setting on that dispatcher in your config. So, for example, if I had a custom dispatcher called `my-dispatcher`, then I could set the mailbox to use for all actor instances that use that dispatcher like this:

```
my-dispatcher{
    mailbox-type = "fully qualified class name"
}
```

You can also scope the mailbox down to an individual actor instance if you need that very fine-grained level of control. To do that, you first need to have a config section that represents the mailbox you want to use. That config would look like this:

```
foo-mailbox{
    mailbox-type = "fully qualified class name"
}
```

Then, with that config in place, you could then explicitly set the mailbox of an actor in your code like so:

```
system.actorOf(
  Props[FooActor].withMailbox("foo-mailbox"), "foo-actor")
```

You could also set that mailbox via deployment config if you didn't want to do it explicitly in code. The deployment config to do that would be as follows:

```
akka.actor.deployment{
  /foo-actor{
    mailbox = foo-mailbox
  }
}
```

Then you would create your actor like this to get it to use that mailbox config:

```
system.actorOf(Props[FooActor], "foo-actor")
```

Keep in mind that like with dispatchers, the config path that you are referencing to the mailbox config section must be fully qualified within the context of your complete config tree.

Refactoring a bad actor to FSM

Now that we have recapped what actors are and understood some of the core features of the Akka actor system, it's time to dive in to our first big refactor. In the `Chapter 1`, *Building a Better Reactive App*, I called out the fact that the current implementation of the `OrderManager` was a poor use of an actor as it was mixing in too much usage of Futures.

This is a complicated actor, in that, it needs to fetch a bunch of data and then make various decisions on whether to stop or continue based on that data. When I end up with something like this, I usually turn to a **finite-state machine** (**FSM**) based actor. This is probably a different use case than what was originally intended or thought of as an FSM, but I think the state representations and transitions lend themselves nicely to complicated flows like this.

This actor will be modified a few more times before the book is done, with this being the first. You may find that some of the other refactors, such as to a **domain-driven design** (**DDD**) approach, don't suit your needs and may be something you aren't comfortable with. If that ends up being the case, then you can consider this the baseline to fall back to for an approach to modeling a complicated actor such as the `OrderManager`.

Modeling the new process flow

One of the first things I do when refactoring a complicated actor flow into an FSM is to draw out the states and transitions using a UML activity diagram. This helps me understand just what is going on in each state and how the whole flow is wired together. We're going to follow that approach here and create an activity diagram for the `OrderManager` refactor. The diagram I came up with for process flow can be seen here:

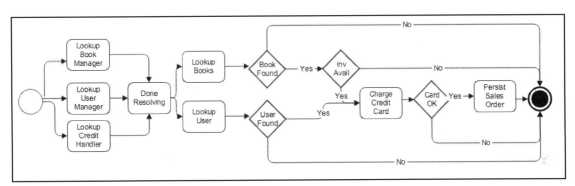

According to our flow, the first thing that we need to do is to lookup (using actor selection) the references to the `BookManager`, `UserManager`, and `CreditHandler` actors. We will do all of that at once, in parallel, as opposed to looking them up one by one.

One quick note about actor selection before we move onto the rest of the code flow. I'm for limiting its use as much as possible (which I discuss more in `Chapter 10`, *Troubleshooting and Best Practices*), opting to pass in direct references to actors when they are available versus looking them up. In this situation, with the way the code modules are structured (not having relationships to each other), we don't have the luxury of passing them in and thus have to look them up. Just keep in mind that you should always prefer passing in dependency `ActorRef` instances when possible, which I will expand upon a bit further in `Chapter 10`, *Troubleshooting and Best Practices*.

Once we are done resolving the services we need for the business logic, the next phase is to look up any entity references that were indicated on the order request. This means looking up the `BookstoreUser` that is making the order and also any book that is referenced on a line item from the order request. Again, we do this in parallel because it will be faster to do so as opposed to doing everything serially.

If, for any lookup, the service responds with an `EmptyResult`, indicating that the entity was not found, we short circuit the process and terminate it, responding with an error. On top of that check, for any book that we look up, if we see that the current inventory amount for that book is less than the amount being requested from the line item, we also terminate and respond with an error.

If everything checks out on the entities we looked up, we proceed to charging the credit card. If the card charges successfully, then we can move on to the last step of persisting the order to the database. Once we finish that, we can respond to the caller.

Coding the new order process flow

Now that we have a rough outline for the code, thanks to our activity diagram, we can focus more on the actual code. One of the first things we need to change in the code is to implement a per-request type model for the actor that is representing this process flow. The FSM actor itself will be stateful in regards to the data it is collecting as it progresses through the flow. This means that we need one per individual request so that state can be tracked on a per-request basis (and so multiple requests don't trip each other up).

We still need a central entry point actor to kick off the per-request actor though, so this ends up being a two-actor process. We will use the existing `SalesOrderManager` as that initial entry point, using a new actor called `SalesOrderProcessor` as the per-request handler of the process flow. The new order-request handling in `SalesOrderManager` is pretty simple, as it just receives the request and then forwards on to a new `SalesOrderProcessor`. This new handling block is as follows:

```
case req:CreateOrder =>
val proc = context.actorOf(SalesOrderProcessor.props)
proc forward req
```

Here, we received the request and created a new instance of `SalesOrderProcessor` to handle that request. The request is then forwarded to that new `ActorRef` to be handled. Forwarding here ensures that the sender of the original request is maintained so that `SalesOrderProcessor` can be the one that eventually responds to that sender.

Defining state and data representations

For the processor actor, which is going to be the FSM, the first thing to do is to model out the different states and the different data representations (state data) that we need to make the flow we modeled work. States and data are the building blocks for modeling FSMs with Akka, and each FSM implementation must define what these two types will be for it. We'll put these definitions in the companion, with the states being defined as follows:

```
sealed trait State
case object Idle extends State
case object ResolvingDependencies extends State
case object LookingUpEntities extends State
case object ChargingCard extends State
case object WritingEntity extends State
```

States will essentially map to the task bubbles from the activity diagram, with each one representing something that we need to do before saving the order. Idle here represents the initial state where this FSM actor is waiting for a request to kick off the process. It is essentially represented by the **start circle** from our activity diagram. All of the other states should map directly to concepts from our diagram and our discussion of that diagram.

The next thing to define is the state data to use as we move through the flow. As we go through different steps, we are collecting more data that we use to get us to the point where we can save the `SalesOrder` to the database. The data types that we define will allow us to collect data within the various states from our flow. The base data definition for our sales order processing flow looks like this:

```
sealed trait Data{def originator:ActorRef}
case class Inputs(originator:ActorRef, request:CreateOrder)
trait InputsData extends Data{
  def inputs:Inputs
  def originator = inputs.originator
}
```

Here, we defined our data type (aptly named `Data`) that we will use throughout the process flow. Any subclass of this data type must support a property called `originator` to provide the original sending `ActorRef`. Basically, this makes sure that we are carrying the original sender forward throughout the flow, making it available at each state, if we ever need to send a response to it.

I also set up a simple case class called `Inputs` to hold the two main pieces of information that we want at every state in the flow: the original sender `ActorRef` and the original `CreateOrder` request that was sent in. Lastly, a trait called `InputsData` is set up to extend from `Data` and provide an instance of `Inputs`. Using this instance of `Inputs`, we can provide a concrete implementation of the `originator` method so that any derived class doesn't have to worry about doing that.

Now that we have these base classes defined, we can write the code for our different data class definitions, which looks like this:

```
case object Uninitialized extends Data{
  def originator = ActorRef.noSender
}

case class UnresolvedDependencies(inputs:Inputs,
  userMgr:Option[ActorRef] = None,
  bookMgr:Option[ActorRef] = None,
  creditHandler:Option[ActorRef] = None) extends InputsData

case class ResolvedDependencies(inputs:Inputs,
  expectedBooks:Set[Int],
  user:Option[BookstoreUser],
  books:Map[Int, Book], userMgr:ActorRef,
  bookMgr:ActorRef, creditHandler:ActorRef) extends InputsData

case class LookedUpData(inputs:Inputs,
  user:BookstoreUser,
  items:List[SalesOrderLineItem],
  total:Double) extends InputsData
```

The `Uninitialized` data class represents the initial state of the FSM before it receives a message. Because it extends `Data`, an implementation of `originator` is required. In this case, since we don't have one yet, the only thing that can be provided is `ActorRef.noSender`. That's not a problem as our code implementation will never require us to have to use this reference.

The `UnresolvedDependencies` class holds data while we are looking up the other actors that we need to execute the flow logic. It has slots on it for each of the actors that we plan to look up via actor selection. These slots are set up as `Option` types that get set to `Some` as we get a response back from each actor lookup.

Once we have resolved our dependencies, we can start to use the ResolvedDependencies data class. This one has non-optional fields for our resolved dependency actors. It also has fields based on Option for the user and books that we plan to lookup with our newly resolved dependencies. Once we lookup the user and books, we will set these to Some, signifying that we are done looking things up.

The final data class we use is LookedUpData. This class has fields that represent all the information we need to produce the SalesOrder that gets saved into the database, including the SalesOrderLineItem instances that we build out from looking up the books.

Implementing the idle state handling

Once we have our state and data representations defined, we can move into the actual event-handling code for the actor. We need an actor class that extends the FSM trait first though. That definition looks like this:

```
class SalesOrderProcessor
extends FSM[SalesOrderProcessor.State, SalesOrderProcessor.Data]{
  val dao = new SalesOrderProcessorDao
  startWith(Idle, Uninitialized)
  . . .
}
```

When we extend FSM, we need to define the two types that represent the states and the data classes. Here, we reference the state and data types that we defined in the companion object. A dao is added to handle any db calls for this actor. Lastly, we declare what state and what data we start with, using Idle and Uninitialized, respectively.

Now that we have declared our intent to start with Idle, we need to add an event-handling block that represents what we do when receiving messages while in that state. That event-handling block is defined here:

```
when(Idle){
  case Event(req:CreateOrder, _) =>
    lookup(BookMgrName ) ! Identify(ResolutionIdent.Book)
    lookup(UserManagerName ) ! Identify(ResolutionIdent.User )
    lookup(CreditHandlerName ) ! Identify(ResolutionIdent.Credit)
    goto(ResolvingDependencies) using
    UnresolvedDependencies(Inputs(sender(), req))
}
```

You probably noticed right away that the message-handling definition for an FSM-based actor is different from that of a normal actor. Instead of implementing the standard receive PartialFunction, you define multiple when(State){...} blocks that define how each state responds to the messages (events) that it receives. Keeping the message-handling code for each state separate from each other (as opposed to one large handling block) makes it easier to visually scan the actor and see what states are there and what is going on in each one.

Each when(State){...} block is essentially similar to the receive PartialFunction of a regular actor, except that it wraps the raw messages in an Event(Any,Data) instance, where Any is the raw message and Data is the current state data you defined for that state. Passing in the data with each event allows you to keep that data scoped to individual states and modify it in response to events, without having to deal with explicit mutable variables. This keeps the code nice and neat and functionally oriented. The state data management within the actor is all about action (event) and then reaction (state data changes or state transition), which is a nice way to reason about its functionality.

After receiving an event, you must always instruct the FSM on what to do next, with there being three possible options:

1. Stay in the current state using stay.
2. Go to a different state using goto.
3. Stop the FSM (and the actor) using stop.

For the Idle state, the only event message we handle is a request to create a new sales order. When we receive this request, as shown in our activity diagram, we first need to look up the actors that we need to process this message. An actor selection based lookup is done for the BookManager, UserManager, and CreditHandler before transitioning to the ResolvingDependencies state, changing the state data to UnresolvedDependencies. Note that we capture the original message sender here and hang on to it so that we can respond to it later.

The lookup method shown here is just a simple method to perform the actor selection and is defined like this:

```
def lookup(name:String) = context.actorSelection(s"/user/$name")
```

Once we have `actorSelection` returned from lookup, we send it an `Identify` request in an effort to get the single `ActorRef` represented by each `ActorSelection`. Because we are sending three parallel requests to identify actors, we need a unique identifier per `Identify` request so that when the responses come back, we will know which `ActorRef` it is. You will see this concept in action when the code for the `ResolvingDependencies` state is shown.

Implementing the ResolvingDependencies state handling

Each event received while in the the `ResolvingDependencies` state is set up as a two-stage process of mapping the received `ActorRef` into the state data and then evaluating the collected state data to see whether everything has been received so that we can transition into the next state. We send out the actor lookup requests in parallel, so there is no guarantee on what order we get them back in. This two-stage process lets us receive the responses in any order, only moving forward once we know we have everything.

In the Akka FSM functionality, this is implemented by wrapping the body of the `when` with the `transform` method, with the logic inside `transform` acting as the gatekeeper for moving on to the next transition. Only when the match inside of there is met will the code flow be allowed to move on to the next state. The outline for our `ResolvingDependencies` state-handling block is as follows:

```
when(ResolvingDependencies, ResolveTimeout )(transform {
  . . .
} using{
  . . .
})
```

Here, we set up the state, using an explicit state timeout represented by `ResolveTimeout`. This protects us from the case where we might not get all of our responses back for some reason. If that happens, we will receive a `StateTimeout` event which will result in the caller getting a failure response.

The inside body of `transform` (where we do the event-handling work) is defined like this:

```
case Event(ActorIdentity(identifier:ResolutionIdent.Value, actor @
Some(ref)), data:UnresolvedDependencies) =>
  val newData = identifier match{
    case ResolutionIdent.Book =>
      data.copy(bookMgr = actor)
    case ResolutionIdent.User =>
```

```
      data.copy(userMgr = actor)
    case ResolutionIdent.Credit =>
      data.copy(creditHandler = actor)
  }
  stay using newData
```

There is only one event that needs to be handled here, and that's the response from the actor lookup, represented by `ActorIdentity`. When we sent out each lookup request, we added an identifier that allows us to see what service each returned `ActorRef` represents. A match is performed to see which of the three it is, and based on that, a part of `UnresolvedDependencies` is set as `Some` for that `ActorRef`. Then, we instruct the FSM to stay in this state, using the new state data that we built by setting the dependency on it. The logic to transition is not done here. It's instead done in the `using` part of the `transform/using` pairing. That part looks like this:

```
case FSM.State(state, UnresolvedDependencies(inputs, Some(user),
  Some(book), Some(credit)), _, _, _) =>

  user ! FindUserById(inputs.request.userId)
  val expectedBooks = inputs.request.lineItems.map(_.bookId).toSet
  expectedBooks.foreach(id => book ! FindBook(id))
  goto(LookingUpEntities) using
  ResolvedDependencies(inputs, expectedBooks, None,
  Map.empty, book, user, credit)
```

The code inside `using` is `PartialFunction` that allows you to match on the state and state data with the intention of transitioning when we have collected what we need. In this case, we indicate that we need `Some` for all three dependencies of `ActorRef` that we looked up.

If we hit a match on that statement, the next thing to do is to look up the user and books tied to the request. For the user, it's a single request. For the books, it's one request for each line item we have on the order. After making these requests, the code transitions into the `LookingupEntities` state where we wait for the results of the entity lookups.

Implementing the LookingUpEntities state handling

In the `LookingUpEntities` state, we are waiting for the results of the user and books that we requested in the previous state. We once again sent out multiple parallel requests and need to wait until we have all of the responses. That means this state will also leverage the `transform/using` method of making sure we have all our data before moving on.

The set of event handling for this state is a bit more complicated than the others thus far as there will be some validation work to do on the books to make sure we have available inventory for them. Because of that, we'll look at the code in smaller chunks to best understand what's happening and why. The first thing to look at is the code that handles the results of the book lookups:

```
case Event(FullResult(b:Book), data:ResolvedDependencies) =>
  val lineItemForBook =
  data.inputs.request.lineItems.find(_.bookId == b.id)
  lineItemForBook match{
    case None =>
    data.originator ! unexpectedFail
    stop

    case Some(item) if item.quantity > b.inventoryAmount  =>
    val invfail = Failure(
    FailureType.Validation, InventoryNotAvailError)
    data.originator ! invfail
    stop

    case _ =>
    stay using data.copy(books = data.books ++ Map(b.id -> b))
  }
```

Here, we are matching on `FullResult` wrapping a `Book` entity, indicating that one of our book lookups was successful. Now that we found have this book, the code makes sure that inventory is available for it. The `Book` entity carries with it the current inventory amount. So, what we need to do is line that up with the line item from the order and make sure that the inventory for that book is greater than or equal to the quantity of the line item.

There are two error conditions handled here that will stop the flow and respond to the caller with an error. The first is that we got a book back where we could not match it back up with a line item from the order. This case is unlikely as the line items were used to drive the book lookup requests, but it's not impossible (if the book lookup code is having issues for example), so it needs to be handled. The second is that we don't have enough inventory for the book to handle the quantity on the line item. If we don't hit either error condition, then the book is copied onto the current state data so that the total state can be evaluated for completeness in the `using` block.

Another event handled in this state is the successful result of a user lookup:

```
case Event(FullResult(u:BookstoreUser), d:ResolvedDependencies) =>
stay using d.copy(user = Some(u))
```

The handling is pretty simple here. If we get `FullResult` for `BookstoreUser`, copy it onto the current state data so that the `using` block can evaluate it.

There is one more possible result that needs to be handled in this event-handling block, and that's getting `EmptyResult` from one of our lookups, indicating that a desired entity was not found. If that happens, we need to stop the process and respond with an error to the caller. The code for that handling is as follows:

```
case Event(EmptyResult, data:ResolvedDependencies) =>
val (etype, error) =
if (sender().path.name == BookMgrName)
  ("book", InvalidBookIdError)
else
  ("user", InvalidUserIdError )
data.originator ! Failure(FailureType.Validation, error)
stop
```

One thing to note here is that we use the sender of that `EmptyResult` message to figure out what error to send back to the caller. If the sender is the `BookManager`, then an invalid book error is sent back. If it's the `UserManager`, then an invalid user message is sent instead.

The last piece of code to look at for this state handling is the code in the `using` `PartialFunction`. That code is evaluating the current state data to make sure we've collected everything we need to proceed with the next step in the process and is as follows:

```
case FSM.State(state, ResolvedDependencies(inputs,
  expectedBooks, Some(u), bookMap, userMgr,
  bookMgr, creditMgr), _, _, _)
if bookMap.keySet == expectedBooks =>

  val lineItems = inputs.request.lineItems.
  flatMap{item =>
    bookMap.
    get(item.bookId).
    map{b =>
    SalesOrderLineItem(0, 0, b.id, item.quantity,
    item.quantity * b.cost, new Date, new Date))
  }
  val total = lineItems.map(_.cost).sum
  creditMgr ! ChargeCreditCard(inputs.request.cardInfo, total)
  goto(ChargingCard) using LookedUpData(
  inputs, u, lineItems, total)
```

The case statement here ensures that we found the user and that we found book entities for each line item on the order. If that happens, then the code will build out the `SalesOrderLineItem` instances to be saved with the order. Then, a request is sent over to charge the credit card, which is the last thing that needs to be done before saving the order. Lastly, the FSM transitions into the `ChargingCard` state, setting the current state data to be `LookedUpData`, which holds the final set of data used to save the order.

Implementing the ChargingCard state handling

The `ChargingCard` state-handling logic is set up to wait for the result of the credit charge request, and if successful, persist the final sales order to the database. The event-handling code for that success case is as follows:

```
case Event(FullResult(txn:CreditCardTransaction), data:LookedUpData)
if txn.status == CreditTransactionStatus.Approved =>

import akka.pattern.pipe
val order = SalesOrder(0, data.user.id, txn.id,
SalesOrderStatus.InProgress, data.total, data.items, new Date, new Date)
dao.createSalesOrder(order) pipeTo self
goto(WritingEntity) using data
```

The result of the DAO call produces a Future that we want to evaluate in the final state. We do this by piping the result of that Future back to this actor so that it can be handled within the actor itself and not via a callback on the Future. If we handled it via a callback, then we'd have to access the internal state of this FSM actor outside of the actor and its mailbox. That's not something we can do (state-handling functionality is private to the actor), or should try to do, hence piping the result back to yourself for proper handling within the actor. After piping the result back to itself, the actor code transitions into the final state of `WritingEntity`.

This state also needs to handle the case that the card was not able to be successfully charged. This will result in an error being sent back to the caller. That requirement is handled with the following logic:

```
case Event(FullResult(txn:CreditCardTransaction),
  data:LookedUpData) =>
  data.originator ! Failure(FailureType.Validation,
  CreditRejectedError)
  stop
```

Implementing the WritingEntity state handling

The final state in our FSM-based process flow is where we are waiting for the result of the DAO call that we piped back to ourselves. That simple block of code looks like this:

```
when(WritingEntity, 5 seconds){
  case Event(ord:SalesOrder, data:LookedUpData) =>
  data.originator ! FullResult(ord)
  stop

  case Event(Status.Failure(ex:InventoryNotAvailaleException),
  data:LookedUpData) =>
  data.originator ! Failure(
  FailureType.Validation, InventoryNotAvailError )
  stop

  case Event(Status.Failure(ex), data:LookedUpData) =>
  data.originator ! unexpectedFail
  stop
}
```

The first case handled is the success case. This means that everything went as planned; we saved the new order to the database, and we can respond with that entity to the original caller.

The second case handles the situation where the database call indicates that inventory is no longer available, even though we checked it previously. It's possible that after checking it, another order came in and took that inventory, which is a situation that we need to plan and account for. In Chapter 1, *Building a Better Reactive App*, we discussed how the DAO used an optimistic database concurrency check to make sure we still had available inventory before we decrement it. This code handles that specific exception from the DAO, informing the caller that inventory is not available. The Status.Failure wrapper around the exception is what happens when you pipe a failed Future back to yourself.

The last case statement here catches some unexpected exception with the DAO call, such as the database not being available for example. It responds with an unexpected failure to the caller.

Handling unhandled events

In Akka's FSM, you have the ability to define catch-all handling for events that did not match on anything in a state's event-handling block. This is a good place to handle certain conditions across all states without having to duplicate the code into each state. For our order process, the unhandled block is defined as follows:

```
whenUnhandled{
  case e @ Event(StateTimeout, data) =>
  log.error("State timeout when in state {}", stateName)
  data.originator ! unexpectedFail
  stop

  case e @ Event(other, data) =>
  log.error("Unexpected result of {} when in state {}",
  other, stateName)
  data.originator ! unexpectedFail
  stop
}
```

The first thing we need to universally handle is a state timeout. For every state that we have represented on our FSM, we defined a maximum amount of time to be in that state. If we end up staying in that state for too long, the FSM code will deliver a `StateTimeout` message to indicate that condition. This protects us from the situation where we are waiting for a response from something and we simply never get it.

As this can happen in any state, it's simpler to define that handling in one place, so this is the best place to put it to accomplish that. If we get a state timeout, we log what happened and then respond with an unexpected failure back to the caller before stopping.

We also define a catch-all case here where we get a response back that's completely unexpected. If we have proper integration testing setup between our components that are communicating in this flow, then this should not happen. It's coded here to gracefully handle it in the off chance that it does happen though, sending a failure back to the caller and not just leaving them hanging.

Summing up the refactor

So, there you have it: our first refactor. We took a stateless, single actor instance that was heavily reliant on Futures and changed it into a stateful, per-request actor instance, using Akka's FSM to model the complex flow. This is a much more actor-oriented implementation as it's using the mailbox of the actor for all message passing that's needed for the flow.

The previous solution only used the mailbox for the initial request message, with all of the other processing being done **out of band** in regards to the mailbox. It just wasn't a good use of an actor, and if you want to go down that kind of route, you might be better off just using Futures as opposed to actors.

I think the code for this solution is also a bit easier to reason about. You see clear demarcation of each state within the flow (with the `when` code blocks). You can also clearly see what events are handled in those states and how that affects transitioning into different states. This allows the code to very closely resemble the activity diagram we produced, making it simple to jump from the diagram (documentation of the process) right into the code (implementation of the process).

All of the code for this refactor is available in the code distribution for this chapter within the order-services project under the following root path: `chapter2/bookstore-app/order-services`.

You can use the same instructions from `Chapter 1`, *Building a Better Reactive App*, to build and run this new version of the bookstore app. You can also use the same JSON files to send some order requests though the new code. Play around with the new app a bit to get a feel of how the refactored code is working when creating orders, even when it is trying to create some of the failure conditions modeled in the code (for example, invalid user, invalid book, or no inventory).

Testing your Akka actors

If you've ever developed in an agile environment, then you should be aware of the importance of automated tests. Continuous, frequent deployment is a big part of agile. It's how you get the feedback necessary to iterate on and improve features.

In the beginning, when your feature set is small, you might be able to get away with manual, full-regression test runs before your deployments. However, as your feature set grows, so does the amount of time required to fully test that feature set. Eventually, you will hit a point where these manual regression runs become an impediment to your ability to deploy frequently, which hurts your agility.

Agile is predicated to have automated test coverage. These automated test runs will shorten your regression testing cycles from potentially days down to tens of minutes (or hours). This will allow you to deploy more frequently and get that feedback that is so important in the agile world. Simply put, if you don't have automated test coverage, then you're not going to be agile.

Within this section, we'll go over the different kinds of automated tests you can create and what purpose they serve. We will then apply some automated testing to the newly refactored sales order processing logic. At the conclusion of this section, you will have a better understanding of how to use the testing-based tools within Akka to add coverage to your actor code, enabling you to be more agile with your Akka applications.

Understanding the testing pyramid

Within any good automated testing infrastructure, there can be up to three different levels of testing:

- Unit testing
- Integration testing
- Acceptance testing

Sometimes, these three levels of testing are referred to as the testing pyramid, which can be seen in the following diagram:

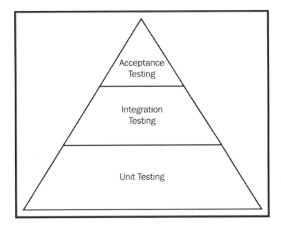

You may have bumped into this pyramid before, with slightly different levels on it. For example, you may see **Unit Testing** at the top instead of **Acceptance Testing**. I think **Acceptance Testing** is a more general term and can incorporate **Unit Testing** as part of it, so that's why it's at the top of this pyramid. Also, not everything you build has a UI. If you are building out an API for your integration partners to consume, you won't have a UI, but you should still have some level of **Acceptance Testing**. These different levels are explained here.

Unit testing

At the base of the pyramid, we have unit testing. A unit test is a single component test where you exercise all of the logic branches in the component (striving for full line and branch coverage). If this component depends on other components (like other actors or perhaps a database), these dependencies will be stubbed out and their behavior simulated. This allows the unit test to focus solely on the logic within that single component and not be corrupted by problems that may exist in other components.

Unit tests serve as the base of the pyramid because they are the most important in terms of logic testing. You will have more of them than any other type of test in the pyramid. This is the layer where you want to catch most of your code logic bugs as these tests will be the least complicated to set up and the fastest to run. This is because they won't have any complicated set up or teardown for things such as databases or other kinds of external dependencies.

Integration testing

The next level up in the testing pyramid is integration testing. At this level, you start to pull in external dependencies such as databases into the test execution. If your component talks to a database, then this is the testing layer where you no longer have that communication mocked out, so it's the first place where you would find problems with your SQL. If you have a multi-actor flow, this is also the place where you would have both actors actually communicating with each other instead of one stubbing the other out (as you did in your unit test).

This is the layer where you can find issues with the actual integrations between multiple components or between a component and an external resource (such as a database). Sometimes, when you stub out an interaction in a unit test, you make an incorrect assumption on the contract for that component. For a multi-actor flow, this may mean misunderstanding the messages that other actors handle and sending the wrong type in your code. Your unit test passes because you stubbed it out according to your code logic, but if you rolled this out to production, it wouldn't work and you'd be left scratching your head. With an integration test between those two actor components, you would find this issue and fix it before you pushed out to production, saving an embarrassing bug for you to deal with.

You will have significantly less integration test scenarios than unit test scenarios. This is because your integration test scenarios should not be focusing on things already adequately covered in your unit tests. They should be very focused on the integration points for a component, things that were not covered in your unit test because they were stubbed out. Retesting the branching logic of the component will be a waste of your time here and will dilute the value of this layer. Stay focused on the integration points here, making sure you are confident in them before moving up to the last layer.

Acceptance testing

Acceptance testing, to me at least, is all about feature-level testing. When you are doing your unit and integration tests, you are very code and component focused. Unfortunately, your business stakeholders don't care about code and components; they care about application features. This is a classic "can't see the forest for the trees situation" where you are so focused on the low-level behaviors and interactions of the code that you forget that you are trying to build out user-facing features.

If all of your tests pass, but no one can log in because you have a feature flag turned off and you don't see that config in your other levels of testing, then you're going to have a real problem on your hands. Acceptance tests serve to answer the question of whether or not the features (and mostly, the critical ones) for your app work at a very high level. You're not looking to test all sorts of corner cases here. Just take a quick pass through the successful path of the feature so that you know its working at the most basic level.

These kinds of tests are generally the most complicated from a setup perspective. They will usually involve having the entire system up and running, including things such as databases. Because of the more complex nature of these tests, you generally don't have a ton of them, hence being at the top of the pyramid. These are your last line of defense, a feature-based sanity check so to speak, before pushing your code out to production.

Unit testing Akka actors

As mentioned in the section on the testing pyramid, unit testing is the foundation of any good automated testing infrastructure. That's the level of testing that we will focus on here in adding some coverage to our refactored sales order processing actor. Before we jump into the code though, it's important to understand what facilities are present in Akka to enable simple and consistent unit testing of actors.

The CallingThreadDispatcher

The CallingThreadDispatcher is probably the most important concept to know for unit testing your actors. Unit tests should be simple and completely deterministic so that things such as asynchronicity don't cause them to occasionally fail. This could happen when the duration on an asserted condition sometimes takes longer than is coded for in the test. The more asynchronous pieces that are involved in your test, the more fragile that test begins to become as each of those parts could exceed the allowed duration of a test condition and thus fail the whole test unnecessarily. If you end up with a bunch of fragile, failing tests, you will probably quickly abandon unit tests with your actors, and that's a dangerous path to follow.

Thankfully, the good people on the Akka team took this into consideration and added a special kind of dispatcher called the CallingThreadDispatcher. If this dispatcher is used for your actor under test, then all communication with it and anything it does inside of its receive handling will be done completely synchronously in the calling thread (hence, the name). If your test thread sends a message to an actor using this dispatcher, then your test thread won't return control to the test until everything that actor needs to do for that message is done. So, by the time control returns to your test, you can reliably start performing assertions on things that need to be done in the actor.

This also means that if your test code is expecting a response from that actor (perhaps using the ImplicitSender trait) then you know you will have that response as soon as control returns to your test code. These types of guarantees make writing actor based unit tests much easier, they remove almost all of the potential fragility that could scare you away from testing your actors.

So how do we use the CallingThreadDispatcher with our actors that we are testing? We'll cover that in the next section.

Using TestActorRefs

When testing your actors, if you wrap them within a TestActorRef when you instantiate them, you get two distinct benefits:

- Automatic setting of the CallingThreadDispatcher as the dispatcher for that actor
- The ability to look at the internal state of that actor from the outside

The first point is pretty straightforward. It's the simplest way to get your actor under test to be associated with the `CallingThreadDispatcher`. Doing so ensures synchronous execution of the actor code you are testing.

The second point is something that is extremely helpful when testing actors that change internal state in response to receiving a message. Say you had a very simple actor coded as follows:

```
object Adder{
  case object Add
  def props = Props[Adder]
}
class Adder extends Actor{
  import Adder._
  var amount = 0
  def receive = {
    case Add =>
    amount += 1
  }
}
```

All this actor does is add to an internal state variable when it receives a message. If you want to test this actor, the assertion you need to make to see if it's working correctly could be one of two things:

- **White box**: Look at the internal state assuming you can, seeing it increased by one
- **Black box**: Add a message to support getting that internal state value and then use it after the request to add to see that it did increase

For unit testing, I'm okay sticking to the first approach, provided you can make it happen. I don't see any need to add new messages to my actor just to be able to test it, provided I have the ability to look at its internal state. Normally, the actor contract does not allow this because all you have is `ActorRef`, and it does not allow you to see the internal state. However, you can wrap it in `TestActorRef` as follows:

```
val testActor = TestActorRef(Adder.props)
```

Then later, after sending the add message to that actor, you can check the internal state like this:

```
testActor.underlyingActor.amount mustEqual 1
```

This ability to look at the underlying actor behind `ActorRef` will come in very handy for certain kinds of actor tests and should be a part of your toolkit when testing your actors.

Using ImplicitSender

If you have a request/response scenario to test with your actor, you probably assume that you need to use the `ask` pattern to get the response to assert against. Your code may look something like this:

```
import akka.pattern.ask
implicit val timeout = Timeout(2 seconds)
val resultFut = (testActor ? GetSomething).mapTo[Int]
val result = Await.result(resultFut, timeout)
result mustEqual 1
```

There are a few problems with this approach that make the code unnecessarily complex. For starters, you always need to keep importing the `ask` pattern. Second, you always need to have an implicit timeout around to use ask even though all this test code is synchronous, thanks to `CallingThreadDispatcher`. Third, you need to get a Future and block to get its result before asserting against it. This isn't a performance issue because it's just test code, but it's just an unnecessary step in my mind. If you use the `ImplicitSender` trait in your test code, then you can simplify the previous example to just this code:

```
testActor ! GetSomething
expectMsg(1)
```

When you pull in `ImplicitSender`, you get an implicit `ActorRef` in scope, which becomes the sender that your actor under test will respond to. This implicit `ActorRef` that you get also supports some specialized assertions (such as the `expectMsg` assertion used in the example) that allow you to verify the responses you receive during testing. This way of testing request/response semantics is much simpler then the ask-based solution and is something you should be using in actor unit tests.

Using TestProbes

The last tool in the essential actor-testing arsenal is Akka's `TestProbe` utility. If you write enough actor code, you're frequently going to find yourself needing to unit test an actor that communicates with another actor to help it do its work. We see this scenario in the `OrderManager` actor for our bookstore app as it needs three other actors in order to complete it's processing. Because a unit test is supposed to only test a single unit, we need a way to simulate the request/response handling from those actors and not include their actual code execution as part of that test. Luckily for us, Akka's `TestProbe` is set up to do just that job.

When you have other actors to simulate behaviors for, you need to substitute `TestProbes` in for them and then stub their behavior for whatever scenario you are testing. If you are doing a request/response interaction, then that interaction will look something like this:

```
myDependencyProbe.expectMsg("foo")
myDependencyProbe.reply("bar")
```

Here, we test both that the actor under test sent the dependency the correct message and that it handled the response correctly. too. If either of these assertions turned out to be not true, the test would fail.

With plain Scala components, you may use mocking to simulate behavior, with something such as Mockito. However, actors, and how they are setup and handle messages, don't lend themselves well to standard mocking. `TestProbes` give you an easy way to this mocking so that you can properly test your actors that use other actors.

Testing the SalesOrderProcessor actor

Let's take what you've learned over the previous sections and now apply it to our `SalesOrderProcessor` actor. I'm fond of ScalaTest as a testing framework, so the examples you will see here, and elsewhere in the book, will be based on that library. The techniques showed could very easily be used with other testing libraries too (such as specs2), so don't feel that this is an approach that can only be used with ScalaTest.

The first thing we should look at for our test is the test class declaration and the variable scoping definition that we will use for our testing. The class definition is shown here:

```
class SalesOrderProcessorUnitSpec
  extends FlatSpec with Matchers
  with BeforeAndAfterAll with MockitoSugar{
    import SalesOrderProcessor._
    implicit val system = ActorSystem()
  . . .
}
```

Our test class extends the ScalaTest `FlatSpec` class, which is required for us to build out a test specification using ScalaTest. The test class also mixes in `MockitoSugar`, which is a ScalaTest trait that allows us to interact with the `Mockito` mocking library in our test spec. For our purposes, `Mockito` will be used to mock the DAO used in `SalesOrderProcessor` as we won't be directly interacting with the database for this test. An `ActorSystem` is also created in the test class to house any actors that we need for testing.

Now, let's take a look at the variable scoping class that I setup for the test. A scoping class defines a sort of mini environment that can be set up for and is isolated to each scenario in the test. For our test, the scoping class looks like this:

```
class scoping extends TestKit(system) with ImplicitSender{
  val userMgr = TestProbe(UserManagerName)
  val bookMgr = TestProbe(SalesOrderManager.BookMgrName)
  val creditHandler = TestProbe(CreditHandlerName )
  val namesMap = Map(
    UserManagerName -> userMgr.ref.path.name,
    SalesOrderManager.BookMgrName -> bookMgr.ref.path.name,
    CreditHandlerName -> creditHandler.ref.path.name
  )
  val nowDate = new Date
  val mockDao = mock[SalesOrderProcessorDao]
  val orderProcessor = TestActorRef(new SalesOrderProcessor{
    override val dao = mockDao
    override def newDate = nowDate
    override def lookup(name:String) =
    context.actorSelection(
      s"akka://default/system/${namesMap.getOrElse(name, "")}")
  })
}
```

This test `scoping` class extends from Akka's `TestKit` class, as this is a requirement for using `ImplicitSender`. We need `ImplicitSender` here to set up `ActorRef` to receive the responses from `OrderProcessor` that is being tested.

For each instance of this `scoping` class (which equates to each test scenario), `TestProbe` instances are created to represent the `BookManager`, `UserManager`, and `CreditHandler` that are needed to process the request. The `namesMap` setup there allows us to substitute these probes when the dependencies are being looked up.

A value is set up called `nowDate` with the intention of overriding the `newDate` method on `SalesOrderProcessor` to return that value. There are a few places in the code that set new `Date` instances on case classes. As we intend to do object equality for the assertions, we need to make sure we have a match on the dates too, and this allows that to happen. A mock DAO instance is then set up to allow us to stub the interaction with the database.

Lastly, we create a new instance of the `SalesOrderProcessor` actor, wrapping it in `TestActorRef` so that it gets hooked into the `CallingThreadDispatcher`. I'm using a direct instantiation (via `new`) as opposed to an instantiation based on `Props` because we need to override a few behaviors on the actor in order to test it. The first thing we override is the `dao`, substituting in the mock DAO that was created. The next thing that is overridden is the `newDate` method, making it always return the `nowDate` value set up previously. The last thing overridden is the `lookup` method. `TestProbe` has a different root actor path, and these probes have dynamic names, so this change allows us to find the probes that we set up and hook them into our test.

Note that instead of code overriding, like I'm doing here, you could have set up dependency injection and injected in things such as the DAO (via the constructor most likely). It's really just a matter of personal preference. There's always more than one way to do things.

Overriding a method like this skips pieces of the component's functionality, so there's always a risk in doing it. However, as long as you have another level of test (integration, acceptance) above this that does not have the overriding, then you mitigate that risk. If we had an integration test that dispatched full instances of `BookManager`, `UserManager`, and `CreditHandler`, then we would not need to override lookup, and that would mitigate the risk of overriding it in this unit test.

The next piece of code to look at is the frame of the test scenario, which looks like this:

```
"A request to create a new sales order" should{
  """write a new order to the db and respond
  with that new order when everything succeeds""" in new scope{
    . . .
  }
}
```

Here, using the ScalaTest `FlatSpec` test structure, we set up the functionality we intend to test (a create order request) and also add a single scenario. I like to start by adding the fully successful scenario first and then working in the error scenarios after, which is what's being done here.

The first piece of logic in that scenario body will involve setting up the inputs and expected outputs for the test:

```
val lineItem = LineItemRequest(2, 1)
val cardInfo = CreditCardInfo("Chris Baxter", "Visa",
"1234567890", new Date)
val request = CreateOrder(1, List(lineItem), cardInfo)
```

```
val expectedLineItem = SalesOrderLineItem(0, 0, lineItem.bookId,
1, 19.99, nowDate, nowDate)
val expectedOrder = SalesOrder(0, request.userId, 99,
SalesOrderStatus.InProgress, 19.99, List(expectedLineItem),
nowDate, nowDate)
val finalOrder = expectedOrder.copy(id = 987)
```

The first three lines involve setting up the input to our test. The next set of lines involves creating the order that will be passed into the DAO and the final order that will be sent back as a response.

Next, we need to provide some stubbing to the mock DAO so that when the correct call happens on it, we can have it return a mocked result:

```
mockDao.createSalesOrder(expectedOrder) returns
Future.successful(finalOrder)
```

Using the `Mockito` syntax, we are saying that if the `createSalesOrder` method is called on the DAO with an argument equal to `expectedOrder`, then we will return a successful `Future` wrapping the `finalOrder` value (which is just the input value with an actual ID assigned to it).

Next, we can send the request to the actor and then set up the stubbed out behaviors on the probes:

```
orderProcessor ! Request
userMgr.expectMsg(FindUserById(request.userId))
userMgr.reply(FullResult(BookstoreUser(request.userId,
"Chris", "Baxter", "chris@masteringakka.com",
new Date, new Date)))

bookMgr.expectMsg(FindBook(lineItem.bookId))
bookMgr.reply(FullResult(Book(lineItem.bookId,
"20000 Leagues Under the Sea", "Jules Verne",
List("fiction"), 19.99,
10, new Date, new Date)))

creditHandler.expectMsg(ChargeCreditCard(cardInfo, 19.99))
creditHandler.reply(FullResult(CreditCardTransaction(99, cardInfo,
19.99, CreditTransactionStatus.Approved, Some("abc123"),
new Date, new Date)))
```

We send the message using tell and then start stubbing the probe behaviors. Each of the three dependent actors are mocked out to return the result that allows the flow to go all the way through without any errors. All probe stubbing has to be done after the message is sent to the actor under test. When you call `expectXXX`, the test stops and waits for that condition to become true (within an allowed amount of time). If you do this before sending the message to the test actor, then that condition will never happen and your tests will always fail.

The last thing in our test is the final assertion, which looks like this:

```
expectMsg(FullResult(finalOrder))
```

Here, we are stating that the implicit `ActorRef` in scope (via `ImplicitSender`) has received a response message equal to `FullResult(finalOrder)`. If this is true, then the test scenario passes.

The full code for this test can be found under the `chapter2` code distribution at the following path: `chapter2/bookstore-app/order-services/src/test/scala/com/packt/masteringakka/bookstore/order/SalesOrderProcessorUnitSpec.scala`

If you want to run this test, you can do so by opening the sbt shell and running the following commands:

```
> project orderServices
> test
```

When you run the test, you should see output indicating that there was one total test, and it passed without any failures.

Testing homework

So, as it stands, our unit test for the `SalesOrderProcessor` actor is woefully short in terms of code coverage. All we have covered here is the success case, and while that certainly hits a lot of the code lines, it does not prove that our error-handling situations work correctly.

Your homework for this chapter (if you choose to accept it) is to finish out the test coverage for this actor, within `SalesOrderProcessorUnitSpec` that was already provided by me. This will get you more familiar with testing a complicated actor and also with the test facilities described in this section. You should focus on covering all of the other possible outcomes that this actor supports as it goes through its flow logic. When done, you should have a fully comprehensive test specification for this actor and feel confident that its flow logic is correct.

Summary

Hopefully, this chapter has served as a nice refresher for you on Akka actors. At this point, you should understand what Akka actors can do and how you can use them to write safe concurrent code. You should now have a good understanding of the FSM trait, and how you can employ it to build complex workflow-like processes with your actors. Lastly, you explored the different levels of automated testing, and how you can use things such as `TestProbe` and `TestActorRef` to test your actors.

Now that we have gotten this refresher out of the way, it is time to start thinking about bigger refactors to the bookstore app. In the next chapter, we will be talking about DDD and how you can use that approach to model your code in a way that more closely relates to the business domain(s) you're working in. So gear up and get ready to change the way you think about modeling software.

3
Curing Anemic Models with Domain-Driven Design

Now that we've had a refresher on the actor model, and how Akka leverages it as a concurrency mechanism, we can start with the first of our big refactors. In the *Assessing the application's domain model* section, in `Chapter 1`, *Building a Better Reactive App*, one of the issues I pointed out with the original bookstore app was that its code model was not a strong representation of the business model. I even went so far as to call the model anemic, which implies that it is a weak representation of the behaviors that are inherent in the business model. So, what can we do to fix this?

The **domain-driven design (DDD)** is a concept that can be applied to domain modeling to transform the business domain into an application model that directly maps to concepts in the business domain. In this chapter, we will use this approach to start making improvements to our app. Following a DDD approach will strengthen the bond between the business domain and the application model, making it easier for people who understand the business domain to work with the code. Here is what you can expect to learn in this chapter:

- An understanding of what DDD is and how you can use it when modeling software
- Knowing the core concepts within the DDD lexicon such as entity, aggregate and bounded context
- Strategic DDD, and how it can be used to draw the boundaries between different bounded contexts
- What anemic domain models are and how they differ from a rich domain model
- How to model your actor based applications to better fit a DDD approach

What is DDD?

The term DDD was coined by Eric Evans in his book, *Domain-Driven Design* (Addison-Wesley, Eric Evans, 2004). It is an approach to software development where the application implementation will completely be a mirror complex and an ever evolving business domain. The core of the focus is on the domain model itself, with other more generic concerns (security, persistence, user interface) being treated as secondary to the domain model itself. The domain model is considered a potential differentiator to the business (unlike the more generic concerns); hence, the increased focused on modeling it within your applications and then representing it within your code, evolving that model as the business evolves.

DDD is all about a set of patterns to facilitate building out complex (enterprise level) applications from the domain model outward. If you have implemented any **Enterprise application integration** (**EAI**) patterns, then some of the DDD patterns may be familiar to you (albeit with different names). The patterns in DDD will help you understand the different subdomains within your business and how applications within those subdomains use each other. You can then use this information to build out loosely coupled application modules, where you can easily understand how changes to one may ripple into another.

For the bookstore application, following a DDD approach will strengthen the bond between the business model and the application model. This approach will also help us draw lines in the sand between different subdomains within our business model. Overall, this will be part of the effort to start separating the different modules of our monolith. In fact, this chapter, along with the next two chapters (Chapter 4, *Making History with Event Sourcing*, and Chapter 5, *Separating Concerns with CQRS*), can really be thought of as one big, related refactor. One main goal of that refactor is to allow us to have completely separate application modules, thus breaking apart our monolith.

Knowing where the domain layer fits

When following a DDD approach, it's important to understand where the domain layer fits into a traditional layered architecture. For example, let's say you worked in an organization that had three separate applications that you were building out for your user base. Using DDD, the layered architecture to support those three separate applications will look like the following diagram:

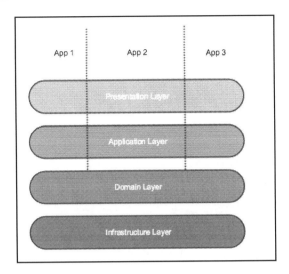

An important thing to note here is that the **Domain Layer** (and less importantly, the **Infrastructure Layer**) runs across logical application boundaries. The domain model is meant to represent the business domain, irrespective of any one application that will be built on top of it. Those separate applications will more than likely have their own **Application Layer**, where the logic and handling specific to that particular app lives. Each application will also have its own **Presentation Layer** to show whatever widgets and controls are needed to support user interactions with that app. However, the **Domain Layer** runs across all of those distinct apps and, as such, is a cross-cutting concern to the multiple applications you build out.

Understanding strategic DDD

Ideally, when building out a domain model, you have a single team that is working on one unified model. If you've worked on big projects enough, you know that this is a pipe dream and unlikely to happen. When you are working in big teams and on large scale projects, the single model generally fragments into smaller models. Strategic DDD is a set of principles and patterns to maintain model integrity in the face of multiple submodels.

Within a smaller system, where you maybe have one model but you still choose to go with a DDD approach, this decision is more of a personal choice and less of a necessity. When you have a big set of systems, all of which need to communicate with each other, DDD becomes a strategic decision in order to deal with the complexities of integrating these systems and models. That's why this particular flavor of DDD is referred to as strategic DDD.

Within strategic DDD, there are some terms that I'll define next, which are set up to deal with maintaining consistency across these multiple submodels. A lot of what you will see in the following paragraphs will come directly from Eric Evans' book.

Ubiquitous language

As mentioned at the beginning of this chapter, DDD is about building a domain model that properly represents the problem domain being built. In order to work on this model together, it's important that both the domain experts (business team) and technical personnel are speaking the same language. We can't have the domain experts referring to a concept as one thing and the engineers referring to the same concept as something else. As such, a DDD approach advocates coming up with a ubiquitous language that is used to define the model and is also used when discussing the model. This language will be represented in diagrams, application code, business presentations, and meetings and conversations in an effort to have everyone speaking the same language.

Bounded context

When you have multiple models in play on a large project, it's important to define the boundaries of what each of those models handle so that concepts from one model don't seep into a negative effect on another. A bounded context draws a line in the sand between what one model will do and not do. By having this clear delineation between models, it makes it very clear what the purpose of that model is so it's not watered down by potentially unrelated concepts. Once you have these context bounds defined, you can figure out ways in which they can and will communicate when and if necessary.

Continuous integration

In Strategic DDD, when you have multiple people working in the same bounded context, it's possible for the model to fragment as each person's ideas of the model diverge. This gets really exacerbated when you are working in large teams. To mitigate this risk, you need to have a process where the application code and other implementation artifacts are being merged frequently, with automated tests used to detect issues (and fragmentation) quickly.

If you've worked on an agile team developing software recently, this is probably not a new term to you. But kudos to Evans for identifying this as a need back in 2004, way before continuous integration became as commonplace as it is today.

Context map

When you have multiple models, it's possible that people won't always be aware of the context bounds. When this happens, teams can make changes that can blur the edges of the boundaries or make intercommunication between contexts overly complicated. To solve this, Evans proposes that you identify each model in play on the project and clearly define its bounded context. You should name each bounded context and incorporate the names into the ubiquitous language. You should also describe the points of contact between the models, showing explicit translation and highlighting any sharing. This effort is called context mapping, and Evans relates it to mapping the terrain of the domain.

Patterns of intercommunication in strategic DDD

When you have multiple models, you are eventually going to need points of communication between them. In his book, Evans describes some standard patterns within strategic DDD to model these communications that are crossing bounded contexts. Those patterns are described in the following sections.

Published language

In this pattern of bounded context intercommunication, instead of translating to and from the models of each language, a shared language is developed outside of those models. When the bounded contexts need to communicate, they do so using that shared language. In this approach, neither model is being subservient (or dominant) to the other. They each use the intermediary and translate to and from that instead of to and from another model.

Open host service

Typically, when integrating with a separate bounded context, a team will develop a translation layer to insulate their own context's model from that other model. But, what if you find that you have one particular subsystem (context) that is in high demand across the other subsystems? Defining a custom translation layer in each context that needs it can slow down the agility of other teams. When this happens, you can create a protocol layer (as perhaps a RESTful web service) that allows others to easily integrate with your model as a set of services. In that layer, you can encapsulate the intricacies of dealing with your model's internal protocols and APIs. In this way, an open host service is similar to the **Gang of Four** (**GoF**) Facade design pattern.

Shared kernel

In some cases, separate teams can push forward in parallel, rather quickly, work on their own models. In doing so, it may end up that what they are producing doesn't end up fitting together well at all. More effort is spent on writing translation layers and retrofitting code than on continuous integration, resulting in code duplication and weakening of the ubiquitous language. If this happens, it's beneficial to create a shared kernel (like a shared library) to represent the model overlap that both teams will use.

Customer/supplier

In multimodel systems, you frequently end up with situations where one model (or subsystem) feeds another. This kind of situation can be referred to as one subsystem being downstream from functionality in the other. With this kind of relationship, you need to make sure the upstream team's agility is not compromised by a rigid change management process with the downstream team or by fear of breaking downstream functionality. You also want to make sure that the downstream team does not feel helpless and at the mercy of differing upstream priorities. To solve this, the downstream team needs to be treated as a customer to the upstream team (which in turn is a supplier to that customer). The customer becomes a stakeholder in the planning meetings for the supplier team, negotiating and budgeting time for their own downstream needs. This ensures that their own needs are known and being taken into account when planning upstream work schedules.

Conformist

The need here is similar to customer/supplier, in that one subsystem (model) needs the functionality of another, but in this case they are not treated as a stakeholder. The downstream subsystem uses the protocols or APIs of that upstream bounded context as-is and has no direct influence over their development. The impact and usage of the other bounded context can be directly seen in the conforming context's model.

Anticorruption layer

This is a similar situation to conformist, in that the downstream is not a stakeholder of the upstream system, and they use the protocols and APIs as-is. The difference here is that the downstream spends development effort building a translation layer to communicate with and map concepts from the upstream system. In this way, the downstream context is protected from corruption from the upstream context's model seeping into its own model, hence the name anticorruption layer.

Visualizing the spectrum of cooperation

In a post on `methodsandtools.com`, Dan Haywood had an interesting way of visualizing these different intercommunication patterns as a cascading chain, where each lower level implied even less cooperation effort than the layer before it. I have recreated that diagram in an effort to show this concept and how it applies to the patterns described above.

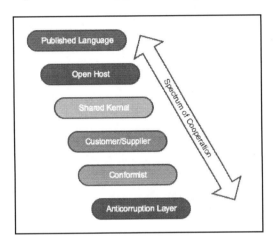

The main point of this diagram is to show that as you work your way down the chain, the level of cooperation for the interactions between two bounded contexts drops. At the top of the chain, with published language, the two contexts are making a very concerted effort to work well together, even coming up with an additional third lingo so that the intercommunication doesn't seem tilted to either side. But, by the time you get to the bottom with the **Anticorruption Layer**, there is little to no cooperation between the two bounded contexts. At this point, one of the models has decided to completely insulate itself from the other rather than trying to work together at all (as with customer/supplier).

Which pattern you choose carries with it the level of cooperation and work necessary to make those interactions work. Keep that in mind when deciding on what strategy to use.

 You can find the full post that this diagram came from on the following link: `http://www.methodsandtools.com/archive/archive.php?id=97`.

Visualizing the relationships in strategic DDD

There's another diagram that I want to share, this one coming from a part of Evans' book (you can also see this diagram on the DDD wikipedia page). The purpose of this diagram is to show the relationships between all patterns and concepts for strategic DDD and how they support maintaining model integrity.

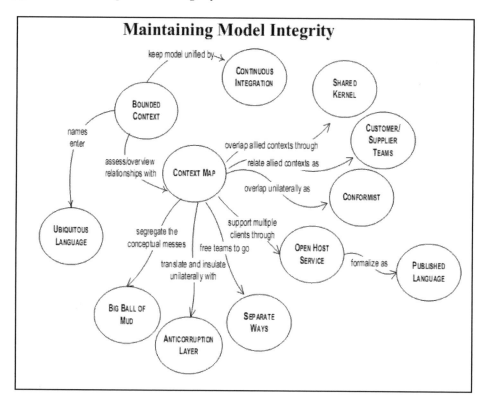

 You can find this diagram on the Wikipedia page for DDD at the following link: https://en.wikipedia.org/wiki/Domain-driven_design.

When I look at this diagram, the big thing that jumps out at me is the fact that everything in strategic DDD flows outward from the context map. This is an important artifact, as it defines the level of cooperation between the multiple bounded contexts in your organization. Because the context map is so important, we will create one as part of our refactor to DDD. It will help us define the relationships between our different application modules of user management, inventory management, credit handling, and order processing.

You may have noticed a couple of bubbles in this diagram that have not been mentioned yet, such as Separate Ways and Big Ball of Mud. I personally didn't think either of these concepts were worth dedicating too many words to, so I left them out of the previous sections.

Basically, a Big Ball of Mud is what happens when you don't constantly plan and refine your models. You end up with something that is amorphous, messy, and tough to deal with, which is where that name comes from.

Separate Ways is a level of cooperation where there is absolutely no cooperation at all. This is a bounded context that has no relationship with any of the other multiple bounded contexts in your system. It will be one level below **Anticorruption Layer** in the **Spectrum of Cooperation** diagram. The idea is that if your context map shows no need to integrate with this context, then it frees that team to go on their separate way and not have to worry themselves with integration concerns.

Building blocks of DDD

Now that we understand some of the higher-level concepts within DDD, it's time to dig into the details of how to structure and build out the domain layer within your organization. DDD describes some core building blocks that you will use to structure your domain model, which I will describe in the following sections. You have probably bumped into some of these building blocks in some form or another as a few are present in other software design approaches too.

Entity

Within DDD, an entity is described as an object instance that is defined by its identity as opposed to being defined by its attributes. This identity will be constant over time, even when the attributes that make up the entity change. This identity allows instances of the entity to be consistently distinguished from each other, and therefore, must be guaranteed to be unique. Because of this unique identity requirement, entities have inherent complexity and overhead associated with them.

Value object

A value object in DDD can be thought of as being fully represented by its attributes and not having an identity. It allows you to model representations without the complexities associated with maintaining an identity. Additionally, it is also meant to be immutable.

A good example of the difference between entity and value object is money. If you were modeling the exchange of money, you would probably treat it as a value object, as you don't care about the individual identity of the bills. But, if you were building a model for the Federal Reserve, you would make the money an entity, as each bill would need to be uniquely identified (by its serial number).

Aggregate

An aggregate is defined as a collection of objects (both entities and value objects) bound together by a root entity. The aggregate root entity is responsible for providing access to and for maintaining the consistency of objects inside its boundary, as well as generating domain events for those objects. External objects will only be able to hold references to the aggregate root and not for any of the contained objects. In OO modeling terms, this is a compositional association where the contained objects are completely owned by the containing objects. In our bookstore app, `SalesOrder` is the aggregate root to the `SalesOrderLineItem` instances.

Domain event

A domain event is a domain object that indicates an important event within the model has occurred. Generally, there is a direct relationship between an action (command) and any number of domain events that occur as the result of that action. Domain events are the backbone of the event sourced world, as they represent the complete history of a particular entity in the system. This is something we will cover in depth in the next chapter.

Service

When a process or responsibility within the domain does not naturally fit into an entity or a value object, then this operation can be accomplished by a service. These services should be completely stateless, as state will imply that it may be better served as an entity or value object. The interface for the service should be defined in terms of the language of the model and the operation name should be a part of the ubiquitous language.

Repository

A repository is a best practice pattern in DDD that delegates the retrieval of domain objects to a specialized object (a repository) such that the alternative storage implementations can be easily interchanged. This is just a best practice to centralize persistent entity loading/storing so that the implementation details associated with persistence don't leak out all over the code.

Factory

A factory is another best practice pattern that centralizes and encapsulates the creation of complex entities and aggregates behind another object. Factories, generally, return abstractions as opposed to concrete classes. This approach allows one to easily swap out implementations without affecting any of the application code that uses those abstractions.

Identifying anemic vs rich models

Now that you've gotten a crash course in DDD, we can start to better articulate the possible weakness in the current bookstore model. In the opening chapter, I called the model anemic, which implies that it is feeble and not strongly representative of the domain we are working in. I didn't really back that up with too much explicit evidence though, so let's dig into how to identify an anemic model.

A major issue with this model, as far as I can see, is that the major entities in the system (`Book`, `BookstoreUser`, `CreditCardTransaction`, and `SalesOrder`) are implemented as simple case classes that have no functionality on them besides the setting of their attributes. All of the functionality related to dealing with those entities is done in manager actors, which is somewhat similar to services in the DDD lexicon.

Services should be ancillary in a DDD approach, but they appear central in our model, robbing the entities of the functionality related to their existence. Also, in general, you should beware of classes that end in `*Manager`, as their function is not truly clear within the context of the business domain, and they generally have too much responsibility. With no functionality in the domain entities, they are just empty husks that weaken the overall representation of our model, hence the anemic name. We need to flip this association around and have these entities become front and center when taking actions against the model. This should reduce the dependency on services, further strengthening the model.

If we need an intermediary between an entity and a requested action, we should make sure that the intermediary is a proper part of our domain model and language. For example, when dealing with books, instead of using a `BookManager` to access them, we can introduce the concept of an `InventoryClerk` that is in charge of accessing the books within our inventory system. This is a more real-world concept and should be properly reflected in our code.

If we make these changes, we can take our currently anemic model and enrich it with the concepts, terminology, and functionality of our domain. Having a model that is well representative of the ubiquitous language of our domain, and one with functionality (methods, commands, events) that directly maps to that language, is what is referred to as a rich domain model. It's just so enriched with domain focused goodness that people refer to it that way. That is our goal for the refactor here, having a more rich model to start to build additional functionality around.

Designing our DDD refactor

Before we get started with laying out the DDD refactor, it bears mentioning that as the code stands right now, DDD is probably a bit much for it. A DDD approach is good for complex domains and large systems, neither of which can really be said about the current bookstore app. You sort of have to use your imagination here and visualize this app being developed by multiple teams within a large organization, with each module being owned by different teams. With that kind of backdrop in place, a refactor like this makes more sense and is a better fit for the DDD problem set.

The two major goals for our refactor are as follows:

1. Enrich the model and have it be more representative of the problem domain, using DDD building blocks such as entities and aggregates.
2. Split the application into four separate bounded contexts for customer management, inventory management, credit processing, and sales order processing.

Before we jump into the code, it makes sense to do a little modeling first. The major artifacts we want to produce to lead us into the code implementation are a context map and also some basic class diagrams for each bounded context.

The bookstore context map

Back when describing strategic DDD, we talked about the importance of producing a context map. This diagram will show the different bounded contexts within the domain as well as the different integration patterns for those contexts. The context map for the changes we'll make to the bookstore app can be seen in the following diagram:

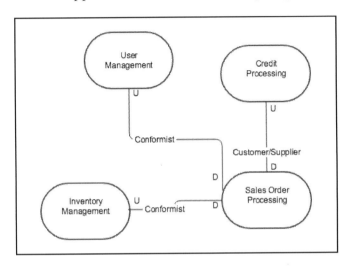

In this diagram, each separate context is represented by a bubble. The lines between the contexts represent the relationships/integrations between them. The **U** and **D** letters represent the upstream and downstream sides of the relationship, respectively, with an upstream context having influence over one that is downstream from it.

In the diagram, you can see that **Sales Order Processing** is highly dependent on the other contexts in the system. The relationship types I have set up between **Sales Order Processing** and the other contexts are sort of arbitrary, but they are what I, reasonably, think would exist in our fictitious organization. A lot of deciding on what strategy to use depends on the teams you have and how they work together. Since I don't really have that, I had to make guesses on how these contexts should depend on each other.

The relationship between **Sales Order Processing** and **Credit Processing** was set up as a **Customer/Supplier** relationship. The reason I chose this versus a **Conformist** is that I believe these two are pretty closely tied together. In fact, **Credit Processing** may exist mostly to serve the needs of the **Sales Order Processing** context. Because **Sales Order Processing** is a primary stakeholder in **Credit Processing** I chose **Customer/Supplier**, as it implies a higher level of cooperation between the teams creating these contexts.

In contrast, the relationship between **Sales Order Processing** and both **Inventory Management** and **User Management** was set up as **Conformist**. My thought here was that these contexts have their own needs above and beyond just being there to support sales. They should not let the needs of sales creep into their models, as sales is probably only a small part of what they do. As such, I saw **Sales Order Processing** needing to conform to whatever these two contexts do without any direct influence into their development plans.

One thing to note in this diagram is that the bookstore-common library is not represented in this context map. Some may have thought of this library as a shared kernel that all other contexts have a relationship with. To me, the things done in that common library are more infrastructure related than domain related. Infrastructure is a separate layer to the domain layer, so that's why you don't see that library in this context map.

Modelling DDD with actors

The idea with this remodeling will be to place the emphasis on the domain entities within each individual context, making them own the majority of the logic related to managing themselves. We will also try and introduce a ubiquitous language around user management, modeling after real-life concepts, and then having the code closely resemble the language and those concepts.

In the old model, the domain entities were just simple-case classes. They didn't have any logic, validations, or operations associated with them other than the simple setting and getting of fields. In the new model, the entities will be modeled as actors who receive messages that represent the operations (or vocabulary) that can be performed against that entity. In this way, the entities themselves will be richer in the functionality that they expose and the logic they handle.

Understanding the vocabulary of a component

When referring to the vocabulary of an entity or aggregate, I'm referring to the commands (requests) as well as the events that it can handle as a result of those commands. This is the language that a certain entity or aggregate can speak, and it's how other components within the system communicate with it. For the code in this book, I am putting the vocabulary on the companions of the actors that the language is for. I think it's a decent enough approach for an actor-oriented DDD system, as it keeps the terminology with the component that speaks it.

Difficulties of DDD and actors

One of the difficulties in doing DDD with actors is that actors don't directly expose their external state. For an actor-based entity, that is, if you request a reference to that entity, all you get is `ActorRef` and getting at the fields won't be so easy. You'd have to send another message after (an ask) to get the field info, and this just seemed a bit clunky to me. For this reason, I created a concept called `FieldsObject` within the model that is a lightweight representation of entities fields or attributes. I intentionally avoided calling it `ValueObject` because the term value object already has meaning within DDD and I didn't want to create any confusion.

In doing this refactoring, I toyed with the idea of returning richer proxies to the actors that had all the full-field values and the operations for that entity directly exposed in order to make calls to an underlying `ActorRef` (via ask), and then return a Future for the new entity in a kind of async copy semantic similar to the copy on a case class. This will be more in line with a properly modeled DDD, but I felt it was pushing away from actors more and that was not a direction I wanted to go in. Bottom line, modeling DDD with actors can be a challenge but that doesn't mean it shouldn't be attempted. This is a stepping stone in our total refactoring effort and it will lend itself well to transitioning to event sourcing in `Chapter 4`, *Making History with Event Sourcing*.

Remodeling the user management context

The first context we will ply our new DDD trade on is the user management context. The new model to show the major players within that context can be seen in the following diagram:

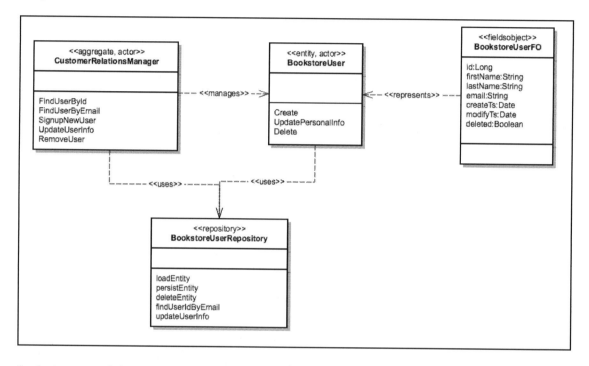

In the new model, you can see that `BookstoreUser` has changed from a basic case class to an actor. The text appearing in the methods section of the class box represents the messages that the actor handles.

Sitting in front of that entity actor (and acting as its supervisor) is `CustomerRelationsManager`. I'm calling this an aggregate because it is responsible for the `BookstoreUser` entities underneath it, and it's where the calls for those entities initially flow through. The items in its methods section represent the actions (or vocabulary) it can handle against the `BookstoreUser` entities.

We also have a DDD repository class, `BookstoreUserRepository`, where the SQL related logic happens. This is a slight change (currently in name only) from the old model where we used DAO classes to handle SQL logic. A repository is meant to be a higher level abstraction than a DAO though, as it deals with objects and collections of objects whereas a DAO deals with lower level data. A repository can use a DAO, to provide a swappable (via dependency injection) abstraction as to how it gets its objects, but for simplicity's sake, we did not do that here. This particular repository class handles all of the lookup and management operations for the `BookstoreUser` entity that go against the relational database.

Lastly, we have `fieldsobject` for the `BookstoreUser` entity called `BookstoreUserFO`. This is what will be returned to anyone who requests an instance of a particular `BookstoreUser` entity.

Remodeling the inventory management context

The next bounded context that need to be remodeled is the inventory management context (formerly the book-services module). A diagram showing the new model can be seen below:

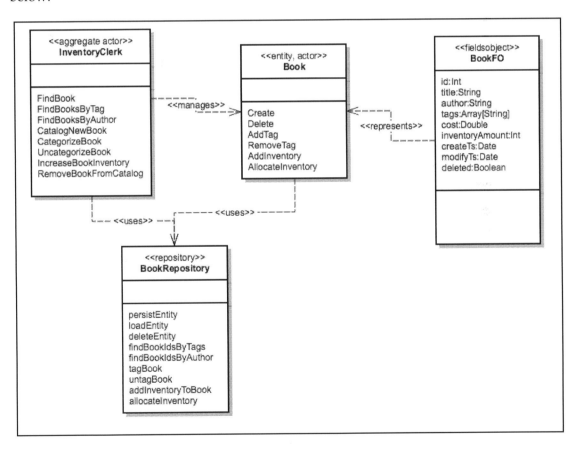

The concepts here are the same as the new user management model, with the aggregate, repository, entity, and fields object used to remodel inventory management.

Remodeling the credit processing context

The next context to look at is the credit processing context. The same approach will be followed here as we did with the other remodeling efforts, having the entity, repository, and fields object. The diagram for this model is as follows:

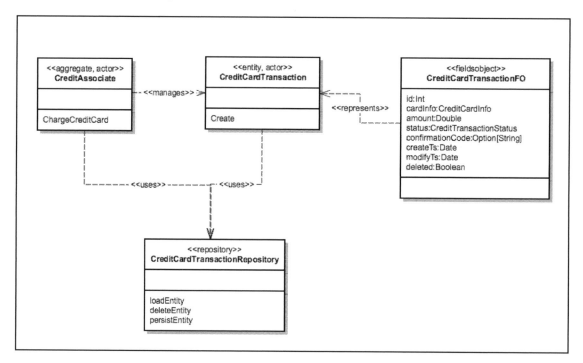

Remodeling the sales order processing context

The last context to remodel is the sales order processing context. The updated diagram for this context is as follows:

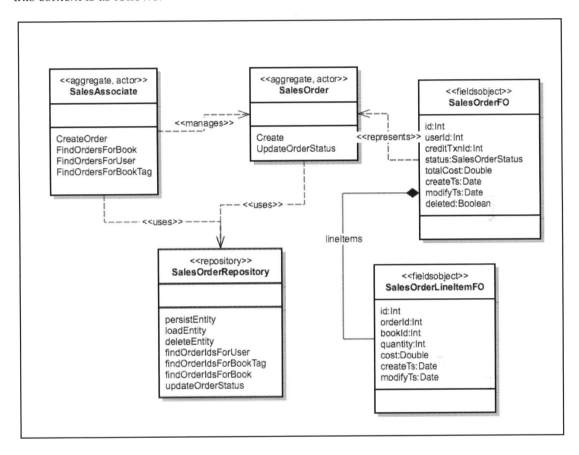

Things get a little more interesting with this model, as we have a DDD aggregate root in the SalesOrder entity. This entity also manages and exposes (via a fields object) the line items that make up the order.

Understanding the refactored bookstore code

So, we have now completed the remodeling effort to get our anemic model into something more rich and more in line with the building blocks of a good DDD. Now, it's time to dive into the code implementation a little, so that you can understand how the code was written to support this model. If you look at the `chapter3` code folder from the code distribution, you will notice that at the top level, it's divided into two root folders: `bookstore-app-incomplete` and `bookstore-app-complete`. The folder marked as incomplete will be the one that I will be referencing the code from. It will also be the place where you will do some homework to complete the refactor later in the chapter. The folder marked as complete will be used by you to compare your homework results against my fully completed refactor.

The EntityActor abstract class

The `EntityActor` abstract class defines the behaviors for our DDD entity actor classes. It's modeled as an FSM, where each of the states in the FSM represent lifecycle stages in creating or loading the entity from the DB and then working with it while it is in the initialized state. The states that this FSM can handle are shown in the following activity diagram.

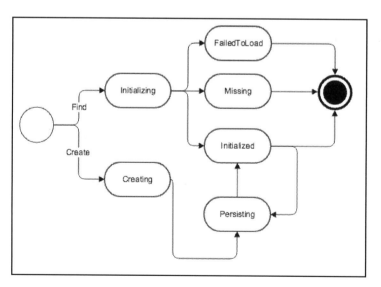

When the actor is started, depending on whether it was given an entity ID or not, it will either go into the **Initializing** state (has an ID) or into the **Creating** state. The **Creating** state is where any pre-create checks can be accomplished before making a call to persist the record (via a repository) and then transitioned into the **Persisting** state. The **Persisting** state is where we check the result of the persist operation (create in this case) and then transition into the **Initialized** State.

If it was not for create, then the actor transitions into the **Initializing** state and makes a request to load the record represented by this entity instance. From here, if it loads successfully, the actor will transition into the **Initialized** state. If no entity record was found, then the actor will transition into the **Missing** state, where requests to get the entity data will always return an `EmptyResult` value. The actor only stays in this state for one second before stopping itself. If there was an error loading the record, then the actor will transition into the **FailedToLoad** state, where requests to get the fields object for the entity will result in failures being returned. Similar to **Missing**, this is also a short-lived state.

If the actor loads or creates properly, it will end up in an **Initialized** state. In this state, requests to act upon that entity can be handled (for instance, changing a field value). When this happens, the code makes an appropriate persistence related call on the repository and then transitions into the **Persisting** state. If the call succeeds, the actor goes back to the **Initialized** state, modifying the cached in-memory representation of the fields object so that subsequent calls to get the fields data return the new state.

The actor will stay in the **Initialized** state for 60 seconds of inactivity before stopping itself. By doing this, the actor instance representing a particular entity is essentially like a cache that will allow quick access to the entity's field values, which will also reflect any recent changes made to that entity (as long as they have flowed through this code).

You can take a look at the full code for this class (and understand what it does) at the following location:
`common/src/main/scala/com/packt/masteringakka/bookstore/common/EntityActor.scala`.

The EntityAggregate abstract class

Another important framework-level class to look at is the `EntityAggregate` abstract class. The code for this class can be found in the same `EntityActor.scala` file that the `EntityActor` abstract class is defined in (a little bit further down in the file).

This class will be used as the extension point for our DDD actors that spawn and delegate to the individual entity instance actors. One important piece of code to look at is the definition for the `lookupOrCreateChild` method. That code can be seen as follows:

```
def lookupOrCreateChild(id:Int) = {
  val name = entityActorName(id)
  context.child(name).getOrElse{
    if (id > 0)
      context.actorOf(entityProps(id), name)
    else
      context.actorOf(entityProps(id))
  }
}
```

Based on the preceding code, when requesting a child actor, one of the three possible things can happen:

1. The child actor (by name, including the ID of the entity) already exists and will be used as is.
2. The child does not exist and this is a create operation (0 for ID); it is created with no specific name because we don't have an ID yet.
3. The child does not exist and we have an ID, we will create a new child with that ID as part of the child's name.

Once a child actor, or multiple child actors (for a multi-lookup request), are created/looked up, then the aggregate will do one of two things, depending on whether there are single or multiple entities involved:

1. **Single entity**: The aggregate will forward a message along to that single entity for final handling.
2. **Multiple entities**: The aggregate will perform a bunch of ask operations on those entities and consolidate the resulting Futures before responding to the caller.

In the second case, a helper method exists on entity to facilitate this multientity interaction. The code for this method is as follows:

```
def multiEntityLookup(f: => Future[Vector[Int]])
(implicit ex:ExecutionContext) = {
  for{
    ids <- f
    actors = ids.map(lookupOrCreateChild)
    fos <- Future.traverse(actors)(askForFo)
  } yield{
    FullResult(fos.flatMap(_.toOption))
  }
```

```
}
```

When you call this method, you supply a by-name function that will return a `Future[Vector[Int]]` representing the IDs of the entities to lookup. This will most likely be a repository method that loads the IDs based on some query against a database table. From there, the actors for those ids are looked up (or created) and then for each one, the fields object representing them is requested.

The fields object requesting happens in `askForFo`, which simply makes an ask request to the actor with the message being `EntityActor.GetFieldsObject`. The resulting list of Futures is then sequenced together into a single `Future[List[FO]]` with any non `FullResult` (empty or failures) being filtered out via `flatMap(_.toOption)`. In a real app, you will probably have error handling instead of just ignoring errors/empty results, perhaps raising a single error up to fail the entire request.

The code in this abstract class serves as the foundation for the aggregate actors delegating to actual entity actors. All the requests that are to go against entities funnel through an aggregate first, which are long lived single instance actors that are easily looked up by name. These actors, and the messages (vocabulary) that they handle, can be thought of as the outward facing interfaces in those different bounded contexts.

The Book and InventoryClerk actors

One of the contexts completed by me within the incomplete bookstore app is the inventory management context. This is where the code related to dealing with the `Book` entity lives. From the earlier model of this context, you may remember that the two main actors are `Book` (the entity) and `InventoryClerk` (the aggregate). You should give both of these actors a thorough look to see how they work together to expose the `Book` entity related functionality. I'll go through a couple of examples in detail here, showing single book lookup, multibook lookup, and a persist operation.

Looking up a single Book

If you want to look up a single `Book` entity by its identifier (primary key), then you send a `FindBook` message to the `InventoryClerk`. The handling of that message in `InventoryClerk` looks like this:

```
case FindBook(id) =>
  log.info("Finding book {}", id)
  val book = lookupOrCreateChild(id)
  book.forward(GetFieldsObject)
```

In the preceding code, you can see that we leverage the `lookupOrCreateChild` method, which was discussed earlier, to find (or create) the `Book` entity actor for the ID supplied. Then we forward a `GetFieldsObject` message to the `Book` instance, delegating the final response handling to that `Book` instance.

When the book is created, because it is given a nonzero id, the entity actor goes into the **Initializing** state and uses its repository to load the fields object from the database. After it finds it, it transitions into **Initialized**. If you look at the code in `EntityActor`, you will see that the definition of the **Initialized** state is as follows:

```
when(Initialized, 60 second)(standardInitializedHandling orElse
initializedHandling)
```

The `standardInitializeHandling` is a `StateFunction` that is fully provided in `EntityActor` while `initializeHandling` is another `StateFunction` that the person implementing `EntityActor` has to provide. The handling of `GetFieldsObject` is done in `standardInitializedHandling` so that you don't have to worry about implementing it yourself for each `EntityActor` you define. The handling is as follows:

```
case Event(GetFieldsObject, InitializedData(fo)) =>
  sender ! FullResult(fo)
  stay
```

In the preceding code, all that happens is that the fields object for this entity (supplied in the **Initializing** state) is returned to the sender and then the FSM stays in the **Initialized** state.

Looking up multiple books

If you want to lookup multiple book records, things are a little different in the `InventoryClerk` handling. As opposed to a simple forward after looking up the entity, the `InventoryClerk` handling needs to perform asks to multiple actors via the previously discussed `multiEntityLookup` method. The handling for looking up by author is shown as follows:

```
case FindBooksByAuthor(author) =>
  log.info("Finding books for author {}", author)
  val result = multiEntityLookup(repo.findBookIdsByAuthor(author))
  pipeResponse(result)
```

In the preceding code, you can see that the function supplied to `multiEntityLookup` is the `findBooksByAuthor` repository method. This will pass a Future containing the ids of the books that match the supplied author. From there, `multiEntityLookup` will find/create `Book` entity instances and pass each a `GetFieldsObject`, which will get the fields object from each entity that represents its field data. Lastly, the multiple Future instances are sequenced together and the `InventoryClerk` handling responds back to the caller with that aggregated set of `BookFO` instances.

Making a persistence action on a book

Entity actor instances can do more than just look up persisted data. They can also make changes to that persisted data, which will also update the cached fields object tied to that entity.

If you want to add some new inventory to a book, then you can start by sending an `IncreaseBookInventory` message to `InventoryClerk`. The handling for that message looks like this:

```
case IncreaseBookInventory(id, amount) =>
  persistOperation(id, Book.AddInventory(amount))
```

The `persistOperation` method is defined in `EntityActor` and it looks like this:

```
def persistOperation(id:Int, msg:Any){
  val entity = lookupOrCreateChild(id)
  entity.forward(msg)
}
```

The handling is pretty simple here. Just lookup or create the entity instance to delegate to and then forward it the message supplied as `msg`.

Inside of the `Book` entity, the `AddInventory` message is received while in the **Initialized** state, within the `initializedHandlingStateFunction`. That code is as follows:

```
case Event(AddInventory(amount:Int), InitializedData(fo)) =>
  requestFoForSender
  persist(fo, repo.addInventoryToBook(fo.id, amount),
  _ => fo.copy(inventoryAmount = fo.inventoryAmount + amount))
```

When we execute the preceding code, the first thing that happens is that we add a request to the mailbox to return the fields object to the sender after the `persist` operation completes. The code then calls the `persist` method, telling it to use the `addInventoryToBook` method on the repository to perform the update and to add the inventory amount to the cached fields object after the persistence completes. The `persist` method is defined in `EntityActor` as follows:

```
def persist(fo:FO, f: => Future[Int],
  foF:Int => FO, newInstance:Boolean = false) = {
  val daoResult = f
  daoResult.to(self, sender())
  goto(Persisting) using PersistingData(fo, foF, newInstance)
}
```

This method takes the following four things of importance:

1. The current fields object for this entity, represented by `fo`.
2. A by-name function that performs the persistence logic, represented by `f`.
3. A transformation function taking an `Int` and returning the modified fields object after the persistence completes, represented by `foF`.
4. A `Boolean` indicator of whether or not this `persist` call is the result of a new entity being created. If it is a new entity instance, then the `Int` from step 3 is used as the ID of the fields object.

The first thing the code does is execute the persistence function specified by `f`. It then pipes that result back to itself before transitioning into the **Persisting** state. The state data for the **Persisting** state includes the transformation function, `foF`, as well as the new instance indicator.

The last piece of the puzzle here is the code for the **Persisting** state that receives the successful result from the persistence operation, which is shown in the following code block:

```
case Event(i:Int, PersistingData(fo, f, newInstance)) =>
  val newFo = f(i)
  unstashAll()

  if (newFo.deleted){
    goto(Missing) using MissingData(newFo.id, Some(newFo))
  }
  else{
    if (newInstance) {
      postCreate(newFo)
      setStateTimeout(Initialized, Some(1 second))
```

```
        }
    goto(Initialized) using InitializedData(newFo)
}
```

The preceding code first invokes the fields object transformation function to arrive on the new instance of that object after the persistence operation is complete. It then unstashes all previously stashed messages in anticipation of going back to the **Initialized** state. This logic uses stash for non lifecycle messages while it is performing a persistence action to defer them until it's done with the persistence functionality.

If the persistence operation was a deletion, then the entity transitions into **Missing** as the record is no more and any requests to get its data should respond accordingly. If it was a create, then the `postCreate` hook is called to provide any necessary entity-specific post create handling logic. It also sets a short state timeout, as this entity instance does not have a name aligned with its ID yet (it didn't have the ID when we created it); so, it's best to just terminate it and let it be recreated on the next request.

Lastly, the code transitions into the **Initialized** state, allowing the persistence cycle to start all over again on the next persistence request.

There's a lot more code in both `Book` and `InventoryClerk` that you should look at to get a feel for how those components handle their logic. This was just a taste of some of the different things that an aggregate and its entities can do together.

Fixing the transaction in the order creation process

Way back in the *Avoiding cross-domain transactions* section, in Chapter 1, *Building a Better Reactive App*, I flagged the fact that we had a cross-domain transaction in the creation of a new `SalesOrder` entity. The SQL logic within that transaction not only created the order header and line items, but it also used the book table directly to decrement the inventory associated with that order. I also stated that this is not a real scalable solution, both from a performance standpoint and the fact that it's creating a strong tie (at the db level nonetheless) between these two contexts that will be difficult to deal with moving forward. It's not the time to start the process of getting rid of that transaction relationship and making it more flexible moving forward.

As part of the refactoring work in the incomplete code folder, I also finished the changes to the sales order processing context. The FSM code that used to be in `SalesOrderProcessor` is moved into the `SalesOrder` aggregate entity. Most of the flow that we showed in Chapter 2, *Simplifying Concurrent Programming with Actors*, modeling the new process flow (in the activity diagram), is still intact. The difference is that the entry point to that flow now happens when it is in the **Creating** state of the `SalesOrder` entity actor. You can take a look at the code in `SalesOrder` to see how the previous flow was fitted into the lifecycle logic of an entity actor.

The big change I made here was to remove the explicit inventory decrement as part of the sales order/line item record creation transaction. Now, instead, the `SalesOrder` entity defines a custom `postCreate` to publish an event that the `InventoryClerk` will listen for. That custom logic is defined as follows:

```
override def postCreate(fo:SalesOrderFO){
  val items = fo.lineItems.map(i => (i.bookId, i.quantity ))
  val event = InventoryClerk.OrderCreated(fo.id, items)
  context.system.eventStream.publish(event)
}
```

In the preceding code, you can see the `SalesOrder` entity publish an `OrderCreated` event to the actor system's event stream. That event contains the ID of the order that was created as well as the book IDs and quantities of each line item on the order. At this point, the order is not yet fully approved as the inventory is yet to be allocated.

When the `InventoryClerk` was created, in the constructor body, it subscribed to the `OrderCreated` event. When it receives that event, it looks up the `Book` entity instances for each book ID on the order and requests that each one allocates inventory for the order. The first part of that logic, where the entity instances are looked up and the requests are made to them, looks like this:

```
val futs =
  lineItems.
  map{
    case (bookId, quant) =>
    val f = (lookupOrCreateChild(bookId) ?
    Book.AllocateInventory(quant)).mapTo[ServiceResult[BookFO]]
    f.filter(_.isValid)
  }
```

In the preceding code, for each line item, we request the appropriate `Book` entity instance. The code then sends each entity instance an `AllocateInventory` message, specifying the amount to deduct from the current inventory allotment. This is done as an ask and the result is checked to make sure it is a `FullResult`. If it's not, the Future resulting from that ask will be failed.

Then, once we have all the Future instances from all those requests, we can sequence them together in an effort to see if even one of them is failed. If there is even one failure, we will consider the order to be backordered and publish the corresponding event. If they are all successful, we can consider the order accepted (and also publish an event). That code looks like this:

```
Future.sequence(futs).
map{ _ =>
  log.info("Inventory available for order {}", id)
  InventoryAllocated(id)
}.
recover{
  case ex =>
  log.warning("Inventory back ordered for order {}", id)
  InventoryBackOrdered(id)
}.
foreach(context.system.eventStream.publish)
```

The two possible events published in the preceding code, `InventoryAllocated` and `InventoryBackOrdered`, are listened for by the `SalesAssociate` actor so that it can modify the status of the order as a result, thus ending this two part back and forth between these two contexts via events. That code looks like this:

```
case InventoryAllocated(id) =>
  persistOperation(id,
  UpdateOrderStatus(SalesOrderStatus.Approved))

case InventoryBackOrdered(id) =>
  persistOperation(id,
  UpdateOrderStatus(SalesOrderStatus.BackOrdered ))
```

Both of these events will result in the status of the order being updated, just to a different status, depending on which event is received.

This concept of using domain events (a DDD concept) is a common way of having one context react to changes in another in a more indirect and decoupled way. In this kind of model, there is an action or a command that is specified in a present tense verb, for instance, `AllocateInventory`. Then, when an action is completed, an event is spawned that reflects the result of that action using a past tense verb. In this particular case, that verb is `InventoryAllocated`.

This concept of an action yielding an event describing that action is going to be an important one moving forward. In fact, we'll start to see it used more in Chapter 4, *Making History with Event Sourcing*, and Chapter 5, *Separating Concerns with CQRS*, when we start introducing event sourcing and CRQS. The idea is that actions in one context can lead to reactions in other contexts via the events that are being generated. This approach will be the foundation for eventually de-coupling our contexts from each other as we refactor the bookstore application.

Improvements needed for the refactor

We made great strides in this chapter and cleaned up some of the issues mentioned in Chapter 1, *Building a Better Reactive App*. We have a richer application model now thanks to our DDD approach, which addresses the concerns from the *Assessing the application's domain model* section, in Chapter 1, *Building a Better Reactive App*. We also removed that ugly cross-domain transaction for inventory allocation, addressing the concerns from the *Avoiding cross-domain transactions* section, in Chapter 1, *Building a Better Reactive App*. Even though we addressed some concerns, there are a few things with the current state of the code that are worth mentioning as areas that need improvement.

For starters, there's a lot of hand-rolled lifecycle related code in `EntityActor` that I feel can go away if it is handled by a framework, preferably Akka. Also, I sort of feel like I reinvented EJB there, and that's not really a good feeling. Thankfully, Akka Persistence, and its `PersistentActor` construct, is somewhat similar in spirit to the code I hand rolled. Akka Persistence also comes with a lot of additional functionality that I feel will be needed in our bookstore app over time. As such, we'll jump right in to switching over to that framework for our persistent entity needs in the next chapter.

The next area that needs addressing is that the back and forth event handling to accommodate inventory allocation is not dependable. It just uses the in-memory event bus of the actor system. If one of the players in that back and forth was not running at the time, then the process will not work. We need something more robust to build this process on top of. Thankfully, this is a big part of what Akka Persistence is all about, so we can fix this in the next chapter as well.

Lastly, the code that we have for caching the current state of an entity instance (in an actor instance) works great if there's just one single server in our system, but it will fall apart quickly if we have more than one server. With more than one server, multiple cached instances of that same entity instance can exist across the multiple servers, each one being different as each may have seen different persistence requests against it. This kind of inconsistency will quickly become a problem for our application, so we need to address it. Thankfully, if we pair Akka Persistence with Akka Cluster Sharding, we can make sure that a single instance of an entity only resides in one consistent server within our cluster. We will take that approach in Chapter 8, *Scaling Out with Akka Remoting/Clustering*, when we start leveraging Akka clustering, which will fix that issue.

DDD certainly is a good starting point, but I feel that we need to do more to get the app to be more robust. I like to think that DDD, event sourcing, and CQRS go hand in hand, so we need to introduce those other two concepts (event sourcing and CQRS) before we see the full picture and benefits. Once we are done with the next two chapters, we can really reflect on how much better we will have made our application. It's too soon (and there are some glaring holes) to do that now.

Refactoring homework

There are two contexts within the incomplete app code base that still need to be refactored to match the models shown earlier in the chapter—user management and credit processing. Your task will be to refactor those contexts in line with the diagrams I created. Changing these contexts will require minor cleanup in sales order processing, so expect a few changes there too. When you are done, you can look at the code in the complete app code base and compare your work with mine to see if we are on the same page in regards to these refactorings.

Summary

The bookstore application changed quite a bit in this chapter as we introduced DDD to the code. We have an application model now that better represents the domain where we do our business. We have also shifted our focus more onto entities and aggregates now, as we moved the core business logic into those classes as part of the refactor. Lastly, we removed that nasty cross-domain transaction, going with an event driven, two-part flow to handle inventory allocation for a sales order.

The changes we made here are important in the big picture of building a more scalable and flexible application. There's more to do though, and we'll start right in on some of those changes in the next chapter when we introduce event sourcing as a means of persistence. This is a big change to how and what you persist for an entity, so come with an open mind and get ready to rethink the way you handle persistent state.

4

Making History with Event Sourcing

When it comes to the persistence needs of an application, the most common, tried, and true approach is to model data in a relational database. Following this approach has been the de facto way to store data until recently, when NoSQL (and to a lesser extent NewSQL) started to chip away at the footholds of relational database dominance. There's nothing wrong with storing your application's data this way—it's how we initially chose to do so for the bookstore application using PostgreSQL as the storage engine.

This kind of approach to storing your data can answer the "What" question, as in "What is the current state of a particular entity?". But there's another question that is sometimes just as important, and that's the "How" question, as in "How did a particular entity get into this state?". This kind of question is not something that is easily handled in a traditional persistence model of storing just an entity's current state. If we want to answer the "How" question, we will need a different approach to persistence, and that different approach is event sourcing.

This chapter deals with event sourcing and how to implement that approach using Akka Persistence. These are the main things you can expect to learn from this chapter:

- What is event sourcing, including the pros and cons of that approach?
- What is Akka Persistence, and how you can use it for event sourcing?
- How does Akka Persistence handle serialization, and how do you build a custom serializer for your events?
- What snapshotting is and how to use it for your entities

- How to use Cassandra for your Akka Persistence journal and for snapshots
- Persistence schema evolution and how to deal with it
- How to use event adapters and Google protobuf to separate domain and data models

Event sourcing primer

I'll try and keep the theory information a little lighter here, as there is a ton of practical, hands on stuff to go over with Akka Persistence. Still, it's worth going over the high-level concepts in a bit more detail first so that you're mentally prepared to attack the code changes that we'll make.

As I stated in the opener, event sourcing is a technique where, instead of storing the current state of the data explicitly, we store the event stream for a particular entity. Using that event stream, we can arrive at the current state when necessary by replaying the events in memory within our code. We also have the added benefit of having a full audit log for each entity instance that can provide all kinds of benefits, which I'll break out in this section.

At the heart of the event sourcing model, there is the simple concept of **Action (command)** and **Reaction (event)**, depicted in the following diagram:

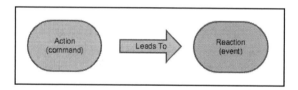

As users interact with your system, their actions (represented in the code as commands such as CancelOrder) will lead to the system having the reaction of creating an event for that action (such as OrderCancelled) if the command can be processed. Different systems can then listen for these events and update their own state as a result of the events.

This is not exactly a new technique. In fact, you will probably see an example of it every month when you are looking at your bank statement. The list of transactions against your bank account is a good representation of an event stream for an entity. Instead of storing the current balance explicitly, it's likely that your bank just stores the transaction (event) stream. From there, it can arrive on your current balance by processing through the transactions in memory when requested, arriving at a final number by adding credits and subtracting debits from some starting value.

One of the drawbacks with just storing the current state is that if I asked you what your balance was on 9/9/2015, you'd have a pretty tough time answering me. But, if you had used an event sourcing approach, all you'd have to do is reprocess a slice of the complete set of transactions and stop on 9/9/2015, and you'd have the answer to that question. An example like this shows a clear benefit to event sourcing, but there are others too, so let's break down the pros and cons quickly to see how they stack up.

The pros of event sourcing

There are quite a few pros of using event sourcing. I'll list some of them here, but I'm sure there are others too. These are the ones that I see as the biggest benefits, which will also answer architectural problems with the current bookstore app.

High performance

Since events are immutable, they can be written to an append-only store. Events also don't have relations to other events (they are standalone). These two factors lead to increased write performance versus a relational model and increased scalability.

Avoidance of Object-relational mapping

Lots of ink has been spilled describing the issue of **Object-relational mapping** (**ORM**) impedance mismatch. In summary, the OO world and the normalized data-model world don't overlap very well. If you use an ORM tool (such as Hibernate), you will probably let one of the two sides spill into and affect the other more than you'd like. Your OO model may end up very fractured like a normalized db model, or your database may end up denormalized to better match your object structure. With simple events that just describe a business occurrence, you avoid the issue of mapping objects to a relational store entirely.

Full audit trail

This one is pretty simple, but it doesn't make it any less of a benefit. If you store the full event stream for an entity, you will also get a full audit trail of when everything happened to that entity to make it what it is now. There was a time in my past where I found myself creating audit tables and triggers to handle something like this when I really should have considered event sourcing.

Enabler for system/context separation

By having a persistent event stream around, we can start to separate our different systems or contexts better. We can have something happen in one context as a result of something that happened in another, and we don't need to do this synchronously and directly tied to the initiating process.

An example of events in one context having an impact on another context is the sales order inventory allocation process that we redid in the *Fixing the transaction in the order creation process* section, in `Chapter 3`, *Curing Anemic Models with Domain-Driven Design*. The two-part process we built there wasn't very robust in being built on top of the actor system's event bus. We need both sides up at all times in order for the back and forth to work. With persistent events, we can write an event and not worry if someone is there on the other side to receive it. The receiver will get the event when they are back up and running, and we won't lose anything during the downtime.

No atomic concerns

You certainly can try an approach with context/system separation where you try to have your cake and eat it too. You can try and store the current state only and then also raise events after (in a separate db table or a JMS queue, for example) that are used to sync up changes with another system. The problem here is that you need to do this in a way that properly guarantees atomicity in the write of the db change and the publishing of the event. If you can't guarantee this, then your systems can end up in an inconsistent state. This may even involve an XA transaction, and that's not a path you want to go down on.

With event sourcing, you just have one thing to write, and that's the event itself. No worries about atomicity here.

A natural fit with DDD

Event sourcing and DDD go pretty much hand in hand. By modeling your system around the Action (command) Reaction (event) model, you really start to see and understand your domain and the sort of things can happen to change your entities. These commands and events will help you develop a strong ubiquitous language that you can use to communicate the concepts through your domain.

The cons of event sourcing

It will be an injustice to you if I don't mention some of the potential drawbacks of event sourcing. No approach is perfect, and there are some things about event sourcing that you should at least consider before moving forward and using it as a part of your architecture.

Querying

Loading the current state of a single entity is pretty simple with event sourcing, but what if you needed to locate all orders that currently have a status of **backordered**. Depending on the storage technology you use, this may involve something like secondary indexes, or in the worst case, needing to scan every single record looking for matches. These can be expensive processes, both, in the query times as well as the load it puts on the data store. Thankfully, if you follow the **Command Query Responsibility Segregation (CQRS)** pattern, which we will discuss in `Chapter 5`, *Separating Concerns with CQRS*, you can mitigate this issue by searching against a query-optimized read model. This approach adds more complexity, though in having to retain this separate read model. It also introduces eventual consistency into your application in that the read model won't be immediately in sync with the write model after a write happens in the write model.

Performance with long lived entities

The longer an entity lives, and the more potential events that occur on it, the slower the process of arriving on the current state will be. We arrive on the current state by replaying the event stream in memory, applying them to some initial state of the entity. If you have a large number of events on a single entity, then this process of loading that record may become slower and slower over time. Thankfully, you can use a process called **snapshotting**, which we will discuss later in this chapter, to reset the initial state to a new value and only process the events that occur after that new snapshot.

Versioning concerns

If your domain event mode evolves, and it will, you will need to be able to process older events that no longer match the model when trying to reconstitute the current state of an entity. Because of this, you will need to have a plan to be able to deal with the different versions of an event that has happened over the course of time. Akka has an answer for this in its persistence schema evolution feature, which is something we will cover in an upcoming section.

It's just different

People like to do what they feel comfortable with, and can be slow to embrace something different. This means that the old standard of using a relational database and storing the current state, even when event sourcing may be a better fit for them. This approach may just seem too radically different to some that they won't ever consider using it. So, as a result, it may be tough to build a good experienced team to implement your DDD and event sourced architecture.

Bookstore-specific example of event sourcing

At this point, we know some of the high-level benefits of using event sourcing as a way to track state and history for our entities. To hammer the point home a little more, I want to present a quick example in the context of the bookstore app. Up until now, the stuff I discussed is more in the abstract sense. Here, we'll get more concrete on how an approach like this might benefit the application we are developing.

Suppose you were looking at an order in the system and this is what you saw on a screen somewhere:

```
OrderId:  Total Cost:  Status:
12344     19.99        CANCELLED
```

Looking at this screen and just seeing the current state of the order, seeing that it's cancelled, doesn't tell me much. It really just tells me what it is now, and not how it got here. I want to know what led to this order being cancelled, but with the current model of just storing the current state in my relational db, I don't have that information.

Now, what if we followed an event sources approach instead, and when looking at the event stream for this particular order instance, this is what we see:

```
Date:               Event:
2016-05-24          OrderCreated
2016-05-24          InventoryAllocated
2016-05-25          OrderShipped
2016-05-27          OrderReceived
2016-05-29          OrderReturned(WrongItem)
2016-05-30          ReturnReceived
2016-05-30          InventoryBackordered
2016-05-30          OrderCancelled(Backordered)
2016-05-30          OrderRefunded
```

Seeing something like this really tells us a much richer story about what happened with this order. By reading through this, I can see that we sent the customer the wrong item and they returned the order. When they did, we tried to reallocate the correct inventory item, but it wasn't available and the order went into the backordered status. The customer then cancelled the order because they didn't want to wait, after which we refunded their initial payment.

If we can get something like this, while at the same time still be able to determine the current state of our entities, it's a big win for our app. Plus, event sourcing will really help us separate our different domain contexts so they can still react to changes in each other without being tied together so tightly. So, let's dive in and start the process of switching to event sourcing using Akka Persistence as the mechanism to do so.

Akka Persistence for event sourcing

Akka Persistence is a relatively newer module within the Akka toolkit. It became available as experimental in the 2.3.x series. Throughout that series, it went through quite a few changes as the team worked on getting the API and functionality right. When Akka 2.4.2 was released, the experimental label was removed, signifying that persistence was stable and ready to be leveraged in production code.

Akka Persistence allows stateful actors to persist their internal state. It does this not by persisting the state itself, but instead as changes to that state, using a configurable Akka Persistence journal to do so. It uses an append-only model to persist these state changes, allowing you to later reconstitute the state by replaying the changes to that state. It also allows you to take periodic snapshots and use those to reestablish an actor's state as a performance optimization for long lived entities with lots of state changes.

Akka Persistence's approach should certainly sound familiar as it's almost a direct overlay to the features of event sourcing. In fact, it was inspired by the **eventsourced** Scala library, so that overlay is no coincidence. Because of this alignment with event sourcing, Akka Persistence will be the perfect tool for us to switch over to an event sourced model.

Before getting into the details of the refactor, I want to describe some of the high-level concepts in the framework. Then, we will apply these concepts into the bookstore codebase and switch it over to an event sourced model.

The PersistentActor trait

The `PersistentActor` trait is the core building block of creating event sourced entities. This actor is able to persist its events to a pluggable journal. When a persistent actor is restarted (reloaded), it will replay its journaled events to reestablish its current internal state. These two behaviors perfectly fit what we need to do for our event sourced entities, so this will be our core building block.

The `PersistentActor` trait has a log of features, more that I will cover in the next few sections. I'll cover the things that we will use in the bookstore refactoring, which I consider to be the most useful features in `PersistentActor`. If you want to learn more, then I suggest you take a look at the Akka documents as they pretty much cover everything else that you can do with `PersistentActor`.

Persistent actor state handling

A `PersistentActor` implementation has two basic states that it can be in—**Recovering** and **Receiving Commands**. When **Recovering**, it's in the process of reloading its event stream from the journal to rebuild its internal state. Any external messages that come in during this time will be stashed until the recovery process is complete. Once the recovery process completes, the persistent actor transitions into the **Receiving Commands** state where it can start to handle commands. These commands can then generate new events that can further modify the state of this entity. This two-state flow can be visualized in the following diagram:

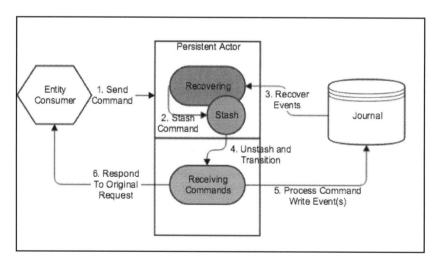

These two states are both represented by custom actor receive handling partial functions. You must provide implementations for both of the following `val` functions in order to properly implement these two states for your persistent actor:

```
val receiveRecover: Receive = {
  . . .
}
val receiveCommand: Receive = {
  . . .
}
```

While in the recovering state, there are two possible messages that you need to be able to handle. The first is one of the event types that you previously persisted for this entity type. When you get that type of message, you have to reapply the change implied by that event to the internal state of the actor. For example, if we had a `SalesOrderFO` fields object as the internal state, and we received a replayed event indicating that the order was approved, the handling might look something like this:

```
var state:SalesOrderFO = ...
val receiveRecover: Receive = {
  case OrderApproved(id) =>
  state = state.copy(status = SalesOrderStatus.Approved)
}
```

We'd, of course, need to handle a lot more than that one event. This code sample was just to show you how you can modify the internal state of a persistent actor when it's being recovered.

Once the actor has completed the recovery process, it can transition into the state where it starts to handle incoming command requests. As I mentioned, and diagrammed, in the *Event sourcing primer* section, event sourcing is all about Action (command) and Reaction (events). When the persistent actor receives a command, it has the option to generate zero to many events as a result of that command. These events represent a happening on that entity that will affect its current state.

Events you receive while in the Recovering state will be previously generated while in the Receiving Commands state. So, the preceding example that I coded, where we receive `OrderApproved`, must have previously come from some command that we handled earlier. The handling of that command could have looked something like this:

```
val receiveCommand: Receive = {
  case ApproveOrder(id) =>
  persist(OrderApproved(id)){ event =>
    state = state.copy(status = SalesOrderStatus.Approved)
    sender() ! FullResult(state)
```

```
        }
    }
```

After receiving the command request to change the order status to approved, the code makes a call to `persist`, which will asynchronously write an event into the journal. The full signature for `persist` is:

```
persist[A](event: A)(handler: (A) ⇒ Unit): Unit
```

The first argument there represents the event that you want to write to the journal. The second argument is a callback function that will be executed after the event has been successfully persisted (and won't be called at all if the persistence fails). For our example, we will use that callback function to mutate the internal state to update the status field to match the requested action.

One thing to note is that the writing in the journal is asynchronous. So, one may then think that it's possible to be closing over that internal state in an unsafe way when the callback function is executed. If you persisted two events in rapid succession, couldn't it be possible for both of them to access that internal state at the same time in separate threads, kind of like when using Futures in an actor?

Thankfully, this is not the case. The completion of a persistence action is sent back as a new message to the actor. The hidden receive handling for this message will then invoke the callback associated with that persistence action. By using the mailbox again, we will know these post-persistence actions will be executed one at a time, in a safe manner. As an added bonus, the sender associated with those post-persistence messages will be the original sender of the command so you can safely use `sender()` in a persistence callback to reply to the original requestor, as shown in my example.

Another guarantee that the persistence framework makes when persisting events is that no other commands will be processed in between the persistence action and the associated callback. Any commands that come in during that time will be stashed until all of the post-persistence actions have been completed. This makes the persist/callback sequence atomic and isolated, in that nothing else can interfere with it while it's happening. Allowing additional commands to be executed during this process may lead to an inconsistent state and response to the caller who sent the commands.

If, for some reason, the persisting to the journal fails, there is an `onPersistFailure` callback that will be invoked. If you want to implement custom handling for this, you can override this method. No matter what, when persistence fails, the actor will be stopped after making this callback. At this point, it's possible that the actor is in an inconsistent state, so it's safer to stop it than to allow it to continue on in this state. Persistence failures probably mean something is failing with the journal anyway so restarting as opposed to stopping will more than likely lead to even more failures.

There's one more callback that you can implement in your persistent actors and that's `onPersistRejected`. This will happen if the serialization framework rejects the serialization of the event to store. When this happens, the persist callback does not get invoked, so no internal state update will happen. In this case, the actor does not stop or restart because it's not in an inconsistent state and the journal itself is not failing.

The persistenceId method

Another important concept that you need to understand with `PersistentActor` is the `persistenceId` method. This abstract method must be defined for every type of `PersistentActor` you define, returning a String that is to be unique across different entity types and also between actor instances within the same type.

Let's say I will create the `Book` entity as a `PersistentActor` and define the `persistenceId` method as follows:

```
override def persistenceId = "book"
```

If I do that, then I will have a problem with this entity, in that every instance will share the entire event stream for every other `Book` instance. If I want each instance of the `Book` entity to have its own separate event stream (and trust me, you will), then I will do something like this when defining the `Book PersistentActor`:

```
class Book(id:Int) extends PersistentActor{
  override def persistenceId = s"book-$id"
}
```

If I follow an approach like this, then I can be assured that each of my entity instances will have its own separate event stream as the `persistenceId` will be unique for every `Int` keyed book we have.

When we will really re-implement the `Book` class later in this chapter, we will need to rethink how we key our entities. In the current model, when creating a new instance of an entity, we will pass in the special ID of 0 to indicate that this entity does not yet exist and needs to be persisted. We will defer ID creation to the database, and once we have an ID (after persistence), we will stop that actor instance as it is not properly associated with that newly generated ID. With the `persistenceId` model of associating the event stream to an entity, we will need the ID as soon as we create the actor instance. This means we'll need a way to have a unique identifier even before persisting the initial entity state. This is something to think about before we get to the upcoming refactor.

Taking snapshots for faster recovery

A few times throughout this chapter, I've mentioned the concept of taking a snapshot of the current state of an entity to speed up the process of recovering its state. If you have a long-lived entity that has generated a large amount of events, it will take progressively more and more time to recover its state. Akka's `PersistentActor` supports the snapshot concept, putting it in your hands as to when to take the snapshot. Once you have taken the snapshots, the latest one will be offered to the entity during the recovery phase instead of all of the events that led up to it. This will reduce the total number of events to process to recover state, thus speeding up that process.

This is a two-part process, with the first part being taking snapshots periodically and the second being handling them during the recovery phase. Let's take a look at the snapshot taking process first. Let's say that you coded a particular entity to save a new snapshot for every one thousand events received. To make this happen, your command handling block may look something like this:

```
var eventTotal = ...
val receiveCommand:Receive = {
  case UpdateStatus(status) =>
  persist(StatusUpdated(status)){ event =>
    state = state.copy(status = event.status)
    eventTotal += 1
    if (eventTotal % 100 == 0)
    saveSnapshot(state)
  }

  case SaveSnapshotSuccess(metadata) => . . .
  case SaveSnapshotFailure(metadata, reason) => . . .
}
```

You can see in the post-persist logic that if we we're making a specific call to saveSnapshot, we are passing the latest version of the actor's internal state. You're not limited to doing this just in the post-persist logic in reaction to a new event, but you can also set up the actor to publish a snapshot on regular intervals. You can leverage Akka's scheduler to send a special message to the entity to instruct it to save the snapshot periodically.

If you start saving snapshots, then you will have to start handling the two new messages that will be sent to the entity indicating the status of the saved snapshot. These two new message types are SaveSnapshotSuccess and SaveSnapshotFailure. The metadata that appears on both messages will tell you things, such as the persistence ID where the failure occurred, the sequence number of the snapshot that failed, and the timestamp of the failure. You can see these two new messages in the command handling block shown in the preceding code.

Once you have saved a snapshot, you will need to start handling it in the recovery phase. The logic to handle a snapshot during recovery will look like the following code block:

```
val receiveRecover:Receive = {
  case SnapshotOffer(metadata, offeredSnapshot) =>
  state = offeredSnapshot
  case event => . . .
}
```

Here, you can see that if we get a snapshot during recovery, instead of just making an incremental change, as we do with real replayed events, we set the entire state to whatever the offered snapshot is. There may be hundreds of events that led up to that snapshot, but all we need to handle here is one message in order to wind the state forward to when we took that snapshot. This process will certainly pay dividends if we have lots of events for this entity and we continue to take periodic snapshots.

One thing to note about snapshots is that you will only ever be offered the latest snapshot (per persistence ID) during the recovery process. Even though I'm taking a new snapshot every 1,000 events, I will only ever be offered one, the latest one, during the recovery phase.

Another thing to note is that there is no real harm in losing a snapshot. If your snapshot storage was wiped out for some reason, the only negative side effect is that you'll be stuck processing all of the events for an entity when recovering it. When you take snapshots, you don't lose any of the event history. Snapshots are completely supplemental and only benefit the performance of the recovery phase. You don't need to take them, and you can live without them if something happens to the ones you had taken.

Serialization of events and snapshots

Within both the persistence and snapshot examples, you can see I was passing objects into the `persist` and `saveSnapshot` calls. So, how are these objects serialized to and from a format that can actually be written to those stores? The answer is—via Akka Serialization.

Akka Persistence is dependent on Akka Serialization to convert event and snapshot objects to and from a binary format that can be saved into a data store. If you don't make any changes to the default serialization configuration, then your objects will be converted into binary via Java serialization. Java serialization is both slow and inefficient in terms of size of the serialized object. It's also not flexible in terms of the object definition changing after producing the binary when you are trying to read it back in. It's not a good choice for our needs with our event sourced app.

Luckily, Akka Serialization allows you to provide your own custom serializers. If you wanted to use JSON as your serialized object representation for example, then you could pretty easily build a custom serializer for that. They also have a built-in Google Protocol Buffers (protobuf) serializer that can convert your protobuf binding classes into their binary format. We'll explore both custom serializers, and the protobuf serializer, when we get into the sections dealing with the refactors.

The AsyncWriteJournal

Another important component in Akka Persistence, which I've mentioned a few times already, is the **AsyncWriteJournal**. This component is an append-only data store that stores the sequence of events (per persistence id) a `PersistentActor` generates via calls to persist. The journal also stores the `highestSequenceNr` per persistence id that tracks the total number of persisted events for that persistence ID.

The journal is a pluggable component. You have the ability to configure the default journal and, also, override it on a per-entity basis. The default configuration for Akka does not provide a value for the journal to use, so you must either configure this setting or add a per-entity override (more on that in a moment) in order to start using persistence. If you want to set the default journal, then it can be set in your configuration with the following property:

```
akka.persistence.journal.plugin="akka.persistence.journal.leve ldb"
```

The value in the preceding code must be the fully qualified path to another configuration section of the same name where the journal plugin's config lives. For this example, I set it to the already provided `leveldb` config section (from Akka's `reference.conf`).

If you want to override the journal plugin for a particular entity instance only, then you can do so by overriding the `journalPluginId` method on that entity actor, as follows:

```
class MyEntity extends PersistentActor{
  override def journalPluginId = "my-other-journal"
  . . .
}
```

The same rules apply here, in which, `my-other-journal` must be the fully qualified name to a config section where the config for that plugin lives.

My example config showed the use of the `leveldb` plugin that writes to the local filesystem. If you actually want to play around using this simple plugin, then you will also need to add the following dependencies into your `sbt` file:

```
"org.iq80.leveldb" % "leveldb" % "0.7"
"org.fusesource.leveldbjni" % "leveldbjni-all" % "1.8"
```

If you want to use something different, then you can check the community plugins page on the Akka site to find one that suits your needs. For our app, we will use the Cassandra journal plugin. I'll show you how to set up the config for that later on, in the section titled *Configuring Akka Persistence to use Cassandra*.

The SnapshotStore

The last thing I want to cover before we start the refactoring process is the **SnapshotStore**. Like the AsyncWriteJournal, the SnapshotStore is a pluggable and configurable storage system, but this one stores just snapshots as opposed to the entire event stream for a persistence ID. As I mentioned earlier, you don't need snapshots, and you can survive if the storage system you used for them gets wiped out for some reason. Because of this, you may consider using a separate storage plugin for them.

When selecting the storage system for your events, you need something that is robust, distributed, highly available, fault tolerant, and backup capable. If you lose these events, you lose the entire data set for your application. But, the same is not true for snapshots. So, take that information into consideration when selecting the storage. You may decide to use the same system for both, but you certainly don't have to. Also, not every journal plugin can act as a snapshot plugin, so if you decide to use the same for both, make sure that the journal plugin you select can handle snapshots.

If you want to configure the snapshot store, then the config setting to do that is as follows:

```
akka.persistence.snapshot-store.plugin="my-snapshot-plugin"
```

The setting here follows the same rules as the write journal; the value must be the fully qualified name to a config section where the plugin's config lives. If you want to override the default setting on a per entity basis, then you can do so by overriding the `snapshotPluginId` command on your actor like this:

```
class MyEntity extends PersistentActor{
  override def snapshotPluginId = "my-other-snap-plugin"
  . . .
}
```

The same rules apply here as well, in which, the value must be a fully qualified path to a config section where the plugin's config lives. Also, there are no out-of-the-box default settings for the snapshot store, so if you want to use snapshots, you must either set the appropriate setting in your config or provide the earlier mentioned override on a per entity basis.

For our needs, we will use the same storage mechanism—Cassandra—for both the write journal and for snapshot storage. We have a multi-node system currently, so using something that writes to the local filesystem, or a simple in-memory plugin, won't work for us. I'll explain in detail how to set up Cassandra as our snapshot storage in the next section, which deals with the Cassandra installation.

Using Cassandra for our persistent store

In Chapter 1, *Building a Better Reactive App*, in the section titled *Cassandra to the rescue*, I talked about why Cassandra will be a good fit for our bookstore application. It's distributed and highly available with great performance on the write side. It seems really tailor-made to fit what an event sourced application needs to do. In this section, we will get it installed and then go over the Akka config, which you will need to use it for both the AsyncWriteJournal and the SnapshotStore.

Installing Cassandra

Thanks to our decision to use Docker, there is no real install that we need to do to get Cassandra set up on our local systems. In this chapter, in the Docker Compose configuration (contained in the `docker-compose.yml` file found at the root of the bookstore app directory structure) we have replaced Postgres with Cassandra. All we need to do is launch the bookstore app as we have done previously (via `docket-build.sh` and then `launch.sh`) and we will have Cassandra up and running in a local Docker container.

Configuring Akka Persistence to use Cassandra

One thing we need to discuss with using Cassandra is how to get Akka Persistence to start using the Cassandra plugin, both for the AsyncWriteJournal and for the SnapshotStore. The first thing you will need to do for this is add the plugin as a dependency in your `sbt` file. The line to add for it is as follows:

```
"com.typesafe.akka" %% "akka-persistence-cassandra" % "0.14"
```

Then, to use Cassandra as the plugin for the AsyncWriteJournal, set the previously mentioned Akka config property for it, as follows:

```
akka.persistence.journal.plugin = "cassandra-journal"
```

The final thing we will need to do is configure the plugin to be our SnapshotStore. We talked about this property earlier too. This property needs to be set like this:

```
akka.persistence.snapshot-store.plugin = "cassandra-snapshot- store"
```

And that's it. Now, we have Cassandra fully installed, up and running, and also configured as the storage for Akka Persistence. Now we can jump into refactoring our entities to use an event sourced model via Akka Persistence.

Refactoring the inventory management module

We'll start out by refactoring the inventory management module, like we did in in the section titled *The Book and InventoryClerk actors*, in `Chapter 3`, *Curing Anemic Models with Domain-Driven Design*. The focus of the next few sections will be to get the `Book` entity to use `PersistentActor` and an event sourced approach to its persistence. This will be a multi-part process where we do an initial simple refactor. Then, we'll layer in some improvements as I introduce a few new concepts from Akka Persistence.

The PersistentEntity abstract class

The `PersistentEntity` abstract class, in the `bookstore-common` project, is the base class that all of our concrete event sourced entities will extend from. It's a similar concept to `EntityActor` from the `Chapter 3`, *Curing Anemic Models with Domain-Driven Design*, DDD refactor, but it's a lot less complex. The majority of the complicated stuff I hand coded is now handled by `PersistentActor`, which `PersistentEntity` extends from. The declaration (and some of the constructor logic) for `PersistentEntity` can be seen in the following code block:

```
abstract class PersistentEntity[FO <: EntityFieldsObject[String,  FO] :
ClassTag](id:String)
extends PersistentActor with ActorLogging{

  val entityType = getClass.getSimpleName
  var state:FO = initialState
  context.setReceiveTimeout(1 minute)
  . . .
}
```

You can see here that we set up this class to extend `PersistentEntity` so we can leverage all of the event sourced goodness that comes with it. Also, we give this class a generic type, `FO`, that represents the fields object that this entity uses to represent its state. Note that we are changing the key type from `Int` to `String` here. This is because, as I mentioned earlier, we will need to generate the IDs before persisting an entity, and I've decided to use UUIDs to handle that requirement.

The constructor here takes that `String` ID as an input and makes it available for any operations that need it. In the constructor body, the class sets up a `val` called `entityType` that is just the simple, not fully qualified class name for whatever the concrete entity is. Then, the class creates the initial state for its fields object using a method that the subclass must implement, called `initialState`. This is the initial value that will be modified during recovery to produce the final state of the entity after it's fully recovered.

Lastly, I will set up a receive timeout to go off after one minute of inactivity. This will be the logic that is used to handle passivation. Similar to the entities in `Chapter 3`, *Curing Anemic Models with Domain-Driven Design*, these instances will stay around in memory, servicing requests, until they hit one minute of inactivity. When that happens, they will be stopped, needing to be started again if another request comes in for the same instance ID.

The next thing to look at is definition of the persistent identifier for this event sourced actor. You may remember that this becomes the identifier which is used to associate all of the events for a particular instance of an entity. For our entities, it's defined like this:

```
override def persistenceId = s"$entityType-$id"
```

The code leverages two things set up in the construction of the actor, the `entityType` and the `id` input to generate a unique persistence id for this entity instance.

Now that we have the persistence identifier defined, we can start focusing on implementing the two states, Recovering and Receiving Commands, which were discussed earlier in this chapter. The recovery handling logic for our entity actors is defined like this:

```
def receiveRecover = standardRecover orElse customRecover

def standardRecover:Receive = {
  case ev:EntityEvent =>
  handleEvent(ev)
}

def customRecover:Receive = PartialFunction.empty

def handleEvent(event:EntityEvent):Unit
```

Here, I set up the required `receiveRecover` PartialFunction to be either `standardRecover`, or if no match there, `customRecover`. The `standardRecover` handling is meant to be things that can be automatically handled for you via this base class functionality. In the `standardRecover` handling, the only handling we have currently is that if we receive `EntityEvent` (a marker trait I created to represent events within this framework), we call an abstract method called `handleEvent` to process that event and modify the internal state. This method will be implemented in each specific entity to handle the events that it generates.

The `customRecover` PartialFunction is there to cover special cases in a derived class that isn't handled by the standard recover logic. This `PartialFunction` is already defined as empty, so derived classes need not worry about it unless they actually have something to do in it.

The definition of `receiveCommand` is similar in spirit to `receiveRecover`, in which it also defines standard handling and then provides a hook to add custom handling. Its definition is as follows:

```
def receiveCommand = standardCommandHandling orElse
additionalCommandHandling
```

There are quite a few cases covered in `standardCommandHandling`. Because of that, I'll break down those cases one at a time so as to not overwhelm you with too much code at once. The first case deals with entity passivation, and is defined as follows:

```
case ReceiveTimeout =>
log.info("{} entity with id {} is being passivated due to  inactivity",
entityType, id)
context stop self
```

Earlier, in the constructor body, I set a receive timeout to occur after one minute of activity as a way to passivate the entity instance. The case `ReceiveTimeout` part here is what will be hit when we get that inactivity timeout. When I get that message, I log the fact that the entity instance is being passivated before stopping the actor.

Now, just plain old stopping the actor here could be a bit shortsighted in that if a message does happen to come in just after getting the `ReceiveTimeout`, you will lose that message. If that is a concern, then you can send a `PoisonPill` back to yourself instead that will auto-stop the actor after any messages in front of it get processed through first. In fact, we will make a similar change later on, in Chapter 8, *Scaling Out with Akka Remoting/Clustering*, when we introduce Cluster Sharding into the application. For now though, this simple approach to stopping will suffice.

The next case to look at deals with handling requests when the entity is marked as deleted or if it's still in the initial state and this is not a create request. That logic looks like this:

```
case any if !isAcceptingCommand(any) =>
sender() ! StateResponse()
```

The `isAcceptingCommand` method is defined as follows:

```
def isAcceptingCommand(cmd:Any): Boolean =
!state.deleted &&
!(state == initialState && !isCreateMessage(cmd))
```

With this logic, if the entity receives any command after it's been marked as deleted, it will not process the command and just move onto responding. This will result in an `EmptyResult` being returned to the caller (as if the entity flat out never existed). This will also be the case if we are in the initial state and the message is not a request to create the entity. The `isCreateMessage` method is something that each entity actor must implement to indicate which command represents their create request.

The code for `stateResponse` is where the decision of how to respond is handled and looks like this:

```
def stateResponse(respectDeleted:Boolean=true):ServiceResult[FO] =
  if (state == initialState) EmptyResult
  else if (respectDeleted && state.deleted) EmptyResult
  else FullResult(state)
```

This is a common piece of code that is used throughout this class to handle responding with the current state to the caller. As mentioned earlier, if the entity is marked as deleted, it will respond with an `EmptyResult`. The `respectDeleted` flag that is evaluated here is used for the case where the entity is getting marked as deleted. In that case, we still want to respond with the current state, showing the entity marked as deleted.

This logic will also respond with an `EmptyResult`, if state matches the initial state, which is an indication that the entity has yet to be created (no events processed against it yet). If neither of those conditions are true, it will respond with `FullResult` for the current state.

The next case to look at with common command handling is the case where the current state is being explicitly requested. That case looks like this:

```
case GetState =>
sender ! stateResponse()
```

This logic is pretty self-explanatory. If someone asks for the current state, via a custom message called `GetState`, then we will use the `stateResponse` to send them the current state.

The last piece of common command-handling code deals with requests to mark the current entity as deleted. That code is as follows:

```
case MarkAsDeleted =>
  newDeleteEvent match{
    case None =>
      log.info("This entity does not support deletion")
      sender ! stateResponse()

    case Some(event) =>
      persist(event)(handleEventAndRespond(false))
  }
```

Here, the delete handling logic is kicked off if we receive a `MarkAsDeleted` custom message. When this happens, we need to check if the entity supports deletion or not. This happens by calling an abstract method, `newDeleteEvent`, that returns an option for the delete event to persist. If the derived class supports delete, then this will be a `Some`, and we will move forward with persisting that event and then responding. Note that when responding that it explicitly passes the `respectDeleted` flag as `false` so that the caller asking for the delete will get the current state back instead of an `EmptyResult`. If it does not support deletion, then we will just respond with the current state.

The Aggregate abstract class

This `Aggregate` abstract class is similar to its counterpart from the DDD refactor, `EntityAggregate`. It is set up to sit in front of the entities that it manages, delegating calls to them as they come in to it. It has two methods that are worth going over as they are important in how it delegates to child entities.

The first is the `lookupOrCreateChild` method. As with `EntityAggregate`, this method is responsible to get the child entity for the supplied ID to delegate a call to. The logic looks like this:

```
def lookupOrCreateChild(id:String) = {
  val name = entityActorName(id)
  context.child(name).getOrElse{
    context.actorOf(entityProps(id), name)
  }
}
```

The logic is pretty basic here. If we have a child for the name already, which included the ID, then just return that. If not, create a new child for that name and return it.

The other method to show is the `forwardCommand` method. This is used when we get a request in the aggregate and as a result, we want to forward a command to the entity. That code looks like this:

```
def forwardCommand(id:String, msg:Any):Unit = {
  val entity = lookupOrCreateChild(id)
  entity.forward(msg)
}
```

The logic here makes use of the `lookupOrCreateChild` method to find the entity to delegate to. It then forwards the supplied message to the child so that it can handle it and respond to the caller.

The JsonSerializer class

The last class from `bookstore-common` to look at before we jump into the `Book` entity is the `JsonSerializer` class. Instead of using the default of Java object serialization to persist our events, we will start using JSON. It's a more flexible and standardized format than Java serialization, so it's not a bad first choice. This class is an Akka custom-serializer that we will plug in (via config) to handle our persistent event serialization. The code for this class is as follows:

```
class JsonSerializer extends SerializerWithStringManifest{
  implicit val formats = Serialization.formats(NoTypeHints)
  def identifier:Int = 999
  def manifest(o:AnyRef):String = o.getClass.getName

  def toBinary(o:AnyRef):Array[Byte] = {
    val json = write(o)
    json.getBytes()
  }

  def fromBinary(bytes:Array[Byte], manifest:String):AnyRef = {
    val m = Manifest.classType[AnyRef](Class.forName(manifest))
    val json = new String(bytes, "utf8")
    read[AnyRef](json)(formats, m)
  }
}
```

This custom serializer extends Akka's `SerializerWithStringManifest`. This is a type of serializer that also saves a `String`-based type hint (a manifest) that will allow you to deserialize the binary data when necessary. Since this is a JSON-based serializer, I set up the class with **json4s** implicit formats, which is required when using that library.

The `identifier` method is just to provide a unique identifier for this serializer. The numbers 0-16 are reserved for Akka, so as long as you don't choose one of those, any other `Int` ID can be used.

The `manifest` method is what provides the type hint (in `String` form) so that you know how to deserialize later. In this case, I chose to use the full class name of whatever the event is that is being serialized.

The `toBinary` method is used to generate the bytes to be saved in the journal. For this serializer, I will use json4s and turn the event into JSON. Then, in the `fromBinary`, I will leverage the previously saved class name to create a Scala Manifest, which I will then pass into json4s to read back into whatever object it was before being serialized. Even though I pass in `AnyRef` as the type, because I explicitly supply Manifest on the read call, I get the correct type back.

In order to make Akka use this serializer for our `EntityEvent` type, we will need to add the following config into our `application.conf` Akka config file:

```
akka.actor{
  serializers{
    json =        "com.packt.masteringakka.bookstore.common.JsonSerializer"
  }
  serialization-bindings {
    "com.packt.masteringakka.bookstore.common.EntityEvent" = json
  }
}
```

Here, we follow the two part Akka-serialization convention of identifying an alias for our new serializer (calling it `json`), and then we bind any type that inherits from `EntityEvent` to use that serializer.

The event sourced Book entity

Now that we've seen the common functionality that we will use to support our event sourced entities, using JSON to serialize them, we can look at leveraging that functionality to refactor the `Book` entity. Let's take a look at the companion object for `Book` where the commands and the corresponding events are defined:

```
private [bookstore] object Book{
  object Command{
    case class CreateBook(book:BookFO)
    case class AddTag(tag:String)
    case class RemoveTag(tag:String)
    case class AddInventory(amount:Int)
    case class AllocateInventory(orderId:Int, amount:Int)
  }

  object Event{
    case class BookCreated(book:BookFO) extends EntityEvent
    case class TagAdded(tag:String) extends EntityEvent
    case class TagRemoved(tag:String) extends EntityEvent
    case class InventoryAdded(amount:Int) extends EntityEvent
```

```
    case class InventoryAllocated(orderId:Int, amount:Int)
    extends EntityEvent
    case class InventoryBackordered(orderId:Int)
    extends EntityEvent
    case class BookDeleted(id:String) extends EntityEvent
  }
  . . .
}
```

The commands here represent the actions we can take against the Book entity. These actions are nothing new as we have supported them in one form or another throughout this book so far. I namespaced them into a new object called Command so it's clear that these are the commands for book. The newer part is the stuff namespaced under Event. These are the events that the Book entity will persist to represent its state changes, and also use to recover its state in the recovery phase. Most of the events here directly relate to an action (command) that can be taken against book.

Next, we can take a look at the class declaration and the definition of the required initialState method, which is as follows:

```
private[inventory] class Book(id:String) extends
PersistentEntity[BookFO](id){
  def initialState = BookFO.empty
  . . .
}
```

For the class definition, we extend PersistentEntity, indicating that the field's object type to use is BookFO. For the initialState method, which is to set the state var to its initial value, we use BookFO.empty. That method just creates a BookFO dummy with default values for all of the fields, which will serve as the starting point when recovering the entity.

Now that we have the basics of the class paid out, it's time to show the important stuff, which is the command handling that's defined in additionalCommandHandling. The first command to look at is CreateBook, which serves as the first event persisted in the lifetime of a Book entity:

```
case CreateBook(book) =>
if (state != initialState){
  sender() ! Failure(
    FailureType.Validation, BookAlreadyCreated)
}
else{
  persist(BookCreated(book))(handleEventAndRespond())
}
```

When receiving this command, the code checks to make sure that we are still in the initial state so that we can't process a `CreateBook` request multiple times in the life of this entity instance. If not, then we can persist a `BookCreated` event. The post-persist handle used here is `handleEventAndRespond`, which does exactly what the name implies. I'll show the custom `handleEvent` code for book after we get through the command handling.

The next two commands we can look at are the `AddTag` and `RemoveTag` commands, which are defined as follows:

```
case AddTag(tag) =>
if (state.tags.contains(tag))
  sender() ! stateResponse()
else
  persist(TagAdded(tag))(handleEventAndRespond())

case RemoveTag(tag) =>
if (!state.tags.contains(tag))
  sender() ! stateResponse()
else
  persist(TagRemoved(tag))(handleEventAndRespond())
```

Each of these handling blocks does the same basic thing. Make sure the action can be taken, and if so, persist the corresponding event, again using `handleEventAndRespond` as the post-persist function.

The last command to look at, for now, is `AddInventory`, which is defined as follows:

```
case AddInventory(amount) =>
  persist(InventoryAdded(amount))(handleEventAndRespond())
```

There are no checks here; the logic just goes right to persisting the corresponding event for the requested action.

All of the command handling is delegated to `handleEventAndRespond`, which in turn calls `handleEvent`. This method needs to be implemented on a per-entity basis, and it's where we make changes to the current state based on an event. For book, it's defined like this:

```
def handleEvent(event:EntityEvent):Unit = event match {
  case BookCreated(book) =>
   state = book
  case TagAdded(tag) =>
   state = state.copy(tags = tag :: state.tags)
  case TagRemoved(tag) =>
   state = state.copy(tags = state.tags.filterNot(_ == tag))
  case InventoryAdded(amount) =>
   state = state.copy(inventoryAmount =
```

```
      state.inventoryAmount + amount)
    case BookDeleted(id) =>
      state = state.markDeleted
  }
```

Each event that we get corresponds to a change we can make to the internal state, which is a `BookFO`. For example, if the event was `TagAdded`, then we will set the state to be a copy of itself with the new tag added to the list of tags it currently has.

You may have noticed that we did not handle a delete request in our custom-command handling for this actor, but we have an event for it here. That's because the delete functionality lives in the standard-command handling logic in the parent class. Also, the parent class will use this same method when recovering the state of the actor when it is reloaded. It's sort of a two-for-one method that handles all logic related to applying events to the state, be it after a command or for a recovery.

The refactored InventoryClerk actor

For the most part, the `InventoryClerk` actor is the same as we left it at the end of Chapter 3, *Curing Anemic Models with Domain-Driven Design*. It extends a different base class now—the newly created `Aggregate`—but for the most part, its functionality is the same. It receives calls, looks up child-entity actors, and delegates commands to them. Let's take a quick look at one of the commands it handles for the request to add a new book to the catalog:

```
    case CatalogNewBook(title, author, tags, cost) =>
    val id = UUID.randomUUID().toString()
    val fo = BookFO(id, title, author, tags, cost, 0, new Date)
    val command = Book.Command.CreateBook(fo)
    forwardCommand(id, command)
```

The big difference here is that we need to generate the ID before persisting the entity, and the ID has changed over to a `String` from an `Int`. I chose to use a UUID here as it was simple and guaranteed to be unique. It's a bit long, and I'm sure there are ways to get Cassandra to generate unique numeric sequences, but I did not consider that in scope for this book. Once I have the ID, I can create the field's object that will represent the initial state of the entity and then pass off a `CreateBook` request to child for that ID, which will be new as it's a new ID, via `forwardCommand`. It's pretty simple, and not much different than what we did in Chapter 3, *Curing Anemic Models with Domain-Driven Design*.

The big difference to note in this actor is that currently, it can't handle any of the multibook lookup requests, such as `FindBooksByAuthor`, so the handling for those is commented out. One of the downsides of an event sourced model (as I mentioned in the pros and cons section) is that it can be tough to support querying against the persisted stream of events. The best approach to handle querying with event sourcing is to maintain a separate read model that is highly optimized for the query cases. We'll be doing just that in `Chapter 5`, *Separating Concerns with CQRS*, when I introduce CQRS; so, for now, these query requests won't be handled. The only lookup functionality that is supported is the single entity lookup by key, which does not require a query.

Trying out the new Book entity

At this point, we have `Book` as our first fully event sourced entity. It makes sense to kick the tires on it a little using the REST API. The code examples from this chapter follow the same convention introduced in the *Understanding the refactored bookstore code* section in `Chapter 3`, *Curing Anemic Models with Domain-Driven Design*, in which there are `-incomplete` and `-complete` folders for the code. The `-incomplete` folder is where the refactor is partially finished and where you will do your homework for this chapter. The `-complete` folder is where I fully finished the refactor so you can compare your code to mine.

Follow the instructions from the *Starting up the example application* section in `Chapter 1`, *Building a Better Reactive App*, to build, package, and run the code, using the `-incomplete` folder as the code base to build. The main difference here is that instead of Postgres running as a Docker container, you will now have Cassandra running as a container.

Once you have the bookstore up and running as a Docker container, you can start to invoke its endpoints. Using the Book-related API instructions from the *Interacting with the Book endpoint* section in `Chapter 1`, *Building a Better Reactive App* , you should try and create a few new books. Once you create a Book, take some actions against it, such as adding/removing tags and adding new inventory to it. One thing to keep in mind is that the ID is now non-numeric, so be sure to grab the ID from the response JSON so that you can use it to make updates to the entity.

There is a fair amount of logging regarding entity recovery and passivation. You should try creating an entity and taking some actions with it. Then, let it sit idle for a minute to see that it gets passivated. Then, try another action against it, seeing that it is fully recovered from using the previous events before applying the latest request.

Viewing the events in Cassandra

When we were using PostgreSQL, it was pretty easy to open up the psql client (via Docker) and take a look at the current state of any database entity. Now that we are using event sourcing for the `Book` entity, we can't look at its current state, but we can, at the very least, see and interact with event records in Cassandra. The event data is binary, so there's not a lot of value to glean by looking at it, but it's comforting to see that the events are being saved properly and we can also clear out events if we want to reset the state of our little app.

The Cassandra client tool is called **cqlsh**. You can use this tool to view and interact with the data stored in your local Cassandra database. To start up this tool via Docker, all you need to do is execute the `cqlsh.sh` file at the root directory of the bookstore app code. If things work, you should see something like this:

```
Connected to OUR_DOCKERIZED_CASSANDRA_SINGLE_NODE_CLUSTER at
127.0.0.1:9042.
[cqlsh 5.0.1 | Cassandra 3.7 | CQL spec 3.4.2 | Native protocol v4]
Use HELP for help.
cqlsh:akka>
```

Once you have the shell running, you can type the following command to see your event data:

```
cqlsh> select * from messages;
```

When you do that, you should see records for each of the events that were persistent when interacting with the book endpoint. You will see a unique `persistence_id` value for each new book that you created, with the `sequence_nr` field representing each unique event within that `persistence_id`. Play around here a little if you want, and then get ready to add some new features to book.

Adding snapshotting to book

Now that we have a basic event sourcing implemented for book, we can start to layer in enhancements. The first of those will be snapshotting. As a reminder, you should snapshot your entities in an effort to speed up the recovery process if they will have a lot of events associated with them. We'll need to make most of the changes in `PersistentEntity`, as we want this to be a framework-level initiative as opposed to only being supported for book.

We'll go with an approach of taking a snapshot after a certain number of events, with that number being defined per entity. To accomplish this, we will need to store the number of events since the previous snapshot and then be aware of this count during recovery and post-persist event handling. Let's take a look at the first few changes, which involve the recovery process:

```
var eventsSinceLastSnapshot: Int = 0

def standardRecover:Receive = {
  case ev:EntityEvent =>
  handleEvent(ev)
  eventsSinceLastSnapshot += 1

  case SnapshotOffer(meta, snapshot:FO) =>
  state = snapshot
}
```

We will start by adding a class-level variable called `eventsSinceLastSnapshot` that will be used to track the count of events since the last snapshot. We will use this as a trigger to indicate when we need to perform a snapshot save.

Then, an update was made to the standard event handling logic during recovery, where we will now increment that new counter for every event we recover. Also, we added a new handling block to the recovery phase to handle an offered snapshot. If that happens, we can simple set the state to that snapshot value.

The next set of changes concerns knowing a snapshot is needed and taking it. That code looks like this:

```
def snapshotAfterCount:Option[Int] = None
def maybeSnapshot:Unit = {
  snapshotAfterCount.
  filter(i => eventsSinceLastSnapshot >= i).
  foreach{ i =>
    saveSnapshot(state)
    eventsSinceLastSnapshot = 0
  }
}
```

The `snapshotAfterCount` method is set up to be overridden in a derived class to provide the number of events to take a snapshot after. By default, it returns `None`, which implies no snapshotting. Then, the `maybeSnapshot` method uses that optional count to decide if a snapshot needs to be taken. If so, `saveSnapshot` will be called and then the event count will be reset back to 0.

The last change to look at for snapshots in `PersistentEntity` is an addition to `handleEventAndRespond`, which now looks like this:

```
def handleEventAndRespond(respectDeleted:Boolean =
true)(event:EntityEvent):Unit = {
  handleEvent(event)
  if (snapshotAfterCount.isDefined){
    eventsSinceLastSnapshot += 1
    maybeSnapshot()
  }
  sender() ! stateResponse(respectDeleted)
}
```

This is the logic that we have used as the post-persist handling function. Here, the event count is increased (if we are using snapshotting), and then we check if the snapshot is needed via `maybeSnapshot`. Putting all of these changes together, we have a system by which an entity can easily opt into using snapshots.

With all of that in place, we need to only make one small addition to the `Book` entity, which is to provide the count to take snapshots after. That addition looks like this:

```
override def snapshotAfterCount = Some(5)
```

This is a really small count to take snapshots after, but it serves well when testing if the snapshots are working. In the real world, this count will be much higher, or the triggering condition may even be based on something such as time.

We also want our snapshots to use the previously created JSON serializer instead of the default of Java serialization. To do that, we just need to update our serialization bindings in the Akka config to look like this:

```
serialization-bindings {
  "com.packt.masteringakka.bookstore.common.EntityEvent" = json
  "com.packt.masteringakka.bookstore.common.EntityFieldsObject" = json
}
```

Now, any class that is derived from `EntityFieldsObject` will use our JSON serializer. This will cover any of the state values for any of our persistent entities.

Play around with the application again now that we have added snapshotting. There will be log entries indicating that a snapshot was taken and also that an entity is being recovered from a snapshot. If you want to look at the stored snapshots, you can do so in cqlsh by running the following commands:

```
cqlsh> use akka_snapshot;
cqlsh> select * from snapshots;
```

You'll see an entry in that table for each snapshot that was taken for each persistence id. There is a column in there called `sequence_nr`, which indicates after which event number the snapshot was taken. The system uses this, both, to select the latest snapshot as well as figure out which events need to be recovered after the snapshot is offered during recovery.

Dealing with an evolving schema

When you have a relational database, there will come a time when you are making changes to the schema after your app first gets into production. This may be something such as the addition (or removal) of a field from a table or maybe just a simple field rename. When you do this, you have to take care not to cause problems with the data that is already in the table. You can't just drop and recreate the table because there's data in it. You will have to have a process in place, such as running incremental deltas, to evolve your schema that handles the data that is already in the table.

Event sourcing is not immune to schema evolution concerns. In fact, the pain may be even more acute and chronic. When you need to keep around serialized versions of events for a very long time, and the event itself can go through many changes during that time period, it's clear that the schema evolution is front and center in the event sourced world. Luckily, Akka has a few tricks up its sleeve to handle an evolving schema and how best to insulate your code from these inevitable changes. I'll go over a couple of those approaches, and then we'll apply one of these techniques to the `Book` entity. This will just be a taste of handling schema evolution. If you want the main course, I suggest referring to Akka's documentation (`http://doc.akka.io/docs/akka/snapshot/scala/persistence-schema-evolution.html`) in the section titled *Persistence – Schema Evolution*.

Using event adapters

An event adapter is a component that can be plugged in between a serializer and receiving the event in your actor. In there, you can inspect what came out of the journal via the serializer and change it before it makes it into your entity actor's code, which is referred to as `ReadEventAdapter`. You can also adapt the events you generate in your entity actor before they hit the serializer and end up in the journal, which is referred to as `WriteEventAdapter`. If you need to handle both concerns in one class, then you can just use `EventAdapter`, which combines both the read and write adaptation.

You can configure any number of adapters per event, stacking them on top of each other to create a chain that will make individual modifications to the event. The following diagram shows how the event flow is handled by introducing adapters into the picture:

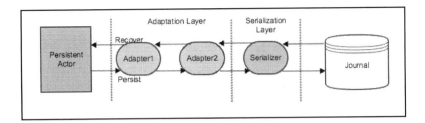

When reading events from the journal, the adapter allows you to specify zero to many events to generate outbound to the actor, or the next adapter, for every event in the journal. One thing this model allows you to do is to expand what was one event in an older version of your event model into multiple in the new model. You can also decide to return nothing if you decide that an old event is no longer applicable in the new model.

Let's go through a quick example of how an event adapter can solve a basic problem with schema evolution within your event sourced application. With the `Book` actor, we have an event called `InventoryAdded` that captures the situation where we increase the inventory of a `Book`. That event has the following structure in the current model:

```
case class InventoryAdded(amount:Int) extends EntityEvent
```

Let's say, way down the road, we decide to make a couple of changes to the event so that the event structure changes to look like this:

```
object InventorySource extends Enumeration{
  val External, Internal, Unknown = Value
}
case class InventoryAdded(inventoryAmount:Int,
source:InventorySource.Value) extends EntityEvent
```

The newer version of the event renamed the `amount` field to `inventoryAmount` and also added a new field to describe the source of the inventory. All new events, after we make this change, will use the new structure; but what can we do about all of the old events that are already in the journal? This seems like a good case for an event adapter, one that only needs to handle the read side of things.

In order to make a model like this work, we will need to make a few changes to some of the common code discussed earlier. The first thing to look at is a change to `EntityEvent` so that it can support identifying the current version of any event. That change looks like this:

```
trait EntityEvent extends Serializable{
  def currentVersion = "V1"
}
```

Now this trait supports identifying the current version of all classes that mix it in while supplying the default of V1. As events start to evolve, they will override this method to provide something other than V1.

Next, we need to modify the `manifest` and `fromBinary` methods on our custom JSON serializer. Those changes are as follows:

```
def manifest(o:AnyRef):String = {
  val className = o.getClass.getName
  val version = o match {
    case event:EntityEvent => event.currentVersion
    case other => "V1"
  }
  s"$version,$className"
}

def fromBinary(bytes:Array[Byte], manifest:String):AnyRef = {
  val Array(ver, clazz) = manifest.split(",")
  val versionedClazz =
  util.Try(Class.forName(s"$clazz$ver")).getOrElse{
    Class.forName(clazz)
  }
  val m = Manifest.classType[AnyRef](versionedClazz)
  val json = new String(bytes, "utf8")
  read[AnyRef](json)(formats, m)
}
```

The updated `manifest` method now saves the version identifier along with the class name. This will allow us to use that version identifier to target the correct class when deserializing. We will make use of this in the new `fromBinary`, first checking whether there is a class name ending with the version identifier. If not, it falls back to just using the class name, which will be what happens when it's the current version.

Then, we will need to keep the V1 version of `InventoryAdded` around on the classpath so we can still deserialize old events to it. We will rename it, though, so that it matches the new logic in our serializer. The V1 version of `InventoryAdded`, along with the current version, is as follows:

```
trait InventoryAddedEvent extends EntityEvent
case class InventoryAdded(inventoryAmount:Int,
source:InventorySource.Value) extends EntityEvent{
  override def currentVersion = "V2"
} extends InventoryAddedEvent
case class InventoryAddedV1(amount:Int)
extends InventoryAddedEvent
```

The current version does not need the version-qualified suffix, but the older version has it added so that it can be properly identified with the version it is tied to. If we follow this convention, we will be able to properly deserialize the old version-aware events. Note that `InventoryAddedEvent` is simply a marker trait that allows us to properly configure the adapter to only work with the `InventoryAdded` family of events.

The last thing we need is our adapter. Even though we are able to deserialize the old events, we don't want them flowing into our entity actor. All we want to ever handle in the entity actor is the current version of the event, so if we see the older versions, we will have to adapt them into the latest version before they make it into the actor. A simple read-based adapter to handle this will be as follows:

```
class InventoryAddedAdapter extends ReadEventAdapter{
  def fromJournal(event:Any, manifest:String) = event match {
    case InventoryAddedV1(amount) =>
    EventSeq(InventoryAdded(amount, InventorySource.Unknown ))
    case other =>
    EventSeq(other)
  }
}
```

When `InventoryAddedV1` flows through this adapter, after passing through the custom serializer, it will be upcasted into the latest version. As we didn't have a value for the source field, we will default it to `InventorySource.Unknown`. If it's any other event type, including the current version, we will pass it through and make no changes to it.

Now that we have the adapter, we will need to configure it so that our journal knows to start using it for the `InventoryAdded` family of events. This config needs to be top level in your Akka config and not nested under the root akka of the config. The config required to use this adapter is as follows:

```
cassandra-journal{
  event-adapters{
    invadded =
"com.packt.masteringakka.bookstore.inventory.InventoryAddedAdapter"
  }
  event-adapter-bindings{
"com.packt.masteringakka.bookstore.inventory.Book$Event$InventoryAddedEvent
" =
    invadded
  }
}
```

This config is similar to the serializer config where you first declare an adapter and then bind it into specific classes.

If we put together all of these changes with the serializer, the multiple versions of the event class, and the adapter, we can start handling schema changes, such as field renames or new fields, appearing in the model. However, this sure seems like a lot of work to handle something common, such as field renames or field additions to our model. It does not seem like a good long-term choice for our event storage needs. It's time to make a change to our serialization layer, one that should provide greater flexibility to our evolving schema.

Detaching the domain model from the data model

Using JSON was a pretty simple approach to store our event and data. It's easy to map to and from with a library such as json4s; it's a very well understood format, and it's human readable to boot. But, it's not very flexible and compact as far as size is concerned. Things that seemed pretty simple, such as field renaming or introducing new fields into the model, ended up being pretty complicated to deal with for our persistent event data. There has to be another kind of serialization format that will meet our needs better.

Google's protobuf framework is an **Interface Definition Language** (IDL)-based binary-serialization framework. You can create a message definition using their IDL specification representing fields as numbers. It supports a wide array of types, and you can also tag fields as being required or optional. You will then use its protoc complier to generate binding classes to serialize into the binary format as well as deserialize back to an object representation. It produces a very compact representation of an object, and it's blazing fast to boot. Akka also has built-in support for it, having an out-of-the-box serializer and config to work with protobuf messages. It's a great choice to start building our new event's serialization framework around.

The protobuf framework is really great for handling things such as field renames. Since the field names are mapped in as numbers, all you have to do is change the field name in your IDL file without touching the field mapping number. Then, you can regenerate the binding classes and accommodate the change in your code. Any previously saved event representations will still be able to be handled without any adaptation because they never stored the field's names to being with just the numeric representations.

Protobuf can also handle new fields relatively easily. All you need to do is add the new field as optional in the IDL file. Then, you will just need to respect that optionality in your code and assigning some default when it's not there, as older versions won't ever have a value for that field. Again, you don't need to create an adapter to handle something like this.

The only problem with protobuf is its Java serialization binding classes, as it doesn't yet support Scala natively, and it is not very Scala-friendly. I wouldn't want to use those classes as our event model as it will be cumbersome in our Scala code base. We need a solution here that allows us to use protobuf as our data serialization format without leaking those Java binding classes into our domain model.

When faced with this kind of problem, the Akka team recommends an approach called **Detaching the Domain Model from the Data Model**. In this approach, you can use one event representation as the data model (optimized for storage) and another to represent that event in your domain model. This kind of approach works perfectly for what we want to do with protobuf, so it's something we will follow.

The approach will involve using an event adapter to convert from the Scala domain model into the protobuf data model. Once we do that, we won't need a custom serializer anymore as we can just use the built-in Akka protobuf message serializer. We'll also have to create the IDL file for our inventory management event model, which I've already done for you, in both the -incomplete and the -complete folders. Let's take a look at an example from that IDL file showing the definition of the BookCreated event. That definition can be seen as follows:

```
message Book {
    required string id = 1;
    required string title = 2;
    required string author = 3;
    repeated string tag = 4;
    required double cost = 5;
    required int32 inventoryAmount = 6;
    required int64 createTs = 7;
    required bool deleted = 8;
}

message BookCreated{
    required Book book = 1;
}
```

Here, there are two messages set up to represent the data to store. The first is a representation of the information from BookFO, which the BookCreated event wraps. The second is the BookCreated event itself, referencing to the book message as its single field.

Notice how all the fields are represented by numbers that must be unique within the scope of each defined message. A format like this allows much greater flexibility to make field name changes without affecting previously stored data. Also, all of the fields here are defined as required as this is the first version, and everything on the domain model is truly required at this point. If new fields were added, we will start using the optional qualifier on those new fields instead so that we can still deal with older messages.

If you want to see the full version of the data model IDL for the inventory management project, it can be found at the following path: `src/main/proto/datamodel.proto`.

I've also generated the Java binding classes for this protobuf model, which can be found at `src/main/java/com/packt/masteringakka/bookstore/inventory/Datamodel.java`.

Now, let's take a look at the generic adapter, which I defined, to handle the domain to data model adaptation, starting with a couple of traits that are needed to support the adaptation process. Those traits are defined as follows:

```
trait DatamodelWriter{
  def toDatamodel:Message
}
trait DatamodelReader{
  def fromDatamodel:PartialFunction[Message,AnyRef]
}
```

The `DatamodelWriter` trait defines a method to support producing a protobuf Message instance from the domain model class that corresponds to it. The `DatamodelReader` trait is used to do the reverse, mapping back from a protobuf Message to the appropriate domain model class. I'm using `PartialFunction` here as the return type because it's possible that when inspecting the type of `Message` instance supplied, it's not what was expected by the `DatamodelReader` and thus can't be handled. In that case, the adapter will throw an exception.

Now that we have the assisting traits defined, we can take a look at the adapter itself, starting with the class declaration and the definition of the `manifest` method:

```
class ProtobufDatamodelAdapter extends EventAdapter{
  override def manifest(event:Any) = event.getClass.getName
  . . .
}
```

This adapter is set as a full read/write adapter as we need translations going in both directions. The `manifest` method simply stores the full class name, as we will need that later in the read-adaptation process.

Next, let's take a look at the `toJournal` method that is responsible to convert from the domain model into the protobuf data model:

```
override def toJournal(event:Any) = event match {
  case wr:DatamodelWriter => wr.toDatamodel
  case _ =>
  throw new RuntimeException(
  s"Protobuf adapter can't write adapt type: $event")
}
```

When the adapter receives a domain model event to adapt, it checks to make sure that the instance implements the `DatamodelWriter` trait. If it does, it leverages the `toDatamodel` method to convert the domain event instance into a data model protobuf `Message` instance. The idea is that the Akka protobuf serializer will pick that `Message` and convert it into binary before being stored in the journal.

The last thing to look at with this adapter is the `fromJournal` method that adapts back from a protobuf `Message` into a domain model event instance. That code is as follows:

```
override def fromJournal(event:Any, manifest:String) = {
  event match{
    case m:Message =>
    val reader = Class.forName(manifest +
    "$").getField("MODULE$").get(null).asInstanceOf [DatamodelReader]
    reader.
    fromDatamodel.
    lift(m).
    map(EventSeq.single).
    getOrElse(throw readException(event))

    case _ => throw readException(event)
  }
}
```

The main idea here is to get a `DatamodelReader` instance that will always be the companion of whatever domain event class was adapter, which is identified via the manifest. Using reflection, the code gets the single instance of that companion and then invokes `fromDatamodel` on it. We then lift that into a full function (it is a `PartialFunction`) and apply it, and then map it into an `EventSeq` with a single event tied to it. If we get a `None`, which implies that the reader cannot handle the type given to it, then an exception is thrown.

Now that we have the adapter coded, we just need to configure it with our Cassandra journal plugin so that it will start being used. This config will be added as top level, which not nested under akka, into our `application.conf` file:

```
cassandra-journal{
  event-adapters{
    proto =
"com.packt.masteringakka.bookstore.common.ProtobufDatamodelAdapter"
  }

  event-adapter-bindings{
    "com.packt.masteringakka.bookstore.common.EntityEvent" = proto
    "com.google.protobuf.Message" = proto
  }
}
```

This config adds a new adapter mapping for our protobuf adapter, giving it the alias of proto. It then adds in two bindings for it, one to handle the write side (`EntityEvent`) and the other to handle the read side when we are recovering an entity (`Message`).

We also need to add the Akka protobuf serializer to handle the message type, as that does not come out of the box. The config for that is as follows:

```
akka.actor{
  serializers{
    proto = "akka.remote.serialization.ProtobufSerializer"
  }
  serialization-bindings {
    "com.google.protobuf.Message" = proto
  }
}
```

With all of that done, all we need to do now is to add the read/write conversion code for each of our events. This is the code where we actually map back and forth between domain and data model—the same code that the adapter drives in a generic manner. I chose to tie this code to the event class (write) and companion object (read). I don't love this solution as it somewhat muddles up the domain model. I chose this approach because it's very light on config. The alternative is that I would have to code and configure a separate adapter per event, and I was less excited about that than what I did here. Just know that my approach for where the mapping code lives is not the only way to do it. Choose whatever approach suits your style and your coding needs best.

Let's take a quick look at a single event so that you can get a feel for what this code looks like. The two-way mapping code for the `InventoryAdded` event is shown as follows:

```
case class InventoryAdded(amount:Int) extends EntityEvent{
  def toDatamodel = {
    Datamodel.InventoryAdded.newBuilder().
      setAmount(amount).
      build
  }
}
object InventoryAdded extends DatamodelReader{
  def fromDatamodel = {
    case ia:Datamodel.InventoryAdded =>
      InventoryAdded(ia.getAmount())
  }
}
```

Things are pretty straightforward with this code. On the write side, via `toDatamodel`, we use a protobuf builder to construct the data-model class that corresponds to the event we want to persist. On the read side, we take the fields from the protobuf data-model class and map them back into corresponding domain events. If you want to see the logic for the rest of the mappings, then take a look at the `Book` entity companion. This is where the domain events for book are defined.

Now that we have the final code for book, you can feel free to build the application again, start it up, and play with the book endpoint. Create a new book and then invoke some of the update operations on it. Let that entity get passivated and then use the endpoint to look it up again. This will show the full cycle of events being written and then read back in during recovery, which should exercise all of the storage related logic.

One thing to note is that we did not change the snapshot system over to use protobuf. We left it as still using JSON. Snapshots don't need to evolve the same way that events do. If you make changes, then you can simply wipe out a snapshot and let it be recreated again when the triggering condition occurs. Snapshots are far less important than the events themselves and thus don't need the same treatment.

The refactored sales order processing module

As with Chapter 3, *Curing Anemic Models with Domain-Driven Design*, I have already completed the sales order processing module's refactor within the -incomplete bookstore app code base. I won't share all of the code for it here as it follows the same approach that we used for Book. If you want to see what I did for that module, you can check out the code within the -incomplete code folder.

There are a couple of things to call out within this module though. The first one is how the pre-create validation works for the creation of a new SalesOrder. In Chapter 2, *Simplifying Concurrent Programming with Actors*, we refactored the creation process to use an FSM. In Chapter 3, *Curing Anemic Models with Domain-Driven Design*, we plugged those FSM steps into the new entity logic as part of the creating state. I was able to do this because I wrote the state handling logic for the base-entity actor code. So, I was able to write it in such a way that I could accommodate a complex pre-create cycle.

In this chapter, I switched SalesOrder over to be an Akka persistent actor. In doing so, I was not comfortable plugging that FSM flow directly into the persistent actor's state management. In Chapter 3, *Curing Anemic Models with Domain-Driven Design*, code, I had control over the stashing logic, which was crucial to the juggling of messages that goes on during that FSM flow. With Akka's persistent actor framework, I didn't have this level of control, so I changed the course a little and separated the validation steps out into a child actor. This child performs the validations and then sends a message back to the parent to complete the persistence of the event.

Another thing to note with this actor is that it still talks to the inventory management system (for inventory allocation) via the Akka event bus. We want to make this system more robust and not need to have both sides up all the time to be working. Persisting events seemed like a great way to make this interaction better, but we're not quite ready for that. In order to make this work, we will need the persistence query functionality from Akka. This will allow one module to listen to and react to the persisted event stream from another module. The persistence query functionality is the main focus of Chapter 5, *Separating Concerns with CQRS*, when we refactor to a CQRS approach.

Refactoring homework

The homework for this chapter will be similar in scope to what we did in the *Refactoring homework* section of Chapter 3, *Curing Anemic Models with Domain-Driven Design*, where you will finish converting the remaining modules of credit processing and user management over to event sourcing. Make your code changes in the code within the -incomplete bookstore app. When you are done, you can check out my fully converted code in the -complete code-base folder.

I've already added in the data model .proto files for each of these two modules and the generated binding classes. This is so you won't have to go through the trouble of installing the protoc compiler. Also, keep in mind that you won't be able to handle the multiuser lookup functionality in the CustomerRelationsManager yet, so just comment that functionality out for now. You'll get that code working again in the *Refactoring homework* section, in Chapter 5, *Separating Concerns with CQRS*,.

With the user-management project, there is a suggestion I would like to give. Since the e-mail address has to be unique, this should become the ID of the BookstoreUser entity. Move the check related to uniqueness into the aggregate sitting in front of the entity. Also, don't let the e-mail be updated anymore as part of the personal info update functionality.

I want to also give a suggestion for the credit-processing module. Move the faked call to the external credit charging service into the aggregate sitting in front of the entity. It just feels more natural here versus it being in the entity now.

Currently, this sales-order-processing module is not compiling. This is because it is expecting the credit transaction ID and user id (e-mail) to be Strings and they still are Ints. When you finish refactoring credit-processing and user-management, this code should compile successfully.

Summary

Throughout the course of this chapter you learned about event sourcing, and how it can be a different approach to persistence versus the more traditional approach of persisting current state. You also learned about Akka Persistence, and how you can use it to implement event sourcing in your Akka-based components. Finally, you also learned about how we can leverage tools such as protobuf to help deal with the reality of a constantly evolving event schema.

We changed the bookstore app quite a bit in this chapter, but we still have some holes to close up. We need to get the query functionality working again, as our switch to event sourcing has broken that capability within the app. That will be the main focus of the next chapter, as we dive into CQRS, and how we can use it to build a separate read/query model for our application.

5

Separating Concerns with CQRS

Within the world of data storage, reading and writing data are really two very distinct things. When writing, you want something that can write quickly and has an efficient storage structure. In the relational db world, this usually leads to normalization of data structures to remove duplication.

If you look at the same problem from the read side, there is a desire to have as many indexes as possible. The more indexes a set of tables has, the faster queries will be against those tables. Also, a highly normalized model, while efficient in storage, can be a burden to query against.

When faced with a problem like this, where you have to satisfy two concerns that are in conflict with their needs, why keep them together in the first place? Wouldn't it be better to separate them into their own storage models and systems, each optimized for their own needs? This kind of approach is at the heart of what we'll cover in this chapter, using a pattern called **Command Query Responsibility Segregation (CQRS)**.

The focus of this chapter is CQRS and how it's enabled by Akka's Persistence Query functionality. Here are the things you can expect to learn throughout this chapter:

- What is CQRS and how does it fit into event sourcing?
- How do we design a read model on top of Elasticsearch using CQRS?
- What are the capabilities of Akka's Persistence Query?
- How do we build views using Persistence Query?
- How do we build a resumable projection?

A brief history of CQRS

Before delving into how CQRS will fit into our event sourced app, I thought it important to at least briefly touch on the origins of this approach. Doing so should help you see how this approach evolved and the kinds of problems it was trying to solve.

CQRS has its origins in the **Command-Query Separation** (**CQS**) principle, which was first conceived by French technologist Bertrand Meyer, who is the creator of the **Eiffel** programming language. According to Wikipedia, the definition of CQS is:

> *It states that every method should either be a command that performs an action, or a query that returns data to the caller, but not both. In other words, asking a question should not change the answer. More formally, methods should return a value only if they are referentially transparent and hence possess no side effect.*

In short, if you are returning a value as part of a method invocation (a query) then you cannot also mutate state as part of that call. Also, if you are going to mutate state (a command), then you must return a void type for that method. This kind of convention makes it clear that void return types are causing side effects and non-void return types are not.

CQRS uses the same terminology of commands and queries that Meyer used for CQS, but takes it one step further. CQRS dictates that command handling and query handling are divided into separate objects, with one containing commands and the other containing queries. It is this kind of complete separation of query and command handling that we will build into our event sourced app when we bring in CQRS.

CQRS in the event sourced world

We know from our work in `Chapter 4`, *Making History with Event Sourcing*, that an event-sourced app is all about commands (actions) and events (reactions to those commands). The events that are generated from these commands are used to represent the state of a given entity over time, with the past events being replayed whenever the current state of an entity is needed. The storage model itself does not store the current state, only the occurrences that lead to a current state for a particular entity.

Given this model, what can I do if I want to query for a particular entity that has the current state with a field matching a specified value? If I don't store the current state, how can I answer this question? Will I have to read every entity in the system, replay its event stream to get its current state, and then see if it's a match? An approach like that will not be tenable, so let's not even consider it.

One answer to this question is to consider commands and queries as two separate concerns and model each with its own data stores that are optimized for its needs. We already have a data store for the command side of things, so it's time to think about the query side. In order to support the query side, we will need separate code to both build the read model from the write model's event stream and to query that read model when requested. This separating of the command-handling code and query-handling code is where CQRS gets its name from.

This idea of separating the read and write code goes beyond just storage concerns. The separation is also a necessity when building the models to represent these two concerns. If you try and build one unified model to handle the needs of both the read and the write side of things, what you will most likely end up with is a model that handles neither one very well. You're better off separating these needs from the start and building the correct model for each so that each model can best support its own needs.

For example, your write model will be designed around efficient storage while your read model will be designed around ease of querying. In your write model, you may store IDs to represent relationships between other entities in an effort to be efficient. In your read model, however, you may store the full related entity, along with all of its attributes, to support querying into that relationship. As such, the representation of that single entity in the write model will be very different than the representation of that same entity in the read model.

Using an approach such as CQRS is not all fun and games though. It comes with some technical complexities that must be taken seriously. Building and maintaining the read model is a fair amount of work; it must be done correctly for the read model to have any real value. If you build a system that misses events, or can't have any downtime because it's not smart enough to pick up where it left off, you'll end up in trouble. You have to put a fairly robust architecture in place in order for this approach to be viable. Hopefully, I'll get you started on the path to that robust architecture with the information we go over in the rest of this chapter.

If Eric Evans is the father of DDD, then Greg Young probably fills the same role for CQRS. If you ever want to really explore CQRS, look for anything on the subject written by him, including his book *Exploring CQRS and Event Sourcing*.

Designing our read model implementation

Now that we have a high-level idea of CQRS, let's set about designing how to use this pattern to support the query needs for our bookstore app. If you remember correctly, in `Chapter 4`, *Making History with Event Sourcing*, we had to remove the comment out of the code that we had previously working to handle multientity queries within our app. We have events for all of our entities stored in Cassandra, via Akka Persistence, currently. Unfortunately, the way this data is stored (binary via protobuf) and the nature of the data itself (events versus actual current state) makes it next to impossible to write queries against it. This means that we can't currently handle things such as looking up books by authors or sales orders by users. In order to get this functionality back, we will have to build read models for our entities.

Selecting our read model data store

Our first order of business in designing our read-model implementation is selecting a good storage engine for that data. We want something that is distributed and highly available so that it won't be a single point of failure in our system. We also want something that is fast and can handle a wide array of different query types. When I started to think about these requirements, there was one application that just kept popping back into my mind and that is **Elasticsearch**.

Elasticsearch is an application that is built on top of the excellent **Lucene** search engine. It has a very expressive query language that allows you to do all kinds of complex matching and Boolean logic. It is clustered and it replicates your data, so it definitely checks the highly available box from our list of requirements. It stores its data in JSON, which is a simple and very well-known format that is easy to work with. Its API is HTTP and JSON based, so there is a low barrier for entry there too. If you haven't bumped into it yet in your programming experiences, I suggest you take a look at it. All in all, I think it's a great choice as our read-model storage engine.

There will be no need for you to install Elasticsearch on your local system. As with Postgres and Cassandra, we will set up Elasticsearch via Docker, running it as a container. You should take a look at Elasticsearch's documentation though in an effort to understand the search, document and update APIs as those will be the ones we use the most. Also read through the Query DSL section as this is the basis for query functionality in Elasticsearch. I have included the link to the documentation root page (`https://www.elastic.co/guide/en/elasticsearch/reference/current/index.html`) for your convenience.

Projecting events into the read model

For each entity we will need a read model for, we'll need a component that represents a view into this collection of entities, which in turn will enable us to query against it. We will refer to this component as a **View**. For each **View** that we have, we will also need a component to listen to the event stream for that entity and project those changes into our read model. We will refer to this component as a **View Builder**. How these components fit into our current event sourced model is shown in the following diagram:

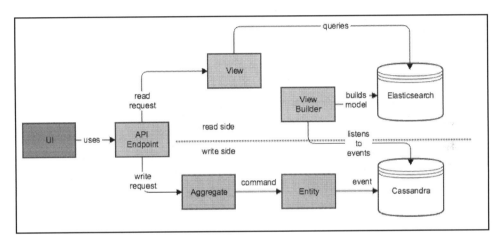

The write side of our system is already built using Event Sourcing as its model. Command requests flow through an **API Endpoint** into an **Aggregate**, which then delegates a command to an entity. That entity processes the command and then writes an event into the write model's data store, **Cassandra**. This is what we built in Chapter 4, *Making History with Event Sourcing*.

The read side of the system is what we intend to build in this chapter. In that flow, once an event is written into **Cassandra**, a **ViewBuilder** component picks up that event by listening for it, which we will cover shortly, and projects it into the read store, **Elasticsearch**. Each **View Builder** component will be entity-specific and will know how to construct the read model for that entity, and how to properly project each event into that model.

When a query request comes into an API endpoint, that endpoint will pass the request off to a new component called a **View**. This component will build the appropriate Elasticsearch request to support that query, execute it, and then send the results back to the requestor.

This model will be our way of implementing the CQRS pattern. We'll still be able to preserve our event sourced write system, but now we'll also have a very rich query system to go with it. The question now is, How can we make all of this work within the Akka Persistence? The answer is with Akka's Persistence Query, which we will cover in the next section.

Using Persistence Query to build our views

In the previous section, I diagrammed a flow to build and query a read model within our app; within that flow, there is a component called a **View Builder**, which is responsible for listening to the event stream of a particular entity and projecting it into **Elasticsearch**. So, how do we make the event listening part work?

We know that Akka has an event bus, which we've used a little, to support the inventory allocation process, but that will not work here. That's an in-memory solution where the sender and receiver of the event are required to be active at the same time for the flow to work. That creates a really strong tie between the sender and receiver and does not allow them to be deployed and run independently of each other. It may work initially, but it's not a good long-term approach for a scalable architecture. We need something more robust that, ideally, is built on top of Akka Persistence.

Akka's Persistence Query is a system that allows you to query into a stream of persisted events. These events are the same ones that were persisted on the write side of the system via Akka Persistence. Persistence Query accomplishes this query capability via a component called `ReadJournal`. Using `ReadJournal`, you can issue a few different types of query, the result of which is an Akka Stream Source of events that you can then project into your read model.

When writing this book, Persistence Query was still an experimental feature. It's the go-forward replacement for a similar piece of functionality called persistent views, which is now deprecated. If you are building a read model, then you should use Persistence Query and not persistent views. To include Persistence Query in your project, add the following line into your `build.sbt` file (where `akkaVersion` represents the version of Akka you are using):

```
"com.typesafe.akka" %% "akka-persistence-query-experimental" %  akkaVersion
```

For the bookstore app, I don't have an explicit import for Persistence Query. That's because it's already included as a dependency for our Cassandra journal provider.

Over the next few sections, I'll break down the features of Persistence Query, identifying how you set up ReadJournal and the types of query it supports. Once we have a better understanding of the capabilities of Persistence Query, we can decide which ones we will need to build our read-model implementation.

Understanding your journal provider's query capabilities

Each journal provider plugin will support different combinations of the query capabilities within Persistence Query. When selecting a journal implementation, you should think of whether or not you will need Persistence Query. If so, you should determine which query capabilities you require and then make sure they are supported by your journal plugin. If there were two journals that you felt were comparable for the write side, and one had significantly better query capabilities, that may be the deciding factor in which of the two will you end up choosing.

Setting up a ReadJournal in your code

When you are ready to use Persistence Query, the first thing you will need to do is to get a reference to `ReadJournal` for your journal plugin. This involves getting a reference to the `PersistenceQuery` Akka extension, calling `readJournalFor` on that extension, and passing in the unique string identifier supplied by your journal provider. For our Cassandra journal, that code looks like this:

```
import akka.persistence.query.PersistenceQuery
import akka.persistence.cassandra.query.scaladsl.CassandraReadJournal

val identifier = CassandraReadJournal.Identifier
val journal = PersistenceQuery(context.system).
readJournalFor[CassandraReadJournal](identifier)
```

One thing to note here is that I'm explicitly identifying the type of my read journal as `scaladsl.CassandraReadJournal` when requesting it from the `PersistenceQuery` extension. `ReadJournal` will generally come in two flavors, a Scala and a Java DSL version, with each having an API that best suits the language it's intended to be used in.

Once you have a reference to `ReadJournal`, you can start making query requests against it. I'll go over the types of queries you can make in the next few sections.

Obtaining all of the persistenceIds in the system

The first pair of queries that I'll go over is about getting all of the available persistenceIds within your event sourced system. Remember that persistenceId is a correlation mechanism that keeps associated events together. For our purposes, each unique entity has its own persistenceId so that it has an isolated event stream of only its activity. If you want to get all of those persistenceIds, then you will use the `allPersistenceIds` query, as follows:

```
val persistIdsSource:Source[String, NotUsed] =
    readJournal.allPersistenceIds
persistIdsSource.runForEach(id => println(id))
```

The type returned here, `Source`, is a type from Akka Streams, which we will discuss in the next chapter. Basically, it gives you a structure that allows you to process matching results one at a time. In this example, I materialize the stream and run it through a for-each processing step where I simply print the persistenceIds. This call returns a "live" stream. As new persistenceIds come into the system, my for-each processing block will continue to be invoked.

If I don't need this live nature, and I want a terminal stream, then I can switch to using `currentPersistenceIds` instead. This query method will give me only the current set of persistenceIds that exist at the point when I make the query. This will result in a finite stream as opposed to the live (potentially infinite) stream that we get from `allPersistenceIds`. This concept of having a pair of query methods, one live and one not, will be present across other queries as well.

This method isn't giving you events; all it's giving you is persistenceIds. So, how can this method be used to listen to a stream of events and build a read model? By itself, it can't, but if you combine it with our next query, then you're in business.

Getting events by persistenceId

The next pair of queries to go over are `eventsByPersistenceId` and `currentEventsByPersistenceId`, with the former being live and the latter not. These queries let you get a stream of events that match a supplied persistenceId. An example of using a query like this is shown as follows:

```
val eventsSource:Source[EventEnvelope, NotUsed] =
journal.eventsByPersistenceId("fooId", 0, Integer.MAX_VALUE)
```

The first argument supplied there is the persistenceId that you want the event stream for. The next two arguments represent the range of sequence numbers that you want to get the events for. Each event within persistenceId has a sequence number that starts at 0 and continues to increase upward. If you want to only see a subset of the full range of events for persistenceId, then you can specify that range with those two inputs. Here, I am basically saying that I want everything by passing in 0 and `Integer.MAX_VALUE`.

If you were to stream the results of an `allPersistenceIds` query into calls to this query method, then you can build a system where you are able to listen to the complete event stream for all of the entities in the system, even as new ones get created. That can be a possibility to build our read models. The thing I don't like about it is that you will need to have a potentially large and ever increasing number of streams materialized in memory to handle this (one for every entity instance of each type in the system). That can get out of hand pretty quickly.

This approach could have merit for some uses of Akka Persistence, but not how we're using it. We will need something better as the backbone to build our read models from. Thankfully, there is one more set of queries that should suit our needs almost perfectly.

Getting events by tag

The last pairing of queries that is supported by the Persistence Query API is `eventsByTag` and `currentEventsByTag`. These queries are based on tagging your events as they are being written, doing so in an event adapter. You can then query by these tags, getting a stream of events that will match your query input.

In order to make this work, you will need to add the adapter code to explicitly tag your events. You only need `WriteEventAdapter` for this, as tagging only matters when writing events and not when replaying them. A simple version of code to handle tagging is as follows:

```
import akka.persistence.journal.Tagged
class TaggingAdapter extends WriteEventAdapter{
  def toJournal(event:Any) = {
    Tagged(event, Set("sometag", "someothertag"))
  }
  def manifest(event:Any) = ""
}
```

In this example, when persisting to the journal, the code wraps the event in a special class called `Tagged`. When the journal sees this, it knows how to save some additional tag metadata along with the event. In this case, the tags, `sometag` and `someothertag`, will be saved along with whatever event this is.

If we follow an event tagging approach like this, then we can query for events matching these tags later on. A query to get a stream of events by tag will look like this:

```
val source:Source[EventEnvelope, NotUsed] =
journal.eventsByTag("sometag", 0)
```

The result is similar to what we got when we queried for events by persistenceId. For inputs, the first argument represents the tag that you want to query for. The second argument is called an offset and is slightly different than the sequence number arguments supplied in `eventsByPersistenceId`; as such, it deserves a bit more explanation.

Getting events by persistenceId, you're scoped into one persistenceId at a time. As a result of that, you can use a basic sequential numbering system to uniquely identify each event within that persistenceId. When you use something such as the `eventsByTag`, you'll get the events for all persistenceIds that emitted events with that tag. You can't use a basic incrementing number scheme as the sequence number for events is scoped to a persistenceId. You will need something that can represent a point to fetch events from that covers all persistenceIds you may be getting those events from. For Persistence Query, this is represented by the offset param.

The offset param will be something that is implemented differently for each journal plugin provider, so read the documentation for whatever journal provider you are using to understand what it is. For Cassandra, the offset type is a `Long` that represents the epoch time of a given event. When you receive an `EventEnvelope` while processing an event stream, that object will contain an offset field on it. The value of that field represents where in the total stream of events this event comes sequentially. If you hang onto this value, then you can resume that stream later on, starting up exactly where you left off last time. This is what's referred to as a resumable projection and is a topic which we will explore later on in this chapter.

Taking a look at what you can do with a tag-based query, I believe this is our best bet for a system from which to build our read-model projection code. We can tag our events with two indicators, which are as follows:

1. A string value representing the entity name this event belongs to.
2. A string value that represents the type of event this is.

We can use step 1 as the mechanism to listen to a complete event stream across all entities of a given type, and then project that into the read model. This will be the mechanism our `ViewBuilder` classes use. Then, if we need something to only listen to a single-event type, across all entities which emit that type, we can use step 2. We can use this technique to implement the inventory allocation back and forth between our inventory management and sales-order-processing systems.

Now that we have a high-level approach for how we'll use Persistence Query, let's get down to the business of making it work within our application. The remainder of this chapter will be about implementing Persistence Query to build out read models and regain our ability to support queries for our entities. We'll also use Persistence Query to finalize the approach for the inventory allocation process, making that process more robust and ready to use in production.

Implementing the Book read model

As usual, we'll take the plunge into our refactor with the inventory management module and the `Book` entity. We want to build out both `ViewBuilder` and `View` for `Book` so that we can build its read projection and be able to query against it again. We'll have to make some changes to our common code first so that we have a good framework to build our CQRS implementation on top of it. I'll start with describing those changes and then we can jump into the Book read-model implementation.

Supporting tagging in ProtobufDatamodelAdapter

When discussing the high-level approach we can use to build our read models, we decided that `eventsByTag` was the Persistence Query feature to leverage. We wanted to tag our events with two `String` tags—the entity type and the event type. We'll implement this tagging process in the `ProtobufDatamodelAdapter` class that we created in *Detaching the domain model from the data model* section in `Chapter 4`, *Making History with Event Sourcing*. Before we go over that code, we'll need a way to identify the entity type per instance of `EntityEvent`. To facilitate that requirement, I added a new method called `entityType` to `EntityEvent`. The new definition of that trait is shown as follows:

```
trait EntityEvent extends Serializable with DatamodelWriter{
  def entityType:String
}
```

Using this approach, whenever I have an `EntityEvent` instance, I can identify what entity it belongs to. For each entity in the app, I'll create a helper trait that extends `EntityEvent` and provides a concrete implementation of `entityType` so that I will only need to define this method once per family of events for an entity. For the `Book` entity, it looks like this:

```
trait BookEvent extends EntityEvent{def entityType = "book"}
case class BookCreated(book:BookFO) extends BookEvent{
  . . .
}
```

Now that we can properly identify the entity type per event, we can add the tagging logic to our adapter class. When I set out to implement this tagging approach, I wanted to chain two adapters together, one to tag and the other to convert to the data model. I know you can configure an adapter chain, so this seemed like a good approach as it separated the concerns of tagging and data-model adaptation. Unfortunately, when I tried it, I found out that you cannot chain multiple write-based adapters together (you will get an exception if you do). So, I had to change course and add the tagging code right into the ProtobufDatamodelAdapter class.

As tagging only happens on the write side (going into the journal), we only need to make a change in the toJournal method in our adapter class. The updated code for that method is shown as follows:

```
override def toJournal(event:Any) = event match {
  case ev:EntityEvent with DatamodelWriter =>
  val message = ev.toDatamodel
  val eventType = ev.getClass.
  getName().toLowerCase().split("\\$").last
  Tagged(message, Set(ev.entityType, eventType))

  case _ =>
  throw new RuntimeException(
  s"Protobuf adapter can't write adapt type: $event")
}
```

The big change to highlight here is that now, instead of returning just the data-model class we adapted to, we are returning a special class type called Tagged. This wrapper class from the Akka Persistence library indicates the underlying journal to save the wrapped message with tags, which are supplied as a set of strings.

For our implementation, we can tag our events with the entity name through our newly added entityType method on EntityEvent and the class name of the event itself. The code used to get the class name of the event may look a little verbose to you. It's coded this way because you can't use getSimpleName on the event class as it's defined in a nested object on a companion. The getSimpleName method can work with one level of nesting but, apparently, not with two. So, this code works around that limitation.

Now that we have tagging coded into our adapter, there is one final thing we need to do to get this to work properly all the way through into our journal. The Cassandra journal plugin that we use, thankfully, supports tagging, and allows you to specify up to three distinct tags per event. In the messages table in Cassandra, these are stored in the tag1, tag2, and tag fields.

In order for the plugin to know in which of those three fields to store each tag, you will need to add some configuration describing all of your possible tags and where they slot in. As this is event-and entity-specific (not general), we will do this per module, adding the config into a `*.conf` file within that module. For inventory management, this is stored in `inventory.conf` (in `src/main/resources`) and looks like this:

```
cassandra-journal.tags = {
  book = 1
  bookcreated = 2
  inventoryadded = 2
  tagadded = 2
  tagremoved = 2
  inventoryallocated = 2
  inventorybackordered = 2
  bookdeleted = 2
}
```

Here, the left-hand side of each config line represents the name of the tag and the right hand side (after the = sign) represents which tag field to store that tag in. In this config, the `book` entity type tag will always be stored in `tag1`, and all of the other event name-related tags will be stored in `tag2`.

Event though we define this same property, `cassandra-journal.tag`, per module, the Akka config handling code is smart enough at runtime to merge all of that into one single property. This single property contains all of the configured values across all modules, as if we configured it all in a single place. It is a good approach to keep the module-specific config in the module that owns it, as opposed to leaking it out into a more common config location, for example, directly in `application.conf` versus an include.

Elasticsearch support traits

As we will be talking to Elasticsearch in this project and writing and reading data to/from it, we will need supporting code to facilitate those interactions. This supporting code will then be used in the `ViewBuilder` classes (writing) and in the `View` classes (reading) to talk to Elasticsearch.

The first set of common Elasticsearch code to look at is the `ElasticsearchApi` object. This object contains case classes that map to and from the JSON that is exchanged between our code and Elasticsearch. That object's definition is shown as follows:

```
object ElasticsearchApi {
  trait EsResponse
  case class ShardData(total:Int, failed:Int, successful:Int)
  case class IndexingResult(_shards:ShardData, _index:String,
  _type:String, _id:String, _version:Int,
  created:Option[Boolean]) extends EsResponse

  case class UpdateScript(inline:String, params:Map[String,Any])
  case class UpdateRequest(script:UpdateScript)
  case class SearchHit(_source:JObject)
  case class QueryHits(hits:List[SearchHit])
  case class QueryResponse(hits:QueryHits) extends EsResponse
  case class DeleteResult(acknowledged:Boolean) extends EsResponse
}
```

The `IndexingResult` class represents the response information from Elasticsearch when we write to the index. This can be the indexing of a new document or a single field update via the update API.

The `UpdateRequest` class represents the request information we pass to Elasticsearch when we are making a single field update via the update API.

The `QueryResponse` class maps the relevant result information from a query that we make to lookup documents in Elasticsearch (note the use of `JObject` for the _source field mapping type). The _source will be the actual JSON field for whatever document type we are looking up. As this will vary per entity, and because any generic typing will be erased and not be available for the parsing logic, I went with the generic `JObject` representation for this field. I don't need to interact with the source at all as this is a read-only code, so this approach works for what we are doing.

The next set of code to look at is the base logic for making calls against and for querying Elasticsearch. The code for it looks like this:

```
trait ElasticsearchSupport{ me:BookstoreActor =>
  import ElasticsearchApi._
  val esSettings = ElasticsearchSettings(context.system)

  def indexRoot:String
  def entityType:String

  def baseUrl = s"${esSettings.rootUrl}/${indexRoot}/$entityType"
```

```
   def callElasticsearch[RT : Manifest](req:Req)
   (implicit ec:ExecutionContext):Future[RT] = {
     Http(req OK as.String).map(resp => read[RT](resp))
   }

   def queryElasticsearch(query:String)
   (implicit ec:ExecutionContext):Future[List[JObject]] = {
     val req = url(s"$baseUrl/_search") <<? Map("q" -> query)
     callElasticsearch[QueryResponse](req).
     map(_.hits.hits.map(_._source))
   }
 }
```

This ElasticsearchSupport is set up to only be mixed into a BookstoreActor class. We will need some actor-based features in this code, hence the self-type restriction. It sets up a settings class, which allows us to get the Elasticsearch hostname from config rather than hardcoding it into this class.

The indexRoot and entityType methods define what index and what type within that index the implementing actor will work with. Indexes in Elasticsearch have a structure where the URL to communicate with them follows this convention: http://localhost:9200/INDEXNAME/TYPENAME.

In that URL, the INDEXNAME part of the path represents what index you want to talk to. For our purposes, we will have an index per module. The TYPENAME part of the path represents a document type within that index that you want to work with. For our code, this will represent the entity type within a module. So, for example, if we are working with the Book entity, then the base URL will look like this: http://localhost:9200/inventory/book.

The baseUrl builds a URL to use, leveraging the host from the settings, the indexRoot, and the entityType method to do so.

The callElasticsearch method contains the generic logic to make a request to Elasticsearch, whether it's a write request or a query request. It takes a generic type called RT that represents the response type to map the JSON response into. The code handles making the Elasticsearch request, then parses the resulting JSON and returns a Future for the type RT.

The last method on this trait to discuss is queryElasticsearch. This method leverages callElasticsearch in order to make a query request. The method returns a Future for a list of JObject with each one representing the _source for a matching document.

One thing to emphasize here is that I am using the simpler URL-based query method versus the richer Elasticsearch JSON query DSL. We're performing pretty simple queries here, so it was much simpler to code against the URL-query API. Using the query DSL will require a complex case-class structure to map into the correct JSON for each query. If the queries were more complicated, we'd probably use the query DSL, but for now this simpler method will suffice.

The last trait that we need to look at, related to talking to Elasticsearch, is `ElasticsearchUpdateSupport`. This trait is used for our `ViewBuilder` classes as they need to write and update documents into the index. Before we dig into the code for this trait, I want to go over one aspect of it that I think needs a bit of an explanation. All updates (indexing a new document, updated to a document) into Elasticsearch for our View Builders are carried out serially. We won't execute an update request until the request in front of it has completed fully. This is because the first request may be the creation of a document and the next request, right behind it, may be an update to that same document. This will happen for sure when we are replaying the full event stream when the server starts up (until we implement resumable projections).

As calls into Elasticsearch are asynchronous, using dispatch, it will be possible for the insert and update to happen at the same time and that won't work properly. In that case, update will fail if the document doesn't exist yet. So, to avoid this, we can execute a request and then switch into a state to wait for the response. Any new request is stashed until we get a response, after which we can continue on our way with the next request. I don't love this process as you really only need to be serial within the context of an individual entity ID, but that wasn't worth implementing here (it will require a separate `ViewBuilder` instance per persistenceId) yet. We'll completely redo this process in the next chapter when we dive into Akka Streams, so this is a temporary solution that works for now.

The first thing to look at with `ElasticsearchUpdateSupport` is the definition of the trait itself, as follows:

```
trait ElasticsearchUpdateSupport
  extends ElasticsearchSupport{ me:ViewBuilder[_] =>
  . . .
}
```

It's important to note the self type of `ViewBuilder[_]` here. After we are done getting a response from Elasticsearch, we will need to switch back to a receive `PartialFunction` that allows us to go back to event handling. The self type here allows me to do that, using `handlingEvents`, which we will go over in a moment.

The next method to look at in this trait is updating the index. That can be either indexing a new document or making an in-place update to a field in that document. The code for that method is shown as follows:

```
def updateIndex(id:String, request:AnyRef, version:Option[Long])
(implicit ec:ExecutionContext):Future[IndexingResult] = {
  val urlBase = s"$baseUrl/$id"
  val requestUrl = version match{
    case None => urlBase
    case Some(v) => s"$urlBase/_update?version=$v"
  }

  val req = url(requestUrl) << write(request)
  callAndWait[IndexingResult](req)
}
```

As we are always dealing with a single document, which will be keyed by the entity ID, we will build a URL that contains that ID. Then, if we get a version ID, we will also add that to the URL as a query param. Elasticsearch supports version checks on updates. If you supply a version that is less than the current version, the update will be rejected. This will be an important feature later when we implement resumable projections. It allows us to reprocess events that we already processed without any consequences as the update will simply be rejected. I'll dig into this concept a little later, when I go over the `ViewBuilder` logic.

Once we have the URL built, we can serialize whatever payload object we get passed in the request param, turning the request into a POST. Then, the code calls the `callAndWait` method to execute the call to Elasticsearch and switch into the state where it waits for the response. The code for `callAndWait` looks like this:

```
def callAndWait[T <: AnyRef : Manifest](req:Req)
  (implicit ec:ExecutionContext) = {
  val fut = callElasticsearch[T](req)
  context.become(waitingForEsResult(req))
  fut pipeTo self
}
```

With this logic, we call Elasticsearch via `callElasticsearch`, which we talked about when discussing `ElasticsearchSupport`. That returns a Future that we pipe back to ourselves and switch into the `waitingForEsResult` receive-handling state. In that other state, we stash any message that is not an index response until we get that response back from Elasticsearch. When that happens, we can unstash and go back to handling events again. That code is as follows:

```
def waitingForEsResult(req:Req):Receive = {
  case es:EsResponse =>
```

```
    log.info("Successfully processed a request against the index for    url:
{}", req.toRequest.getUrl())
    context.become(handlingEvents)
    unstashAll

    case akka.actor.Status.Failure(ex) =>
    log.error(ex,
    "Error calling elasticsearch when building the read model")
    context.become(handlingEvents)
    unstashAll

    case other =>
    stash
}
```

With these two traits, we have a framework to talk to Elasticsearch for our View Builders and Views. Now, we can start to build those components to finish the process of building our read models.

The ViewBuilder trait

The ViewBuilder trait is where the common functionality to build an entity-based View lives. It's here we leverage Persistence Query to tap into a stream of events for an entity and project it into Elasticsearch to serve as the data store for a read model. This trait does the majority of the heavy lifting to create those projections so that the derived classes only have to implement a small set of entity-specific functionality.

Acknowledging the flaws with the current code

Before we jump into the code, I want to talk a little about how I approached the code for this chapter. In my mind, creating projections with Persistence Query is really all about using the rich functionality of Akka Streams. As we have not yet covered that functionality, I took a more simple approach here, using techniques that we've already covered. As a result, it's a less than ideal implementation that has a few flaws.

The biggest flaw, to me, is that it has to serialize the stream of events and completely process them one at a time-request and response against Elasticsearch. We can't have a create for a document and an update for that same document happening at the same time against Elasticsearch. The update will fail in that case, and our read model will not be accurate and lose its value as a result. Ideally, we'd serialize at the level of an individual entity, but there will be a bit more code here, and it will be much easier with Akka Streams, which we will cover in the next chapter.

Another flaw here is that the stream of events to Elasticsearch has no back-pressure mechanism at all. If we have a huge stream of events to process, it's possible that we can inundate Elasticsearch and take it down, which is never a good thing. Again, I could have added some throttling code here, but it will be much easier when we redo this implementation in Chapter 6, *Going with the Flow with Akka Streams*.

The last flaw to discuss is the one we will fix in this chapter. The first cut of this trait does not do what I've referred to as a resumable projection. What I mean is that, if I shut down the server and then start it back up again, the query I use for events will use 0 as the starting offset, which means that I want the whole stream again. This is not ideal because, as the stream grows over time, the time required to completely rebuild it will get longer and longer. We will require a mechanism to keep track of where we left off and resume from there on a server restart. We'll do that later in this chapter, and then make that process even better when we do Akka Streams in the next chapter.

Discussing the code

Flaws and all, the code still works well at getting the event data synced into Elasticsearch to serve as the data for our read models. Let's take a look at it and see how it does the work of projecting those events into Elasticsearch. The first two things that we can look at are a helper trait to identify read-model classes and the companion to the ViewBuilder trait. The definitions are as follows:

```
trait ReadModelObject extends AnyRef{
  def id:String
}
object ViewBuilder{
  import ElasticsearchApi._

  sealed trait IndexAction
  case class UpdateAction(id:String, expression:List[String],
  params:Map[String,Any]) extends IndexAction
  object UpdateAction{
    def apply(id:String, expression:String,
    params:Map[String,Any]):UpdateAction =
    UpdateAction(id, List(expression), params)
  }
  case class InsertAction(id:String,
  rm:ReadModelObject) extends IndexAction
  case class NoAction(id:String) extends IndexAction
  case object DeferredCreate extends IndexAction
}
```

The `ReadModelObject` trait will be used on the case classes that represent the read model for a particular entity. This trait provides a method to get the ID of that read-model object, which we need to properly index and update the document in Elasticsearch.

The companion to `ViewBuilder` defines an `IndexAction` trait that serves to define an action to be taken against the index based on receiving an event. There are four possible types of actions represented as extensions of that trait: updating an existing document field, inserting a new document, doing nothing, and a deferred create. Each concrete `ViewBuilder` implementation will use these types when deciding what to do for each event that it receives. The deferred create is used when we need to pull in some additional information on a create before indexing the document. We'll cover that in more detail when we go over the sales order processing refactor.

The next thing to look at is the definition of the trait itself, as well as the constructor body code to establish the event stream. The code is shown as follows:

```
trait ViewBuilder[RM <: ReadModelObject]
  extends BookstoreActor with Stash
  with ElasticsearchUpdateSupport{
  clearIndex
  val journal = PersistenceQuery(context.system).
  readJournalFor[CassandraReadJournal](CassandraReadJournal   .Identifier)
  val eventsSource = journal.eventsByTag(entityType, 0)
  implicit val materializer = ActorMaterializer()
  eventsSource.runForeach(self ! _)
  . . .
}
```

Every implementation of this trait needs to define `ReadModelObject`, which it works with. This trait also pulls in `ElasticsearchUpdateSupport` as it needs to be writing to the index. It pulls in `Stash` because we need that capability to support the one-at-a-time model of writing to the index.

The first thing that happens when a subclass of this trait gets created is that it clears the index. This is a method on `ElasticsearchUpdateSupport` that I didn't go over because it wasn't very interesting code and this approach is temporary anyway (all that code does is perform an index delete). Then, the first event we process will result in the index getting recreated automatically by Elasticsearch. We're rebuilding from scratch until we implement resumable projections, and clearing the current state in the index is just part of making that work.

The next few code lines are around setting up our query against the read journal. We get a reference to our `CassandraReadJournal` extension and then use it to issue an `eventsByTag` query. We get the event-type tag to use for that query via the `eventType` method, which a subclass must implement, as defined by `ElasticsearchSupport`. Note that I'm explicitly using 0 as the offset param to the query. We'll fix this later, when we make this projection resumable.

The query returns a `Source[EventEnvelope, NotUsed]`, which is an Akka Streams type that can be used to consume an event stream. The code immediately materializes this stream, after creating an `ActorMaterializer` to do so, running a simple `foreach` type loop over it. Inside that loop, I'm delivering the event to myself so that I can handle it in the receive-handling code for this actor. I kept things as simple as possible here in relation to the stream processing. This code will be redone quite a bit in the next chapter, as there are better ways of reading and processing this live event stream. For now, this logic will suffice as it minimizes the exposure to Akka Streams and leverages the techniques we are already comfortable with.

Next, we can look at the receive-handling code for this actor, which processes the events and figures out what actions they will result in against the index. The code for that handling looks like this:

```scala
def receive = handlingEvents

def actionFor(id:String, offset:Long, event:Any):IndexAction

def handlingEvents:Receive = {
  case env:EventEnvelope =>

  val id = env.persistenceId.toLowerCase().drop(
  entityType.length() + 1)
  actionFor(id, env.offset, env.event) match {
    case i:InsertAction =>
    updateIndex(i.id, i.rm, None)

    case u:UpdateAction =>
    updateDocumentField(u.id,
    env.sequenceNr - 1, u.expression, u.params)

    case NoAction(id) =>
    updateDocumentField(id,
    env.sequenceNr - 1, "", Map.empty)

    case DeferredCreate =>
    //Nothing happening here
  }
```

```
}
```

The code starts out by setting the initial receive-handling logic to be a custom `Receive` called `handlingEvents`. As we write to the index, the code will toggle back and forth between `handlingEvents` and `waitingForEsResult` as it's a technique for completely handling the events one at a time. The code then defines an abstract method called `actionFor` that will be used to determine the appropriate `IndexAction` for each specific event that is received.

In the `handlingEvents` receive-handling block, we only need to handle one possible message type, `EventEnvelope`. This is the type that we emit to ourselves when reading the live stream of events from the query we made. Upon receiving a message of this type, we will first split out the entity's ID from the persistenceId on the event envelope. We used a consistent naming structure on our persistenceIds, so we can pretty easily use one to determine what ID the event is for. Next, the code leverages `actionFor` to see how the specific subclass wants to handle this event. Then, based on the action type, we will take the appropriate action against the index.

If the action calls for an insert, we'll be inserting a new read-model object into the index. We will use the `ReadModelObject` tied to the `InsertAction` as the payload to save to Elasticsearch. If the action calls for a document field update, then we will leverage a method called `updateDocumentField` to make that update work. If no action, we will still touch the document so that the version gets bumped, even though no fields change. The reason for this is further explained in the next few paragraphs.

An important concept shown here is how to leverage the versioning code of Elasticsearch to make sure we don't apply the same event multiple times into our index. Consider the `InventoryAdded` event and what impact it will have on the read model. When we get this event, we will need to increment the inventory amount on the document in the index by the amount specified on the event. Since we are incrementing, and not just setting the final value, we will need to be careful to not process the same event multiple times or else we will have the wrong inventory amount value in the index. It is possible that, when we resume our projections later, we may encounter this very situation, and as such we will need to handle it properly.

The way that I chose to handle it was to keep the event-specific sequence number from Akka Persistence in sync with the automatic version-rolling code in Elasticsearch. Each time you touch the document, Elasticsearch will roll the version forward by one. As each event touches the document, including tones that result in no action, we can pretty reliably keep these numbers in sync and leverage the event-sequence number as our version identifier. Elasticsearch supports external version-number handling, as opposed to doing it by itself, but you can't use that with the update API and our logic is based on using that API.

Note that the reason I'm using the one less than the current sequence number is because what we specify is what we think is the the current version of the document. If that matches our input, then our update for the next sequence is allowed, which rolls the version forward by one. This is Elasticsearch's implementation of the **Optimistic concurrency control (OCC)** pattern.

The last piece of code to look at, on this trait, is the `updateDocumentField` method, which is used when we need to make a version-controlled update to an existing document. That code is as follows:

```
def updateDocumentField(id:String, seq:Long,
expressions:List[String],
params:Map[String,Any]):Future[IndexingResult] = {

  val script = expressions.map(e =>
  s"ctx._source.$e").mkString(";")
  val request = UpdateRequest(UpdateScript(script, params))
  updateIndex(id, request, Some(seq))
}
```

Elasticsearch's update API allows you to a specific script expression that can act against fields in the document and change their values. That's the reason we turned scripting on when we installed Elasticsearch. For our purposes, each specific `ViewBuilder` will identify that expression per event, as well as the params to plug into them. Once we have the expressions, we can make a call to update the index, and pass an `UpdateRequest`, which models the JSON for an update, to be serialized into JSON as the POST body. We pass the version here so that we can make this change in a version-aware manner. When we have no action to take, we will simply pass an empty expression, which does nothing to the document, but still rolls the version forward, keeping it in sync with our event-sequence numbers.

Building the BookViewBuilder

Once we have all of that framework code in place, we can build out an actual `ViewBuilder` implementation. I've already done that for you with a class aptly named `BookViewBuilder`, which is in the inventory management project. All `ViewBuilder` extension classes need `ReadModelObject` to work with, so let's take a look at that first:

```
case class BookRM(id:String, title:String,
author:String, tags:List[String], cost:Double,
inventoryAmount:Int, createTs:Date, deleted:Boolean = false)
extends ReadModelObject
```

Read-model representations can add in additional data (denormalize) to make querying against the read model easier. We didn't need to do that here, so this class looks pretty much like its counterpart, `BookFO`. When we get to the sales order processing refactor, we will see a read-model class that is a bit different from its fields object counterpart.

Now we can take a look at the definition of `BookViewBuilder` and a simple helper trait, which are shown as follows:

```
trait BookReadModel{
  def indexRoot = "inventory"
  def entityType = "book"
}

class BookViewBuilder extends BookReadModel
with ViewBuilder[BookViewBuilder.BookRM]{
  . . .
}
```

Both `BookViewBuilder`, and `BookView` needed to identify the entity type and the index root as they use Elasticsearch. I created the simple trait, `BookReadModel`, to capture these common values for book and then mix them into each of those classes.

Now, the real work in this class is being done in the `actionFor` method. This is where we look at each event and figure out how to apply it to the index. I've pulled in some of that code to show here. If you want to see the rest, go and take a look at the full class in the `chapter5` code distribution:

```
def actionFor(bookId:String, off:Long, event:Any) = event match {
  case BookCreated(book) =>
  val bookRM = BookRM(book.id, book.title,
  book.author, book.tags, book.cost, book.inventoryAmount,
  book.createTs, book.deleted )
  InsertAction(book.id, bookRM)

  case TagAdded(tag) =>
  UpdateAction(bookId, "tags += tag", Map("tag" -> tag))

  case InventoryBackordered(orderId) =>
  NoAction(bookId)
  . . .
}
```

When the builder receives a `BookCreated` event, it first builds out the read model representation for a book, `BookRM`. It then responds with an `InsertAction` for that read-model object. The framework-level code then kicks in and completes the insert of that new index document.

If the code receives a `TagAdded` event, it needs to update the previously stored `BookRM`, adding the new tag to it. It does so by returning an `UpdateAction` with a script expression on it. This script expression will add the new tag into the existing tags on the indexed document. This **in-place** edit is a somewhat newer feature with Elasticsearch and it fits what we're doing very nicely. Before this feature existed, we would've had to read the document, update it in memory, and then resave the entire document back to the index. This newer approach is more streamlined as it saves an I/O round trip. Remember that this update is also version-aware (via the framework code previously discussed) so, if it has already been processed, it will be simply rejected. It's not idempotent, meaning it can't be processed multiple times without having a bad effect, so we need to prevent that from happening.

The last case that the code shown here is handling is an event where it doesn't need to do anything other then bump the version on the indexed document. When the builder receives an `InventoryBackordered` event, indicating that the inventory allocation process failed for a sales order, there's nothing that it needs to do. We didn't model any representation of this on the document, so we don't need to change it. By responding with `NoAction`, the framework-level code from `ViewBuilder` will perform an update request with an empty expression, which is a noop of sorts. This will roll the version but, otherwise, will not touch the document.

The rest of the events that were elided from the code sample do more of the same from the update path. They evaluate the event, form an expression to change the document in accordance with the event, and then return an `UpdateAction`. Take a look at the full code if you are interested in seeing the rest of what's going on with this component.

Building the BookView

Now that we have `ViewBuilder` in place to build out the read model, we will need a View component to read that new model to service query requests. For book, we call this component `BookView`. This is where we will re-implement the queries that we had to comment out in Chapter 4, *Making History with Event Sourcing*. This component also represents the Q in CQRS, as it's separated the query-handling code so it's not comingled with the command-handling code.

There's not a lot of code here (which is nice), so I'll show the entire actor in one code posting, which is contained as follows:

```
class BookView extends BookReadModel
  with BookstoreActor with ElasticsearchSupport{
  def receive = {
```

```
      case FindBooksByAuthor(author) =>
      val results = queryElasticsearch(s"author:$author")
      pipeResponse(results)

      case FindBooksByTags(tags) =>
      val query = tags.map(t => s"tags:$t").mkString(" AND ")
      val results = queryElasticsearch(query)
      pipeResponse(results)
    }
  }
```

Here, I've taken the previously supported `FindBooksByAuthor` and `FindBooksByTags` query requests and moved them from `InventoryClerk` to this new component. When we receive either of these query requests, we will build a Lucene query expression that will be plugged in as a URL query against Elasticsearch. With Lucene, via Elasticsearch, we will get automatic partial matching. This means that, for the author query, I only need to pass in a matching first or last name to get a search hit.

We're barely scratching the surface of the query capabilities of Elasticsearch here. We can do a lot more exotic stuff if we have more complicated search requirements. Elasticsearch is an excellent search-based system, so hopefully this little taste, has shown you some of the stuff you can do with it when using it to build a read model.

The last change I had to make in order to get the API-query requests to work was to make the `Book` endpoint use this new actor when it receives the query requests. That's not very interesting code, so I did not include it here. You can take a look at the code distribution if you are interested in how I made that part work.

Building a resumable projection

When discussing the `ViewBuilder` framework code, I mentioned that it was not ideal in how it set up its events query. It's always passing 0 as the offset, which means that whenever we start up the server, it will rebuild an entire view from scratch. This is probably okay in the beginning, but as we get more and more new entities, this approach will eventually not be tenable. We will need an approach to track the offsets that we have seen so that when we restart the server, we can pick up where we left off.

In order to make our resumable projection concept work, we will need a place to store the combination of entity type and current offset, and updating that offset value whenever we receive events for that entity type. Then, when we restart the server, we can look up the offsets per-entity type and pass them into our `eventsByTag` queries so that they essentially pick up right where they left off. It's a pretty simple approach, and it makes our view building code much more production-ready.

When thinking about what data storage to use for the entity type or offset mappings, you'd probably be best off using a persistent key/value store, such as Redis, if you are already using something like that within your organization. A key/value store is schema-free, so you don't need to lug around SQL-like concepts for something that really is as simple as key-to-value mappings. You could also consider using Akka Persistence itself for offset management, setting up persistent actors to handle commands for updating the offset as events happen, using a persistenceId that relates to the particular projection that you want to be able to resume. For our bookstore app, I decided to piggyback on top of Cassandra directly (not via Akka Persistence) as we are already using it and the code was pretty simple. Just know that the storage system here is not the important take-away; it's the approach to store the offsets and then use them again to resume a projection.

Defining the resumable projection framework

I built a little abstraction around the resumable projection concept to further highlight the point that the underlying storage here (implementation) is less important than the concept itself (abstraction). Let's start by looking at the abstract class that defines a resumable projection:

```
abstract class ResumableProjection(identifier:String){
  def storeLatestOffset(offset:Long):Future[Boolean]
  def fetchLatestOffset:Future[Option[Long]]
}
```

This abstract class is pretty simple, with only two methods needed for us to be able to support a resumable projection. It accepts a `String` identifier field that defines the key to associate the stored offset with. This key should be unique per situation where you need to have a resumable projection. The `storeOffset` method is used to store the latest offset number from the event stream as you are processing events. The `fetchLatestOffset` method will be used when starting up a projection so that it can fetch the last stored offset and resume the stream from there.

There is also a factory-type class to get an instance of the concrete type of projection that is used in the app. That code, as well as the Cassandra implementation class, is shown as follows:

```
object ResumableProjection{
  def apply(identifier:String, system:ActorSystem) =
  new CassandraResumableProjection(identifier, system)
}
class CassandraResumableProjection(identifier:String,  system:ActorSystem)
extends ResumableProjection(identifier){
  val projectionStorage = CassandraProjectionStorage(system)
```

```
def storeLatestOffset(offset:Long):Future[Boolean] = {
  projectionStorage.updateOffset(identifier, offset + 1)
}
def fetchLatestOffset:Future[Option[Long]] = {
  projectionStorage.fetchLatestOffset(identifier)
}
}
```

The factory class just returns instances of `CassandraResumableProjection`. The implementation class contains the read and write methods from the abstraction, delegating them to an Akka Extension class called `CassandraProjectionStorage`, where all of the magic happens. I don't want to go into that code in too much detail, because it's not all that important in the grand scheme of this process. I will go over the high-level details of how it works though.

The extension class takes care of creating a new keyspace called `bookstore` and a new table called `projectionoffsets` where the offsets will be stored. It then uses async Cassandra driver calls to handle writing to and reading from that new table. If you want to look at this code a bit more, and see the inner workings of the calls to Cassandra, then you can look at the `ResumableProjection.scala` file in the bookstore-common project.

Note that, on saving the latest offset, I am adding one to the supplied value. I'm doing this to avoid picking up the last event for a given projection again when starting up the server. It seems that the query is inclusive of the supplied offset, so adding a millisecond of precision here (as the offset is an epoch time value) fixes that issue.

Applying ResumableProjection into our code

Now that we have the framework defined to work with resumable projections, we can plug it into our code. The only place this code needs to go is into is the `ViewBuilder` class trait. I made a few modifications to show how that trait works compared to the code that I showed earlier for it. I'll highlight the main changes in this section so you can see where the new `ResumableProjection` code fits into that logic.

The first change to discuss is what happens in the constructor logic for any `ViewBuilder` class. Previously, this is where the `eventsByTag` call happened, setting up the stream of events to listen to. We still need to do that, but first we need to fetch the correct offset to start that stream from. The code to fetch that offset replaces the event-query code in the constructor body and looks like this:

```
val resumableProjection =
ResumableProjection(projectionId, context.system)
resumableProjection.
```

```
fetchLatestOffset.
map(LatestOffsetResult.apply).
pipeTo(self)
```

This code creates a new resumable projection class, passing in an identifier `String` specified by a new abstract method called `projectionId`. Then, it fetches the latest offset, piping the Future-based result back to itself to process, wrapping it in a new custom class called `LatestResultOffset`.

Now we will need to handle that new message type representing the offset result. When we get it, we can now make our event query with the correct offset. The code, which is a new case in the receive block, looks like this:

```
case LatestOffsetResult(o) =>
val offset = o.getOrElse(0L)
if (offset == 0){
  clearIndex
}
val eventsSource = journal.eventsByTag(entityType, offset)
eventsSource.runForeach(self ! _)
```

Here, if we get a `None` value, which means that there is no record in the offsets table for the projection identifier, then we will set the offset to 0. This implies a full index rebuild, so the index will be cleared in this case. The fetched offset is then passed into the `eventsByTag` query so that we can pick up right from where we left off. After that, the code follows the same approach of piping the events from the stream back to itself to process.

The second half of this process will involve tracking the offsets as we see them on events. The code is accomplished inside the case statement, where we receive the events from the stream and plug them into the index. Any time we see an event, we will update the index. After that, we will need to store the latest offset. An example of the code, for the case where we are updating an index field, is shown as follows:

```
case u:UpdateAction =>
updateDocumentField(u.id,
env.sequenceNr - 1, u.expression, u.params).
andThen(updateProjection)
```

`updateProjectionPartialFunction` is defined as follows:

```
val updateProjection:PartialFunction[util.Try[IndexingResult], Unit] = {
  case tr =>
  resumableProjection.storeLatestOffset(env.offset)
}
```

After the index update finishes, the code will update the projection offset for that projection identifier.

This code probably will need a little hardening if we want to move forward with it more permanently. It needs better error handling in how it handles updating the projection offset. Right now, it does it regardless of what happens when talking to the index. But, because we will refactor this code quite a bit in `Chapter 6`, *Going with the Flow with Akka Streams*, using Akka Streams, this will suffice for now.

Putting all of this together, we now have a way to properly resume our projections. Each time we see an event, we track the offset tied to Cassandra. Each time the server starts backup, it fetches the correct offset for whatever projection is starting and applies that offset into the Persistence Query. That simple process allows us to always pick up right where we left off instead of having to always start over. Our resumable projection approach can even be used outside of `ViewBuilder` classes when syncing events between contexts. We'll see this approach in action in the next section.

Refactoring sales order processing

As part of the work in this chapter, I also completed the refactor for the sales order processing module. In doing so, I built out a new read model with a `ViewBuilder` class and View to support the `SalesOrder` entity. I will not go over all of that code here, because, for the most part, it's on par with what we just covered for book. I will highlight some of the differences here though. I'll also detail how I redid the inventory allocation process so its not based on Persistence Query and our resumable projection framework.

Denormalization in the SalesOrder read model

One of the benefits of a read model is that you can denormalize the data a bit to better suit some of the queries you need to do. As this model is to be optimized to make queries more efficient, then denormalization is an acceptable practice, even though something like this is frowned upon in the write model, which is less efficient for storage. We took advantage of this ability when building out the `SalesOrder` read model to allow us to support all of the queries we had back in the beginning of the app.

If you remember the old SQL-based model we used to query SalesOrders, we had two queries that needed to find the `SalesOrder` entities by attributes, which were on the books that were tied to the line items. I had done this initially by some nasty cross-context joins that were not a good long-term solution. They tied the two contexts together too much, creating a fragile dependency in the database layer. That's something that we can finally remedy now that we're implementing separate read models.

The approach I took here was to define a `SalesOrder` read-model object that also included information from the books on the line items. Then, I'll be able to query against that information directly, via Elasticsearch, when I need to be able to search for sales orders by book-related information. Let's start by taking a look at the `SalesOrder` read-model object definition:

```
case class LineItemBook(id:String, title:String, author:String,
tags:List[String])
case class SalesOrderLineItem(lineItemNumber:Int,
book:LineItemBook, quantity:Int, cost:Double, status:String)
case class SalesOrderRM(id:String,
userEmail:String, creditTxnId:String,
totalCost:Double, lineItems:Map[String, SalesOrderLineItem],
createTs:Date, deleted:Boolean = false) extends ReadModelObject
```

For the most part, this is similar to what we did with book and its read model. The big difference is that I have enhanced the line-item class to contain a reference to the book information of the book for that line item.

Now that we have defined this new model, we need to be able to build it when we get an order-created event. Normally, in a `ViewBuilder`, we will get an event and take an immediate action against the index. In this case though, we can't directly save the `SalesOrderRM` instance until we load the necessary book information first. If you remember back to the four actions that can be taken when you receive an event, one of them was called `DeferredCreate`. If you use that action, nothing happens in the index right away as more work needs to be done to finish that create. That's the action we will use in `SalesOrderViewBuilder`. The event-handling logic for that is shown as follows:

```
def actionFor(id:String, offset:Long, event:Any) = event match {
  case OrderCreated(order) =>
  order.lineItems.
  foreach(item => invClerk ! FindBook(item.bookId))
  context.become(loadingData(order,
  offset, Map.empty, order.lineItems.size))
  DeferredCreate
  . . .
}
```

Upon receiving the `OrderCreated` event, the code loops over the line items and makes requests to look up each book against the `InventoryClerk`. Then, we will switch into a new receive-handling state called `loadingData`, passing some context into that receive block, which will be needed to finish the create-handling logic. The code returns `DeferredCreate` here because we are deferring the create until we have loaded the necessary book information.

It's inside the `loadingData` receive-handling block where we can finally finish that create. There's a fair amount of code there, so I won't show it here. All that really happens is that the code waits for each book response until it has the ones that it needs. When it does, it finishes building the `SalesOrderRM`, commits it to the index, and updates the resumable projection to correctly mark progress. You can see the full code for this process inside `SalesOrderViewBuilder`, which is in `SalesOrderReadModel.scala`, if you are interested.

Using Persistence Query for inventory allocation

Up until now, the back and forth inventory allocation process between the sales order processing and inventory management contexts happened over the Akka Event Bus. That was never intended to be a long-term solution. It's not fully reliable, as both sides of the system have to be up at all points in time for it to work properly. That's not very realistic or dependable.

To make this process better, we will change it to be based on the events that we've persisted on our entities. Then we can use Persistence Query and our resumable projections to set up subscriptions for those events. Having persistent events and resumable projections makes this process much more reliable. This doesn't really have anything directly to do with CQRS, but as you learned Persistence Query in this chapter, this seems like the right place to do the refactoring.

You may have noticed when viewing the `SalesOrder` read-model case classes that status was no longer present at the top level of the order and was instead on a per-line item basis. In evaluating this redo, it made more sense to me to push the status down to each line item as the inventory needs to be allocated per book per line item. That also allows us to listen for each book's allocation related events (`InventoryAllocated` and `InventoryBackordered`) separately instead of collecting them and then trying to send an aggregate status along with it to the relevant `SalesOrder`, which is what we were previously doing. This new flow can be represented by the following set of steps:

1. A `SalesOrder` entity persists an `OrderCreated` event.

2. `InventoryClerk` listens for that event via a resumable Persistence Query.

3. Upon receiving that event, `InventoryClerk` passes it along the `AllocateInventory` commands to each `Book` entity represented on the order.

4. When processing an `AllocateInventory` command, the book either persists an `InventoryAllocated` event (inventory available) or an `InventoryBackordered` event (inventory not available).

5. The `SalesOrderAssociate` listens for either of those events (also via a resumable projection). When it receives them, it passes the `UpdateLineItemsStatus` commands on to the relevant `SalesOrder` entity.

6. `SalesOrder` entity processes that command and locates the line item on the order that the event is for and updates it to reflect the inventory allocation status, persisting a new `LineItemStatusUpdated` event as a result.

You can see that full set of steps visually in the following diagram:

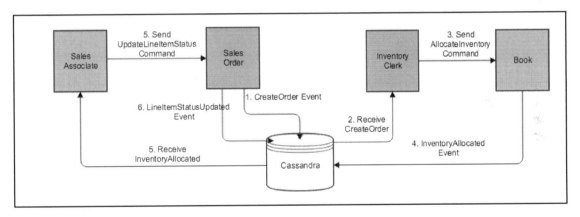

Now that we understand the high-level flow, let's take a look at some of the code for these steps. We'll start out in `InventoryClerk`, taking a look at the new receive-handling case where it receives an event from its event query:

```
case EventEnvelope(offset, pid, seq,
order:SalesOrderCreateInfo) =>

order.lineItemInfo.
foreach{
  case (bookId, quant) =>
```

```
      forwardCommand(bookId, AllocateInventory(order.id, quant))
    }
  projection.storeLatestOffset(offset)
```

This code essentially mirrors step 3 from the previously described flow. Notice the explicit call to update the projection offset. This ensures that we only ever pick up where we left off.

Another thing to emphasize here is related to how this code receives an event that is defined in another project. Currently, the sales order processing project has a dependency on inventory management, but not vice versa (it will be a circular dependency). We will need to receive the `OrderCreated` event here, but we don't have a reference to that class.

Bigger picture, I wanted to just redefine the relevant protobuf IDL information I required for that event here and read it in against an inventory-centric view of that same event. That's one of the good things about a format such as protobuf. It's well understood, via its IDL, so a piece of code can read that same event, even though it didn't write it, as long as it knows the format. The problem with that here is that the adapter layer expects that the class used to read it out and map it into the domain model has a name matching the manifest set up during adaptation. For `OrderCreated`, it will be as follows:

```
com.packt.masteringakka.bookstore.order.SalesOrder$Event$OrderCrea ted
```

I would need to define that same class structure in the inventory management project in order to make the reading process work properly. It's not really that big deal, except for the fact that we're still running this whole app as a monolith, and it all shares one class loader. I can't define the same class twice (it already exists in its original form in the sales order processing project) without all kinds of bad stuff happening. I wanted to use this approach, but it will have to wait until we fully separate and isolate the modules later on in the book.

We still need an approach to read this event here, so I created a trait in inventory management called `SalesOrderCreateInfo`, which lets me access basic information on the order event without having to know the exact class itself. I then implemented this trait on `OrderCreated` to provide that information outward to the `InventoryClerk`. This is a bit of a hack and it depends on the fact that, at runtime, we do indeed have access to that class as everyone shares a class loader. This is something that will eventually be fixed with a more permanent and palatable solution. Just look the other way in the mean time.

The other piece of code worth taking a look at for this process is what happens in the `SalesOrderAssociate` when it receives the inventory allocation events. The code is shown here:

```
  case EventEnvelope(offset, pid, seq, event) =>
  event match{
    case InventoryAllocated(orderId,
```

```
    bookId, amount) =>
    forwardCommand(orderId,
    UpdateLineItemStatus(bookId, LineItemStatus.Approved))

    case InventoryBackordered(orderId, bookId) =>
    forwardCommand(orderId,
    UpdateLineItemStatus(bookId, LineItemStatus.BackOrdered ))

    case other =>
    //ignore
  }
```

If we get either of those two events, we make the appropriate update to the line item that they are for. The subscription I set up here is for the tag book versus being for two event specific tags (as we need to listen for two separate events). That's why we will need the match statement and the ignored case in here. We'll redo this part in the next chapter, using Akka Streams to combine two separate queries into a single stream for those two events as opposed to listening to the entire entity-based stream. We'll also get rid of some of the repetitive code related to the resumable projections used here. I didn't put any time into consolidating the repetitive code here, knowing that it will change quite a bit in the next chapter.

Playing around with the new application

At this point, we have two modules completely refactored, so it's a good time to take the app for a test drive and check out how the newly added query support works. To get the app up-and-running, first build it via `docker-build.sh` and then start it up via `launch.sh`. You should create a new `BookstoreUser` and then a new book via the REST API, being sure to add an inventory to it. Refer to the *Interacting with the Book endpoint* section from `Chapter 1`, *Building a Better Reactive App*, if you need help remembering the endpoint calls to make. Then, using the ID of the newly created book, craft up the correct JSON to create a new `SalesOrder` and then use the REST API to do that.

With those three entities created, you can start to use the query-API calls. The API stayed the same in relation to the query calls, so you can use the instructions from `Chapter 1`, *Building a Better Reactive App*, to run queries. Try looking up books by author and then try looking up your `SalesOrder` by a tag from one of the books on it. When you make these calls, you are now using the newly created read models that were enabled by Persistence Query. You are seeing all of our CQRS work in action!

Refactoring homework

Just like the previous two chapters, your homework in this chapter will involve finishing the refactor for the other two modules. You'll be doing your work in the `-incomplete` codebase for this chapter, just as you did earlier. You will need to set up a few new queries for user management as what was previously a query, find by email, now is the ID-based lookup and thus not a query. Try supporting querying by name, where a single input will match against either the first or last name.

For the credit-processing project, there isn't even a REST endpoint there yet, as it wasn't needed up to this point. For extra credit, if you feel so inclined, add an endpoint and support a way to lookup credit transactions by the card holder's name.

Closing comments

There are a few final comments that I wanted to make about the code that we refactored in this chapter. I feel that these things needed a little further explanation, so you're not left scratching your head.

The first thing that I wanted to comment on is the fact that I did not do the single-entity lookup inside the read model even though this is technically a lookup operation. I felt that the single-entity lookup, by ID, should always return the most current state of that entity, and the read model won't guarantee this. It's always possible that the read model is slightly behind the write model due to the nature of how it's built. This was a judgment call that I made, going for being pragmatic versus being a purist.

The purist would say that all lookups go to the read model. The pragmatist in me however thought that single entity lookups should always give you the most up-to-date info, avoiding potential read model lag in these cases. This is a decision you can certainly change when you implement CQRS in your codebase, directing single entity lookups to the read model if you want to follow more of a purist approach.

Another thing I wanted to cover is fully separating the read and write code. If this was a real app, I would have probably split each project down the middle, with the read code in one project and the write code in another. This would give us eight separate contexts instead of the four we have now. Taking an approach like this would allow the read code to have a separate scaling profile from the write code. I think this is the correct approach to take with CQRS, but it seemed an overkill for this chapter. It's something to consider if you adopt CQRS in your applications.

Summary

In this chapter, we supplemented our event sourced entity model with a separate read model, following the CQRS pattern. We implemented our separate read models by leveraging Akka's Persistence Query feature to listen to event streams from our entities and project those events into Elasticsearch, which serves as our read model data store. Following this approach gives us rich query capabilities against the current state of our entities while still preserving the event sourced nature of those entities for the write model. We also leveraged Persistence Query to finalize the back-and-forth interaction between the inventory and sales modules when allocating an inventory to a new sales order.

The code we created in this chapter to listen to the event stream was a good starting point, but we really didn't leverage some of the cool features from Akka Streams, such as proper back-pressure handling. We'll plunge right into this in the next chapter, when we introduce Akka Streams as a mechanism to build back-pressure-aware data processing pipelines and graphs.

6

Going with the Flow with Akka Streams

The concept of data processing, that is, taking data from point A to point B with all kinds of transforms in between, is not a new concept in the world of programming. It's the basis of the age old processes of **Extract, Transform, Load (ETL)** and, to a lesser extent, **Electronic Data Interchange (EDI)**. For decades now, programmers have had to produce, transform, and then consume data between two systems. So, if this isn't a new problem, why would anyone need a new paradigm to handle this age-old process? What's changed in this day and age to cause us to have to rethink data processing?

The biggest change is the volume of data that's out there and available to process now. We're living in the age of big data now, and there are massive amounts of data that people want to consume and make use of within their apps, one such example being the Twitter Firehose. These data sets are very large, way too big to try and fit into the application memory, which is why you can't process them in bulk.

To solve a problem like this, you will need to shift gears and process this data in a nonblocking, asynchronous, streaming fashion, in an effort to use all of your CPU cores. Something like this doesn't seem too hard by itself, but what happens if one of the components in your async processing pipeline starts to get overwhelmed with the amount of data and number of calls it's receiving? We need the components within the processing pipeline to be able to signal that they are falling behind, and therefore slow the data flow down. This type of signaling, called back-pressure, will allow you to continue to asynchronously process large volumes of data without worrying if the volume of data is going to take down one of your critical systems. This is the concept that we'll be exploring more in this chapter, building back-pressure-aware, data processing pipelines using an API from Akka called Akka Streams.

Here is what you can expect to learn in this chapter:

- Understanding the core Reactive Streams API components
- Understanding the dynamic push/pull modes of back-pressure handling in Reactive Streams
- Understanding the core of the Akka Streams API and its building blocks of `source`, `sink`, and `flow`
- Building complex processing graphs with the Graph Builder DSL
- Handling streaming I/O and framing
- Handling buffers and rates within the Akka Streams

Understanding the Reactive Streams API

Before we jump into the design of the Akka Streams API, it's important for us to take a quick look at the Reactive Streams API, which is where Akka Streams gets its roots. The Reactive Streams API started out as an effort to design a standardized way of handling asynchronous stream processing with nonblocking back-pressure. Their main focus was to build a nonblocking, event-driven API, and therefore making it reactive, to govern the interchange of streaming data across asynchronous processing stages or boundaries.

The Reactive Streams group is made up of contributors from companies such as Twitter and Netflix, and includes the team from Akka too. They set out to define a very low-level API that can serve as the foundation for other streaming APIs, such as Akka Streams, to be built on top of. The Java API was designed as a mechanism to process a potentially unbounded number of elements in sequence, asynchronously passing elements between components-with mandatory nonblocking back-pressure. The core components used to make all of that happen are `Publisher`, `Subscriber`, `Subscription`, and `Processor`.

Within the Reactive Streams world, a `Publisher` component is a producer of a potentially unbounded number of sequenced elements. It publishes these elements in response to demands from a downstream `Subscriber`. When a `Subscriber` component is hooked into a `Publisher` via `Publisher.subscribe(s:Subscriber)`, a `Subscription` object is created to represent the relationship between that `Publisher` and `Subscriber`. It is through this `Subscription` that the `Subscriber` can signal demand upstream, requesting between *1-n* elements via `Subscription.request(n:Long)`.

When this demand happens, the `Publisher` component can respond by doing one of the following three things:

- Invoke `onNext` on the `Subscriber`, up to the number of elements demanded, if it has any more data elements to send
- Invoke `onComplete` if and when there are no more elements to send downstream
- Invoke `onError` if there is some sort of a failure sending elements downstream

The subscribing relationship between a `Publisher` and a `Subscriber` can be terminated at any point, even prior to completion of the data stream, by calling the `cancel()` function on a `Subscription`.

A `Processor` is a special component that is meant to represent a processing or transformation stage within a data flow. This component is a `Publisher` and a `Subscriber` implementing both the Java interfaces, so it must adhere to the contract of both components. By having this component be both, a `Publisher` and a `Subscriber`, it can be snapped in between any other `Publisher` and `Subscriber`, brokering the supply and demand relationship between those two. You can also snap `Processor` components together; it allows you to create processing chains of any length, with each step having it's own supply and demand cycle with the components adjacent to it in both upstream and downstream directions.

I've created a couple of diagrams to show how these components interact with each other. The first one is a very simple flow where we have just a single `Publisher` and `Subscriber` hooked together.

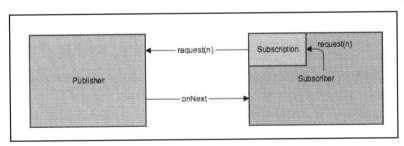

In this simple diagram, we have a single `Publisher` component hooked up to a single `Subscriber` component. At this point, the `Subscriber` has already called subscribe on the `Publisher`, passing in itself, which resulted in a `Subscription` being created for that `Subscriber`. Once the `Subscriber` has this `Subscription`, it can start to signal demand upstream, which it does by calling `request(n:Long)` on that `Subscription`. The `Subscription` then makes this demand known to the `Publisher`. The `Publisher` can then signal elements downstream by calling `onNext` any number of times, up to the maximum demand specified by the `Subscriber`.

In a relationship like this, there is no real transformation of the data elements being exchanged. The elements flow directly from the originating source, the `Publisher` into the requesting sink, the `Subscriber`, without anything else happening in the middle. If you wanted to include data transformation steps, which will be a common requirement when processing data, then you will need the fourth component, the `Processor`. In the following diagram, I have added two separate transformation stages into this flow, showing how this affects the messaging between the original `Publisher` and `Subscriber`.

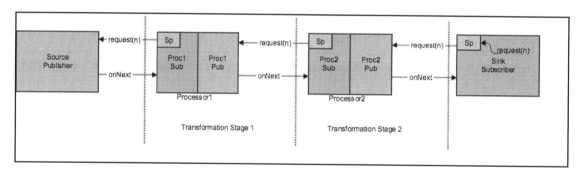

In this flow, we now have multiple processing stages sitting in between the source `Publisher`, which is where the data elements start, and the final sink, `Subscriber`, which is the last place the data elements end up. The transformation stages are represented by the `Processor` components that act as a `Publisher` and a `Subscriber` at the same time. By having the behavior of both of those components, a `Processor` can be snapped in between an existing `Publisher` and `Subscriber` pairing, in order to make changes to the data before it flows to the `Subscriber`.

As the preceding diagram shows, when you snap a transform stage into an existing `Publisher`/`Subscriber` pairing, the `Processor` faces its `Subscriber` handling logic upstream to the `Publisher` and it faces its `Publisher` handling logic downstream to the `Subscriber`. Now, the `Subscriber` sink is signaling its demand to a `Processor` instead of directly demanding it of the source `Publisher`. The `Processor` then signals its own demand upstream in an effort to satisfy the demand of that downstream `Subscriber`. The element(s) to meet that demand then flow downstream through all of the stages, eventually reaching the sink `Subscriber`.

By creating this kind of indirection between source and sink, you can create processing chains of any length, each supplying their own demand and back-pressure without any changes needed to the source and sink. This is a very simple, yet powerful, construct that serves as the backbone of the Reactive Streams implementation.

The Reactive Streams API itself is very low level, and was not really designed to be a user facing/friendly API. It was designed to represent the common concern of asynchronous, back-pressure oriented data movement across processing boundaries. Real implementation libraries, such as Akka Streams, will wrap their own user-facing APIs on top of the Reactive Stream's low-level APIs and protocols, mostly hiding those interfaces in the process. The Reactive Streams API also serves as an interoperability mechanism between different implementations of that API, such as using **RxJava** and Akka Streams together. In this way, it's more of a **Service Provider Interface** (**SPI**) for interoperability versus a true user-facing API.

> If you want to read more about the Reactive Streams specification, you can visit the following link: `http://www.reactive-streams.org/`.

Back-pressure in action

In the previous section, I talked a lot about back-pressure without really explaining what it is and how it's implemented within Reactive Streams. As it's such an important concept in Reactive Streams, let's spend a little time going over what it is and why it's so important in the stream-based processing of data.

Simply put, back-pressure is a technique to affect the flow of data, slowing, and possibly even stopping it in response to some condition within that flow. For example, if a Subscriber is having trouble processing the data elements being sent to it, then it might slow the signaling of demand or stop signaling demand entirely. As elements are only sent downstream from a Publisher in response to explicit demand, the flow of data will naturally slow or stop when demand is slowed or stopped. It's this ability to propagate backwards-pressure upstream to slow the data flow that gives back-pressure its name.

Within Reactive Streams, the back-pressure process has been referred to as a dynamic push/pull mode system. This system will switch back and forth between push and pull modes, depending on whether the downstream side is able to keep up with the upstream's production rate. This model is best explained with specific scenarios, as it's easier to visualize the purpose of each mode that way.

If a Subscriber is faster than the Publisher, then all is well in stream processing land. The Publisher will not need to be slowed down in this case. As the Subscriber is consuming at such a fast rate (even more than one element per request upstream), there will always be demand queued up in the Publisher. As a result, it will never have to queue/buffer elements, and it will always push them to the right downstream as soon as they are available. That's why this mode is referred to as the push mode.

Now if things change, and we suddenly have a Subscriber that is having trouble keeping up with the rate of data coming from the Publisher, the mode will switch into pull mode. It's named this way because in this mode, the Subscriber is now pulling the data elements downstream to it when it signals demand. As part of the contract of Reactive Streams, a Publisher can never send more elements downstream than what is demanded of it. When back-pressure starts to flow upstream from this slow Subscriber, the Publisher is left with three possible choices:

1. Stop generating elements. Not all Publisher components will be able to stop generating elements though (a timer driven one for example), so this won't always be an option.
2. Try buffering the elements in a bounded manner until more demand shows up.
3. Drop elements until more demand shows up.
4. Stop the stream if it can't take any of the preceding actions.

Option 1 is a pretty interesting one to try and think about. Imagine that you have implemented a `Publisher` that was reading a very large file and sending lines downstream one by one to a `Subscriber` who was then performing inserts into a database based on those lines. If the insert calls started to slow down because the database was getting swamped with the writes (as they might be parallelized), the `Subscriber` can stop signaling demand upstream for a while. In this situation, if you have implemented the `Publisher` in such a way that it was reading the lines one at a time, based on demand, then you can simply stop reading the lines until demand returns.

You can also envision using option 1 perhaps if your `Publisher` was paging its way through a very large JDBC `ResultSet`, sending those results downstream for additional processing. In this case, as demand comes in, the `Publisher` can issue a JDBC query against the database, using the limit/offset combination to read a page of data at a time, with some specified page size. In this scenario, you can also stop issuing queries when back-pressure takes place, resuming again when the downstream `Subscriber` starts requesting elements again.

Not every kind of `Publisher` will be able to stop generating elements, so the next course of action, if that's the case, is to try and buffer elements in memory until demand returns. Think about a timer-based `Publisher` that's sending elements downstream every second. This is not a situation where you can just stop the generation of elements when demand slows or stops. In this kind of case, the `Publisher` can set up an overflow buffer to hold elements in the hope that demand returns quickly. These buffers need to be bounded, because if you introduce an unbounded buffer here, and demand does not return, you run the risk of running out of memory.

Option 3, where you start dropping elements, can be used on its own or combined with a buffering strategy. When used with a bounded buffer, you can try things such as dropping from the head or tail of that buffer when you have reached maximum capacity. This will not work for all data flows as you won't be able to process those dropped elements. This technique is a good option if you can tolerate data loss though, as it allows you to keep processing the stream in cases where you need to start dropping elements due to back-pressure.

When all else fails, you are left with the option to shut down the entire stream. This is a last resort, but it is required in some cases, where you will need to be sure you only process the stream in its entirety. In these kinds of cases, it's better to just stop the processing and then perhaps resume it later manually, after remediating whatever caused the back-pressure, if possible.

The Akka Streams API

Akka Streams is an API that is built on top of the Reactive Streams core Java library. This, somewhat, newer API defines its own components, which we will discuss shortly, to represent stream processing versus directly exposing the Reactive Streams API. This library handles all of the complicated concerns of back-pressure, and helps you to better focus on the real problems, such as how you'll process your data.

Being built on top of Reactive Streams, Akka Streams is fully interoperable (pluggable) with any other Reactive Streams compatible library, such as Slick or RxJava. This means that you can easily incorporate data processing steps into your Akka Stream flows that are not themselves built from Akka Streams. The possibilities of building back-pressure-based streams on top of Akka Streams can be endless as more and more Java/Scala libraries start to adopt the Reactive Streams protocol.

Throughout the next few sections, I'll break down the main components from the Akka Streams library. I'll also go over how to use those components to build simple processing pipelines, and also more complex processing graphs. This will prepare us for making some Akka Streams-based changes to our bookstore app.

The building blocks of Akka Streams

When discussing the Reactive Streams API, you learned that stream processing can be built by connecting a `Publisher` and `Subscriber` together. Within this relationship, the `Subscriber` signals demand upstream and the `Publisher` sends elements downstream in response to that demand. You can also snap any number of `Processor` components in the middle of that `Publisher`/`Subscriber` relationship to transform the data as it flows downstream. Akka Streams has the same three component concepts within its API too, and they are represented by source, sink, and flow, respectively.

An Akka Streams source is similar to the concept of a Reactive Streams `Publisher`. When building a data processing pipeline or graph, a source is where the data elements originate from. A source can only have a single output, and no inputs, which means the data can only flow out of it and never into it, hence its need to be the origination point for a data flow. Being similar to a `Publisher`, a source is responsible for receiving demand from a downstream element, and to send data downstream in response to that demand. A source also has two types of parameters—one for the type of data element it emits and another to represent what value it materializes to, which I will explain in more detail shortly.

An Akka Streams sink is the component that is similar to a Reactive StreamsSubscriber. It is the final place where the data flows to, after starting out at the source and passing through whatever processing stages you define in your flow. A sink only has a single input and no outputs, and as such, data can only flow into it and never out of it. Being like a Subscriber, a sink is responsible to signal demand upstream to a source and back-pressuring whenever necessary. Just like source, a sink has two type params—one representing the data element it accepts and the other representing what value it materializes to.

Within Akka Streams, a flow is similar to a Reactive Streams Processor component. It's where a data transformation or processing step occurs within your data pipelines or graphs. A flow has exactly one input and one output, using those ports to connect its upstream and downstream together while transforming the data along the way. You can chain any number of flow components together, using familiar combinators, such as map, filter, fold, and a whole lot more, to keep adding more transformation steps into your flows. A flow has three, total type params—one to represent the type of data coming in, another to represent the type of data coming out, and the last representing the materialized value of that flow.

Learning the basics of Stream building

At this point, we've covered the core components of Akka Stream; so, now it's time to start playing with those components to get a better understanding of how they fit together when creating data processing flows. Let's start with an example of something very basic—connecting a simple Source and Sink together. That code is shown as follows:

```
val source:Source[Int, NotUsed] = Source(1 to 5)
val sink:Sink[Int, Future[Done]] = Sink.foreach[Int](println)
val dataflow:RunnableGraph[NotUsed] = source.to(sink)
```

I am using explicit typing on the val here so it's clear what the type params are on each of the classes being used. I will start by creating a very simple Source, using the Source.apply that takes an instance of an Iterable, passing in an Iterable for the range of 1 to 5. The first type on the Source represents the Int elements that will be sent downstream. This means that this Source can only be hooked into a downstream component that accepts Int elements as its input. The second type on the Source is a specialized type called NotUsed, which is basically a glorified unit. This type represents the materialized value of the Source, which, in this case, is nothing.

The Sink that is created here is purely side effecting, performing a loop over a stream of Int elements that were sent downstream to it. The Int type param specifies that this Sink can only be hooked into an upstream component that is emitting Int elements downstream, making it a good fit for the Source created on the line above it. The second type on the Sink represents the materialized value for the Sink, which, in this case, is Future[Done]. The Future there will be completed when the Sink has finished processing all of its elements, with the Done type also being a glorified unit.

After creating the Source and Sink, I hook them together by using the to method on the Source. I am able to do this because the Source is emitting the same element type, Int, that the Sink happens to accept. The result of linking the two components together is a RunnableGraph that will materialize to a NotUsed, which comes from the materialized type from the Source.

At this point, this data flow is still just a blueprint and, therefore, does not do anything. If I want it to start processing the numbers from the Source, then I need to run it. Running this stream requires the following code:

```
implicit val system = ActorSystem()
implicit val mater = ActorMaterializer()
dataflow.run
```

Stream components are built on top of actors, which is probably no surprise, so you need an ActorSystem to run the actors underneath those components. Also, in order to run a stream, you need to have an implicit Materializer instance around, which, in this case, is being satisfied by the ActorMaterializer created in the second line. This ActorMaterializer contains a bunch of configurable options on how to run the stream, including things such as what dispatcher to use and how to size the input and output buffers for the processing stages. After we have the necessary implicits in place, we can actually run the stream processing, which is kicked off via a call to run.

If you were to execute this code, you will see the numbers 1 to 5 printed out on the screen, which isn't very exciting in the grand scheme of data processing. Additionally, because of how we connected our Source and Sink together, no real tangible output value is produced, as NotUsed is essentially the same as Unit. Let's make some minor changes to this flow so that we can use it to perform a calculation and then get the final result when it's done:

```
val sink2:Sink[Int, Future[Int]] = Sink.fold(0)(_+_)
val dataflow2:RunnableGraph[Future[Int]] =
source.toMat(sink2)(Keep.right)
val fut:Future[Int] = dataflow2.run
fut.onComplete(println)(system.dispatcher)
```

Here, I changed the `Sink` to do a `fold` instead of a `foreach`, so now it will materialize to a `Future` that wraps the result of that `fold`. Also, when connecting the `Source` to the `Sink`, I used `toMat` instead of just plain `to`. By using `toMat`, I can specify here that I want to keep the materialized value from the right-hand side of the two components being connected, which equates to the `Sink` in this example. When I run this new stream, I now get a `Future` that, when completed, will contain the number 15, which is the result of the `fold` operation.

So this is pretty nice, seeing that we can use Akka Streams to perform a stream-based computation and asynchronously yield a result that can be used when completed. We've now seen `Source` and `Sink` in action, but where does `Flow` come into the picture? As a `Flow` is similar to a Reactive Streams `Processor`, it can be used to perform transformations to the data as it flows between a `Source` and a `Sink`. Let's add some transformations into the example from earlier to see how we can get `Flow` involved in the action:

```
val flow = Flow[Int].map(_*2).filter(_ % 2 == 0)
val fut2 = source.via(flow).toMat(sink2)(Keep.right).run
fut2.onComplete(println)(system.dispatcher)
```

In the first line in that code example, we will create a `Flow` using the no-args `Flow.apply`, indicating that `Int` is the type of element we expect as an input. It means that this `Flow` can be hooked into an upstream component that is emitting `Int` elements downstream.

Once the `Flow` is created, I will apply two simple transformations to it, using two familiar combinators, `map` and `filter`. In the `map` step, I'm taking the input element and multiplying it by 2. In the `filter` step, I'm preventing any element that is not even from flowing downstream. Stream components are immutable, so applying these combinators will of course create a new `Flow` each time you apply one.

Once the transformation steps are set up, they can be hooked into upstream and downstream components so that a complete `RunnableGraph` is created. In this code example, I will hook the `Flow` into the upstream `Source` with the via method. At that point, all the data flow that needs to run is to be hooked into a downstream `Sink`, which happens as it did earlier with the `toMat` method. Now the graph can be run, with it still producing the same `Future[Int]` as the first example showing the `fold`. The difference is that we get a different final result, 30 here versus 15 previously, due to weaving in the transformation steps in between the `Source` and `Sink`.

 There are a lot of useful ways to create source, sink, and flow components using their respective companion objects. You should review the API documents for each of those companion objects to see all the ways they can be constructed.

Understanding Stream Materialization

There is a concept called Stream Materialization that I've mentioned a few times so far that needs a bit of an explanation. A completed (closed) stream itself, and even the individual stages that make it up, is merely a set of instructions or blueprints. It's only when the stream is materialized (run) that those blueprints come to life and perform some sort of action for you.

To make this clearer, think of the concept of architectural blueprints for a house. Those blueprints describe everything that needs to be done to construct a house. They may contain multiple distinct sets of specifications, things such as plumbing and electrical layouts, all linked together to describe the final output, which is a home. From those blueprints, builders can build many actual instances of the home described within them, materializing them from the specifications contained in the blueprints. This is the same concept of building reusable stream blueprints and then materializing them into a running data flow.

Consider the following stream example where I'm reading a file, doing something to the data within it, and then sending the output to another file:

```
implicit val system = ActorSystem()
implicit val mater = ActorMaterializer()

val file = this.getClass.getClassLoader().
 getResource("current_inventory.csv")
val inPath = FileSystems.getDefault().
 getPath(file.getPath())
val outPath = FileSystems.getDefault().
 getPath("no_inventory.csv")
val fileSource = FileIO.fromPath(inPath)
val fileSink = FileIO.toPath(outPath)

val csvHandler = Flow[String].drop(1).map(_.split(",").toList)

val lowInventoryFlow = fileSource.
via(Framing.delimiter(ByteString("\n"), Integer.MAX_VALUE)).
  map(_.utf8String).
  via(csvHandler).
  filter(list => list(2).toInt == 0).
  map{ list =>
    ByteString(list.mkString(",")) ++ ByteString("\n")
  }.
toMat(fileSink)(Keep.right)
```

In this example, I will start by setting up my file-based `Source` and `Sink`. I will then create a separate transformation stage called `csvHandler` that expects a `String` input. This stage will drop the first line, that is, the header, and then split every other line into a list using the standard csv comma delimiter. Note that this `csvHandler` represents a common type of processing concern for csv-based handling, and can be woven into any number of concrete processing flows. It is a mini blueprint for the concern of csv-based handling.

Once I have all of those parts set up, I can build out my main processing flow. I will start with the file-based `Source`, adding in some processing stages to delimit the content on a new line and also convert it into a `String` before sending it through the `csvHandler`. After I have it as a list of fields, I can filter it on items that have a 0 value for the third field (second here as we index by 0) before converting back to strings and sending it through the file output `Sink`. I will assign all of these instructions to a variable called `lowInventoryFlow`, which has a type of `RunnableGraph[Future[IOResult]]`.

The `lowInventoryFlow` variable represents the blueprint for my process of reading in inventory information and outputting the lines that have a current inventory amount of zero. But as it stands right now, it will not do anything. That's because, in order for it to start up and actually read in and produce out a new file, it has to be materialized. It's the materialization process itself that will open the files and allocate actors to run the stages. I can materialize this `RunnableGraph` any number of times, each time being a completely separate and fully isolated process with its own set of resources. If I materialized it two times in a row, those two processes will have nothing in common, that is, share no common resources, other than the fact that they were built off the same blueprint.

If I wanted to materialize this blueprint, all I would have to do is run it with the following code:

```
val fut = lowInventoryFlow.run
```

This flow represents a closed graph, meaning it has no open, nonconnected, ports on it's components. As such, it is a runnable graph and can be materialized simply by calling `run`, provided I have an implicit `Materializer` handy. If I want to, I can schedule the materialization of this graph to happen once a day, and each run will be a completely separate instantiation of this blueprint.

Having these processes, and even the individual stages themselves, such as `csvHandler`, be reusable and composable blueprints that don't allocate resources until materialization, is a very powerful technique within Akka Streams. It gives you near limitless options to compose all sorts of modular subprocesses together into larger and more complex processing flows. If you want to see more about the composability of Akka Streams components, then check out the Akka Streams documentation section (`http://doc.akka.i o/docs/akka-stream-and-http-experimental/2..3/scala/stream-composition.html`) titled *Modularity, Composition and Hierarchy*.

The full code for this example is contained in the `samples` folder under the `chapter6` code distribution, in a file called `BlueprintExample.scala`. You can run the example via sbt by getting into the root `samples` directory, opening the sbt shell, and executing the following command:

```
> runMain code.BlueprintExample
```

It's worth noting that Akka Streams contains a few shortcut methods if you want to connect `Source` and `Sink` together and run everything in one fell swoop. Those methods follow the naming convention of `runXXX` and will have the requirement of having an implicit `Materializer` around as they materialize those flows. I've put together a couple of examples of those shortcuts, as follows:

```
val source = Source(List(1,2,3,4,5))
val sink = Sink.fold[Int,Int](0)(_+_)
val multiplier = Flow[Int].map(_*2)
//Hook source and sink into flow and run
multiplier.runWith(source, sink)
//Hook flow to sink and then run with a source
multiplier.to(sink).runWith(source)
//Connect a flow with a source and then run with a fold
source.via(multiplier).runFold(0)(_+_)
```

These are just a few of the available shortcuts to connect up and materialize a process in one step. There are more, so check out the API documents if you are interested in seeing the full set.

Operator fusion within streams

Akka Streams 2.0 introduced a new concept about how streams are built and run, called Operator Fusion. This was a performance optimization to mitigate the cost of passing elements between the different stages, allowing all of the steps to be processed by a single actor instance. The Akka documents list three main consequences of this approach on stream-operator fusion and they are as follows:

1. Starting up a stream may take longer due to the execution of the fusing algorithm.
2. Passing elements between fused stages is much faster due to the avoidance of asynchronous messages passing overhead.
3. Fused stages no longer run in parallel with each other, meaning only one CPU core is used for each fused part.

The first item from the list can be easily countered by pre-executing the fusing algorithm when building your stream blueprints, thus avoiding this cost at the time of stream materialization. An example of doing that is as follows:

```
val flow = Flow[Int].map(_*3).filter(_ % 2 == 0)
val fused = Fusing.aggressive(flow)
Source(List(1,2,3,4,5)).via(fused).runForeach(println)
```

In this example, we start by creating the transformation parts of our process as a `Flow`. Then, we take this `Flow` blueprint and create a copy of it that is pre-fused using `Fusing.aggressive` to do so. This gives me a new blueprint that can be materialized any number of times, and also woven into other materialized flows any number of times, mitigating the cost of the fusing algorithm. Also, note that I am using one of the materialization shortcuts here, `runForeach`, which attaches a `Sink.foreach` and materializes the flow in one step.

The third consequence from that list is an important one to understand. It means that each element being sent downstream needs to be processed fully, by all possible downstream stages, before the next element will be processed. It's not possible with a fully fused flow for two elements to be processed at the same time. This means that it will be a one-in, one-out situation unless explicit async boundaries are added.

If you want to be able to run stages in parallel, you will now need to explicitly insert async boundaries when constructing your flows. You do so by using the `async` method, which is available on all three `Source`, `Sink` and `Flow`. Adding a boundary like this into a stream essentially draws a box around all previous stages that are not already part of an async boundary, making them run in parallel to other stages or other async boundaries in the flow.

Let's start with a simple example to first show that a fully fused flow will process it's stages sequentially. That code is shown as follows:

```
Source(1 to 5).
map{x => println(s"pre-map: $x");x}.
map(_*3).
map{x => println(s"pre-filter: $x");x}.
```

```
filter(_ % 2 == 0).
runForeach(x => s"done: $x")
```

In this example, I've built a flow where I've added some dummy map calls to print out an identifier for where each element in the process is. If you run this flow, you will always see the following output:

```
pre-map: 1
pre-filter: 3
pre-map: 2
pre-filter: 6
done: 6
pre-map: 3
pre-filter: 9
pre-map: 4
pre-filter: 12
done: 12
pre-map: 5
pre-filter: 15
```

From the output here, you can see that each element goes from source to sink, in order, and sequentially, one at a time. Now, if we need to add an `async` boundary into this flow, before the filtering stage, in an effort to run parts in parallel, we can add in an explicit `async` boundary, as follows:

```
Source(1 to 5).
map{x => println(s"pre-map: $x");x}.
map(_*3).async.
map{x => println(s"pre-filter: $x");x}.
filter(_ % 2 == 0).
runForeach(x => s"done: $x")
```

By adding the `async` method after the real `map` operation, that step, plus any steps that upstream from it, will be separated into their own async region. This means that the remaining steps downstream from that boundary can run in parallel to any steps within that boundary. This simple change enables us to use two CPU cores to process this data flow. If we ran this updated code example, the output could be slightly different each time due to the non-determinism of running in parallel, but it will look something like this:

```
pre-map: 1
pre-map: 2
pre-map: 3
pre-map: 4
pre-map: 5
pre-filter: 3
pre-filter: 6
done: 6
```

```
pre-filter: 9
pre-filter: 12
done: 12
pre-filter: 15
```

You can see from the output here that multiple elements are able to flow into the first map stage before the very first element gets to the filter. This is distinctly different from the first example where you saw each element going all the way through before the next element's processing started.

If you need to be able to leverage multiple CPU cores for your data flows in an effort to improve throughput, you basically have two options to choose from. The first, as demonstrated, is to add explicit `async` boundaries in your flows. The other option is to disable operator fusion entirely. You can disable fusing by setting the following property in your Akka config:

```
akka.stream.materializer.auto-fusing=off
```

Just be aware that this will affect the performance of your flows as you will incur costs for the asynchronous message passing between stream stages. This may hurt a little if you have flows with lots of stages that need to be completed very quickly, so keep that in mind. You can, however, still explicit fuse where needed after disabling auto-fusing by using `Fusing.aggressive`.

Using buffers to control rate

In a happy Akka Streams data processing flow, downstream demand is faster than the elements can be produced upstream. As I mentioned previously, in the section titled *Back-pressure in action*, when this happens, the back-pressure handling is in push mode. This means that elements are being signaled downstream as fast as they are available because downstream demand is always there. But when the situation flip-flops, and the rate of upstream element generation outpaces downstream demand, the stream needs to figure out what to do with those elements for which it does not currently have in demand.

One of the ways Akka Streams allows you to handle back-pressure is by introducing buffers into your streams. There are two types of buffer handling Akka supports on streams—implicit (internal) buffers, and explicit buffers. I'll break down those types in detail in the following sections.

Internal buffers on async stages

In a previous section, dealing with *Operator fusion within Streams*, I discussed how one can add explicit asynchronous boundaries to their flows, with the `async` method, to enable different sections of the flow to run in parallel. Generally, this can improve throughput of the flow due to multiple CPU cores being used, but in practice, there is cost associated with passing an element through an `async`, and thread context, boundary.

The Akka streams team was aware of this cost, and they have employed a mitigation strategy to help reduce the overhead from it. The strategy they use when sending elements across the async boundaries is referred to as windowed, batching back-pressure. They use the term windowed here because they do not just stop and wait when sending elements across the boundary. It's possible that there are multiple elements in flight concurrently. They use the term batching here because the protocol requests and drains multiple elements at a time from the window buffer. The cost of transferring elements across an async boundary will be the same, regardless of the number of elements being sent. That's why it makes sense to batch up and send multiple elements at once to mitigate the total cost of sending all of those elements across that boundary.

This internal buffering protocol is something that you won't often have to deal with directly. In a normal data flow, the processing rate of that flow is strictly coordinated by the back-pressure signals that propagate up through the flow, which means that each stage can process only as fast as the total throughput of that flow. However, there are facilities within Akka Streams to allow you to detach the processing rate of individual segments so that they can process at a rate that is different from the total flow itself. You can also use external timing sources within flows to govern the rate of processing. If you decide to use either of these approaches, then you will need to be aware of, and have to deal with, these normally transparent internal buffers.

If you want to control the size of the internal buffers used on the async stages, you have a few options, each with a different granularity of effect. To change the buffer sizes universally, you can add the following settings to your config:

```
akka.stream.materializer.initial-input-buffer-size = 4
akka.stream.materializer.max-input-buffer-size = 16
```

Note that the preceding values shown for these settings match the defaults set by Akka. These buffers are only meant as an optimization strategy, so we will set them as high as necessary, to meet the throughput requirements of your flows. Setting them higher than required can lead to odd behaviors in your flows due to things like buffer prefetching, which I will show in a moment.

If you want to set this at a more fine-grained level, for example, an individual flow that you are materializing, then you can use the settings on ActorMaterializer, as shown in the following example:

```
implicit val materializer = ActorMaterializer(
  ActorMaterializerSettings(system)
  .withInputBuffer(
    initialSize = 16,
  maxSize = 32))
```

Following an approach, such as the preceding example, gives you a finer-grained control, down to the level of an individual materialized flow, with all async stages in that flow using those settings. If you want to get down even further in granularity, you can control the buffers for individual stages within a flow, as the following code example shows:

```
val separateMapStage = Flow[Int].map(_*2).async.
withAttributes(Attributes.inputBuffer(initial = 1, max = 1))

val otherMapStage = Flow[Int].map(_/2).async

val totalFlow = separateMapStage.via(otherMapStage)
```

By separating the first async map stage into its own Flow, I can tweak just that stage's buffer settings using withAttributes. In the preceding example, I am setting the initial and max buffer settings for that separate stage to 1. The other async map stage, represented by otherMapStage, will use the default settings for internal buffers.

When you use async stages, you need to be aware of the potential side effects of the internal buffers that they employ. The following code example intends to demonstrate one such problem:

```
case class Tick()
val fastSource = Source.tick(1 second, 1 second, Tick())
val slowSource = Source.tick(3 second, 3 second, Tick())

val asyncZip = Flow[Int].zip(slowSource).async

fastSource.
conflateWithSeed(seed = (_) => 1)((count, _) => count + 1).
via(asyncZip).
runForeach{case (i,t) => println(i)}
```

In this example, we have two sources producing at different rates—one at 1 element per second and another slower one, at 1 element every three seconds. On the faster of the two sources, I'm applying a conflate step to count the number of ticks it has to wait until the slower source produces its element. I will then zip the two sources together using an async stage to do so, before printing the results from the conflate step.

Looking at this code, one may think that it will continually print the number 3. But when you run it, what you actually see is the number 1 printed a bunch of times instead. This has to do with the internal buffer of the async zip step prefetching it's 16 element buffer, resulting in the conflate step running 16 times without waiting for the slower source first. You can fix this by setting the internal buffer to 1 on the async zip step, although you will still see a single leading 1 because there is still a buffer prefetch there.

 If you want to see this code sample in its entirety, and tweak and run it yourself, you can find it in the `samples` code distribution for `chapter6`, in a file called `BufferProblems.scala`.

Adding explicit buffers to data flows

In the previous section, you learned about the implicit buffers used on asynchronous stages within data flows. Those are buffers that you generally don't have to think much about or interact with. But, there is another kind of buffer that can be explicitly added to data flows as part of the logic for that flow. These buffers are explicitly set up to handle back-pressure, and detailing a strategy on what to do when downstream can no longer handle the rate of elements being produced.

You can add these explicit buffers to your flows using the `buffer` combinator. Say, for instance, you had a queue somewhere that held events to be processed. As part of your work, you need to write a data flow to consume those events periodically, pumping them into possible, multiple downstream systems. Each element being processed through the flow may take a while, and you want to dequeue a whole bunch of events at once, up front, to alleviate any backlog in the queue itself.

If you want to follow an approach like that, you could employ an explicit buffer in your flow. The code to perform something like that will look like this:

```
val eventsSource = eventsConnector()
val processingFlow = eventsProcessingFlow()
eventsSource.buffer(500, OverflowStrategy.backpressure).
to(processingFlow)
```

In this example, after setting up the fictitious event source, we will add an explicit buffering stage to it. By adding that stage, I ensure that 500 events, and no more, pulled from that source are stored in the buffer, in memory. Once that buffer fills, elements can start to flow downstream into the processing flow. As the buffer starts to drain, more demand can flow upstream from it in order to fetch elements, but it's really there to deal with the situation of demand being slower than the rate of elements being produced. To show this a little more concretely, consider the following code example:

```
Source(1 to 1000000).
map{x => println(s"passing $x");x}.
buffer(5, OverflowStrategy.backpressure).
throttle(1, 1 second, 1, ThrottleMode.shaping).runForeach(println)
```

In this sample, I've set up a simple source that has the elements from 1 to 1000000 in it. Underneath this source, I will set up a dummy `map` step to show when demand is flowing upstream to that source. Then, I will put in an explicit buffer that will hold up to five elements before it starts to back-pressure. After that, I'll insert a throttle that will only demand elements once per second. The situation created here should result in the rate of upstream elements outpacing downstream demand. If you run this code, you should start to see output that looks like this:

```
passing 1
passing 2
passing 3
passing 4
passing 5
1
passing 6
passing 7
2
passing 8
3
passing 9
```

What you see in the first five lines is the buffer prefilling itself, irrespective of the downstream demand. Then, as the ticks start to happen, the elements will flow down from the buffer into the sink. As the buffer starts to drain, it will then send the demand upstream to pull more elements from the source. If you want to play around with this code a bit, you can find it in the `samples` code distribution for this chapter, in a file called `ExplicitBuffer.scala`.

Whenever you add an explicit buffer, you will need to pick an overflow strategy to use. In the two samples provided thus far, I used `OverflowStrategy.backpressure`. In this mode, when the buffer fills, demand will stop flowing from the buffer stage, which will cause upstream back-pressure. This is a decent strategy to choose if you want to try and preserve all of the upstream elements.

If you don't care about the occasional loss of data, there are a few other strategies to consider. The first one is `OverflowStrategy.dropTail`. In this strategy, if an element arrives when the buffer is full, the youngest element (the tail of the buffer) gets dropped so that the new element can be enqueued. This strategy preserves fairness, in which, the oldest elements in the buffer will get priority. If you want to completely toss out the new element and not even bother enqueueing it, you can switch to using `OverflowStrategy.dropNew` instead.

If you have a situation where you want to start dropping the oldest items in the buffer first, you can use `OverflowStrategy.dropHead`. In this strategy, the incoming element will move to the front of the buffer, replacing the element that was at the head when the new element arrived. This can be useful if an element gets resent if it's not processed or acknowledged within a certain amount of time. If this is the case, it's likely that the resent element is already in the buffer again, so dropping it from the front is a good idea.

The next strategy to consider is a little more drastic than the ones already discussed, and it is called `OverflowStrategy.dropBuffer`. In this strategy, when the buffer is full, and a new element arrives, you can completely clear the buffer before enqueuing the new element. There is high-data loss here, but if that is less important than getting elements through the flow, this may be a good choice for you.

The last strategy to consider is called `OverflowStrategy.fail`. In this strategy, when the buffer gets full, the entire stream is failed and terminates. This is a good choice if you need to strictly enforce limits on elements being in flight within a flow. Something like this can be used to implement a rate limit (perhaps per client for an API you develop) where exceeding the `max` in flight requests causes all current requests to fail.

Transforming rate within flows

It will not always be possible to tell an upstream source of data to slow down via back-pressure. An example of this can be a timer-based source. That source will continue to tick away at a fixed rate, regardless of the back-pressure signals from a downstream component. Additionally, there may be times when downstream has continual demand that just can't be met by the upstream source. When faced with situations like these, you may need to add stages into your flows to manipulate the rate of data flowing through them. We'll discuss how to do that in the following sections using two opposite options.

Reducing data flow rates with conflate

The first kind of situation where you may need to manipulate the flow rate is when you have a slow downstream and a fast upstream that won't respond well to back-pressure. If you find yourself in a situation like this, where you can't slow down an upstream source, you can try and incorporate a conflate stage into your flow as a solution.

The idea behind conflate is that you can write a function to combine elements from upstream until a demand signal comes from downstream. This particular strategy won't work for all situations as there will be data that just doesn't lend itself to combining, which implies some loss of precision in the process. But there certainly will be situations where this is a good option, particularly with streams of numeric data where summing or averaging elements can work when combining them.

Imagine a scenario in our bookstore app where we had a data mart type table that showed the total number and amount of all sales orders for a particular day. To get this information, we will listen to the event stream for sales orders and atomically increment the count and amount columns in our data mart table for each order event we get. In this example, the event stream is the source and the relational database is the sink.

For our app, it's possible that we may get bursts of orders, say a flash sale or something, and in those situations, the database may get overburdened and propagate back-pressure back upstream. This can be a good situation to use a `conflate` operation, summing the counts and amounts when we have to combine events. If you follow this approach, you are essentially batching the count and amount updates together to reduce the total number of calls that you will need to make to the database. A rough sketch of the code that I just described is shown as follows:

```
val eventsSource:Source[OrderCreated,NotUsed] = ...
val dbSink:Sink[(Int,Double),NotUsed] = ...
eventsSource.
conflateWithSeed(Seq(_))(_:+_).
```

```
map{ events =>
  (events.size, events.map(_.amount).sum)
}.runWith(dbSink)
```

The `conflateWithSeed` step here will combine events into `Seq` when there is no pending demand from downstream. Once demand resumes, the `map` step will take care of compressing the combined information back down to a single element to send downstream. Here, that single element is a tuple of the count of events and sum of the amounts across all of those events. The end result is that the data mart is still updated with the correct count and amount numbers, incrementing by larger numbers when back-pressure caused events to be combined.

Note that there are two forms of `conflate` operations—`conflateWithSeed` and `conflate`. The former is like a `fold` in that it requires an initial value to accumulate info. The latter is like a `reduce` in that it does not require an accumulator.

Increasing data flow rates with expand

There's one more operation that you can use if you need to manipulate the rate of information flowing through your streams. This operation is called `expand` and it behaves in the opposite way that a `conflate` operation does. You can use `expand` in situations where you have a slow upstream source that is not able to produce enough elements to keep up with the downstream demand. If you use `expand` in your flows, you have to understand that when it kicks in, it will be sending an element downstream that you have already seen. This sort of implies that whatever action happens as a result of receiving that element is idempotent. As long as you can handle this fact, then you can use expand in situations where you need to keep sending elements downstream even if the upstream source currently cannot produce them.

A simple example of using `expand` within a flow is as follows:

```
eventsSource.
expand(Iterator.continually(_)).
runWith(sink)
```

The `expand` combinator takes a function that takes the type of element being processed and returns an `Iterator` for that element. In this example, when there are no elements to meet the downstream demand, then the last received event will be continually sent downstream until new elements become available from the upstream source.

Building processing graphs with the graph builder DSL

Up to this point, the data flows we've built were linear in nature. They have involved data flowing sequentially through a straight-line process. These types of flows lend themselves well to the fluent DSL that we've used so far to string process stages together. But, what if your data flow cannot be modeled as a simple linear process? What if your process is better modeled as a computation graph instead? When you have a graph-based processing flow that you want to solve with all the benefits of Akka Streams, then you need to leverage the graph DSL.

Graph building basics

A graph-based problem is one that typically involves the concepts of fanning out and fanning in. In Akka Streams terms, fanning out is going from a single input port to multiple output ports. Conversely, fanning in is going from multiple input ports to a single output port. Within the graph DSL, these types of operations are enabled via components called junctions. When building a graph, you can use junctions to connect up any of the other core Akka Streams building blocks (source, sink, and flow) to build more complex, graph-based processing flows. In fact, some of the more simple operations, such as zip or concat (both fan-ins), are available directly on source, sink, and flow, and are implemented under-the-hood as graph junctions.

The graph DSL is quite different in appearance to the DSL we have used to build linear flows. It uses a `GraphBuilder` component to add junctions into. Once you have added all of the necessary junctions, you can wire your source, sink, and flow components into those junctions using the special ~> operator. The idea here is that your code will end up actually resembling the graph that it is modeling. Consider the following graph that you want to create, modeled as a simple activity diagram:

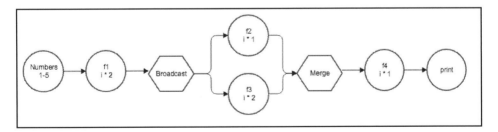

In the preceding diagram, the circles represent concrete flow steps, being either source, sink, or flow. The hexagons represent the junctions for our graph, where we are implementing fan-out and fan-in behaviors. Any step marked with the letter **f** represents a transform where we are performing some sort of math operation to the incoming number element.

If you want to implement the graph depicted in the preceding diagram, you can do so, using the graph builder DSL, with the following code:

```
val g = RunnableGraph.fromGraph(GraphDSL.create() {
    implicit builder: GraphDSL.Builder[NotUsed] =>

    import GraphDSL.Implicits._
    val in = Source(1 to 5)
    val out = Sink.foreach[Int](i => print(s"$i "))
    val f1 = Flow[Int].map(_*2)
    val f2 = Flow[Int].map(_ * 1)
    val f3 = Flow[Int].map(_*2)
    val f4 = Flow[Int].map(_+1)

    val bcast = builder.add(Broadcast[Int](2))
    val merge = builder.add(Merge[Int](2))

    in ~> f1 ~> bcast ~> f2 ~> merge   ~> f4 ~> out
    bcast ~> f3 ~> merge
    ClosedShape
})
g.run
```

In order to start building this particular graph, you will need to call `RunnableGraph.fromGraph`, passing in any external components needed in the flow. I'm passing no external components for this example; I'll show you that technique later on in this section. Then, you will need to implement a function that takes the implicit `GraphDSL.Builder`. Inside the body of this function is where you build out the graph, using the `GraphDSL.Builder` to add your junctions to that graph. Another important concept here is the importing of `GraphDSL.Implicits._` inside the graph building function. This enables the usage of the `~>` operator so that I can start to link my steps together.

Inside the graph building function, I set up a `Source` and `Sink` to represent the start and end points of the flow from the diagram. Then, I set up the individual transform steps from the diagram using the `Flow` components, each with a single `map` step to model those steps from the diagram. After I have all of the basic components set up, I add two junctions to the graph via the `builder`; one `Broadcast` and one `Merge`. The `Broadcast` junction will represent the fanning-out step from the graph in the diagram. It has a single input port and two output ports, so every element that comes in will be sent out two times, one on each of the output ports. The `Merge` junction will handle the fanning in from the diagram. It has two input ports and a single output port. It will send each element it gets, regardless of port, downstream through the single output port.

Once all of the components and junctions are defined, you can start to tie them together with the `~>` operator. The idea here is that the code and the arrows are supposed to mirror the graph you are modeling. The arrows will connect inputs and outputs together so that you don't have any open ports remaining. If you do this, then you have a closed, or complete, graph that is ready to be run. We indicate that by returning `ClosedShape` at the end of the building function.

If you run this graph, the output for it will be as follows:

```
3 5 5 9 7 13 9 17 11 21
```

One thing to note here is that I only put in five elements, but I got 10 elements out. This is an effect of the `Broadcast` and `Merge` pairing used in the graph. The `Broadcast` junction will duplicate the elements it receives, passing them multiple times downstream, one for each output port. The `Merge` component does not de-duplicate things, it just accepts whatever is coming from upstream and merge it in to a single downstream output port.

There are a bunch of predefined junctions out there to handle fan-in and fan-out logic, each having their own behaviors. You should take some time and get familiar with them within the Akka Stream documentation (`http://doc.akka.io/docs/akka-stream-and-http-experimental/1.-M2/scala/stream-graphs.html`), on the page *Working with Graphs*, in the section *Constructing Flow Graphs*.

The graph produced in this example is materialized to an `akka.NotUsed` object. That may work for some situations, but you may find situations where you want the computation performed within the graph to produce some kind of output. If you want to do that, then you will need to import some components (the ones that produce an output) into the graph as opposed to creating the in-the-graph-building function. A modified example of the graph we just created, to now produce an output, is as follows:

```
val foldSink = Sink.fold[Int,Int](0)(_+_)
val g = RunnableGraph.fromGraph(GraphDSL.create(foldSink) {
  implicit builder => (sink) =>
    . . .
    in ~> f1 ~> bcast ~> f2 ~> merge  ~> f4 ~> sink
    bcast ~> f3 ~> merge
    ClosedShape
})
```

Here, the sink component that is to be used is created outside of the graph and then passed into the `GraphDSL.create` method. Then, it's redeclared, as sink, inside the graph building function, allowing us to use it inside of that function. The imported component is then hooked into the graph where the internally created sink previously was. If we set things up like this, then materializing the graph will result in a `Future[Int]`, which matches the materialized value of the `Sink` component that we imported into the graph.

Here, we bring in a single component into the graph. However , you're not limited to one. If you want, you can import many components into your graphs and then use those imported components to customize the materialized values of your graphs.

Building a real-world graph example

Now, a graph to perform some math on a bunch of numbers is not a very real-world example. I'll try and provide something a little more concrete to show the power and simplicity of the Akka Streams Graph API. Imagine that you stored a bunch of events in a storage system, such as Amazon S3. These events come from your client's log files, and the value your business is providing to these clients is to add additional contextual information to these events before storing them in Amazon Redshift and building analytical models from them. You will need a process where you can consume events from S3 (as the source), feed them into a bunch of transforms (in parallel, as each one can take some time), and then pump them into Redshift (the sink). Let's start by looking at the case classes used in this graph, as well as some methods to build the components and fetch the extra data:

```
case class Event(eventType:String, date:Date, imageUrl:String,
  weather:Option[WeatherData], imageInfo:Option[ImageInfo])
case class WeatherData(temp:Int, rain:Boolean)
case class ImageInfo(tags:List[String], colors:List[String])

def s3EventSource:Source[Event, NotUsed] = ...
def fetchWeatherInfo(date:Date):Future[WeatherData] = ...
def fetchImageInfo(imageUrl:String):Future[ImageInfo] = ...
def redshiftSink:Sink[Event, Future[Done]]= ...
```

The `Event` class is the main type that will flow through the graph. It is what comes from the `Source` and flows into the `Sink`. The `WeatherData` and `ImageInfo` classes represent the additional context data that we'll be fetching from external services in order to enhance the information on the `Event` class. The methods included here are only meant to show return types so it understands what types they are contributing to the graph. The details of what those methods will need to do is not important to this example.

Now that we've laid out some of the necessary structure and operations required, let's take a look at the graph itself:

```
val g = RunnableGraph.fromGraph(GraphDSL.create() {
  implicit builder: GraphDSL.Builder[NotUsed] =>
  import GraphDSL.Implicits._
  val eventsSource = s3EventSource
  val eventsSink = redshiftSink
  val weather =
  Flow[Event].mapAsync(4)(e => fetchWeatherInfo(e.date))
  val imageInfo =
  Flow[Event].mapAsync(4)(e => fetchImageInfo(e.imageUrl))

  val bcast = builder.add(Broadcast[Event](3))
  val zip =
  builder.add(ZipWith[Event,WeatherData,ImageInfo,Event]{
    (e, w, i) =>
    e.copy(weather = Some(w), imageInfo = Some(i))
  })

  eventsSource ~> bcast ~> zip.in0
  bcast ~> weather ~> zip.in1
  bcast ~> imageInfo ~> zip.in2
  zip.out ~> eventsSink
  ClosedShape
})
```

As with the first graph example, we start by setting up the components that make up the graph. Here, it means setting up the S3-based source and the Redshift-based sink. Then, we will set up two separate flow steps that are meant to go out to the external services and fetch the additional event-context data. Both these steps will use mapAsync, which let's you plug in transforms that return a Future. As we don't want to block during processing, this seems like a good choice to use to integrate with the fictitious web services that are providing data. Note that the first argument (4 in both cases) represents the amount of parallelism that step can have. This parallelism allows that step to process multiple requests at a time, even though it will eventually send them downstream in the order they came in. If you don't care about the order in which the elements flow downstream then you can use mapAsyncUnordered instead.

Once the basic components are set up, I add two junctions to the graph. The first is the same kind of `Broadcast` we saw in the first example, except that this one is broadcasting three times instead of twice. The second junction is new so far, and is called `ZipWith`. This junction allows you to take any number of inputs, and after receiving all of them, sends a single element downstream. This allows us to rendezvous the original `Event` with the `WeatherData` and `ImageInfo` for it. As the elements come out of those two parallel tasks in the order received, we will know that we are linking up the data correctly. Once we have all three pieces, we can add the new context data to `Event` and then send it downstream to sink to be written into Redshift.

Once we have all of the components and junctions ready, the last step is to weave them all together. In this example, the `Event` hits `Broadcast`, and then immediately splits out into the first input port of the downstream `ZipWith`. At that point, it's just waiting for the other data to join up with it. The `Broadcast` then fans out the event to the two other processing stages. Each processing stage does its work and then fans back into `ZipWith` to tie back to the event that it's for. From there, `ZipWith` has its single output port tied into the sink as the final destination for the data.

So, this is very similar to the first basic example but it's a little more real world. We built something pretty powerful rather simply. If we were to do this via actors, or just plain Futures, the code would be a bit more complex and not give us the benefit of back-pressure. Hopefully, this demonstrates the beauty and simplicity of the Akka Streams graph DSL.

Working with partial graphs

In the previous section, all of the graphs discussed and all of the examples provided were of closed graphs. This means that the graph itself was fully self-contained and complete. It does not have any open input and output ports. It is a closed circuit, hence the closed designation. However, Akka Streams does not limit you to creating just closed graphs. They have the concept of open or partial graphs too, and that's what we will explore in this section.

When you have a closed graph, all of the input and output ports are connected. In this case, the graph building function returns a `ClosedShape`, which is what you saw in the previous examples. A closed graph is a `RunnableGraph`, meaning that it's ready to be executed. There are other shapes though; ones that imply that input and output ports are open and need to be satisfied. These graphs are classified as partial because they are not yet complete and therefore cannot be run. A partial graph allows you to return the set of ports—both in and out—that need to be connected, which is specified by a shape. After that, all you need to do is connect up those ports and you can run your graph.

To provide a concrete example of creating a partial graph, let's take our event example from the previous section and turn it into one. In that example, we hooked in a source that was pulling events from S3. We also hooked in a sink that was storing the enhanced events in Redshift. That's what made that example a closed graph. But, what if we wanted the middle processing piece where we fan out and then in, adding the additional context to the events, to be able to be hooked into any upstream and downstream that were dealing with the event type?

If we want to follow an approach like that, one option will be to turn that middle part into a partial graph with a single open input and output port. The code for that change will look like this:

```
val eventsFlow = Flow.fromGraph(GraphDSL.create() {
  implicit builder: GraphDSL.Builder[NotUsed] =>

  import GraphDSL.Implicits._
  val weather =
    Flow[Event].mapAsync(4)(e => fetchWeatherInfo(e.date))
  val imageInfo =
    Flow[Event].mapAsync(4)(e => fetchImageInfo(e.imageUrl))

  val bcast = builder.add(Broadcast[Event](3))
  val zip = builder.add(ZipWith[Event,WeatherData,ImageInfo,Event]
  {(e, w, i) =>
    e.copy(weather = Some(w), imageInfo = Some(i))
  })

  bcast ~> zip.in0
  bcast ~> weather ~> zip.in1
  bcast ~> imageInfo ~> zip.in2
  FlowShape(bcast.in, zip.out)
})
```

The code is pretty similar to the original example, at least pertaining to the steps where the events are being enhanced. The first difference to note is that we are no longer wrapping the call to `GraphDSL.Create` with a call to `RunnableGraph.fromGraph`. Instead, we are wrapping the graph creation with a call to `Flow.fromGraph`. This is because we are no longer creating a closed, runnable graph; we are creating an open `Flow` component instead.

The second change to note is at the end of the graph building function—I'm returning a `FlowShape` instead of a `ClosedShape`. The `FlowShape` is specifying the single inlet port of `Broadcast` as the input and the single outlet port of `ZipWith` as its output. This will allow you to plus in any upstream that is sending events downstream and any downstream that is receiving events from its upstream.

There are many different types of `Shape` instances you can use when constructing your partial graphs, each allowing different combinations of inputs and outputs. You should check out the Akka API documents, using the following link to see what other possibilities exist: `http://doc.akka.i o/api/akka/2.4/#akka.stream.Shape`.

Now, if we want to plug this new component into a data flow, it will be as simple as it is shown in the following example:

```
otherEventsSource.
  via(eventsFlow).
  runWith(otherEventsSink)

def otherEventsSource:Source[Event,NotUsed] = ...
def otherEventsSink:Sink[Event,Future[Done]] = ...
```

Because `otherEventSource` has an output type matching the inlet type of my graph component, I can tie them together using `via`. Also, because `otherEventSink` has an input type matching the outlet of that graph component, I can connect the graph to that sink. So, here, my complex graph just looks like a basic flow component, but under the hood, it's a complex processing graph. That's one of the beauties of creating partial graphs and then plugging them into basic data flows. You can encapsulate the complexities of some of your processing tasks behind a partial graph component, which serves as a blueprint that you can then weave into your data flows.

Handling streaming I/O

Before the advent of Akka Streams, if you wanted to perform I/O in Akka, for instance, maybe, to build a TCP server, you'd have to use the Akka I/O library. That library is very low level, forcing you to handle back-pressure signals on your own. While it's certainly possible to do so, it's rather complex and requires one to write quite a bit of code to do so. Thankfully, Akka Streams has I/O-handling capabilities that allow you to produce simple, stream oriented, back-pressure aware I/O code on top of Akka I/O. This section will detail some of the ways you can leverage Akka Streams for I/O-based operations.

Streams and TCP

One of the ways that you can leverage the power of Akka Streams for I/O handling is by building a TCP server. This is one of the things that you can already do with Akka I/O, but it was pretty complicated to do correctly in regards to back-pressure. With Akka Streams, it's much easier, lowering the barrier to creating simple TCP servers built on top of Akka.

It's best to start out with an example first, to show the simplicity of building a TCP server with Akka Streams. For this example, we'll implement a simple calculator that accepts two numbers, which is separated by an operator. The calculator will perform the operation and then return the result. Let's start by taking a look at the subflow that will do the calculation work based on the input String:

```
val Calculation = """(\d+)(?:\s*([-+*\/])\s*((?:\s[- +])?\d+)\s*)+$""".r
val calcFlow = Flow[String].
map{
  case Calculation(a, "+", b) => a.toInt + b.toInt
  case Calculation(a, "-", b) => a.toInt - b.toInt
  case Calculation(a, "*", b) => a.toInt * b.toInt
  case Calculation(a, "/", b) => a.toInt / b.toInt
  case other => 0
}
```

There's nothing too special here. We have a regex that is used to extract the two numbers and the operation. Then, based on the operation, a calculation is performed. The code is not very robust in terms of error handling, but it will suffice for this example.

The next thing to look at is the code to bind to the local port so that you're ready to start handling connections:

```
val connections:
Source[IncomingConnection, Future[ServerBinding]] =
Tcp().bind("localhost", 8888)
```

Here, we're using the `Tcp` extension to bind to the local port, `8888`. This produces an Akka Streams `Source` that will produce `IncomingConnection` elements for each incoming connection request to our server. This `Source` will also materialize to a `Future`, which will wrap a `Tcp.ServerBinding` that can be used to unbind the local port if necessary.

Now that we've connected the last piece of code, all we need is something to handle the incoming connections. That code looks like this:

```
connections runForeach { connection =>
  println(s"New connection from: ${connection.remoteAddress}")

  val calc = Flow[ByteString].
```

```
        via(Framing.delimiter(
        ByteString("\n"),
        maximumFrameLength = 256,
        allowTruncation = true)).
        map(_.utf8String).
        via(calcFlow).
        map(i => ByteString(s"$i\n"))

        connection.handleWith(calc)
    }
```

On the first line, we're immediately materializing the connections source, connecting it to a Sink.foreach, and running the flow, all via the helper method, runForeach. Inside of the foreach function, we will get an instance of IncomingConnection each time someone connects to our server.

For each connection that we receive, we will set up a bi-directional flow instance that accepts ByteString and also outputs ByteString. The incoming ByteString represents the data coming in from the client that is connected to our server. The outgoing ByteString represents the data that our server wants to send back to that client.

The first action that we will take on the incoming ByteString data is to apply a framing handling on it. For our calculator app, we will delimit operation requests on the newline character. With the way TCP sends data, it's possible that a single request gets fragmented into multiple separate ByteString elements that will come into our calc flow. The frame-handling logic, added via Framing.delimiter, will take care of aggregating the data into a single ByteString, only sending it downstream after it receives the necessary newline delimiter.

The next step in the flow maps the now complete ByteString into a UTF-8 string since our regex is based on parsing a string. We will then apply the calcFlow that was set up earlier to handle that string and perform the calculation that it represents. Lastly, we will take that Int result and map it back to a ByteString to be sent back to the client with a trailing newline delimiter.

Once that flow is established, we hook it in as the logic used to handle the incoming connection via handleWith on the IncomingConnection. This method takes a Flow[ByteString, ByteString, Mat] so it matches the handling flow that we built out nicely. It's important to note here that the calc flow that we built out to handle the incoming connection is not a reusable blueprint like most of the other examples we've built in this chapter. It is intrinsically tied to an open connection that it's handling and, therefore, can only ever be materialized one time. That's why it's created inside the foreach loop instead of outside.

With all of this code set up, we can start up our server and send a calculation into it. To start the server, you can open an sbt window in the root `samples` directory from the `chapter6` code distribution. From there, the command to start the server is as follows:

```
> runMain code.TCPCalculator
```

Once the server is running, you can connect into it and send calculation requests via `telnet`. An example of using `telnet` to send a few calculations is shown as follows:

```
$ telnet 127.0.0.1 8888
1+2
3
9*9
81
^]
telnet> quit
```

Framing your streaming I/O handling

In the previous section, I discussed the need to add framing handling into your streaming I/O-based code. This is because of the nature of TCP and how it can lead to packet fragmentation. What you push onto the TCP layer as a single message may be split into multiple parts as it gets routed to its destination. When it arrives at its destination, there is no guarantee that the handling code on that side will receive it as a single message. Instead, the handling code may receive it as multiple `ByteString` messages that will need to be aggregated into a single `ByteString` so that the downstream code can process it properly.

This need to aggregate and then process the received data as a single message is referred to as framing. Within Akka Streams, you can add framing into your stream processing by using the `akka.streams.scaladsl.Framing` object. This object has a bunch of methods on it that will allow you to add common frame handling into your streams.

The first useful method on the `Framing` object is the `delimiter` method. This is the method that we used in the TCP calculator example (and the CSV example) to properly set the boundaries for each calculation request. This method allows you to specify a simple `ByteString` based delimiter as the separator between messages. For the TCP calculator, we used a newline character as the delimiter. This method returns a flow that both accepts and transmits `ByteString` elements, performing the delimiter-based aggregation inside of its internal logic. You can snap this flow into your data flows by using the `via` method.

Another useful method on the `Framing` object is the `lengthField` method. One of the problems with delimiter-based processing is that the content of the messages themselves may be text in nature and may contain popular delimiter characters already. This makes it hard to select a really good delimiter character that won't naturally occur in your data. When faced with a problem like this, a good option is to add a length-based indicator into your data, most likely as a prefix, to indicate the total length of the payload. Then, you can use the `lengthField` method on `Framing` to decode your payloads, specifying the total size, in bytes, of the length field, which is usually four bytes for an `Int`, as well as the offset of that length field from the front of the message, which is usually 0, meaning at the very front.

Refactoring the view building code

Hopefully, at this point, you have a pretty good understanding of what you can do with Akka Streams. It's a pretty big topic, certainly enough to fill a book on it's own. I've tried to cover all of the areas that I thought were important for someone who was learning Akka Streams for the first time. Armed with that knowledge, we can now take care of some unfinished business, which was leftover from `Chapter 5`, *Separating Concerns with CQRS*.

When we built out the `ViewBuilder` framework in `Chapter 5`, *Separating Concerns with CQRS*, we had the source from our `eventsByTag` query essentially piping the events back to itself and then processing them as if they were regular inbound actor messages. This works, and it's pretty simple, but you won't get any of the benefits of back-pressure handling. The actor that receives the messages will dequeue events as fast as possible, which can possibly lead to memory issues with its mailbox. Also, whatever is happening downstream from the events being received, can be flooded during times of high event volumes.

These types of potential issues are certainly ones to be avoided if possible. As such, it makes sense to continue to use Akka Streams throughout the whole processing flow for each event, taking advantage of the built-in back-pressure handling. The code will still live in the `ViewBuilder` trait as it did earlier. Let's start by looking at a couple of utility-case classes that will be used to transfer information through the flow:

```
case class EnvelopeAndAction(env:EventEnvelope,
  action:IndexAction)
case class EnvelopeAndFunction(env:EventEnvelope,
  f: () => Future[IndexingResult])
```

The EventEnvelope is something that we will need to carry through most of the processing flow, hence, it's inclusion on these two classes which are used in the flow. The EnvelopeAndAction is the pairing of EventEnvelope and the associated IndexAction that should result from that event. The EnvelopAndFunction class is the pairing of EventEnvelope and the function that should be invoked for IndexAction for the event.

One more class that we should look at is the DeferredCreate class that represents the situation where we need to look up some more information first before adding an item to the index. We will use this in the SalesOrderViewBuilder when loading the book information to denormalize into the SalesOrder index. This class is redefined as follows:

```
case class DeferredCreate(
  flow:Flow[EnvelopeAndAction,EnvelopeAndAction,akka.NotUsed])
  extends IndexAction
```

This class used to be a simple case object earlier. Now, it needs to hold a subflow that the main event-handling flow will use to load the extra information before saving the item into the index. This is sort of a conditional branch, inserted into the flow when we have a DeferredCreate situation.

Next, we can take a look at the changes made to the code that is actually handling the events. This code just used to pipe the events back to itself. Now, it's redefined as follows:

```
val eventsSource = journal.eventsByTag(entityType, offset)
eventsSource.via(eventsFlow).runWith(Sink.ignore)
```

Here, we're materializing and running this flow, using a Sink.ignore as the Sink. This is a Sink that you can use when you are performing the important processing upstream and don't have anything else to do afterwards, which is how I modeled this flow. I'll discuss why we have to use Sink.ignore in more detail after describing the complete processing flow.

The main work for this event processing is being done in eventsFlow, which is defined at the class level, as a blueprint, and then pulled into the flow with a call to via. There's a fair amount going on in that flow, so I'll break it down section by section. The first part of that flow to look at, which is the definition and the first processing stage, can be seen as follows:

```
Flow[EventEnvelope].
map{ env =>
  val id = env.persistenceId.
  toLowerCase().drop(entityType.length() + 1)
  EnvelopeAndAction(env, actionFor(id, env))
}.
```

Each time we receive an `EventEnvelope` from the upstream `Source`, we will determine the action for that event and map it over to an `EnvelopeAndAction` instance. That instance will then be handled in the next processing stage, which is defined as follows:

```
flatMapConcat{
  case ea @ EnvelopeAndAction(env, cr:DeferredCreate) =>
  Source.single(ea).via(cr.flow )

  case ea:EnvelopeAndAction =>
  Source.single(ea).via(Flow[EnvelopeAndAction])
}.
```

This is the processing stage where we will conditionally plug in the alternate branch to the flow where additional data is loaded for a `DeferredCreate` action. We will do this with a special combinator called `flatMapConcat`. This combinator is really meant to return a `Source` for each input element that will then be flattened into the resulting output stream, having the effect of increasing the number of elements flowing downstream. For our purposes, it allows us to conditionally insert our branch into the flow, taking that subflow from the `DeferredCreate` action from the previous step. If it's not a `DeferredCreate` action, we will essentially perform a no-op, giving a `Flow` that will just pass the input straight through to the output, unchanged.

Once we have the conditional branch handled properly, we can continue with the handling of the event. The next stage is shown as follows:

```
collect{
  case EnvelopeAndAction(env, i:InsertAction) =>
  EnvelopeAndFunction(env, () => updateIndex(i.id, i.rm, None))

  case EnvelopeAndAction(env, u:UpdateAction) =>
  EnvelopeAndFunction(env,
  () => updateDocumentField(u.id, env.sequenceNr - 1,
  u.expression, u.params))

  case EnvelopeAndAction(env, NoAction(id)) =>
  EnvelopeAndFunction(env,
  () => updateDocumentField(id, env.sequenceNr - 1, Nil,
  Map.empty[String,Any]))
}.
```

In this stage, we are transforming `EnvelopeAndAction` from the previous stage into `EnvelopeAndFunction`, which holds the function that is used to update the index. We're using `collect` here as a combination of both `filter` and `map`. At this point, we only care about the cases that are not `DeferredCreate`, hence the filter part of the processing. Depending on the `IndexAction`, we will either be inserting into the index or updating it, which is what's shown in this code. But, we're not performing the actual updating here. We're just returning functions that will perform the update in the next stage. That next stage code is as follows:

```
mapAsync(1){
    case EnvelopeAndFunction(env, f) => f.apply.map(_ => env)
}.
```

In this stage, we will use `mapAsync` to execute the actual function against the index, which returns a `Future`. I'm using a parallelism argument of 1 to serialize the flow of events through this stage. This is the same problem we had in the previous chapter, where we needed to completely process the events in the order that they were received, per persistence identifier. In the *Elasticsearch support traits* section in Chapter 5, *Separating Concerns with CQRS*, we followed a process of switching receive handling and stashing while we were executing each update against the index. In this new code, we are just throttling down to one update at a time to ensure that we don't process events out of order. We can probably get cute and try to serialize per persistence ID here, maybe using a `groupBy`, but this seemed much simpler and will probably be good enough.

The last stage to look at in the flow is where we update the projection offset. That code looks like this:

```
mapAsync(1){env =>
    resumableProjection.storeLatestOffset(env.offset)
}
```

We're following the same approach as we did with the previous stage, throttling down to a parallelism of 1 to make sure we are not updating the offsets out of order. Inside this `map` stage, we will make the call to update our projection offset.

As this is the last part of our processing flow, we can consider plugging it into a `Sink.foreach` as shown in the following example:

```
Sink.foreach{ env =>
    resumableProjection.storeLatestOffset(env.offset)
}
```

The problem with that approach is that the call inside of the `foreach` is returning a `Future` that's not guaranteed to be complete before the next element is processed by the `Sink`. We want the `Sink` to be aware of the completion of each `Future` before it signals demand back upstream. This is so the `Sink` can correctly back-pressure when the processing of those calls to update the offset store slow down. As there is no out-of-the-box `Sink` implementations that can properly handle elements that are of type `Future`, we can push that part upstream by one stage using `mapAsync` instead, which also allows us to throttle down to the one-at-a-time semantic that we need. As we are performing the final processing in the `mapAsync` step, we don't need to do anything in the `Sink`, hence the use of `Sink.ignore`.

Putting all of these stages together, we have a data flow that can handle our deferred create case, and will update Elasticsearch and our projection offset store, all with the benefits of back-pressure handling. I like this solution much better than what we did in the previous chapter, because it's much simpler (no juggling of events with stash/unstash while updating) and is back-pressure aware.

As things stand, our event-handling flow is missing one thing, and that's the logic for what to do in case of failure. If a single stage fails, the entire flow will stop, and that's not what we want. We want to be aware of the failure, and depending on the type, be able to resume the flow or stop the flow. If this sounds a bit like supervision, it's because it is. When you set up the `Materializer` for your flows, you can give it an optional supervision strategy, just like you can do with your actors. The default behavior is to stop the entire flow. If you want to change that, and we do for our flow, then you need to set up a custom supervision strategy and set it onto the `Materializer`. For the `ViewBuilder` trait, the code is as follows:

```
val decider: Supervision.Decider = {
  case NonFatal(ex) =>
  log.error(ex, "Got non fatal exception in ViewBuilder flow")
  Supervision.Resume
  case ex  =>
  log.error(ex, "Got fatal exception in ViewBuilder flow, stream    will be
stopped")
  Supervision.Stop
}
implicit val materializer = ActorMaterializer(
  ActorMaterializerSettings(context.system).
  withSupervisionStrategy(decider)
)
```

If we get a non-fatal exception, we will log it and then allow our stream to continue to handle elements. If we get something that is fatal, then the stream will be stopped. Adding this supervision strategy will allow our flow to continue on when it encounters exceptions, such as failures from Elasticsearch on individual indexing operations. This makes our view-building code much more robust and production ready.

Refactoring homework

There are still a couple of more places in the code that need Akka Streams based refactoring work, which will be done by you as homework. The first place is really a continuation of the work that we did in the previous section. As part of that refactoring, we built a system where a `ViewBuilder` class can define a subflow to handle the `DeferredCreate` situation. We have one such situation with the `SalesOrderViewBuilder` class where we need to define that subflow. This is one of the pieces of work that you will need to do for this chapter. Go into the `-incomplete` code folder for this chapter and fill in the subflow implementation for the `OrderCreated` event handling. Currently, I have stubbed that flow out, as follows:

```
val flow = Flow[EnvelopeAndAction]
```

As it stands, this `Flow` will do nothing, just passing the input `EnvelopeAndAction` back out as it is. You will need to add processing stages to this `Flow` so that it loads the books for each line item and then uses that information to build out the `SalesOrderRM` that will eventually be saved into the index. When done, you can take a look at the implementation that I provided within the `-complete` bookstore app codebase for this chapter.

The other area that needs attention is the event listening back and forth for the inventory allocation process. Both, the `InventoryClerk` and the `SalesAssociate`, have event-listening code where the events are being piped back to itself where the remainder of the processing occurs. We'll keep this convention because the handling involves looking up or creating child actors and we don't want to close over the context of the actor within our stream processing. As such, we don't need to touch `InventoryClerk`, but there is an improvement that we can make to `SalesAssociate`. In the `SalesAssociate`, we are listening to all events for the book entity instead of the two events that we really care about-`inventoryallocated` and `inventorybackordered`. See if you can set up two separate streams there and merge them together for processing. When done, you can see how I implemented this change within the `-complete` bookstore code for this chapter.

Summary

In this chapter, we learned how to perform stream based processing in a reactive manner. You now have a better understanding of the core Reactive Streams components, and how they fit together to build data processing flows. You also understand how Akka Streams builds upon the Reactive Streams initiative to allow you to build back-pressure aware data flows and graphs. Lastly, we used this new found knowledge to enhance the streams based processing used in our CQRS and Persistence Query oriented components.

Now that we have a solid understanding of Akka Streams, it's time to think about replacing our HTTP libraries (Unfiltered and Dispatch) with something that's more stream oriented and back-pressure aware. Thankfully, Akka provides that exact functionality via Akka HTTP, which is built on top of Akka Streams. This work will be the primary focus of the next chapter.

7
REST Easy with Akka HTTP

When building out a services-oriented or microservices architecture, you'll expose your services so that they can be called remotely over a network. You can choose to do so by leveraging whatever remoting protocol is native to your programming language of choice. In the Java world, this could mean using Java serialization and RMI, or even EJB, to communicate between your services. The problem with this approach is that it locks you into that language, making it difficult or even impossible to introduce services written in another language.

As your architecture grows bigger, it's not realistic to think that all of your services will always be written in the same language and will communicate with that language's native remoting protocol. Additionally, if you ever want to expose some of your business functionality outside your own software, like an external API, then having a language-specific API will only limit that API's adoption. When faced with such problems, it makes sense to consider another way of externally communicating with your services, something that is programming-language-agnostic.

Representational State Transfer (REST) is an HTTP-based protocol to expose and consume services over a network. It's a concept we are already using in the bookstore app, but we'll refactor our usage to leverage Akka's HTTP library, which has all the goodness of Akka Streams and back-pressure built into it. In this chapter, we will cover the following topics:

- What it means to build RESTful interfaces
- Understanding the differences between Spray and Akka HTTP
- How to build RESTful-service APIs on top of Akka HTTP
- How to unit-test your inbound HTTP routes
- How to consume external REST APIs with Akka HTTP

Creating RESTful HTTP interfaces

The REST concept was formulated back in 2000, but I don't think it really gained steam until later on in the 2000s. This was a protocol that was designed to leverage concepts that the browser already understood, built on the following three core concepts:

- Using HTTP verbs, for example, GET and POST, to specify the action you want to take, such as a read or a create action
- Using HTTP status codes when responding to requests to indicate the success or failure of that request back to the caller
- Using the URL of the request to indicate what resource (entity) you want to act against

These three concepts were already baked into the browser, so using them with a browser language such as Javascript seemed like a good fit. Then, using JSON as the data protocol on top of REST was a great match too as JSON was already native to Javascript. Parsing and generating JSON was a snap within Javascript, so much easier than parsing and generating SOAP and XML, as it was previously done up to that point.

The idea behind these JSON RESTful interfaces was that you were acting against a resource, or an entity, from the backend web service. If you have a particular entity (let's use Book here) for which you had already written some basic **create, read, update, delete (CRUD)** service logic, and you want to now expose that logic over a RESTful interface, you can do so pretty easily. For instance, a single-entity lookup request will look something like this: GET /api/book/123.

In this request example, we are specifying the following three things to the backend server:

- **Action**: This is the GET HTTP verb, which specifies we want to perform a lookup
- **Entity**: This is the book part of the URL path, which specifies that we want to work with the Book entity
- **ID**: This is the last part of the URL, 123, which specifies the ID of the Book entity we want to lookup

With these three pieces of information, the server can now service this request. An example of how the service can respond to this request is as follows:

```
HTTP 200 No Error
Content-Type: application/json; charset=UTF-8

Content-Length: 51
```

```
{"id": 123, "title": "20000 Leagues Under the Sea"}
```

Here, the backend service used a 200 level status code to indicate that the request could be properly serviced and it found the entity we requested. If it hadn't found that particular entity, it could have instead responded with a 404 Not Found status code. The backend also sent us the JSON representation of that entity so that we can use that data to render some frontend screen element(s).

You can also add query params to GET requests if you want to lookup multiple instances of a particular entity, specifying something like a filter criteria as a query param. By not including a specific ID in the URL, the implication is that you are potentially looking for multiple entities instead of a single one. An example of a GET request like that is as follows: GET /api/book?tag=fiction.

Now, if I want to create a new instance of the Book entity, the request will look something like this:

```
POST /api/book
Content-Type: application/json; charset=UTF-8

{"title": "Fight Club", "author": "Chuck Palahniuk"}
```

The POST action signifies that I want to create a new resource/entity on the backend. Unlike GET requests, this type of request is not idempotent, in that it does change the state of data on the backend and therefore cannot be retried in the case of a transient failure. Also, here we are communicating the information of what we want to create within the POST body. I'm using JSON in this example, but you can also do a form-urlencoded body of key/value pairs. That request will look like this:

```
POST /api/book
Content-Type: application/x-www-form-urlencoded; charset=UTF-8

title=Fight+Club&author=Chuck+Palahniuk
```

Either of those two content types works, json or form-urlencoded, so pick whichever one you prefer. With a request like that, the server can respond like this:

```
HTTP 201 Created


Content-Type: application/json; charset=UTF-8
Content-Length: 51

{"id": 456, "title": "Fight Club", "author": "Chuck Palahniuk"}
```

The backend service here decided to respond with a 201 status code to indicate that the create was successful. That's not required though, and any of the 2xx level status codes could have sufficed there to indicate success. The extent to which you strictly follow the status code to use for each situation will be up to you. Just be sure that you are using the correct ranges (2xx for success, 3xx for redirection, 4xx for client error, and 5xx for server error) when you do so.

Besides the GET and POST requests, the following are the other basic conventions that are supported within REST:

- A PUT request to perform an entity update where the ID of the entity to update is part of the URL. This request will contain the updated entity information as JSON in the request body.
- A DELETE request to delete an entity from the system, also with the ID of the entity as part of the URL. This request will not contain anything in the request body.

Those four basic actions, GET, POST, PUT, and DELETE, make up the majority of the types of request that you will use when designing your RESTful APIs. There are other actions you can use, such as the aforementioned patch to perform a partial update if you want to go down that route, but those four will be bread-and-butter for your RESTful APIs.

Comparing Akka HTTP to Spray

Before Akka HTTP came about, the most popular choice for a HTTP framework to use with Akka was Spray. The Akka team liked what they saw with Spray, so they decided to collaborate with the Spray team to create a new back-pressure aware I/O layer for Akka. This collaboration went so well that the Akka team decided to go all in on an internal HTTP framework which would be based on Spray. Development was to stop in Spray and continue in Akka HTTP. Developers could still use Spray, but any new features and enhancements would only be available within Akka HTTP.

So Akka HTTP has its roots in Spray, and for the most part the APIs for inbound and outbound HTTP are the same across the two libraries. This means that it's pretty easy to migrate from Spray to Akka HTTP. There are some key differences though, things that you should be aware of when making the switch from Akka HTTP to Spray. I'll do my best to highlight the most important differences between the two frameworks in the following subsections. There will be subtle differences that won't be highlighted here as I'll just focus on macro-level differences.

If you want to see some of the more minor differences, you can check out the *Migration Guide from Spray* section of the Akka HTTP documents.

Akka Streams and back-pressure

Probably the biggest difference between Akka HTTP and Spray is the fact that Akka HTTP is completely built on top of Akka Streams and Spray is not. This means that, when using Akka HTTP, whether for inbound or outbound HTTP handling, you get all the benefits of Akka Streams-based back-pressure handling. For inbound HTTP, the logic to handle each individual connection is a Flow, with the upstream Source being the HTTP request content itself. For outbound HTTP, the request/response cycle (and connection pool handling) is also modeled as a Flow.

By having inbound and outbound HTTP handling built on top of Akka Streams, you can have both reactive and back-pressure-aware handling of your HTTP needs. This means actions such as slowing down the flow of outbound requests into a connection pool if the requests through that pool start to slow and the pool back-pressures. For inbound HTTP, this means actions such as propagating back-pressure back up the TCP connection, possibly slowing down the writing side, when the receiving side is getting backed up. These are things that you just can't easily do with Spray.

Other differences

The rest of the differences between Akka HTTP and Spray, to me, are pretty minor. One of those minor differences is that the IO layers are completely different. Spray had its own internal IO layer and so did Akka via Akka IO. Most of the initial work of porting Spray to Akka HTTP involved getting the Spray code to work on top of Akka IO. Initially, this led to some performance lags on the Akka HTTP side. But this gap was closed by focusing on some improvements in Akka IO, and now the two frameworks perform pretty much the same, with Akka HTTP even outperforming Spray in some areas.

Another difference to call out is the lack of an outbound-pipeline API in Akka HTTP. For those of you who are familiar with using outbound HTTP in Spray, when making a request, you can chain a bunch of actions, such as compression and JSON handling, together via the ~> operator, forming a processing pipeline. This exact API does not exist in the outbound Akka HTTP code. Instead, you can use the Akka Streams constructs to handle pre and post request processing. It's a subtle difference, but one worth calling out nonetheless.

Creating RESTful interfaces with Akka HTTP

Now that we have a little background on REST in general, and how Akka HTTP evolved from Spray, it's time to dig in and understand how we can use the inbound Akka HTTP API to front our services with RESTful interfaces. Here, the goal for me will be to provide details on the low-level and high-level inbound HTTP APIs within Akka. Although refactoring later on will use the high-level routing, DSL-based API, it's important to understand what's happening under the hood with the low-level API first.

Before jumping into descriptions of the low and high-level APIs, it's important to understand the different modules that make up Akka HTTP. These modules are as follows:

- `akka-http-core`: This is where the code for the low-level server and for the client-side HTTP API lives.
- `akka-http`: This is where the high-level inbound HTTP API lives with things such as the routing DSL, marshalling, and compression/decompression included.
- `akka-http-testkit`: This is where the testing infrastructure-related code lives, with utilities to test your server-side HTTP interfaces.
- `akka-http-spray-json`: This is where some predefined marshalling/unmarshalling-related code for requests and responses lives, built on top of the spray-json library. We will switch over to using this JSON library, from json4s, during the refactoring.
- `akka-http-xml`: This is similar to `akka-http-spray-json` but for XML-based marshalling/unmarshalling. As we will be building around JSON as a data format, we will not be using this library.

For the first part of this section, we will use concepts that come from the `akka-http-core` and `akka-http` modules. When I introduce concepts from another module, I will be sure to mention which dependencies you will need to include in your `sbt` file. For now, those two dependencies are as follows:

```
"com.typesafe.akka" %% "akka-http-core" % akkaVersion
"com.typesafe.akka" %% "akka-http-experimental" % akkaVersion
```

As the time of writing, the `akka-http` module is still carries the experimental designation while the `akka-http` module does not. That's because the high-level API, with items such as the routing DSL, are still in a bit of flux as the Akka team tinkers to get things right. When you use an API that's marked as experimental, you basically opt into dealing with potentially breaking changes as the experimental API continues to evolve. I would not interpret the experimental designation here as an indication that the library may go away, like Typed Channels did. It's just more of an indication of potentially high volatility in the API until it gets completely locked down. That module is here to stay and ready for you to build on top of.

Using the low-level server-side API

As part of the `akka-http-core` module, the Akka team has provided a fully asynchronous, reactive-streams compliant, HTTP/1.1 server that leverages Akka Streams. Being a fully HTTP/1.1 compliant server, it has support for all of the features within that specification, including things such as Websockets, optional SSL/TLS encryption, HTTP pipelining, and HTTP streaming via **chunking**. The design and features of this low-level server were very much focused on just being an HTTP/1.1 server, which includes the following:

- Connection management
- Parsing and rendering of messages and headers
- Timeout management for requests and connections
- Response ordering in order to implement transparent pipelining

To put it another way, this low-level server is really just focused on the basics of serving HTTP requests. Any helpful functionality around complex routing and creating RESTful interfaces will be contained in the high-level API, which is in the `akka-http` module. This doesn't mean that you can't use this API directly. It's fully capable of having HTTP APIs built on top of it; it just doesn't have some of the bells and whistles that the high-level API has.

As this API serves as the core server functionality regardless of which API you choose to use, it's important to understand its inner workings a little. This will allow you to understand how your requests are being handled under the hood. Over the next few sections, we'll go over the key aspects of the low-level API in an effort to understand how it works.

Akka Streams in the low-level API

As mentioned previously, Akka Streams is at the heart of what the low-level server-side API is doing. Refer to the *Streams and TCP* section in Chapter 6, *Going with the Flow with Akka Streams*, where we used Akka Streams to handle binding a local TCP socket and handling inbound connections. In that model, we had a Source[IncomingConnection] that was sending IncomingConnection downstream each time someone external connected into our server. The Akka Streams-based model in the low-level API will be very similar to that TCP server model.

Like in the TCP model, binding an HTTP socket with the low-level API will also return a Source[IncomingConnection], just a slightly different IncomingConnection though, setup for handling HTTP requests. Then, to handle each incoming request, you will need to provide a Flow[HttpRequest, HttpResponse, _], which will take the inbound HttpRequest, handle it, and turn it into an HttpResponse that will be sent back to the caller. That Akka Streams-based concept of HttpRequest in and HttpResponse back out is the foundation of how the low-level API works.

Handling requests with the low-level API

Now that we know the Akka Streams based structure of the low-level API, let's dive into how you will start up an HTTP server and handle requests with it. First, we'll take a look at the code required to start up your server, which is shown as follows:

```
implicit val system = ActorSystem()
implicit val materializer = ActorMaterializer()
val serverSource: Source[Http.IncomingConnection,
Future[Http.ServerBinding]] = Http().bind(interface = "localhost", port =
8080)
```

As the low-level API uses Akka Streams, we will need both an ActorSystem to run the stream's actors in and a Materializer to materialize the flows. We will set these two requirements up with the first two lines of code in this example. Then, the code will bind the local server socket by first getting the HttpExt extension class via Http.apply and then calling the bind method in it. We will pass in both the address to bind to (localhost here) as well as the port to bind to (8080) when calling the bind method.

There are a bunch of other arguments that can be supplied to the bind call to handle things such as socket options and other connection handling-based configuration. You should take a look at the full-method description for that call in the API documents if you are interested in knowing the other available options.

The result of the call to `bind` is a `Source` that will emit `IncomingConnection` elements downstream, one for each connection to the server. This `Source` will materialize to a `Future[ServerBinding]` that can be used to unbind the server if necessary. But, as it stands right now, incoming connections will not start being handled, and that's because we have yet to hook this `Source` into a `Sink` and materialize the resulting `RunnableGraph`. This is a requirement to kick off the inbound connection-handling logic. The code to do that is as follows:

```
val sink = Sink.foreach[Http.IncomingConnection]{ conn =>
  . . .
}
val bindingFut = serverSource.to(sink).run
```

Here, we will set up a `Sink.foreach` to drain the incoming connections into. This `Sink` will iterate through each incoming connection, allowing you to handle the request that comes from it, which is currently not shown in this example. Then, we will connect the `Sink` to our `Source` and materialize it with a call to run. This will return the materialized value from the `Source`, which is a `Future[ServerBinding]`, and start up the flow to handle the incoming connection requests.

Inside the `foreach` handling block on the `Sink`, you will have access to each incoming connection. It's here that you can attach handling to that connection to allow you to service its `HttpRequest` and return an `HttpResponse`. There are three possible methods on the `InboundConnection` that allow you to provide handling logic to service the request. The first of those methods is called `handleWith[Mat]`. This method takes a single argument of the type `Flow[HttpRequest, HttpResponse, Mat]` that acts as a transformation flow, going from an `HttpRequest` to an `HttpResponse`. An example of using that method to handle a connection is shown as follows:

```
val flow =
  Flow[HttpRequest].
    map{ req =>
      HttpResponse(StatusCodes.OK)
    }
conn.handleWith(flow)
```

In this example, regardless of what the request is—method type, URL, and so on—I'm just returning a 200 OK status. It's not a very real-world example, but it at least shows the concept of using a map operation to transform the incoming HttpRequest to an HttpResponse. In fact, since mapping a request to a response is probably the most common flow built to handle a connection, there is a helper method on InboundConnection called handleWithSyncHandler to do the flow part of the work for you. To use that method, all you will need to pass in is a function of type HttpRequest => HttpResponse, which represents the mapping operation. The preceding example, simplified to use that method, is as follows:

```
conn.handleWithSyncHandler{ request =>
  HttpResponse(StatusCodes.OK )
}
```

This type of handling is synchronous in how it services the request. If you do anything of substance when servicing a request, such as looking up data in some data store, and you want to be nonblocking, then you'll have to switch over to the asynchronous-based handling method. That method is called handleWithAsyncHandler, and it takes a function argument with the signature HttpRequest => Future[HttpResponse], and also an Int representing the level of parallelism to use in the processing, which defaults to 1. Under the hood, this method creates a flow that does a mapAsync operation instead of the normal map operation, hence the required input for parallelism. An example of using this method to asynchronously service a connection is shown as follows:

```
conn.handleWithAsyncHandler{ request =>
  val fut = talkToDatabase()
  fut.map{dbentity =>
    val respEntity =
    HttpEntity(ContentTypes.`application/json`,
    s"""{"id": ${dbentity.id}}""")
    HttpResponse(StatusCodes.OK, entity = respEntity)
  }
}
```

The HttpRequest class is a case class, as are the other compound fields on it, so it's possible to build out some detailed match statements to represent how you want to handle all kinds of requests. With a little bit of utility/glue code, it will certainly be possible to build out RESTful interfaces on top of the low-level API. The kinds of matching and handling will look very similar to the current unfiltered RESTful API that we have in the bookstore app. I still lean towards the high-level API as it's far more elegant, and allows for less repetition in the handling, but if you prefer it, you can definitely build on top of the low-level API instead.

Controlling parallelism within your server

If you build out an HTTP server that can only handle one request at a time, in a serial fashion, it won't be very useful in real-world request handling. You need to be able to handle multiple requests at a time, in parallel, to give you the kind of throughput and lower latency needed to serve your user's requests. Thankfully, Akka HTTP supports the ability to parallelize your inbound request handling, giving you two separate control mechanisms to do so.

The first technique you can use to control parallelism is the ability to serve and handle multiple connections at once. As a connection's request comes in, we will give it its own handler flow, which will be processed asynchronously using the dispatcher tied to the `Materializer` in scope. This works great at handling requests in parallel, but what if you need to limit the total number of simultaneous open connections in an effort to prevent your server from being overloaded with requests?

If you want to limit the number of open connections within your server, you can set the config setting to `akka.http.server-max-connections`, which has a default value of `1024`. This setting will only come into play when you use the `bindAndHandleXXX` methods to set up your server-handling logic. If you use the lower-level bind call, then you will have to add throttling logic yourself by applying a combinator-like throttle to the flow that you pass into the call to bind. Doing so will apply back-pressure to the incoming connection flow, slowing the flow of the `InboundConnection` elements downstream into your handling logic.

The second way you can support parallelism with your Akka HTTP server is via HTTP pipelining. HTTP pipelining allows the client to send multiple requests on a single connection without waiting for the responses first. This technique is generally discouraged and is disabled by default by most browsers, but it's still fully supported via Akka HTTP. As this is another possible way that your sever can end up overloaded by requests, there are ways to limit and control it.

The first way to control pipelining is to set the config setting to `akka.http.server.pipelining-limit`. This setting carries an initial value of 16 and must be set to a value between 0 and 1024. This setting ensures that no more than that specified number of outstanding requests is passed into the per-connection handler flow.

The second way to limit pipelining is via the parallelism argument that is available on the `bindAndHandleSync` and `bindAndHandleAsync` methods. The default value for this setting is 1, which means that pipelining is disabled completely unless you supply an explicit value for it that is greater than 1. If you opt to use the lower-level `bind` or `bindAndHandle` instead, then you will need to apply back-pressure yourself by adding the appropriate combinator to the handling Flow. As it's possible for the config setting and the explicit parallelism to have different values, the Akka code will use the smaller of the two possible values when deciding how to limit pipelining on your flow.

Low-level server example

In order to better understand what you will need to do to service RESTful requests with the low-level API, I've created a simple example server to show that process. This example is to demonstrate the types of things you will need to do when using the low-level API to service requests against actors. The idea with this example is that we have an actor representing a data store for an entity called `Person`. We will then build an HTTP interface in front of that actor's functionality to add new `Person` entities and view all the `Person` entities. The definition for the `Person` entity and for the actor is as follows:

```
case class Person(id:Int, name:String)

object PersonDb{
  case class CreatePerson(person:Person)
  case object FindAllPeople
}

class PersonDb extends Actor{
  import PersonDb._
  var people:Map[Int, Person] = Map.empty

  def receive = {
    case FindAllPeople =>
    sender ! people.values.toList

    case CreatePerson(person) =>
    people = people ++ Map(person.id -> person)
    sender ! person
  }
}
```

There's nothing particularly complicated going on here. It's just an actor that contains an internal `Map`, which represents the data store of `Person` entities. In the real world, you'd more than likely use an external data store, but this will suffice for our little example app.

Next, we'll take a look at the outline for our server class, which is shown as follows:

```
trait MyJsonProtocol extends DefaultJsonProtocol {
  implicit val personFormat = jsonFormat2(Person)
}

object LowLevelHttpServer extends App with MyJsonProtocol{
  implicit val system = ActorSystem()
  implicit val materializer = ActorMaterializer()
  import system.dispatcher
  import akka.pattern.ask
  implicit val timeout = Timeout(5 seconds)

  val personDb = system.actorOf(Props[PersonDb])
  . . .
}
```

The `MyJsonProtocol` trait is something we need in order to use spray-json for the marshalling and unmarshalling of the JSON data for this app. It defines an implicit class `personFormat`—that knows how to map back and forth between JSON and our `Person` case class. If you're not familiar with spray-json, you should take a look at the API (`https:/ /github.com/spray/spray-json`) as we will be using it going forward in this chapter.

Then, we will set up our server class, mixing in the JSON protocol trait so that we will have access to its features. In the constructor for our server class, we will set up the necessary stuff to be able to bind and run our HTTP server. This includes creating an instance of the `PersonDb` actor to handle the requests.

The next thing to look at is the request-handling function to map from the inbound `HttpRequest` to the outbound `Future[HttpResponse]`. We'll take a look at this on a case-by-case basis so as to not show too much code at once. The first case is where we will handle the request to lookup all of the `Person` entities we have in the system, as shown in the following code:

```
val requestHandler:HttpRequest => Future[HttpResponse] = {
  case HttpRequest(GET, Uri.Path("/api/person"), _, _, _) =>
  val peopleFut =
  (personDb ? PersonDb.FindAllPeople).mapTo[List[Person]]
  peopleFut.map{ people =>
    val respJson = people.toJson
    val ent = HttpEntity(ContentTypes.`application/json`,
    respJson.prettyPrint )
```

```
          HttpResponse(StatusCodes.OK, entity = ent)
    }
    . . .
}
```

We're using basic pattern matching here to capture a request where the method is a GET request and the path is /api/person. If that's the case, then we will make a request to our db actor using ask. Then, we will map over the resulting Future, turning it into an HttpResponse using spray-json to build out the entity for that response.

The next case we can look at is where we are receiving a request to create a new Person entity. That case is as follows:

```
case HttpRequest(POST, Uri.Path("/api/person"), _, ent, _) =>
val strictEntFut = ent.toStrict(timeout.duration)
for{
  strictEnt <- strictEntFut
  person = strictEnt.data.utf8String.parseJson.convertTo[Person]
  result <- (personDb ? PersonDb.CreatePerson(person)).
  mapTo[Person]
} yield {
  val respJson = result.toJson
  val ent = HttpEntity(ContentTypes.`application/json`,
  respJson.prettyPrint )
  HttpResponse(StatusCodes.OK, entity = ent)
}
```

It's the same general idea as the first case. We're matching on the HTTP verb and on the URI path to figure out what action to take. One thing to pay attention to is the fact that the incoming request entity, our Person JSON, is itself a stream-based component, being a Source[ByteString, Any]. This allows you to read the request entity in a streaming fashion, and also allows the incoming entity to be nonstrict (not all in memory at once). This comes in handy when reading large or multipart requests where you don't get everything at once, and will have memory issues if you read it all into memory.

That's not the case here, so I'm forcing it to a strict representation where we will have all of the data in memory. Once we have the entity in memory, it can be parsed into a Person case class and then sent along to the PersonDb actor shown earlier. We will then take the response from the PersonDb actor, which is the input echoed back, and respond with it with the code looking similar to what we did in the lookup-request handling.

The last case to look at is the default handling when we don't match on either of the other two cases, as follows:

```
case req:HttpRequest =>
```

```
req.discardEntityBytes()
Future.successful(HttpResponse(StatusCodes.NotFound ))
```

The idea here is that, if we get a request that we don't have handling for, we will return a `404 Not Found` response. The important thing to note here is that we must explicitly drain the request entity's byte stream before responding, which we do with a call to `req.discardEntityBytes()`. If we don't consume the entity here, it will be seen as a back-pressure signal to the other side of the TCP connection, stalling the handling of that connection. The ability to back-pressure the other side, based on the consumption of the HTTP entity, is actually a very useful feature. It can be used as a technique to prevent our server from being overwhelmed with additional in-memory data when it is struggling to handle the request load it currently has. That's not what's happening here, but we will need to adhere to the rules of the system and discard the entity bytes so that our actions are not interpreted as a back-pressure signal.

The full code for this example server can be found under the `samples` project in the `chapter7` code distribution, in a file called `LowLevelHttpServer.scala`. If you want to play with the API a bit, you will need to first start up the server. Get into the `samples` project directory and open up the sbt shell. From there, you can execute the following command:

```
> run code.LowLevelHttpServer
```

Once the server is up-and-running, you can start sending requests to it. It's probably best to create a couple of `Person` entities first before looking them up. To create some `Person` entities, open up a command prompt and get into the `json` folder under the samples project-root directory. Once in there, you can execute the following two commands:

```
http POST :8080/api/person < person1.json
http POST :8080/api/person < person2.json
```

This will execute the `POST` request handling that we added to our API to add `Person` entities to the db actor. On success, you should see the same JSON that was sent in on the request echoed back on the response. Once you have created these two entities, you can look them back up with the following command:

```
http :8080/api/person
```

When you do that, you should see a response body that looks like the following code:

```
[
  {
    "id": 123,
    "name": "Chris Baxter"
  },
```

```
  {
    "id": 456,
    "name": "Jules Verne"
  }
]
```

This is about as far as we'll dive into the low-level server API. It's important to understand how it's set up, as the high-level routing DSL is built on top of it, but it's not a good choice for us to build our bookstore RESTful API around. It's too cumbersome and lacking in helpful features for us to build out an elegant API on top of it. If you have more interest in low-level APIs, then you should check out the low-level server-side API section of the Akka HTTP documentation. From here on, we will be discussing the high-level API with the intention of using it when refactoring the bookstore RESTful API.

Using the high-level server-side API

If you're building RESTful APIs with Akka HTTP, then you will more than likely be using the high-level API to do so. The high-level API builds upon the low-level API, adding enhancements such as a routing DSL and a path-matching system, things that were sorely missing in the low-level API. If you've used Spray before, a lot of this will seem familiar, as the high-level API is based on Spray's routing API.

I think, here, it's best to start with a side-by-side example, comparing high and low-level APIs and showing how much more convenient and elegant the high-level API is. I've taken the example server that was created in the previous section and adapted it to use the high-level API. Let's start by looking at the shell of the class, showing the class declaration, and what's going on in the constructor:

```
object HighLevelHttpServer extends App with MyJsonProtocol with
SprayJsonSupport {
  implicit val system = ActorSystem()
  implicit val materializer = ActorMaterializer()
  import system.dispatcher
  import akka.pattern.ask
  implicit val timeout = Timeout(5 seconds)
  . . .
}
```

The definition here is the same as what we did with the low-level server example. We will mix in the `MyJsonProtocol` trait so that we will have access to the JSON serialization formats for the `Person` case class. In the constructor, we will set up the same instances we did earlier as we still need an `ActorSystem`, a `Materializer`, and an implicit `ExecutionContext` in scope.

Next, let's take a look at the route definitions, as that's where things will start to look much different. Those route definitions are shown as follows:

```
import akka.http.scaladsl.server.Directives._
val routes:Route = {
  path("api" / "person"){
    get{
      val peopleFut =
      (personDb ? PersonDb.FindAllPeople).mapTo[List[Person]]
      complete(peopleFut)
    } ~
    (post & entity(as[Person])){ person =>
      val fut =
      (personDb ? PersonDb.CreatePerson(person)).mapTo[Person]
      complete(fut)
    }
  }
}
```

The first line in this example, where I'm importing everything under `akka.http.scaladsl.server.Directives._` is important as that's one way you can enable routing-DSL functionality (the other being mixing the `Directives` trait into your class). The routing DSL is made up of a bunch of implicits, and this is how you can bring them into scope. This import also makes all of the separate functional areas of directives-path matching, future handling, and so on available with a single import.

Under the `import` statement, I'm declaring my routing tree as being of type `Route`. This is a custom type that represents the function type `RequestContext =>` `Future[RouteResult]`. We'll delve into this structure a bit later; so, for now, just know that this route definition defines all of my possible matching scenarios and returns responses for each of them.

The first thing I will do to define my routes is use the `path` directive to match on the `/api/person` path for both of my possible route options. Directives are things you can apply to route definitions to do things such as matching on parts of the request, extracting params, and formulating the eventual response. We'll cover these in more detail later on in this chapter.

Using the `path` directive at a high level in my routing tree allows me to not have to repeat myself with the matching criteria throughout each specific request I want to handle, like I had to do with the low-level API. This hierarchical nature of the routing DSL, allowing you to define common matching criteria at a higher level and then nest specific criteria inside that section, is one of the biggest strengths of the high-level API.

The code body inside of the `path` directive represents additional matching criteria to check when we have a proper path match. The first case checked in there is to see if we have a GET request, via the `get` directive. If we do, then the code flow enters the body of that directive. In there, we will have a full match on a request that we know how to handle, and we can actually go about servicing the request. Here, we will send the request to our actor via ask and get a Future in return.

After making the request to the actor, I will apply the `complete` directive on the Future to build out my response based on the result of that Future. As we will have an implicit in scope, via `MyJsonProtocol`, which knows how to marshall the type of the Future (a `List[Person]`), we can neatly convert it to an `HttpResponse` via `complete`. I'll go over the marshalling magic here in a subsequent section.

If the request is not a GET request, then I will join in another set of criteria to check via the ~ operator, which is used for route concatenation. If the request is POST, then I will match on it via the `post` directive. Coupled with the check for a POST is a check to extract the body and parse it as a `Person` via the entity directive. By using the `&` operator on those two directives, they both must match (the AND condition) in order to enter the function body that follows. The entity directive will pass its extracted value into the resulting function when it matches, hence the person argument being passed in there. Once in that function body, we will call our actor, get the response, and complete the route, as we did with the GET request.

Once we have the routes defined, we will still need to bind to the local port and add the code to handle the incoming connections. For our high-level server example, that code looks like this:

```
val serverSource =
  Http().bind(interface = "localhost", port = 8080)
val sink = Sink.
  foreach[Http.IncomingConnection](_.handleWith(routes))
serverSource.to(sink).run
```

For the most part, this code is the same as what we performed previously with the low-level server example. The thing to pay attention to is the line where we are applying our route's definition to the handling of each inbound connection. The `handleWith` method on the `IncomingConnection` class takes a `Flow[HttpRequest, HttpResponse, _]`, but here we are using a `Route` as the input to that method. The reason why this works is that there is an implicit method in scope here that will call `Route.handlerFlow` to convert the `Route` into a conforming `Flow`. Under the hood, this method will create a `Flow`, which will use `mapAsync` with a parallelism of one to asynchronously handle the incoming request, using the `Route` supplied.

The code shown above to bind and handle connections is the long form in order to explicitly show the flow that gets created and run. That code could be cut down to a single line using `bindAndHandle` as follows:

```
Http().bindAndHandle(routes, "localhost", 8080)
```

So that's it. We have all the same logic we had with the low-level API example, but with considerably less code. The code is much more elegant too, as its nested structure is reflective of the types of checks and matching that is going on as the evaluation continues down into the tree. This full example can be found under the `samples` project in `chapter7`, in the `HighLevelHttpServer.scala` file. If you want to run this server and play around with it, you can first start it up by opening an sbt prompt in the `samples` project-root folder and running the following command:

```
> run code.HighLevelHttpServer
```

Once it's running, you can make the same HTTP requests used against the low-level server example as it responds to the same API.

Hopefully, this quick example shows the power of the high-level API. There's a lot more to learn though, so over the next few sections I'll break down the main functional areas of the high-level API. We will then use that information to refactor our bookstore endpoints to use Akka HTTP via the high-level API.

Completing, rejecting, or failing routes

When building out the high-level example in the previous section, the type we used to represent our different pieces of request matching/handling was a route. This type, which is really an alias for a function with the `RequestContext => Future[RouteResult]` signature, is the main building block of Akka HTTP's routing DSL. All of the structures that you build to handle requests, whether simple, single matching blocks or complex composed trees, are of this route type.

Each time your Akka HTTP server receives a request, it spins up an instance of `RequestContext` to represent that request. Then, it passes it into the top-level route that you passed into the `handleWith` for the `InboundConnection`. When a route receives a request via `RequestContext`, there are a few possible things that it can do to handle it. They are as follows:

- Accept it and complete it synchronously
- Accept it and handle it asynchronously by returning a `Future`

- Accept it and handle it asynchronously, returning a `Source` to support streaming data back to the caller
- Not accept it via rejection
- Fail it

If a set of matching directives hits on a request, it means that you found what you are looking for, so you can accept it and start the work to generate a response. When done, the route component that has accepted the request will call `complete(ToResponseMarshallable)` on `RequestContext`, passing something that can be turned into a `HttpResponse`. Calling the `complete` method will return a `Future[RouteResult]`, satisfying the right-hand side of our route function definition, which completes the request/response cycle.

The first scenario I listed accepting and completing a route is synchronous, and probably won't apply too much of our handling since we'll be using actors to handle requests asynchronously. Thankfully, there is a way to also accept a request and return a `Future` that, when completed, will be used to determine the `RouteResult` for that request.

If a route component sees a request and it does not match its given criteria, then that component can reject the request via a call to `requestContext.reject(Rejection*)`. This does not mean that the entire request itself has been rejected and thus, not handled. It just means that this individual route component does not handle it, and the request-processing logic should move on to the next possible route in the tree instead. The rejections added to the `RequestContext` will accumulate and can later be evaluated if the request is not handled by any route. The reject call will also return a `Future[RouteResult]`, satisfying the right-hand side of the `Route` function. We'll go over rejections in depth in a later section.

If, for some reason, a request needs to be failed by a route, that route can do so by either explicitly calling `fail(Throwable)` on the `RequestContext` or by throwing an exception somewhere in the handling logic. Like complete and reject, fail will also return a `Future[RouteResult]` to satisfy the right-hand side of the `Route` handling function.

The following diagram represents the above described flow that is taken when evaluating a request against the set of possible routes:

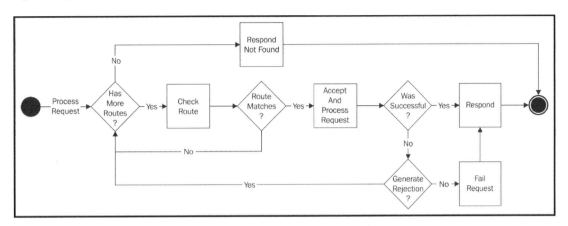

The RequestContext class

In the previous section, we talked about how the left-hand side of a `Route` handling function—the input—is of the `RequestContext` type. This class wraps the inbound `HttpRequest`, making it available to the routing directives so that they can see if they match against it. This class also exposes an `ExecutionContext` that can be used to schedule asynchronous work to service requests as well as `Materializer`, which was used to materialize and run the flow that is handling the connection. If you need to log messages when handling a route, the `RequestContext` also exposed a `LoggingAdapter` instance, which you can use.

Part of the logic in matching a request is determining whether the request-URI path matches any of the route definitions within the routing tree. As that tree is hierarchical, and you can nest individual components of the path as you work your way inward, something needs to keep track of what parts of the path remain unmatched. This is so that the inner path-based directives underneath a directive, such as `pathPrefix`, only needs to specify and check against what the remaining unmatched path is up to at that point. This unmatched path information is also something that is kept on the `RequestContext`.

The `RequestContext` class contains a bunch of methods to change its internal state. However, being a good functional construct, the class is immutable and any of those methods to change its internal state will return a copy of the instance with the change instead of truly mutating the internal state.

Building out a routing tree

One of the core concepts of building out your `Route` handling is the ability to nest and concatenate simple route definitions together, and building what is referred to as a routing tree. In fact, to build out more complex routes from simpler ones, there are three techniques that can be used:

- **Route transformation**: This is a nesting-based approach, where the handling of a request is delegated to an inner route, but only after manipulating or changing something about the request, the response, or both.
- **Route filtering**: This is another nesting technique where the handling will only be passed to the nested route(s) if some condition is satisfied. If not, the handling will be rejected by that outer route.
- **Route chaining**: This technique allows for the processing logic to try another route if the previous route rejects the request.

The first two items from the preceding list are handled by directives, which we will be covering in more detail in the next section. The last item is made possible with the ~ route-concatenation operator, which is enabled here by importing `akka.http.scaladsl.server.Directives._`.

When the request-handling logic is processing a request against your routing tree, it starts at the outermost directive and works its way inward, continuing to match until it either hits a rejection point (filtering) or it accepts the request against a particular route. This means that, when building your tree, you should start with the more specific routes first, and then let the logic fall into the default cases, if they exist, further down into the tree. To demonstrate how the handling logic will process a routing tree, consider the following numbered set of routes that you want to implement:

1. A GET request to `/api/person` with no additional path elements or query params.
2. A GET request to `/api/person` with a numeric-ending path element.
3. A GET request to `/api/person` with no numeric path element, but a query param called `foo`.
4. A POST request to `/api/person` with a JSON body.

If you want to build out a routing tree to handle that set of requirements, then it will need to look something like this:

```
pathPrefix("api" / "person"){
  get{
    path(IntNumber){ id =>
```

```
    //Route 2
      . . .
  } ~
  pathEndOrSingleSlash{
    parameter('foo){ foo =>
      //Route 3
        . . .
    } ~
    //Route 1
    . . .
  }
} ~
(post & pathEndOrSingleSlash){
  entity(as[Person]){ person =>
    //Route 4
      . . .
  }
}
}
```

What's represented here is itself a route, starting with the `pathPrefix` directive at the very top of this tree. It's built out by nesting some directives inside of each other and adding the filtering concept to the tree. It also uses the chaining concept by concatenating routes together so that the processing logic has another sub-route to evaluate when it's in a particular level of the tree. These two concepts together allow me to build out a tree that can handle the requirements that were given to me.

When a request is processed against this tree, the first check is that it has a root URI path of `/api/person`. If so, the processing logic is allowed to enter into the body of the `pathPrefix` directive. Once inside there, the logic will check the request method to see if it's a GET or not, via the `get` directive. If so, it can start to evaluate which of the three possible GET request types it has.

If the path ends in an `Int` number, then we have the route shown in step 2 from our requirements. If not, that route rejects the request and then, via route chaining, with the `~` operator, we will move on and check if we have the `foo` param on the request, which will be the route shown in step 1. If not, we will fall into the default logic for a GET to that path, which is the route shown in step 3. Note that, here, we had to define the more specific criteria first, the ones that looked for things above and beyond a GET to `/api/person`, before allowing the request to hit the more general handling for that method and path.

On thing to note with this example is that, when using the `parameter` directive, I'm representing the parameter name as a Scala Symbol (denoted by the single quote preceding the parameter name). Symbols will perform very fast comparisons by doing a simple object reference equality check (via `eq`). You can use a String for that directive instead, but it's not a guarantee that a repeated String is properly interned by the JVM and therefore, comparing them may require checking character by character. Using a Symbol here is not a requirement, but it's a good performance optimization, especially for repeated parameter names and routing trees with lots of parameter name checks in them.

Using directives to build your routing tree

Within Akka HTTP's routing DSL, directives are the core building blocks that allow you to define your complex routing structures. It's the combination of a set of directives that equates to an individual route within your application. For instance, if you need to handle a GET request to the `/api/book` path that accepted a tag-query param, then that route can be defined as follows:

```
path("api" / "book"){
  get{
    parameter('tag){ tag =>
      //This is where your route is handled
      . . .
    }
  }
}
```

In order to properly define that route, I will need to use three separate directives: `path`, `get`, and `parameter`. So, it's the combination of those three directives that equals my route to fetch books by tag.

In general, directives conform to the following structure:

```
name(arguments){extraction =>
  //inner route
  . . .
}
```

A directive will always have a name and that name can optionally be followed by a list of arguments. Following the optional argument list is the nested body of the directive where any values extracted by the directive are made available for use. Inside that body, you can further nest additional directives.

At some point in the nesting, you will need to do something that will create the
`Future[RouteResult]` that is required to satisfy the right-hand side of the `Route`
function. Once you add that part, via one of the `RouteDirectives` such as complete or
reject, then you have fully defined a route within your routing tree.

Directives can be used to perform a whole bunch of common operations on request. For
instance, you can use directives to transform the `RequestContext` and the information it
wraps, before passing control onto the inner routes. So, if you want to do something, such
as always switching `PUT` requests to `POST` requests, you can apply the `mapRequest`
directive as follows:

```
put{
  mapRequest(_.copy(method = HttpMethods.POST)){
    . . .
  }
}
```

Now, any nested directive and route-handling logic inside of the `mapRequest` block will
see the request as being a `POST` instead of a `PUT`.

You can also use directives to filter the `RequestContext`, only passing along to the inner-
handling logic, rejecting it otherwise, if some condition is met. We've seen this concept in
action along with previous examples showing the `path` or `get` directives. These directives
look at information on the request such as the URI path and request method, respectively,
and will reject it for that route if there is not a match.

Another thing you can use directives for is to perform an extraction and make that
information available to the inner-route logic. For example, if you need the full
`HttpRequest` inside of some inner-route handling logic, then you can do so using the
`extractRequest` directive like this:

```
extractRequest{ request =>
  //Do something with request here
  . . .
}
```

If you need to modify the response by adding something to it before it is ultimately sent
back to the caller, then you can use directives for that too. An example of this is to add a
custom-response header via `respondWithHeader`, which is shown as follows:

```
path("api" / "book"){
  get{
    respondWithHeader(RawHeader("X-Foo", "bar")){
      complete(OK, "hello")
    }
```

```
    }
  }
```

The last type of thing that you can do with directives is use them to complete a route definition by supplying the `Future[RouteResult]` to do so. This can be done by completing, rejecting, or failing a request, via `complete`, `reject`, or `fail`, respectively.

 There are many predefined directives within Akka HTTP. You should peruse the full set at the following link to get a feel for the kinds of things you can do when building your routing tree: http://doc.akka.io/docs/akka/current/scala/http/routing-dsl/directives/alphabetically.html.

Composing directives together

In the previous section, you learned that you can compose directives together through nesting. When you nest directives, all of the criteria through the nesting must be met for a route to be activated. Consider the following example from the previous section again:

```
path("api" / "book"){
  get{
    parameter('tag){ tag =>
      //This is where your route is handled
      . . .
    }
  }
}
```

In this example, we will need a GET request to the URI path, /api/book, which has a tag-query param on it. This nested structure is one way to convey that three-part requirement. There is another way, via the & operator, which allows us to compose directives together with the AND semantics across the directives. Using the & operator, we can rewrite the preceding example as follows:

```
(path("api" / "book") & get & parameter('tag)){ tag =>
  //This is where your route is handled
  . . .
}
```

This is semantically the same as the longer, nested form preceding it. All the three directives must match in order for the logic to enter the body.

You can also combine multiple directives together which, each extract a value. When you do so, the extracted value that gets passed into the inner route is a tuple with both of the extracted values. So, for example, if you want to extract a header value and extract a parameter, you can do so, as follows:

```
(headerValueByName("X-Foo") & parameter('bar)){(foo, bar) =>
    . . .
}
```

You can combine any number of extracting directives together, up to the 22 limit imposed by Scala for tuples.

If you find that you are commonly combining the same few directives together, and using them in your routing tree, you can get a good reuse by assigning the combined directives to a named `val` and then reusing it within your tree. Using the preceding example, we can create a new named directive, as follows:

```
val fooHeaderAndBarParam =
headerValueByName("X-Foo") & parameter('bar)
```

All we are doing here is setting up a new directive that is the combination of those other two. It's not being used yet as it's not part of a routing tree and is therefore not yet being applied. Then, we can plug this new directive into our routing tree, as follows:

```
fooHeaderAndBarParam{ (foo, bar) =>
    . . .
}
```

If you want to use the OR behavior, as opposed to AND, across two or more directives, then you can use the | operator instead of the & operator. This operator can be useful in eliminating duplication within your tree where you have multiple possible filter criteria funneling into the same route-handling logic. For example, say you had one URI path that you used to support, and then you changed it somewhere along the way, but you still wanted to support the old path for backwards compatibility. Without using the | operator, your code will look something like this:

```
path("oldpath"){
  get{
    val fut = (actor ? message).mapTo[Foo]
  }
} ~
path("newpath"){
  get{
    val fut = (actor ? message).mapTo[Foo]
```

```
    }
  }
```

There's clear duplication in that tree section, and something like this is a good case to use the | operator, which will shrink that code sample down to the following:

```
  (path("oldpath") | path("newpath")){
    get{
      val fut = (actor ? message).mapTo[Foo]
    }
  }
```

As with the & operator, you can assign multiple directives combined via | to a val and then reuse them anywhere in your routing tree. There is, however, a key difference between using & and | that you should be aware of. When using the & operator, each directive you combine will contribute its extracted type, if it has one, to the final tuple value that is passed into the inner route. As combining with & only has the possible effect of adding a tuple slot, there is no requirement for the combined types to be of the same produce or the same extracted type. So, with &, I can easily do something like this:

```
  (path("somepath" / IntNumber) & get & parameter('foo)){(i,f) =>
    . . .
  }
```

Here, I'm combining a directive that extracts an Int (path), a directive that extracts nothing (get), and a directive that extracts a String parameter. This code compiles, and the combined directive will produce a Tuple2[Int,String]. If we try the same example with the | operator in place of the & operator, it will not compile. That's because, when using | operator, all of the directives that you combine must be of the same type. In this example, we have a Directive1[Int], a Directive0, and a Directive1[String]. As those three types are different, you cannot combine them via |. If the types do match, then you can use the | to combine them, as the following example shows:

```
  (parameter('foo) | headerValueByName("X-Foo")){ param =>
    . . .
  }
```

Even though these are two different directives, because they both extract a String value (they are of type Directive1[String]), they can be combined together via |.

The most common mistake made when combining routes is to forget to chain separate routes together via the ~ operator. This code will still compile, but only the bottommost routes will be used as that is what's returned to the enclosing parent route as its child. Keep this in mind as the first thing to look at if you see certain routes not being matched on.

Marshalling and unmarshalling JSON with spray-json

Akka HTTP has a rather sophisticated marshalling and unmarshalling infrastructure that allows you to convert to and from higher-level representations of your wire-data format, such as JSON, XML, and so on. There are a lot of low-level constructs and processes there, which we won't be covering directly. This section will be at a higher level, showing you how to use spray-json within your routes to convert request and response data to and from JSON. If you are interested in that lower-level stuff, check out the following links to view Akka's documents on marshalling and unmarshalling:

- http://doc.akka.io/docs/akka/current/scala/http/common/marshalling.html
- http://doc.akka.io/docs/akka/current/scala/http/common/unmarshalling.html

The spray-json library is a standalone JSON-processing library developed by the team at Spray.io. This is the library we will use as we move forward within the bookstore app for JSON handling related to inbound and outbound HTTP requests. It's a very good library in terms of features and performance, and it plugs very nicely into Akka HTTP, which is really helpful. In order to use spray-json with Akka HTTP, you will need to include the following dependency in your sbt build files:

```
"com.typesafe.akka" %% "akka-http-spray-json-experimental" %  akkaVersion
```

This module includes the code that is required to use spray-json for both marshalling and unmarshalling JSON, and will automatically pull in spray-json as a transitive dependency.

Once you have the correct dependency setup, you will need to go about defining the spray-json specific formats for whatever types you need to convert to and from JSON. This is already something we did when developing the low and high-level server examples, but I didn't spend any time explaining how everything worked. Let's take a look at the JSON protocol class that we created for those servers and dissect how it all works with Akka HTTP:

```
import akka.http.scaladsl.marshallers.sprayjson.SprayJsonSupport
import spray.json._
```

```
case class Person(id:Int, name:String)
trait MyJsonProtocol extends SprayJsonSupport with  DefaultJsonProtocol{
  implicit val personFormat = jsonFormat2(Person)
}
```

The first important thing to do in order to use spray-json is to add an import for `spray.json._` into whatever Scala file you are adding your JSON formatting code to. This will pull in all of the necessary implicit goodies from spray-json, allowing you to easily define your formatting classes.

The next thing to do is to define a construct-class, trait, or object to store your JSON formatting definitions. Here, I've chosen a trait called `MyJsonProtocol` that I plan to mix into my route-definition classes. This trait is set up to extend from two other traits that will give it the functionality required to use for marshalling/unmarshalling in Akka HTTP.

The first of those traits is `SprayJsonSupport`, which is on the Akka side of things. This trait provides a bunch of implicit methods to convert spray-json `RootJsonWriter` and `RootJsonReader` instances into Akka's `ToEntityMarshaller` and `FromEntityUnmarshaller` respectively. This means that as long as you have your spray-json format instances in scope, they can be implicitly converted into either an unmarshaller to read a request entity, or into a marshaller to write a response entity.

The second of those two traits is `DefaultJsonProtocol`, which is on the spray-json side of things. This trait pulls in all of the implicit conversions that allow you to build your JSON format instances and to have them treated as both `RootJsonReader` and `RootJsonWriter`. Combined with `SprayJsonSupport`, this functionality gives you the ability to define very simple JSON format classes and then have them seamlessly plug into the Akka HTTP marshalling/unmarshalling frameworks.

Once we have that trait defined, we can define a class where the routes will be defined, mixing in that trait so that we have access to the implicits and formats that are required to plus into the marshalling and unmarshalling frameworks for Akka HTTP. Once we do that, we're in the business of defining routes that will leverage the marshalling and unmarshalling features via spray-json. If we want to define a route that unmarshalled to a class instance that is supported by the `MyJsonProtocol` trait, then it's as simple as this:

```
entity(as[Person]){ person =>
  . . .
}
```

Here, we're using both the `entity` directive and the `as` directive to read and unmarshall the request entity into our `Person` case class. The `entity` directive accepts an instance of `Unmarshaller[HttpRequest, T]` that will be used to perform the unmarshalling from the request into the type `T`, which, in this case is `Person`. This argument is supplied by the `as` directive, which has a requirement to have an implicit `FromRequestUnmarshaller[T]` in scope in order to be used. Thankfully, this implicit is available via our `MyJsonProtocol` trait, so there's nothing more we need to do to get this to work.

When we need to marshal instances of `Person` into a response entity, we can also do so pretty easily thanks to all of the functionality brought in via `SprayJsonSupport`. One such way of responding and leveraging the marshalling framework to build the response entity is shown as follows:

```
val peopleFut:Future[List[Person]] =
(personDb ? PersonDb.FindAllPeople).mapTo[List[Person]]
complete(peopleFut)
```

The magic here is done via the `complete` directive, with a little help from the implicits made available from the `MyJsonProtocol` trait. The `complete` directive has the following signature:

```
def complete(m: => ToResponseMarshallable):StandardRoute
```

So, that means, in order to use `complete`, we will need to pass it a function that will return an instance of `ToResponseMarshallable`. In this example, all we are passing in is a `Future[List[Person]]` function, so there is obviously some implicit magic at work here. In fact, if you were to try and expand all of this functionality to understand the long-hand form of what's going on, it would look similar to the following code:

```
extractRequest{ request =>
  val trm = implicitly[ToResponseMarshaller[List[Person]]]
  val peopleFut =
  (personDb ? PersonDb.FindAllPeople).mapTo[List[Person]]
  val fut = for {
    people <- peopleFut
    resp <- Marshal(people).
    toResponseFor(request)(trm, system.dispatcher)
  } yield resp
  onComplete(fut){
    case util.Success(resp:HttpResponse) =>
    complete(resp)
    case util.Failure(ex) =>
    complete(StatusCodes.InternalServerError)
  }
}
```

In this more explicit code sample, we will get the Future from the actor request, and when that's completed, we will explicitly use the marshalling framework (and the implicit `ToResponseMarshaller[List[Person]]` function brought into scope via `MyJsonProtocol`) to turn the `List[Person]` function into an `HttpResponse`, producing a new `Future` to hold that response. When the second Future is completed, we can leverage the `complete` directive, this time passing in a fully formed `HttpResponse` to send back to the caller. This is not exactly what will happen, but it's pretty close, and it shows just how much boilerplate is handled via all the implicit magic of the marshalling framework and `SprayJsonSupport`.

There are a lot of predefined implicits to convert different combinations of things such as status codes, strings, and so on, into a `ToResponseMarshallable` to meet the contract of the `complete` directive. If interested, you should take a look at the `PreDefinedToResponseMarshallers` trait within the Akka API documents to get a better understanding of the different ways you can communicate a response to the framework code.

Handling rejections within your routes

When you build out your full routing tree, you will typically be composing directives together, via nesting or the & operator, to create individual route definitions and then chaining individual route definitions together via the ~ operator. As the Akka HTTP framework starts to process a request against your tree, it will evaluate its way down from the top of the tree, looking for a full match where the request is accepted against all filtering directives. If that happens, the route can be successfully completed and a response is generated for the caller.

This process works great when you have a match on the first set of directives evaluated, but what happens when you don't? If the processing logic finds a directive, say a `get`, but the request is a POST, what happens? If the processing logic were to stop there and send an exception back to the caller indicating a nonmatch (404), then that will be a problem. You need the processing logic to continue on and start to evaluate the next route definition chained into the tree, and this is where rejections come in.

Each time the request-processing logic hits a filtering directive that is not a match for the request, that directive will reject the request. This means that the directive is calling `requestContext.reject`, producing `Future[RouteResult]`, which is required to complete that route definition. In this case, the `RouteResult` will be of type rejected, which is a signal to the processing logic that it needs to continue on and try the next route defined in the tree.

Rejections will accumulate on the `RequestContext` as they are encountered. If the request cannot be handled at all, then all of those accumulated rejections will be available to evaluate when deciding on how to respond to the caller. When you want to handle the accumulated rejections, possibly turning them into a response, then you do so with `RejectionHandler`, which has the following definition:

```
trait RejectionHandler
  extends (immutable.Seq[Rejection] => Option[Route])
```

So, by this definition, `RejectionHandler` is essentially a function that can optionally convert a sequence of `Rejection` instances into a final `Route`. If the logic wants to handle the accumulated rejections, then it can return a `Some` wrapping a response to send back to the caller. If it does not want to handle the accumulated rejections, then it can return a `None`, which will cause the processing logic to continue on, unless it's already at the very top of the routing tree.

Rejections will accumulate within the process of looking for a matching route, but there are also points where some of the accumulated rejections will be cancelled when certain filtering directives let the request pass through. Consider the following route snippet:

```
path("book"){
  get{
    . . .
  } ~
  post{
    parameter('foo){ foo =>
      . . .
    }
  }
}
```

As the request-handling logic starts to process an inbound request against this tree, it'll first check if the request is a GET. If it's not, then a `MethodRejection` will be added to the `RequestContext`. Then, the processing logic will see if the request is a POST. If it is a POST, then the logic will check if the `foo` query parameter exists on the request. If not, then the only exception that will end up bubbling up to `RejectionHandler` is a `MissingQueryParamRejection`. So, what happened to the previously added `MethodRejection`? When the `post` directive accepted the request, it cancelled any previously encountered `MethodRejection` instances, removing them from the `RequestContext`. This is something to be aware of when thinking about rejections within your routing tree.

You can include `RejectionHandler` anywhere in your routing tree via the `handleRejections` directive. This directive has the following signature:

```
def handleRejections(handler:RejectionHandler)
```

If you have the need, you can define multiple distinct `RejectionHandler` instances and use them at different levels in your routing tree via `handleRejections`. Consider the following example:

```
handleRejections(topLevelHandler){
  pathPrefix("api"){
    path("book"){
      get{
        . . .
      }
    } ~
    path("order"){
      handleRejections(orderRouteHandler){
        (get & parameter('tag)){ tag =>
          . . .
        }
      }
    }
  }
}
```

In this example, we have a top-level, default `RejectionHandler` at the very top of the routing tree. This is the catch-all `RejectionHandler` that will be invoked if a specific rejection is not handled elsewhere in the routing tree. Then, we nest a lower-level `RejectionHandler` underneath the `order` path, which is meant to transform rejections from that path. For instance, if the request is GET to the `/api/order` but it does not contain the `tag` parameter, then the parameter directive there will produce a `MissingQueryParamRejection`.

At this point, the closest parent, `RejectionHandler`, where the rejection was generated, will have a chance to handle that rejection. In this case, that's the `RejectionHandler` represented by `orderRouteHandler`, the definition of which is not shown in this example. If the handler does handle that specific rejection, then it can produce a response that will complete the route and end the handling for that request. If not, then the rejection will just be added to the `RequestContext` and can potentially be handled by another parent `RejectionHandler` set up further up the tree. In the case of this example, that's the `RejectionHandler` represented by `topLevelHandler`. As this handler is at the very top of the routing tree, it won't be invoked until the entire set of possible routes is tried and none of them accepted the request.

Regardless of whether or not you add explicit `RejectionHandler` instances into your routing tree, there is always a default implicit one there that acts as the topmost handler of rejections. This means that, if you are okay with the behavior of the default rejection handler, then you don't need to add any additional rejection handling into your tree. You can, however, override this default handler by plugging in your own custom one, if you want to control the top-level rejection handling behavior.

To understand how this works, you will first need to look at the definition of `RouteResult.route2HandlerFlow`, which is the implicit method that turns your route into the Flow the low-level API needs. That method has the following implicit input required on it:

```
rejectionHandler: RejectionHandler = RejectionHandler.default
```

So, when `RouteResult.route2HandlerFlow` is implicitly invoked, it looks for an implicit `RejectionHandler` in scope to use as the top-level handler. If it does not find one, it falls back to using `RejectionHandler.default`.

Building a custom RejectionHandler

So far, I've talked about how to include a `RejectionHandler` in your tree, but I've yet to discuss how you can go about creating that `RejectionHandler`. To create a `RejectionHandler`, Akka HTTP has a builder-like API that allows you to specify handling by chaining together one of the following three methods—`handle`, `handleAll`, and `handleNotFound`. An example of building a `RejectionHandler` using these methods is shown as follows:

```
RejectionHandler.newBuilder.
handle{
  case AuthorizationFailedRejection =>
  complete(Unauthorized, "You are not allowed!!!")
}.
handle{
  case MissingQueryParamRejection(p) =>
  complete(BadRequest, s"Param ${p.name} is required!!!")
}.
handleAll[MethodRejection]{ rejs =>
  val allowed = rejs.map(_.supported.name)
  complete(MethodNotAllowed ,
  s"Bad request method, we only allow ${allowed.mkString}")
}.
handleNotFound{
  complete(NotFound,
  "Are you sure you know what you are doing?")
```

```
}
```

In this example, we are using all three possible methods to add rejection-handling behavior. The plan-handle method takes a `PartialFunction[Rejection,Route]`, and can be used to handle a single rejection type. The `handleAll` method takes a function accepting a `Seq[T]`, where `T` is a type of rejection, and returns a route. This can be used to handle a bunch of accumulated rejections of the same type. The `handleNotFound` method allows you to customize the response when the route processing logic does not find a match at all for the request that is supplied.

The most important thing to realize about how the rejection-handling behavior is built is that the order in which the different handle blocks are added reflects the order in which the rejections will be handled. Given that the handle takes a `PartialFunction[Rejection,Route]`, you might think you can just provide a bunch of case statements to that `PartialFunction` and just do all of their handling via a single call to handle. The problem with this is that the rejection-handling logic will pass the first rejection in the list and that will hit one of your case statements and will be handled, even though that may not be the rejection type you want to handle first. By adding separate handle calls in order, you get the ability to define the rejection-handling behavior by your explicit priorities as opposed to the potentially random order in which the rejections appear on the `RequestContext`. There will more than likely be certain rejections that you want to treat as the highest priority and thus be the ones that the error response will reflect, such as authorization-related ones, and chaining calls to handle is the correct way to make that happen.

Testing your routes with route TestKit

The routes that you define for your application contain logic in what they match and what they do as a result. As such, they are a type of component that should be tested. When the time comes to add unit testing to your routes, then you will use Akka's route TestKit to do so. In order to start using the route TestKit, you will need to add the following `import` to your `sbt` build file:

```
"com.typesafe.akka" %% "akka-http-testkit" % akkaVersion
```

Once you have that dependency set up, you are in business to start writing tests. In order to show the basic features of a route unit test, I have crafted a simple example test to test the routes defined in the `HighLevelHttpServer.scala` file in the `samples` code folder. This test class is called `HighLevelServerRoutesSpec.scala` and can also be found in the samples code distribution, under the `test` folder structure. I'll break down the main components of that test here, starting with the class declaration and some basic setup code, as follows:

```
class HighLevelServerRoutesSpec
extends WordSpec with Matchers
with ScalatestRouteTest with HighLevelHttpRoutes{

  val person1 = Person(123, "Chris Baxter")
  val person2 = Person(456, "Bill Williams")
  val people = List(person1, person2)

  def withProbe(f:TestProbe => Unit):Unit = {
    val probe = TestProbe()
    f(probe)
  }
  . . .
}
```

Here, I'm setting up a test class that extends from `ScalatestRouteTest`, which pulls in Akka's `RouteTest` trait and also brings in some facilities to test routes with `ScalaTest`. I'm also mixing in `HighLevelHttpRoutes` so I will have access to the routes definition that I will be testing. Inside the body of the test class, I will create a few `Person` instances that will be used throughout the tests. Then, I will set up a method that will be used, for each scenario, to inject a new `TestProbe` into that scenario. As these routes use an actor, we will need to stub that part out with a `TestProbe` so that we are only exercising the route logic as part of the test.

Once the basic setup stuff is in place, we can start adding route testing scenarios. The first scenario is for the GET request that these routes handle. The code for that scenario test is as follows:

```
"A GET request to the /api/person path" should{
  "make a FindAllPeople request to the personDb and respond with     the
results" in withProbe{ actorProbe =>
    val result =
    Get("/api/person") ~> routes(actorProbe.ref) ~> runRoute
    actorProbe.expectMsg(PersonDb.FindAllPeople)
    actorProbe.reply(people)
    check{
      status shouldEqual StatusCodes.OK
```

```
        responseAs[String] shouldEqual people.toJson.prettyPrint
    }(result)
  }
}
```

Inside the body of this test, the first thing that we will do is set up a GET request to the `/api/person` path. Then, we will apply this request to our route's definition from `HighLevelHttpRoutes` by using the `~>` operator. Then, we will take the result from that call and execute it by chaining to `runRoute`, again, via the `~>` operator. This will start up the process of the request execution, getting it to the point where it has sent a message to our probe. We will trap the result from running the request in a `val` called `result` so that we can use it later when performing out checks.

The next step, after kicking off the request-execution process, is to provide the stubbing for our actor `TestProbe`. Here, we will indicate that we expect to receive a `FindAllPeople` message. If we do get that message, we will send a reply that is a `List[Person]`, which is what the route expects in that situation. Once these two parts are done, the request is completed to the point where it's returning a response.

Once we have a response, we can go about the process of checking that result. We will do this by making a call to the `check`, which has the signature:

```
def check[T](body: => T):RouteTestResult => T
```

The `body` function argument that's passed into check is where you will perform any assertions against the result of running the route. There are a variety of things that you will be able to check in there, for instance, whether or not the request matched and was handled by the route, the status code of the response, and the body of the response. To see the full list of what's available to assert against in the `check` method, take a look at the route TestKit section under the *High-level Server-Side API* section of the Akka HTTP documents, the link to which is shown as follows: `http://doc.akka.io/docs/akka/current/scala/http/routing-dsl/testkit.html`.

The call to the `check` returns a function of type `RouteTestResult => T`, which, when applied, will run the assertions defined in body. I will apply that function immediately after calling `check` and passing in the `RouteTestResult` set up earlier by running the request. The majority of the test scenarios you write that involve an actor will have this same basic flow to them, which is as follows:

1. Set up a request and apply it to the route using the `request ~> route ~> runRoute` convention, holding on to that result for later use.
2. Stub out the interaction with the actor `TestProbe`.

3. Invoke `check` to build out a function to perform your assertions against the response.
4. Apply the route running `result` to the function returned from calling `check`.

I have also added a couple of test scenarios for the POST request that creates a new `Person`. I'll show one of those scenarios here as it's a bit different than the basic steps that I just described. This scenario is one where the request will not hit the actor because the route will reject it as it's missing a required piece of information. That scenario is shown as follows:

```
"reject the request when there is no json body" in   withProbe{
actorProbe =>
  Post("/api/person") ~> routes(actorProbe.ref) ~> check{
    handled shouldEqual false
    rejections should not be empty
    val rej = rejections.
    collect{case r:MalformedRequestContentRejection => r}
    rej should not be empty
  }
}
```

In this scenario, I'm making a POST request, which is one of the accepted method types, but I'm not supplying the required JSON request entity that the POST route needs. As such, this request will be rejected by the routes that are being tested against and it will not hit the actor `TestProbe`. As we don't need to add the logic to stub the `TestProbe` actor in between the request execution and the assertions, we can instead go right into the checking logic by chaining in the `check` call to the request-execution flow. Inside of the checking logic, I'm adding assertions to verify that the request was indeed not handled, as well as what kind of rejection it yielded. This convention will be what you use when you are writing tests that demonstrate rejections and do not involve stubbing of your `TestProbe`.

If you want to run this test, you can open an sbt prompt in the `samples` root folder in `chapter7`, and run the test action. As this is the only unit test in the project, it will be the only thing that will run. The output should be green, indicating that everything has passed successfully.

Invoking RESTful APIs with Akka HTTP

We've spent quite a bit of time, up to this point, discussing how to build RESTful interfaces to support receiving inbound external requests to delegate to your actors. Now, we'll flip things around and talk about how we can make those external calls to a RESTful API using Akka HTTP. You can use this approach if you need to consume some external service over the internet, such as our dummy credit card charging service in the bookstore app, or to invoke your own internal APIs if you go with a microservices-like approach in your infrastructure.

Over the next few sections I'll break down the main features of Akka's client-side HTTP functionality so you will understand the main usage patterns for that library. Then, you can use this knowledge to remove dispatch from the bookstore code base and replace it with client-side Akka HTTP.

Client-side Akka HTTP and streams

Like the server-side API, the client-side API for Akka HTTP is built on top of Akka Streams. This means that all of the wonderful features of streaming and back-pressure are available when you use Akka HTTP to consume HTTP interfaces. Regardless of what connection model you choose (Connection-Level, Host-Level, or Request-Level), the basic idea is that you will be pumping in `HttpRequest` instances via a source; they will flow through a connection Flow that will execute them against the desired host and transform them into `HttpResponse`, and then those responses will flow into whatever `Sink` you attach into the flow. So, from a code perspective, those steps look something like this:

```
val respFut =
requestSource.
via(connectionFlow).
runWith(responseSink)
```

In this example, I will execute a request, or multiple requests, against a host via its connection flow, and then collect the response or responses and expose it/them as a Future via the materialized value of `Sink`. This is, of course, a very simplified example, and one will normally have additional steps in the data flow, but it shows the high-level basics of all outbound requests.

Consuming the response entity

Just like the server-side API and the request entity, the entity tied to `HttpResponse` from a request is streaming in nature, being represented by `Source[ByteString,Any]`. This allows for things such as chunked responses, where the initial response will not contain the entire payload data yet. And, just like in the server-side API, you must remember to consume the response entity or else you will back-pressure the underlying TCP connection. In the case of pooled connections, this also means that you will leak that connection, making it no longer available to the pool as it will forever think it is still handling that request. This need will span all of the connection models. No mater which one you use, you will still have to make sure you always consume the response entity.

There are a couple of ways you can go about consuming the response entity that I'll describe here to you. The first such way, which is the safest way to actually read, not discard, the response, involves using built-in streaming facilities to read and handle the data bytes. Say, for instance, that you are using an API that allows long-running connections, and it keeps sending you JSON lines representing some data you care about, similar to the Twitter streaming API; this will be way too much data to read into memory, and on top of it, the stream itself is never really complete as the server keeps sending chunks of the response along. Handling a situation like that will look something like this:

```
Source.single(request).
  via(connectionFlow).
  flatMapConcat(_.entity.dataBytes).
  via(Framing.delimiter(ByteString("\n"), 1024)).
  map(parseLineAsJson).
  mapAsyncUnordered(16)(saveToDatastore).
  runWith(Sink.ignore)
```

In this example, after making the request and getting the response, we will take the entities data source and flatten it into the flow with `flatMapConcat`. At this point in the data flow, the elements that will start flowing downstream are those that are coming from the `Source[ByteString,Any]` that represents the response entity. Then, we will frame that response stream using the newline character to delimit each line of JSON. After that, we will parse the JSON and send it into some data store. This example will be a live stream as the server on the other side can keep sending response-entity data back to us and we will continue to consume it, until it ends of course. It will also be back-pressure-aware, in that if the data storage step starts to slow down, it can send a back-pressure signal upstream that will slow/stop the reading of additional bytes into memory from the TCP stream.

The earlier listed technique works well if you potentially have a lot of data to consume and you don't want to read it all into memory. But, sometimes you know the response won't be too large, and you will need to read the entire payload using some JSON parsing framework to convert it into a higher-level object structure. When this is the case, you can force the response entity to be strict, making sure all of the content is received (*total bytes received == content-length*) before continuing. Using this technique to handle a response entity will look something like this:

```
val fut:Future[SomeEntity] =
  Source.single(req).
  via(conn).
  mapAsync(1)(_.entity.toStrict(10 seconds).map(_.data)).
  map(parseAsJson).
  runWith(Sink.head)
```

Here, we are using the `toStrict` method on the response entity to force it into being entirely in memory. This method takes a timeout that indicates the maximum amount of time to wait before failing the resulting Future if we don't have all of the data yet. If the entity was strict already (unchunked), then this call to `toStrict` is essentially a no-op. Once we have the resulting `Future[HttpEntity.Strict]`, we will map over it and get the underlying `ByteString` so that we can parse it as JSON.

The first two techniques can be used when you actually care about the entity data being returned. However, there may be situations where you are getting a response entity but you don't care about reading it; maybe you just want to rely on the status code to indicate whether or not your request succeeded. If this is the case, you will still need to fully consume the response entity or else you will inadvertently back-pressure the underlying TCP connection and can potentially leak a pooled connection too. If you want to safely discard the response entity, then you can leverage the `discardEntityBytes` method on `HttpEntity`, as shown in the following example:

```
val fut =
  Source.single(req).
  via(conn).
runWith(Sink.head)

fut.onComplete{
  case util.Success(resp) =>
  resp.discardEntityBytes()
  . . .

  case util.Failure(ex) =>
  . . .
}
```

In this example, I'm capturing the response in a Future first. Then, when it's successful, I will make a call to discard the entity bytes before moving on with the rest of my logic. Semantically, this has the same effect as hooking up the entity's source to `Sink.ignore` and running the resulting graph. Either of these two actions will free up that connection and avoid back-pressuring the underlying TCP connection. Forgetting to do so can be a common gotcha that you should be aware of when using the client-side HTTP functionality in Akka HTTP.

Parsing the response entity as JSON

More often than not, you'll want to parse your response entities as JSON, converting them to some higher-level object representation. Thankfully, we can do this pretty easily by using the spray-json functionality, which we discussed earlier. Say we want to invoke the GET request from our example high-level server, and have the resulting Future be of type `Future[List[Person]]` as opposed to `Future[HttpResponse]` or `Future[ByteString]`. If we want to do something like that, then as long as we have `MyJsonProtocol` mixed in, the code will look like this:

```
val fut:Future[List[Person]] =
Source.single(HttpRequest(GET, "/api/person")).
via(connectionFlow).
mapAsync(1){ resp =>
  Unmarshal(resp.entity).to[List[Person]]
  }.
runWith(Sink.head)
```

Here, I'm leveraging the unmarshalling framework from Akka HTTP to do some of the heavy lifting to consume the response-entity stream and then convert it to the `Person` type. The call to the method works here because `MyJsonProtocol`, and its inherited `SprayJsonSupport` functionality, define a conversion from `ResponseEntity` to our custom `Person` type. With spray-json and Akka HTTP, reading your outbound calls' response entity as JSON and mapping to your custom classes are as simple as that.

Understanding the outbound connection models

When the time comes to make an outbound HTTP request using Akka HTTP, you will have three possible connection-handling models to choose from. Each of these different models has its purposes, and it's certainly possible that you may use two or even all three of them together at various places in your code. I'll do my best to highlight the differences between them and what situations they work best in. This should help you decide which of them suits your different needs.

The three outbound connection models that are supported in Akka HTTP are as follows:

- **Connection-level API**: This is a low-level model where you have full control over the opening and closing of individual connections
- **Host-level API**: This is a connection pool-based model where Akka HTTP will manage pools to individual host/port combinations
- **Request-level API**: This is a higher-level API than the host-level API, where you delegate all connection management to Akka HTTP

As you work your way up from the connection-level API through the host-level API and finally up to the request-level API, you will cede more and more control to the Akka HTTP framework. But in trading control over connection management, in return you will get a simpler API. Over the next few sections, I'll break down these outbound connection models in more detail, help distinguish them more, and show you what situations they most suitable for.

The connection-level API

The connection-level API is one where you have full control over the opening and closing of individual connections to the hosts where you are issuing your requests. There is no pooling here, so keep in mind that you will incur TCP connection overhead each time you connect to a host. Also, if you are using SSL, you will incur SSL handshake costs each time you connect.

This is a model you can consider using when you don't have high-volume or high-performance needs. I find that it's appropriate for low-volume calls that happen at fixed intervals, such as a timer that wakes up and hits an external service to fetch information. You don't need a pool in those situations, and if you are making other more high-volume calls to the same host/port combination, using pooling, you don't want these calls to eat up connections from those pools.

This is also the right model to use when you have long-running connections, where the service on the other side is streaming response-entity data back to you. That's another situation where pooling will run into issues as those long-running requests will be hogging the connections in the pool.

The way you get a connection using the connection-level API is via the `HttpExt` class, using a method called `outgoingConnection`, which has the following signature:

```
def outgoingConnection(host:String, port:Int = 80,
localAddress:Option[InetSocketAddress] = None,
setts:ClientConnectionSettings=ClientConnectionSettings(system),
```

```
    log:LoggingAdapter = system.log
    ):Flow[HttpRequest, HttpResponse, Future[OutgoingConnection]
```

Calling this method will return a `Flow` that can be used to make requests using the HTTP protocol to whatever host you supply. At a minimum, all you have to supply is a host, with the port being defaulted to `80`, which is the standard HTTP port. The `localAddress` argument can be used to determine which local address and port the outgoing connection will use, which defaults to `None`, and which will let the framework make that decision for you. The `ClientConnectionSettings` can be used to tune a bunch of settings related to the behavior of the connection. This includes things such as what socket options are used when connecting or how long to wait for a connection to be made before time-out. The `log` argument allows you to supply a `LoggingAdapter` for any sort of connection-based logging to use, which will default to the system's log if you don't explicitly supply one.

The `Flow` that is returned is set up to accept an `HttpRequest` from its upstream and output an `HttpResponse` to whatever is downstream from it. When this `Flow` is materialized, it will produce a `Future[OutgoingConnection]`, which can be used to obtain some information about the connection that was established. This `Flow` can be used as a blueprint and materialized multiple times, which each materialization producing a new outgoing connection to the host/port combo supplies.

An example of using the connection-level API to make an HTTP request is as follows:

```
val connFlow = Http().outgoingConnection("localhost", 8080)
val fut:Future[HttpResponse] =
Source.single(HttpRequest(HttpMethods.GET, "/api/person")).
via(connFlow).
runWith(Sink.head)
```

In this example, we'll make a GET request to the following URL: `http://localhost:88/api/person`.

We will start out by getting a reference to the `HttpExt` class by using the apply method on the `Http` object. Then, we will chain in a call to `outgoingConnection`, passing in localhost for the host and `8080` as the port to use. This produces the `Flow` that represents the outgoing connection we will use to make the request.

Once we have the connection `Flow`, we will need to set up the `Source` and `Sink` to hook up to it, making a fully runnable graph that represents the request/response cycle. The `Source` is set up as a single element `HttpRequest` that specifies `HttpMethods.GET` as the method and a relative URI of `/api/person` as the URI to use. The `Sink` is set up as `Sink.head`, meaning that we only care about capturing the first element that flows into the `Sink`. As we are only putting one element in, we should only get one element out, so this `Sink` should be appropriate.

With the `Source` and `Sink` set up, we can materialize and run the flow, starting with the `Source`, passing through the connection Flow and then ending up with the response going into the `Sink`. When we materialize and run the total flow, it produces a `Future[HttpResponse]` that, when complete, will hold the response from the remote host we communicated with.

 If you want to make an HTTPS request, the flow is similar, but you will be using `outgoingConnectionHttps` instead when getting the outgoing connection Flow.

In that example, we were only using a single outgoing request. If, instead, we decided to use a `Source` with multiple requests set up on it, then it's possible that those requests will be pipelined across the connection. The normal TCP process is that a request is sent and a response is received before another request is sent. In pipelining, multiple requests are sent before the initial response is received. Pipelining is not supported by all HTTP servers, so be aware of this effect when using the connection-level API. If you need to make multiple requests at once, then the host-level API may be better as it supports pooling, which should negate the need to pipeline multiple requests.

The host-level API

The host-level API is set up to alleviate the need for you to have to manage individual outgoing connections. The API does this by managing instances of connection pools that are keyed by the combination of host and port. Requests can then be made against this pool and the framework will figure out which underlying connection to actually use to execute each outgoing request.

As the connections are pooled, and therefore won't need to be explicitly opened and established for each request, you have significantly less connection overhead with this API. As such, it's a good choice for situations where you have a high volume of requests and/or you need low latency for the responses. It's also a good choice when you have to make multiple parallel requests to a single host and you don't want to rely on pipelining support on the host server.

If you want to get a connection pool to a specific host/port combination, then you do so by using the `cachedHostConnectionPool` method on the `HttpExt` class. That method has the following signature:

```
def cachedHostConnectionPool[T](host:String, port:Int,
settings:ConnectionPoolSettings = defaultConnectionPoolSettings,
log:LoggingAdapter = system.log)(implicit m:Materializer)
:Flow[(HttpRequest, T), Try[(HttpResponse, T)],
HostConnectionPool]
```

Similar to the `outgoingConnection` method, this one accepts a host and port to specify where to connect to. It also takes an instance of `ConnectionPoolSettings` that can be used to tune a whole bunch of settings related to the behavior of the pool, such as size and how it handles retries.

A key difference here is that this method takes a generic type `T` that is then incorporated into the upstream and downstream elements that the `Flow` works with. This type represents an identifier that must be tied to each request via a tuple that will subsequently also be tied to the response from that request, again via a tuple. With a pool, it's possible for you to send in multiple requests to the same pool at the same time, via a `Source` that emits multiple elements downstream. As each separate request will have its own call time associated with it, it's not guaranteed that the responses come out in the same order that the request went in. So, this arbitrary user-supplied identifier allows you to correlate what response came from which request.

Consider the following example, where we want to load a bunch of entities by their identifiers using a RESTful interface to do so:

```
val conn = Http().cachedHostConnectionPool[Int]("localhost", 8080)
val ids = List(1,2,3,4,5)
val fut:Future[Map[Int, HttpResponse]] =
Source(ids).
map(id => (HttpRequest(GET, s"/api/book/$id"), id)).
via(conn).
runFold(Map.empty[Int, HttpResponse]){
  case (map, (util.Success(resp), id)) =>
   map ++ Map(id -> resp)
  case (map, (util.Failure(ex), id)) =>
```

```
    //log error
    map
}
```

In this code example, we will start by getting a cached host-connection pool, specifying that we are using `Int` as the correlation-type identifier. After that, we will set up a `List` that contains the multiple IDs that we want to fetch. Taking that `List`, we will build a `Source` of type `HttpRequest, Int`, which represents each request that we want to make, and then the ID that will be used to correlate that request to a response. We will then run those requests through the connection pool and then use a fold on the `Sink` to collect our results. The final output we want to produce is a `Map[Int, HttpResponse]` where the key is the ID of the entity loaded and the value is the raw response for that request. As the pool framework sends the correlation ID back out to me as the output of the connection `Flow`, I can very easily associate this with the request that spawned it without having to parse the response body.

In this example, I'm not showing the code where the response entity is consumed. As it's not happening in the flow itself, you will need to explicitly do it for each response when the Future completes or you will leak connections in whatever pool is used.

Like the connection-level API, the host-level API also has a HTTPS variant, `cachedHostConnectionPoolHttps`, which you can use when making secure requests.

One important thing to note here is that the `Flow` returned by the `cachedHostConnectionPool` can be materialized multiple times, but it will always use the same underlying cached connection pool. This prevents multiples of the same host/port combination pools from being created for each materialization of that Flow. Also, multiple calls to `cachedHostConnectionPool` for the same host/port combo will use the same underlying pool instance.

The request-level API

The request-level API is built on top of the connection-level API, providing an even more simplified way to use host connection pools. It's designed to be really simple to use for very basic request and response cases. Aside from having a flow-based way to use it, it also has one that completely hides the details of using Akka Streams, instead being completely Future based. This Future-based API is a good one to consider using if you have really simple request/response semantics and you're always only making a single request at a time.

Let's start by first looking at the flow-based variant of this API. In this model, you will obtain the `Flow` that will execute your request/response cycle by calling the `superPool` method on the `HttpExt` class. The signature for that method is shown as follows:

```
def superPool(connectionContext: HttpsConnectionContext =
defaultClientHttpsContext, settings: ConnectionPoolSettings =
defaultConnectionPoolSettings,
log: LoggingAdapter = system.log)(implicit m:Materializer):
Flow[(HttpRequest, T), (Try[HttpResponse], T), NotUsed]
```

This method returns a `Flow` that essentially acts as a router, dispatching the request to whatever actual underlying HTTP or HTTPS connection pool the request should go out through. It will inspect the request URI, check the protocol and host, and then route accordingly. That's why you will see both connection-pool related and HTTPS-context related arguments for this method. In the servicing of an individual request, it may need to actually spin up a host-connection pool, and it will use those settings to do so. Also note that the `Flow` type returned is the same as the the host-level API, requiring you to pass along an identifier on requests. This means that you can send multiple requests at a time through this API and still be able to properly correlate the responses with the requests they came from.

The main benefit of this approach is, of course, simplicity. You don't have to worry about the creation of and settings of the pools for each host you connect to. Also, you don't have to worry about distinguishing between HTTPS and HTTP requests, as the host-level and connection-level APIs force you to do. You can just send any request across this `Flow` and let the framework do the dirty work for you. Of course, the potential downside is that you can only have one set of connection-pool and HTTPS-context settings across all of the underlying pools that will be created. If you need more fine-grained control than that, then you will need to drop down to the host-level API instead.

Sending a request across this API is as simple as the following code:

```
val conn = Http().superPool[Int]()
val request = HttpRequest(GET, "http://localhost:8080/api/person")
val fut:Future[(util.Try[HttpResponse], Int)] =
Source.single((request, 1)).
via(conn).
runWith(Sink.head)
```

One important point here is that this request is the first time I'm passing in a nonrelative URI on the `HttpRequest`. In the connection-level and host-level API, the protocol and host/port part of the URI will be tied to the connection or connection pool you are using. You must specify this information when asking for the connection or connection pool, so you can send in relative paths for all requests going through those flows. In this case, because we are not creating individual pools ourselves, the pool creation/routing logic needs to know this information so it can create and route to the correct host-connection pool. If you were to pass in a relative URI, it would produce a `Failure` coming out of the `Flow`.

Now, let's take a look at the even simpler Future-based variant. This variant is based on using the `singleRequest` method on the `HttpExt` class, which has the following signature:

```
def singleRequest(request: HttpRequest,
  connectionContext: HttpsConnectionContext =
  defaultClientHttpsContext, settings: ConnectionPoolSettings =
  defaultConnectionPoolSettings, log: LoggingAdapter = system.log)
  (implicit m:Materializer):Future[HttpResponse]
```

The arguments here are similar to the `superPool` method, with the exception of also passing in the `HttpRequest` that is to be executed. Under the hood, this request will still travel through either a HTTP or HTTPS host-connection pool, hence the requirements around the settings for those two concerns. As it's always a single request, you won't need to pass in any request/response identifier, which simplifies the handling a bit. If we were to execute the same request we did for the `superPool` example, but using this `Future`-based variant instead, the code will look like this:

```
val request = HttpRequest(GET, "http://localhost:8080/api/person")
val fut:Future[HttpResponse] = Http().singleRequest(request)
```

The code here is clearly very simple. If you want to deal with Future instead of the Akka Streams types, and you are always only executing a single request at a time, you can't beat this variant for simplicity.

So, that's it for us with the connection models for Akka HTTP's outbound HTTP handling. The main point I hope I got across as we discussed these three models is that, as you work your way upwards from the connection-level API, you will lose functionality and control, but you will gain simplicity of use. Choosing the right model for the different situations in your app will really be about how much control you need over your outbound request/response handling. If you find the answer is not much, then it's always a good idea to try and keep things as simple as possible and look at the much higher-level API variants. You can always drop down to the models that allow more control if you find things that will change for you.

Refactoring homework

The refactoring homework for this chapter will involve getting rid of unfiltered and dispatch it in the bookstore-code base and replacing it with Akka HTTP. I have done the work of creating the framework-level code that you will build on top of. I'll break down what needs to be done for both outbound and inbound HTTP changes separately, in the following sections. As always, you will do your work in the -incomplete code base, and you can consult what I did in the -complete code base if you get stuck.

Inbound HTTP changes

Your inbound HTTP homework will involve creating Akka HTTP routes for the sales-order-processing and user-management modules. I have already fully updated the routes handling code in the inventory-services module. You can look at it and let it serve as the guide on how you finish the changes in the other modules. One thing you will notice is that the api root is not contained in the routes definition. As this is a common concern across all routes, it is pushed up to the top of the routing tree, which is defined in the Server class in the server project. Also, look at the framework-level changes in BookstoreRoutesDefinition to help you get started.

Outbound HTTP changes

I did the bulk of the outbound HTTP changes already in an effort to remove dispatch from the code. A lot of this work involved updating the Elasticsearch related functionality, so if you are curious how that was done, check out how things look now in the Elasticsearch.scala file in the common project.

The one piece of outbound HTTP-related homework concerns some code in the CreditAssociate actor class. This is where the external call to the fake credit card charging service lives, which is still using dispatch. Your assignment is to update this call to use Akka HTTP, which will remove the last place in the code that was still using dispatch.

Summary

Hopefully, at this point, you have a good understanding of Akka HTTP and what you can do with it. You should know how the low-level server-side API leverages Akka Streams to support a back-pressure-aware HTTP server. You should also have a good understanding of how the high-level server-side API works on top of the low-level API, allowing you to build and compose complex route combinations with the routing DSL. If you need to consume those server-side RESTful APIs, then you know how to do so via Akka HTTP's outbound HTTP-handling API. This includes knowing which connection model to use for specific situations.

In the grand scheme of the bookstore refactor, this chapter may not have seemed very important in our plan to build a more scalable app. In reality, HTTP will be a very important concept in fully separating our service dependencies. It will allow us to go away from any tightly-coupled inter-module dependencies where we make direct actor calls across module boundaries. Instead, we will satisfy these kinds of calls by going over HTTP, which will loosen up the coupling a bit. As HTTP will become a very important concept within our application, we should be on a modern framework that fits well with our use of actors, and now we are.

We'll see HTTP come back to the forefront in Chapter 9, *Managing Deployments with ConductR*, where we will fully decouple our services and use ConductR to orchestrate between them. Before we do that, we'll add a clustering support app in Chapter 8, *Scaling Out with Akka Remoting/Clustering*. That will get us a step closer to highly available, loosely coupled services, which we will then finish up in Chapter 9, *Managing Deployments with ConductR*.

8
Scaling Out with Akka Remoting/Clustering

Within the realm of scaling, there are two main techniques that people use to scale their software. The first of those techniques is called scaling up, or vertical scaling. In this technique, you can increase the horsepower of the box the software is running on. This can include adding more CPUs or increasing the memory. The idea here is that by increasing the headroom on the box, the software now has the ability to do more work than before. Akka is a great framework for scaling up as it will allow you to take advantage of those multiple-CPU cores as you add them.

This seems like a pretty simple technique as it doesn't involve any re-architecture of your software. Unfortunately, it may not be the most cost-effective. With most cloud providers, you pay a steep premium for the bigger boxes. It may be smarter to try and spread your work over many smaller boxes, and that's where the second scaling technique comes into play.

Scaling out, or horizontal scaling, is a technique where you add more boxes to increase the total throughput capabilities of your software. Commodity hardware can be pretty cheap, as are the smaller boxes in the major cloud providers. If you can string a bunch of these together and distribute the work onto them, you can get the same effect as vertical scaling at potentially a fraction of the price.

Within Akka, there are two concepts that enable scaling out / horizontal scaling – remoting and clustering. We will explore these two features in this chapter, eventually applying clustering to the bookstore app to tie up a few loose ends. In this chapter, you can expect to learn the following topics:

- How to enable Akka Remoting and Clustering in your projects
- How to look up and deploy actors remotely
- The core architectural principles of Akka Clustering
- How to use Cluster Sharding for your persistent entities
- How to use the Cluster Singleton pattern within your cluster

Using Akka Remoting

Akka Remoting allows you to look up and communicate with actor instances that reside in actor systems which are not in the local JVM. The caller does not need to know where that actor instance itself is. They just need a reference to that actor as well as knowledge of what message(s) to send to it.

To the caller, the actor instance behind the `ActorRef` they are using exhibits what is referred to as **location transparency**. This is a technique where local calls are made to look like remote calls and is a core concept within Akka. Regardless of whether the actor you are communicating with is local or remote, the API and underlying framework are designed around the failure and error possibilities of dealing with something that is possibly remote.

By embracing location transparency, Akka forces you to think about some concepts that you might not have to consider on a purely local system. This includes things such as asynchronicity, serialization, and non-guaranteed message delivery. Because you have to account for these concepts regardless of whether or not you use remoting, you can easily switch your system onto remoting without having to change any of your code. That will allow you to scale out with little to no effort if the need arises.

Location transparency is a term within remoting that can sometimes be confused with another term in that realm called **transparent remoting**. Transparent remoting is what you see with something like Java RMI. In this model, how the caller sees things is actually the opposite of location transparency in that remote calls are made to look like local calls. This seems like a subtle difference, but the impact is actually pretty big. By taking the fact that a remote call is possibly happening, and sweeping it under the rug, the caller is not prepared to embrace the potential failure and error modes that come from a remote call. It may seem more convenient to the caller to hide this stuff, but it makes their code more prone to error.

By making you think of these failure points, regardless of whether the call is local or remote, location transparency is the far more resilient of the two models.

Due to location transparency, you can very easily build out a system to run in local mode initially, and then switch to a remote model simply by making configuration changes. The code itself won't have to change at all, even though remote interactions are now taking place. This allows pretty simple scale-out semantics with Akka Remoting, and it is a concept that we will explore over the next few sections.

Enabling Akka Remoting in your projects

If you want to use Akka Remoting in your projects, there are a couple of quick steps that you will need to take. The first of those steps will be to add the following dependency to your sbt build file:

```
"com.typesafe.akka" %% "akka-remote" % akkaVersion
```

Once you have that dependency included, then you will need to inform your actor system that you will be using the remoting features when looking up or creating actor instances. This is done by adding the following config to your project in the `application.conf` file:

```
akka {
  actor {
    provider = "akka.remote.RemoteActorRefProvider"
  }
  remote {
    enabled-transports = ["akka.remote.netty.tcp"]
    netty.tcp {
      hostname = "127.0.0.1"
      port = 2552
    }
  }
}
```

The first config change to call out here is the explicit setting of the `akka.actor.provider` setting to `akka.remote.RemoteActorRefProvider`. This setting controls how actors are looked up and created. If you don't have an explicit value for this setting, it defaults to `akka.actor.LocalActorRefProvider`. This default provider only knows how to work with local actors, so if you want to use remoting, you need to change it. By setting it to `RemoteActorRefProvider`, you will now be able to look up and create actors in nonlocal actor systems.

Inside of the remote config section, the enabled-transports section indicates that Netty is used as the TCP transport layer for remoting. The value shown here for this setting is the default, so you don't need to explicitly include it if you don't want to. Under that, there is a specific section to configure that Netty TCP transport layer. In there, the hostname property indicates the host address/name where other remote-actor systems can reach this system. The port setting then indicates what port the Netty TCP layer binds to. Be sure to set these two properties to a host/port combo that is reachable by the outside world or else remote actors won't be able to route responses back to senders from this system. Setting your host to something like the loopback address, as shown here, means that only other actor systems running on the same host can communicate with you. Additionally, if you do run multiple actor systems on the same machine, each with remoting enabled, you will need to make sure the port is unique for all of them, or you will run into bind issues.

Interacting with remote actors

Once you have remoting enabled in your project, you can start interacting with actors in remote actor systems. If you want to work with a remote actor, you will need to get either an `ActorRef` or an `ActorSelection` to proxy to that actor. You can do this by either looking up a remote actor via the `actorSelection` method or by deploying an actor to a remote node and then using its `ActorRef`. We'll go over these two techniques in two upcoming sections using examples to demonstrate how they work.

Akka Remoting and serialization

Before we dive into remoting examples, I thought it was important to first discuss the dependency between Akka Remoting and Akka Serialization. When sending messages across the network, the remoting system uses Akka Serialization to handle the serialization of those messages. By default, if you don't make any additional config to the serialization framework, then Java object serialization will be used. This works fine, albeit with poor performance, but if you don't have the same class definition on both sides of the system, then you will get a failure on the receiving side when it receives the message. This can be a common pitfall as people start to play with remoting, so it's something to be aware of.

In summary, if you plan on using remoting heavily in your projects, then be aware of the dependency on Akka Serialization and plan accordingly. Additionally, if you do use it heavily, you should consider another serialization protocol, such as Protobuf or Avro, instead of the default setting of Java object serialization.

Looking up remote actors

If you're only familiar with using local actors, then you've probably only used a relative path reference when looking up those local actors via `actorSelection`. So, for instance, if you were looking up a local actor with the name `foo`, then the code will look like this:

```
val ref = context.actorSelection("/user/foo")
```

The default `LocalActorRefProvider` understands this relative path construct and is able to locate the correct actor instance and return an `ActorSelection` for it. Now, what if that actor lived on a remote-actor system and you want to look it up and interact with it? If that actor lived in an actor system called `MySys` and was on a host with the address `10.1.2.3` and port `2552`, then as long as you have remoting enabled, on both, the local and remote systems, then you can look up that actor like this:

```
context.actorSelection("akka.tcp://MySys@10.1.2.3:2552/user/foo")
```

Using a path like this allows the `RemoteActorRefProvider` to properly figure out where the desired actor instance is, so calls can be routed to it. If you look at that path, you can see that there are some distinct components to it that allow the provider to locate actors. The convention of these remote paths is as follows:

```
akka.<protocol>://<actor system name>@<host>:<port>/<actor path>
```

Once you have an `ActorSelection`, you can either send a message through it as you normally would when using `ActorSelection` locally. Also, you can use the `Identify` or `resolveOne` functionality to get an individual `ActorRef` out of that `ActorSelection` if need be.

In order to demonstrate this interaction, I drafted up a quick sample application that will show remote look up and usage of that remote actor. All of the code that is shown can be found in the `samples` project in the `chapter8` code distribution in a file called `RemoteLookupExample.scala`. Some of the less important code from that file will be omitted here for brevity's sake. This will be a two-system example, where we have a sending-actor system sending a message to an actor in a remote-receiving system. Let's start by looking at the very simple code for the actor that will receive the message and respond to it:

```
object DateActor{
  case object GetCurrentDate
  case class CurrentDate(date:Date)
  def props = Props[DateActor]
}
```

```
class DateActor extends Actor with ActorLogging{
  import DateActor._
  def receive = {
    case GetCurrentDate =>
    val caller = sender()
    log.info("Received a request from {}", caller.path)
    caller ! CurrentDate(new Date)
  }
}
```

There's nothing really special going on here. It's just a regular actor that receives a custom message and then routes a response back to the sender. I added a `log` message in there so you can see the full path of the sender during this interaction.

Next, let's take a look at the following code, which sets up the receiving-actor system where this actor will live:

```
object ReceiverSystem extends App with RemotingConfig{
  val config = ConfigFactory.parseString(remotingConfig(2552))
  val system = ActorSystem("ReceiverSystem", config)
  system.actorOf(DateActor.props, "dateActor")
}
```

Here, I've set up a class with a main entry point that will start up an actor system and create an instance of our `DateActor` within it. The `RemoteConfig` trait that's mixed in here is a custom trait I wrote to give me the ability to build out the necessary Akka config, which was shown earlier, to enable remoting. It provides a method called `remotingConfig` that takes the `Int` port to bind to and produces the full config string to use for our remote-enabled system. Here, this system is binding to port `2552`, which means that messages sent to it must come on that port.

The last thing to look at for this example is the code representing the sending side of the relationship. That code is as follows:

```
object SenderSystem extends App with RemotingConfig{
  import DateActor._
  val config = ConfigFactory.parseString(remotingConfig(2553)) ·
  val system = ActorSystem("SenderSystem", config)
  val path =
  "akka.tcp://ReceiverSystem@127.0.0.1:2552/user/dateActor"
  val selection = system.actorSelection(path)

  implicit val timeout = Timeout(5 seconds)
  import akka.pattern.ask
  import system.dispatcher
```

```
    val result =
    (selection ? GetCurrentDate).mapTo[CurrentDate]

    result.onComplete{ tr =>
        println(s"Received result from remote system: $tr")
        system.terminate
    }
}
```

The first few lines of code here are similar to the receiver-system code. They set up a remote-capable actor system using port 2553 as its port binding. It's important that this port differs from the 2552 port used on the receiving side because we'll run this on the same host and we don't want port-binding issues. Then, after getting the system up and running, we will issue an `actorSelection` to look up the remote actor from the receiver system using the path convention laid out earlier. Once we have the `ActorSelection` for that remote actor, we will send a message through it using `ask` and get a `Future` representing the expected result type. When that `Future` completes, we will print the result and shut down the sender-actor system.

If you want to run this example, you can do so using two separate sbt processes. Start by opening up an sbt prompt in the root of the `chapter8/samples` project. Once you do that, you can type the following command to start up the receiving system:

> **runMain code.ReceiverSystem**

When you do that, you should see some log output in the window about how the system is starting up remoting and what host/port combo it's binding to. At this point, the receiving system will be up and running, waiting for requests. Next, open up a new terminal window and start up sbt in the same `samples` folder as you just did for the receiver system. Then, execute the following command:

> **runMain code.SenderSystem**

When you do that, the sender system will start up and send a request to the receiving system. You should see a log message in the terminal window for the receiver system that looks something like this:

```
Received a request from
akka.tcp://SenderSystem@127.0.0.1:2553/temp/$a
```

Then, after that, in the sender system's terminal window, you should see a print statement, which looks something like this, indicating that a response was received:

```
Received result from remote system: Success(CurrentDate(Thu Jul 28
08:34:09 EDT 2016))
```

To better demonstrate exactly what's going on in this code sample, I've created the following diagram of the interactions:

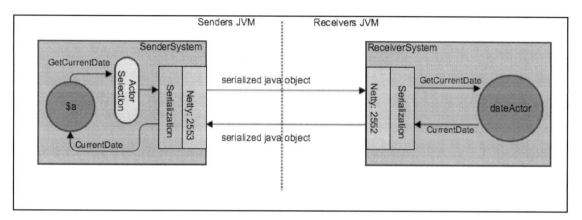

The flow in the diagram starts out with the temporary actor $a, which is created under the Future used for the ask operation. This actor, via the ActorSelection to the remote system, sends out a GetCurrentDate request that is to go to the dateActor on the other side. This message flows through the serialization framework, where it is converted into a serialized Java object. From there, it flows through outbound Netty TCP code and onto the network wire.

On the other side, there is another Netty TCP instance waiting for inbound requests. That instance receives this request and passes it through the serialization framework again, converting it back to a GetCurrentDate object. Then, the request is routed to the correct actor instance for handling. From the request perspective, which is the first part, that is the end of the flow. When that actor responds, it's the same process of sending outbound information, but this time the direction is reversed, with the response message eventually landing back with the $a actor that started it.

The key thing to note here is that this flow is actually two separate remote calls. It's not a synchronous request/response over TCP where the send-side writes to the socket and then reads back from it to get the response. It's a decoupled two-way communication over a remote and asynchronous boundary. The sender sends a one-way request, including the address information necessary to send a response back. The receiver then sends a separate one-way message back to that address.

Deploying actors to remote systems

In the first interaction example, we showed how to look up an actor that was already created in a separate remote-actor system. This is one of the ways that you can interact remotely with actors. In that model, the sending side of the system has to know that a certain actor already exists on the other side, having little control over that situation. But that's not the only way that things have to work. You can also explicitly deploy actor instances to other remote systems and then make use of them, and that's what we will explore in this section.

Consider an example where you have a fair amount of work to be done. You have limited CPU processing power across all of the machines you have, but you do have a lot of machines to use. Doing all of this work on a single machine will take way too long, but if you can enlist the CPU horsepower of all of your available machines, you can get that work done in a reasonable amount of time. In this model, you will have a master node that distributes a bunch of work and then multiple remote-worker nodes to get that work done.

I've created an example piece of code to represent this model. Now, of course, we will be performing all of this on one machine as I don't expect any of you to have three available machines on a connected network in order to run the example. Just use your imagination a little and imagine that the three JVMs we use are actually running on separate machines. This example is a distributed word-count application. It's made up of a master node where the work is distributed to the multiple-worked nodes. The master then waits for all of the responses and when done, outputs the top 10 words found. All of the code for this sample is in the RemoteCreateExample.scala file within the samples code distribution for this chapter.

We'll skip showing the code for the worker actor as it's not important to show how we remotely deploy actors. It's just a regular actor with nothing special done to it to allow it to be remotely deployed. We'll start looking at the code that starts up the worker nodes, which is as follows:

```
object WorkerNode extends App with RemotingConfig{
  val port = args(0).toInt
  val cfg = remotingConfig(port)
  val system =
  ActorSystem("WorkerSystem", ConfigFactory.parseString(cfg))
}
```

This main entry point leverages the `RemotingConfig` trait we used in the remote look up sample to enable remoting for this actor system. It expects an `Int` port to be passed in as a program argument, which will easily allow us to start up multiples of them to represent our two worker nodes. One thing to notice here is that no actor instances are started up. We just have an actor system with remoting enabled, which will serve as an actor-deployment target for our master node.

Next, let's take a look at the master actor that will be reading in a file and then distributing word-count requests to the workers. The class definition, constructor body, and receive definition for that class is as follows:

```
class WordCountMaster extends Actor with ActorLogging{
  import WordCountMaster._

  val workerA = context.actorOf(WordCountWorker.props, "workerA")
  val workerB = context.actorOf(WordCountWorker.props, "workerB")

  def receive = startingReceive
  . . .
}
```

Here, we have an actor that has two child-actor instances of type `WordCountWorker`. Note that there is no explicit remote-related code there, just normal child-actor creation. We also set up our receive-handling to be represented by `startingReceive`, which is the initial starting state for this actor. The code for that receive-handling is as follows:

```
def startingReceive:Receive = {
  case CountWordsInResource(name) =>
  log.info("Received request to count words in {}", name)
  val in = getClass.getClassLoader().getResourceAsStream(name)
  val lines = Source.fromInputStream(in).getLines
  var expected = 0
  lines.zipWithIndex.foreach{
    case (line, index) =>
    expected += 1
    val worker = if (index % 2 == 0) workerA else workerB
    worker ! CountWords(line.split(" ").toList)
  }
  context.become(waitingForCounts(sender(),
  expected, Seq.empty))
}
```

When a request is received to count words in a file, the actor reads in the file lines one by one and sends request to the workers to count the words. It explicitly alternates back and forth, round-robin style, in order to evenly spread the request across the two workers. Once the master has sent out all of the work requests, it switches state to wait for the responses to come back. Again, for brevity's sake, I won't show that code here, but just know that it aggregates all of the individual responses back, summing counts when it sees the same words again, and then prints some output when it has all of the responses.

Now, let's take a look at the main entry point to start up the master actor and run the program. This is where you will finally see what makes this completely normal looking actor code become remote capable. The definition of that class, plus the config for the creation of the actor system, is as follows:

```
object WordCountApp extends App with RemotingConfig{

  val config = ConfigFactory.parseString(remotingConfig(2552))
  val deployConfig = ConfigFactory.parseString("""
  akka {
    actor {
      deployment {
        /wordCountMaster/workerA {
          remote = "akka.tcp://WorkerSystem@127.0.0.1:2553"
        }
        /wordCountMaster/workerB {
          remote = "akka.tcp://WorkerSystem@127.0.0.1:2554"
        }
      }
    }
  }
  """)
  val system = ActorSystem("MasterSystem",
  config.withFallback(deployConfig))
```

The key to the remoting aspect of this code is the deployment config. In that config section, we indicate that the `workerA` and `workerB` children of the `wordCountMaster` actor will be deployed remotely. The `workerA` child will be targeted to a separate local system listening on port 2553 and the `workerB` child on a system listening on port 2554. With this config in place, the creation of those children, which happens normally in the master-actor constructor, will be remote, with each child going to a separate node. That's one of the beauties of remoting—you don't need any explicit code to enable something like this. You can make a program remote simply by making some config changes. This is where you see a concept like location transparency in action.

Once we have that setup in place, the only thing we need to do is kick off the program. That is done by creating the master and sending it a request to perform a word-count. The code is as follows:

```
val fut = (master ?
CountWordsInResource("declaration.txt")).mapTo[WordCounts]
```

There's quite a bit more code after that to handle the response and perform the output, but it's not worth showing here as it's not remoting specific.

If you want to run this example for yourself, to see how things work, then you will first need to start up two separate worker nodes. You can start the first worker by opening up an sbt prompt in the root of the `chapter8/samples` project. From there, you can execute the following command:

```
> runMain code.WorkerNode 2553
```

After running that command, you will see some basic information about starting up remoting on the worker node. Next, you need to start up another worker, so open another sbt prompt in the same directory and run the following command:

```
> runMain code.WorkerNode 2554
```

At this point, we have the two remote-actor systems that line up with our deployment config. We're now ready to run the master that will execute our word-count program. To run the master, open up a third sbt prompt in the `samples` directory and run the following command:

```
> runMain code.WordCountApp
```

Upon doing this, you will see some output indicating that the word-count process is kicking off. When completed, you will see an output showing the top 10 words found in the content that the program was analyzing. If you take a peek at the two worker-node windows, you will see the output indicating that they are receiving requests to do work, showing that the work was indeed being done remotely.

Similar to the serialized messages going back and forth, the remote system must have access to the class definition for any actors that are being created remotely.

Aside from using config to handle remote deployments, you can also opt to use code to deploy your actors remotely. If you want to use code to deploy `workerA` inside the master actor, then the code will look like this:

```
import akka.actor.Address
import akka.remote.RemoteScope

val workerAAddress = Address("akka.tcp",
"WorkerSystem", "127.0.0.1", 2553)
val workerA = context.actorOf(WordCountWorker.props.
withDeploy(Deploy(scope = RemoteScope(address))), "workerA")
```

This can be another avenue to use for remote deployment if you prefer code over config. Just know that if you happen to define both config-based and code-based remote deployment for an actor, the config-based will always win.

Hopefully, this example shows the simplicity of creating actors on remote systems and then having them do work for you. There is one aspect of this example that is ripe for improvement, and that's the explicit round-robin sending of messages to the two workers. This logic seems perfect for an Akka router. We'll explore how to make that change to a router work with remoting in the next section.

Using remote routers

Routers are an aspect of the Akka framework that can seamlessly be used with Akka Remoting. If you are building a remote-work distribution app, like the one in the previous example, then you are probably going to want to use a router to distribute that work for you. Using routers with remoting can be enabled very simply, via config, without any effect in the code itself.

To show how simple this pairing can be, I created another work distribution example using a lot of the code in the previous example, but this time leveraging a remote-capable router. You can see this code in the `RemoteRouterExample.scala` file in the `samples` code distribution for this chapter. As this sample is basically the same as the previous work distribution example, I will only show the relevant changes here. Let's start by taking a look at the deployment config for our router, which is defined in the `RouterWordCount` object, as follows:

```
val deployConfig = ConfigFactory.parseString("""
akka {
  actor {
    deployment {
      /wordCountMaster/workerPool {
        router = round-robin-pool
        nr-of-instances = 4
        target.nodes = [
        "akka.tcp://WorkerSystem@127.0.0.1:2553",
        "akka.tcp://WorkerSystem@127.0.0.1:2554"
        ]
      }
    }
  }
}
""")
```

For the most part, this looks like your basic router definition within the deployment config. The thing that is new is the `target.nodes`, which here identifies an array of remote systems to deploy the actors to. In this config, I have two target nodes and I am specifying four total workers, so the expectation is that there will be two workers per node.

Now, we can take a look at the code in the master actor where the router is created. That code looks like this:

```
val workerPool = context.actorOf(Props[WordCountWorker].
withRouter(FromConfig()), "workerPool")
```

There's nothing remoting specific about this code at all. It's just your run-of-the-mill actor creation with a config-based router. The magic happens under the hood as long as we have the right config in place for our router.

That router replaces the two explicit worker children the previous example had. It also allows us to remove the explicit round-robin code, for which I had to distribute the work myself so that the code to send a message to perform work now is as simple as this:

```
lines.foreach{line =>
  expected += 1
  workerPool ! CountWords(line.split(" ").toList)
}
```

If you want to run this new router-based example, then the instructions are similar to the previous example. Start by getting two worker nodes started up in separate sbt terminals. Then, run the master node with a third sbt window by running the following command:

```
> runMain code.RoutedWordCountApp
```

When you do that, you should see both worker node JVMs performing the work. Also, you should see two separate actors, based on their names, performing the work per JVM, as we specified four total workers across the two nodes.

This is about as far as we'll go with remoting. It's a great feature, but it's not something we'll directly use within the bookstore app. It was important to discuss because it's a building block to another feature that we will be using. That feature is clustering, and it will be the focus for the remainder of this chapter.

Using Akka Clustering

Akka's clustering framework allows you to build fault-tolerant, decentralized, peer-to-peer based clusters without any single point of failure. It's a good system to build on top of if you want dynamic elasticity in your application services. It allows you to add and remove nodes on the fly, increasing or decreasing your total CPU power as the need arises.

The clustering system is somewhat complex, both in how it works and in the different things you can do with it. I definitely suggest that you read through the documentation for it on the Akka site if you plan on using it in your apps. I'll do my best to first give a high-level overview of the basics, such as how it works and how to enable it. Then, we'll shift gears into two specific features within—**Clustering Sharding** and **Cluster Singleton**—and how we will use them in the bookstore app.

Core architectural principles of clustering

Before we delve into enabling and using clustering in your projects, it's important to understand some of the core architectural principles of this feature. We'll start with a couple of key clustering terms that you should understand, as they will appear throughout the rest of this section. They are as follows:

- **node**: This represents a logical member of a cluster. There can be multiple nodes on a single physical machine, each differentiated by their `hostname:port:uid` tuple.
- **cluster**: This is a set of nodes joined together through the membership service for the purpose of performing work.
- **leader**: This is a single node in a cluster that performs certain duties, such as managing cluster convergence and member-state transitions.

Every cluster is made up of a set of member nodes, with each member node being identified by a `hostname:port:uid` tuple. As each member-actor system comes up, it can specify the `hostname:port` part of that identifier via config. Then, the cluster framework itself will assign a UID to that node so that it can be uniquely identified within the cluster. Once a particular `hostname:port:uid` tuple joins a cluster, it can never join again after leaving. If the three-part identifier for a node is quarantined—through the remote death watch feature—it can never rejoin the cluster again. So, if a node shuts down and then comes back up and wants to rejoin the cluster, a new UID will be generated for that node. This will give it a unique `hostname:port:uid` tuple again, and allow it to join back in.

The membership state within the cluster itself was modeled to be a very dynamic thing. Nodes are able to join and leave the cluster at will, making it so that the membership state is a very fluid thing. Even though the state is dynamic and can be constantly changing, every node needs to know the current membership state in case it needs to communicate with a component within the cluster. In order to deal with this requirement, the Akka team looked to Amazon's dynamo whitepaper for inspiration, using a decentralized gossip protocol-based system to manage membership state throughout the cluster.

The important feature of this membership management system is that there is no master of information. It's not like the leader holds and manages the current state and then broadcasts it to the cluster. The state itself is managed within each member node, and the nodes then gossip the current state information randomly throughout the cluster, with a preference to nodes that have not seen the latest membership state version.

As different changes can happen concurrently (where node A can come up and node B can go down at the same time), the state data in each node uses a data structure called a vector clock to reconcile and merge state differences on the information being gossiped throughout the cluster. As nodes are seeing the latest state, they are modifying the gossiped information to indicate that they have seen those changes. Gossip convergence occurs when a node can prove that the membership-state information he is seeing is also seen by all other nodes in the cluster. When convergence has occurred, the member-state information is consistent throughout the nodes in the cluster.

Once the cluster has achieved gossip convergence, a leader can be determined. This is not an election process though, as you may see in other cluster-based systems. Selecting the leader is a deterministic process that can be conducted by each node once convergence has occurred. At that point, each node just selects the first sorted node in the list of members that is able to fulfill this role and selects it as the leader. As this list is the same in all nodes, via convergence, every node deterministically selects the same node to be the leader with no voting process and/or quorum required. Additionally, the leader can change at each new point of convergence. This is because the list of nodes changes and so the first sorted node may change as well.

The leader is the node responsible to shift members in and out of the cluster. If a new node comes into the cluster, the leader is the one responsible for changing it from the joining state into the up state. Conversely, if a node is exiting the cluster, the leader will shift it from the exiting state into the removed state. The leader also can auto-down nodes, if configured to do so, if the failure detector has indicated that the node is unreachable after a certain amount of time.

Within the cluster, a sophisticated failure detector is employed to continually monitor whether or not the members are currently reachable. This system is based on *The Phi Accrual Failure Detector* by Hayashibara and others. In this model, instead of a simple yes/no answer for whether a node is reachable, you get a phi score, which is based on a history of failure statistics that are kept over time. If that phi score goes over a configured threshold, then the node will be considered down.

A system like this can be configured to be as sensitive or as lenient as your needs may be. You may be running in the EC2, where transient network blips are part of life, so you may want a more lenient phi-threshold score. On the flip side, you may be running in your own data center, and immediate detection of, and removal of, failed nodes is critical, so you may use a lower phi score.

Within the cluster, it is the responsibility of the individual nodes themselves to monitor and track failure scores for each other. This means that each node will be monitored by a few (default five) of its own peers through a heartbeat process. Once a node detects that another node is unreachable, it will gossip that information throughout the cluster, and decisions can be made based on that information, such as, potentially, auto-downing of that node by the leader. It only takes one of the monitoring nodes to detect a failure before that node is marked as unreachable in the current cluster state; this is again not a voting-based/quorum process.

One last thing to mention when setting up your cluster is that all clusters need at least one seed node. A seed node is a consistent contact point where a new node can contact into and start the gossip process. This gossip initiation will lead to convergence with the new node, which is now an established member. You should try and configure multiple seed nodes when setting up your cluster, as that will allow for nodes to still join into the cluster if an individual seed node is down.

Dealing with unreachable nodes

Part of the failure detection process within Akka Clustering includes marking a node as unreachable when the failures to contact that node exceed the configured phi value. Nodes that become unreachable must be dealt with rather quickly or else you can run into some issues with your cluster. This stems from the fact that when a node is unreachable, gossip convergence cannot occur in your cluster. Convergence requires acknowledgment of the current cluster state from all members, and this cannot happen if a node cannot be reached.

When a node becomes unreachable, it needs to either be manually downed by an explicit user action (via JMX or provided command-line tools) or "auto-downed" by the leader if that option is enabled. If this node is not downed, then it will more than likely form a cluster of one, as it will see the rest of the cluster as unreachable too and then become its own leader. Over time, this can leave you with a situation where you have a lot of single node clusters instead of one large multi-node cluster.

Using the auto-downing feature may seem like the right thing to do always. It avoids you having to take explicit user actions when nodes become unreachable, but you should be careful when deciding to enable it. It works great for node crashes, but not so well when you run into a network partition. If your cluster is spread out across multiple subnetworks, perhaps EC2 regions, and suddenly a partition is formed (the different sides can't see each other) and this condition persists for a while, auto-downing can cause a split-brain condition to be formed.

In a split-brain cluster, what was once one homogeneous cluster, with a single brain, is now split down the middle, with each side thinking it's running its own show. If you have auto-downing on, when a network partition forms, both sides will see all the nodes on the other side as unreachable. When in this state, gossip convergence cannot happen, so no state changes can take effect and no new leader election can happen. But, if all the other unreachable nodes were marked as down, then each side can perform its own convergence and elect a new leader.

At this point, you now have two separate multi-node clusters split apart by the network partition that is caused by the automatic downing of nodes. In fact, you might have not even noticed that this happened in the first place. That's why it's best in production to not use auto-downing. Manually intervening in situations like this is best anyway. It allows you to properly survey the situation, remediate the issue, hopefully, and get the cluster back up and running with its normal topology.

Understanding the membership life cycle

As nodes can come in and out of the cluster at will, there needs to be a process to assess each node's state to dictate how it can participate in the cluster. It's important to understand these states, and the transitions between them, so you can know what's going on as nodes come in and out of the cluster. The following diagram, taken directly from the Akka documents, shows the possible states and transitions that you can expect from the nodes in your cluster. Note that this diagram shows the states where weakly-up states are turned off. If you want to see the diagram including weakly-up states and get a better understanding of that state, check out the documents on the Akka site:

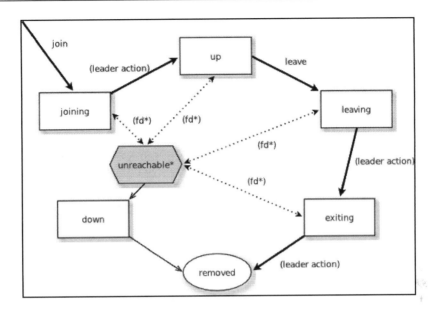

A new node coming into the cluster starts out in the **joining** state. Once convergence happens with the new node, the leader can transition that node into the **up** state, which is the normal operational state of a node in the cluster. If the node then wants to leave, through a graceful departure via JMX or command-line tools, it will transition into the **leaving** state. From here, the leader will transition that node into the **exiting** state and then into the **removed** state. Once removed, the node is no longer part of the cluster, and after another convergence, it will not be present in the list of nodes.

During any of those states, besides **removed**, the failure detection process, that is, **fd*** in the diagram, can detect failures to reach the node, and if the configured phi threshold is reached, the node will transition into the **unreachable** state. These transitions are represented by the dotted lines in the diagram. Once the node is unreachable, it will stay that way until one of the following things happens:

- The node can be contacted again, and it will then transition back to **joining**
- An explicit user action happens, via JMX or command-line tools, to take the node into the **down** state.
- If enabled, the auto-downing feature takes the node into the **down** state.

Once **down**, the node can then transition into the **removed** state and be safely removed from the cluster.

Enabling clustering in your projects

At this point, you should have a decent understanding of clustering, so it's time to take it for a test drive with a few samples. In order to start using clustering, you must first include the appropriate dependency in your sbt build file. That dependency is shown as follows:

```
"com.typesafe.akka" %% "akka-cluster" % akkaVersion
```

Akka Clustering is built on top of Akka Remoting, so by including this dependency, you will also pick up the remoting library.

Once you have the right dependency in place, you need to add some config to your `application.conf` file to enable clustering. An example of the basic config you need to add is shown in the following code:

```
akka {
  actor {
    provider = "akka.cluster.ClusterActorRefProvider"
  }
  remote {
    netty.tcp {
      hostname = "127.0.0.1"
      port = 2552
    }
  }

  cluster {
    seed-nodes = [
      "akka.tcp://WorkerSystem@127.0.0.1:2553",
      "akka.tcp://WorkerSystem@127.0.0.1:2554"
    ]
  }
}
```

The config here looks a lot like the config that you need to enable remoting, but there are a few subtle differences. The first thing to call out is that the `akka.actor.provider` is set to the `ClusterActorRefProvider`. This is the provider that is specific to clustering, and adding this config will allow you to look up and create actors across your cluster.

The `akka.remote` is similar to what you will need when enabling remoting, with a host and port being specified for Netty to bind to. Note that you can set the port setting to zero here if you want the framework to pick any available local port. You can do this when your node is not a seed node, as it won't need a consistent port to contact it on in that case.

The one noticeable difference here is the inclusion of the seed-nodes config section. This section indicates what seed node contact points a new joining node should use when joining into the cluster. As mentioned earlier, it's best to have more than one configured seed node to avoid issues in joining when an individual seed node is down.

Refactoring the remote worker example for clustering

Now that we know how to get clustering configured for a project, let's take the remote worker example that we did earlier and refactor it to use clustering instead of plain remoting. The purpose of this refactor and example is to show the following concepts:

- The dynamic and elastic nature of the cluster and its members
- How to listen to cluster state-change events
- How to use cluster-aware routers

This example will be similar to what we did earlier. There will be a master that can be instructed to read in and count the words in a file. That master will use a router to distribute the work across the workers on the remote nodes. The main change is that the driver program, with the main method, will do this word-count process in a loop, sending 10 total requests into new master actors, with pauses in between. The purpose of this is to start and then stop nodes, while this processing is happening, to show how the cluster and the router are dynamic and responding to membership changes on the fly. The remoting example was very static in what nodes it used to perform the work. This example will be much more dynamic in who is doing the work.

 All of the code that we're about to go over can be viewed in the ClusterWorkerExample.scala file in the samples folder for chapter8.

Let's start out by looking at an actor that was set up for this example to listen to cluster state-change events. You can use an actor like this to perform actions in response to certain conditions being met within your cluster, for example, certain number of nodes achieved, members leaving, and so on. In this example, we're logging a few choice events, but you are certainly not limited to just that. The definition for this actor, plus the preStart and postStop methods is as follows:

```
class ClusterStateListener extends Actor with ActorLogging{
  val cluster = Cluster(context.system)
  override def preStart(): Unit = {
```

```
        cluster.subscribe(self,
        initialStateMode = InitialStateAsEvents,
        classOf[MemberEvent], classOf[UnreachableMember]
        )
    }

    override def postStop(): Unit = cluster.unsubscribe(self)
        . . .
}
```

As you can see, by how this actor is declared, it's just a regular actor class. There is nothing cluster specific in the definition of the class itself. But, inside of the actor there is something that is indeed cluster specific. In the body, we created an instance of the cluster class by calling `Cluster.apply` and passing in the local `ActorSystem`. The cluster instance which is returned there allows me to take actions against the entire cluster, such as listening to cluster-wide events as opposed to only doing that against the local system.

Inside of the `preStart` method, we make immediate use of the cluster to subscribe to some cluster state-change events, namely `UnreachableMember`, and then the more general `MemberEvent`. The `initialStateMode` argument on the subscribe call allows me to specify how I want to see the initial set of member events that occurred prior to this node joining the system. By specifying `InitialStateAsEvents`, I'm essentially requesting that the cluster send me all of the previous member events individually, as if this node was there listening the whole time. If I wanted just a single event indicating the current state of the cluster, I could have used `InitialStateAsSnapshot` instead. Also, note that this actor will unsubscribe from the cluster-event stream when it is stopped via the logic in `postStop`.

With the actor declaration and event subscription code covered, let's now take a look at the receive-handling block for this actor, which is shown as follows:

```
def receive = {
  case MemberUp(member) =>
  log.info("New member in cluster: {}", member.address)

  case UnreachableMember(member) =>
  log.info("Member is unreachable: {}", member)

  case MemberRemoved(member, previousStatus) =>
  log.info("Member has been removed: {} after {}",
  member.address, previousStatus)

  case _: MemberEvent =>
  //Nothing to do here for other MemberEvent types
}
```

Again, there's nothing cluster specific here. Just a normal receive block where we handle the events that we subscribed to earlier. There's a lot more we can do here if need be, for instance, kicking off processes once the cluster has reached some desired size, but for now, we're just logging things.

The next thing to look at is the code that starts up a cluster node that will support having workers deployed to it. It's similar in spirit to the `WorkerNode` code that we did for the remoting examples, but with a few subtle differences, which are as follows:

```
object ClusterWorkerNode extends App with ClusterConfig{
  val port = args(0).toInt
  val cfg = clusterConfig(port, "worker")
  val system =
  ActorSystem("WordCountSystem", ConfigFactory.parseString(cfg))
}
```

The main differences revolve around the config being used for this system. The config, which comes in via the new `ClusterConfig` mixing, sets up configuration to enable clustering. When you call the `clusterConfig`, you will pass in a port, which is what we did in the remoting examples as well, but you will also pass in a role that the node will play within the cluster. Roles allow you to target the deployment of actors to only nodes that have that role. We'll use that later when we set up our work router. In this example, the worker nodes are using the role of worker. Take a look at the full code for `ClusterConfig` to see how this input is incorporated into the config.

Another thing to note is that we are enabling auto-downing for this example in `ClusterConfig` as we will be shutting down a node as part of the example, and we want it removed from the cluster automatically. That's fine for a little self-contained example like this, but as stated earlier, this is not a good thing to use in real production scenarios.

The `ClusterWordCountApp` object is the main entry point for this example. It also contains the deployment config that the router in the master actor uses. This is something to look at as it contains cluster-specific config to make our router cluster-aware. That config is as follows:

```
val deployConfig = ConfigFactory.parseString("""
akka {
  actor {
    deployment {
      /wordCountMaster/workerPool {
        router = round-robin-pool
        cluster {
          enabled = on
          max-nr-of-instances-per-node = 2
          allow-local-routees = off
```

```
                use-role = worker
            }
        }
      }
    }
  }
""")
```

The thing that's new in this config is the cluster section. Inside that section, we will indicate that cluster-awareness using the `enabled` property. Next, we will set the desired number of actor instances per cluster node to 2 via the `max-nr-instances-per-node` setting. Multiply this value by the number of cluster nodes you have that can host these actors, by role, and you will get the total instance count across your cluster.

We turn local routees off explicitly here, via `allow-local-routees`, as we only want to use this work remote to where the master is. This is probably unnecessary here due to the fact that the master and worker nodes have different roles, and we are targeting deployment based on role, but I left it here so you are aware of this setting and what it can do. Lastly, we will set the node role to target our actors, which is `worker`, using the `use-role` property.

I won't show the rest of the `ClusterWordCountApp` or any of the slightly changed master actor code here because it's not super relevant. Just know that in this example, the master receives a work request and repeats it multiple times, with a pause in between. This will allow us to add and remove a third node during the processing and see what effect that has on who is getting what work.

To run this example, you should first start up the initial two cluster-worker nodes. Start up the first one by opening an sbt prompt and running the following command:

```
> runMain code.ClusterWorkerNode 2553
```

Then you can start up the second worker node by opening up another sbt window and running the same command, but with a different port argument:

```
> runMain code.ClusterWorkerNode 2554
```

Once the two workers are started up, we can kick off the main program that will start submitting work across the clustered pool. Open another sbt window and run the following command:

```
> runMain code.ClusterWordCountApp 10 10
```

The first argument supplied here is the total number of cycles that the master actor will run before stopping. The second argument is the pause, in seconds, between cycles. With this setup, the master will run 10 total cycles and pause 10 seconds in between cycles. This will give us plenty of time to introduce a new node into the cluster and then remove it.

With the program now running, if you take a look into the windows where the worker nodes are running, you should see periodic output when the master sends work their way. At this point, we can now introduce a third worker node into the cluster to see that it too will start receiving work via our cluster-aware router. Start up that third node by opening a new sbt window and running the following command:

```
> runMain code.ClusterWorkerNode 2555
```

With this third node running, keep an eye on its window and you should see that it too will start receiving a piece of the total workload that is being periodically distributed by the master. Our router recognized this new code as being another worker and has started to send work its way. Also, when this worker came back up, if you looked into the master nodes window, you should see a message printed by our ClusterStateListener acknowledging this new node.

The last thing we can do with this example is to stop that third node. You can do so by hitting *Ctrl + C* in that node's sbt window. Try to time this to be during one of the pauses between cycles so that you don't disrupt that node while it's actually performing work. When this node becomes unreachable, after killing it, you should see a bunch of messages from the other nodes complaining about not being able to contact it anymore. At this point, no more work will be sent its way, and only the existing two workers will receive work from the router. After 10 seconds, the auto-downing functionality should kick in and the node will be completely removed from the cluster, which you should be able to see via the ClusterStateListener output.

Hopefully, this example showed the true dynamic nature of the cluster and its ability to add and remove nodes at will. Clustering is a powerful tool, and there's a ton of features within it. You should read through the full documentation on the Akka site to get a more in-depth idea of what it can do. From here on out, we will focus on two specific features—Cluster Sharding and Cluster Singleton—and how we can use them in the bookstore app.

Using clustering in the bookstore application

The original bookstore app was set up to run in a multi-server configuration, with each server containing and running a full copy of the application code. This was your basic example of simple horizontal scalability; if you need more throughput, just add another server with the full application deployed to it. The problem with this approach is that it treats all application components equally in how they need to scale, and that's a naive way to view things. In reality, we will want to fully separate our components and allow each to have its own scaling profile.

In this section, we will introduce clustering into the bookstore app. We won't fully separate out our components yet, as that will be the primary focus of the next chapter. This also means that we won't introduce any remote interactions when leveraging actors from different modules, like the sales-order-create flow does in its use of the inventory and user systems. We can set that up here using a cluster-aware routing group so that the actors can be running on different nodes, but that approach will change anyway in Chapter 9, *Managing Deployments with ConductR*, so it's not worth solving it here. It is possible to follow an approach like that, but we'll take it a step further in Chapter 9, *Managing Deployments with ConductR*, using HTTP and ConductR's service location functionality to locate and invoke our remote dependencies.

The big focus of clustering in this chapter is to solve a couple of problems related to our use of event sourcing and **Command Query Responsibility Segregation (CQRS)**. We'll introduce two new clustering features, namely Cluster Sharding and Cluster Singleton, and talk about how they will fix these issues. In the end, we'll be one step closer to fully separating out our components, which we can then wrap up in Chapter 9, *Managing Deployments with ConductR*.

Using Cluster Sharding in the bookstore application

Way back in Chapter 5, *Separating Concerns with CQRS*, we introduced event sourcing into the bookstore app. Within that model, whenever we get a request for a particular entity, by ID, we will first check to see if the actor for it was already in memory or not. If not, it will be created, and then its state will be recovered from the persistent store. At that point, it can process whatever command is being requested using the current state in memory to make any decisions. The actor instance will then stay in memory for a period of time, passivating (stopping) after a certain amount of time of inactivity.

This model worked well, and was efficient in keeping state in memory for a while, avoiding frequent hits to the persistent store. But there are a couple of potential issues with this approach. If we only use a single server, it's possible that in a large system with lots of entities, we may run out of memory if we have a lot of requests to different entity instances. We can fix this issue using multiple servers with something simple, such as a load balancer, in front of them to spread out requests. That should fix the potential memory issues using multiple JVMs to house our entity instances.

Unfortunately, our multi-JVM approach creates another problem. Let's consider the following scenario:

1. A request goes into server 1 for entity instance A. It's loaded from the store first. Then, its state is changed to S1, persisting it back to the store.
2. Another request comes in for entity instance A, this time in server 2. Server 2 loads the entity from the persistent store and has state S1.
3. The request in server 2 changes entity A's state to S2, persisting it to the store.
4. A third request comes in for entity A, back in server 1. The entity is already in memory, but it has state S1, which is stale.

This same flow can be visualized in the following diagram:

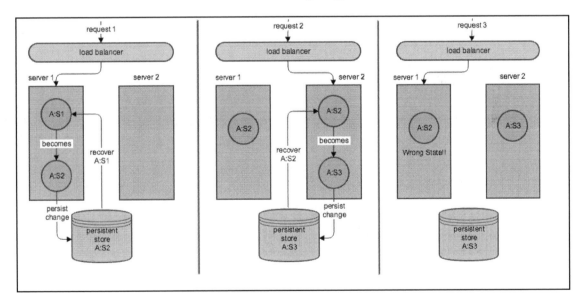

When you hit step 4 in this flow, when the third request comes in, you've got a problem. If you're looking at the state of that entity in order to make a decision, you are looking at the wrong state and, therefore, you might make a bad decision. We will need all requests to a particular entity actor to be processed serially, and in order, by the same actor instance. This works great with a single server, but a single-server approach won't scale and, therefore, is not an option.

In order to solve this problem, we will employ a feature within Akka Clustering called Cluster Sharding. If you've worked with data storage systems for long enough, you've probably bumped into the term sharding before. When you shard data, you spread it out over multiple backend stores, which allows you to store more data than you could on a single-server node. A big part of this approach is that the system always knows where any piece of data is as long as it knows its key. Most systems use a process of consistent-hashing to hash a key against a ring of nodes to arrive on what node to store that key on. This is a deterministic process that easily allows the distributed data to be located.

Akka's Cluster Sharding is a similar approach to standard data sharding, spreading actor instances out over a set of nodes and always being able to determine where they are by their keys (persistence IDs for us). If we use an approach like this, we know that for a given persistence ID, there will only ever be one actor instance currently in memory in the cluster to represent that persistence ID. That actor instance may not be local to wherever the request that wants to work with it is, but that won't be an issue thanks to the features of remoting and clustering. With a single instance in the cluster per persistence ID, we will know the requests for that instance will be processed in order and we won't run into the stale state issue, which was previously described.

Basic concepts of Akka Cluster Sharding

Before we refactor the bookstore code to use Cluster Sharding, it's important to at least understand some of the basic concepts for how the system works. Within Cluster Sharding, the most core concept to understand is ShardRegion. This is a special actor that will be started in each cluster node that can host your persistent actors, and you will start one per entity type that you want to be sharded. So, for example, if you have two persistent entities, foo and bar, and you want to shard them both, then you will start up two separate ShardRegion actor instances, one for each entity, per cluster node.

When a request comes in for a particular entity, it needs to be routed through the
`ShardRegion` actor. The `ShardRegion` will look at the request and, via two user-defined
functions, figure out what shard is responsible for this request. If the `ShardRegion` does
not know about this shard yet, it will contact a central `ShardCoordinator` to ask for
information about this shard. At this point, one of the following two things can happen:

- The `ShardCoordinator` responds that the shard is local to where the requesting
  `ShardRegion` is. The `ShardRegion` will create that shard, and supervisor, locally
  and delegate the request to it, where the entity actor will then be created as a
  child.
- The `ShardCoordinator` indicates that this shard is owned by another
  `ShardRegion`. In this case, the request is forwarded from the first nonowning
  `ShardRegion` to the second one, where the process starts over again.

The flow of information for both of these scenarios, including the actor parent/child
hierarchy, is shown in the following diagram:

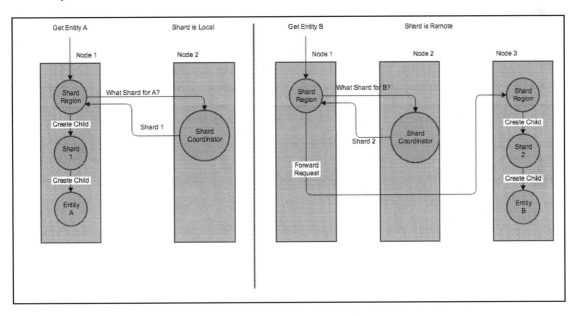

Once a `ShardRegion` actor has resolved the home of a particular shard actor, it can cache
this knowledge and skip the call to the `ShardCoordinator` for subsequent requests to that
same shard. One other thing to note is that `ShardCoordinator` runs as a Cluster Singleton,
which we will cover later in this chapter, meaning that it only runs on one node in the
cluster.

In the preceding diagram, I always show it running on a separate node from the other two nodes where the sharding-related actors are running. This was just to keep the diagram clean and easy to understand. In reality, this actor can, and will, run on the same nodes where the shards themselves are hosted.

It should be noted that the `ShardCoordinator` actor uses Akka Persistence to persist the state of the shard locations. Without any specific config changes related to this feature, the state will be persisted using the default journal and snapshot stores configured for your system. For us, this means that the `ShardCoordinator` actor will use Cassandra to persist its internal state.

One of the useful features within Cluster Sharding is the ability for the system to respond to the addition or removal of a node in the cluster. When this happens, a process called rebalancing is used to move entire shards (and the entity actors that are part of them) to other nodes in the cluster in an effort to properly balance out how many shards each node is responsible for. When a shard actor is being rebalanced, requests to it are buffered until it is properly relocated. Once relocated, those requests can be forwarded to the new location and be properly serviced.

Refactoring the code for Cluster Sharding

With the basics of how Cluster Sharding works under our belt, it's now time to implement this feature in the bookstore app. The first thing that we need to do to get things working is to add the Cluster Sharding dependency to our sbt build file. That dependency is as follows:

```
"com.typesafe.akka" %% "akka-cluster-sharding" % akkaVersion
```

For every entity that we want to enable sharding for, we need to start up `ShardRegion` in each node which we will host shards on. In our current model, messages flow to an aggregate first, and then that aggregate passes along to the appropriate child entity. We will still keep the aggregate concept with this new model and use it to direct messages to `ShardRegion` for the entity that the aggregate works with. So, every aggregate will start up a `ShardRegion` actor, which is done via the `ClusterSharding` extension, with a piece of code similar to the following, using `Book` as the example entity:

```
val bookRegion: ActorRef = ClusterSharding(system).start(
  typeName = "Book",
  entityProps = Props[Book],
  settings = ClusterShardingSettings(system),
  extractEntityId = extractEntityId,
  extractShardId = extractShardId)
```

Right off the bat, using this approach will cause us to have to make some refactors to our common code around aggregates and entities. As the shard itself is the parent for any created entity actor, it needs to have the props for that entity—here, via `entityProps`. In our current model, each entity has a reference to its own ID via a constructor `arg`. This means that the `Props` for this entity have to be aware of that ID on a per entity basis. That won't fit this model as the `Props` here have to be more general. As such, I have made the following changes in the `PersistentEntity` abstract class:

```
abstract class PersistentEntity[FO <: EntityFieldsObject[String,  FO]:
ClassTag]
extends PersistentActor with ActorLogging{

  val id = self.path.name
  override def persistenceId = s"$entityType-$id"
  . . .
}
```

You can see here that the ID is no longer being passed in via the constructor as it was before. But, the Cluster Sharding system will always use the ID of the entity, as obtained from the command messages themselves, as the name of the actor. Knowing this, we can easily get the ID from the actor's path without having to have it as an explicit input.

We also need to do a little cleanup in the aggregate abstract class. This class has functionality on it to look up and create child actors as well as forward messages to them. As this actor no longer owns the entity actors it works with, we can greatly simplify its internal functionality. The only three methods this actor now needs are as follows:

```
def entityProps:Props

private def entityName = {
  val entityTag = implicitly[ClassTag[E]]
  entityTag.runtimeClass.getSimpleName()
}

def forwardCommand(id:String, command:Any) =
entityShardRegion.forward(command)
```

The `entityProps` method here is a slight change from earlier as it no longer needs to take the entity ID as an argument. The `entityName` is completely unchanged from before and still serves to identify the simple name of the entity class that this aggregate works with. Now, the `forwardCommand` just needs to forward a command on to the `ShardRegion` actor, which this aggregate works with.

One of the most important concepts in starting up a `ShardRegion` actor is the definition of the `extractEntityId` and `extractShardId` partial functions. These are partial functions that you will need to implement, per sharded entity, to arrive on the entity ID and the shard ID per request message, which those entities handle. To extract the entity ID, this means that any message that gets forwarded through the `ShardRegion` must carry an entity identifier on it. In order to accommodate that requirement, I've added a new trait into the common code, which is as follows:

```
trait EntityCommand{
  def entityId:String
}
```

All of the commands that go to our entities will need to implement this trait in order to be properly routed through a `ShardRegion`. Once we have that in place, we can focus on how to make the `extractShardId` functionality work. This function will take a given entity ID and figure out what shard ID it will be assigned to. This function should be deterministic so that the same entity ID will always produce the same shard ID when it runs through that `PartialFunction`. A good approach here is to take the absolute value of the entity ID's hash code, which could be negative, and get the modulo of that hash against the maximum total expected number of shards. As a rule of thumb, you should consider the maximum number of shards to be 10 times the expected maximum number of cluster nodes. This will allow future room for growth in the number of nodes without having to do any rebalancing of what entities belong to what shards.

For our bookstore application, I've combined these two partial functions into a class, which is as follows:

```
class PersistentEntityIdExtractor(maxShards:Int) {
  val extractEntityId:ShardRegion.ExtractEntityId = {
    case ec:EntityCommand => (ec.entityId, ec)
  }

  val extractShardId:ShardRegion.ExtractShardId = {
    case ec:EntityCommand =>
    (math.abs(ec.entityId.hashCode) % maxShards).toString
  }
}
object PersistentEntityIdExtractor{
  def apply(system:ActorSystem):PersistentEntityIdExtractor = {
    val maxShards = system.settings.config.getInt("maxShards")
    new PersistentEntityIdExtractor(maxShards)
  }
}
```

To extract the entity ID, we will depend on the fact that all commands coming through the system will extend from the newly created `EntityCommand` trait. We will use that trait to get the entity ID and return it as part of a tuple with the actual command itself. For the shard ID, we will again leverage the `EntityCommand` requirement to get the `entityId` and mod the absolute value of that against the maximum number of shards. This will give us the consistent shard ID that we need per entity ID. Note that I also added a companion here with an apply method to facilitate creating an instance of `PersistentEntityIdExtractor` given an `ActorSystem`. This apply will use the system's config to get a setting that I set up to represent the maximum number of shards our system will host.

With this class defined, we can now set up our aggregate class with a `ShardRegion` to route messages through. We can set up that `ShardRegion` with the following code:

```
val idExtractor =
PersistentEntity.PersistentEntityIdExtractor(context.system)
val entityShardRegion =
ClusterSharding(context.system).start(
  typeName = entityName,
  entityProps = entityProps,
  settings = ClusterShardingSettings(context.system),
  extractEntityId = idExtractor.extractEntityId,
  extractShardId = idExtractor.extractShardId
)
```

Each aggregate gets an instance of `PersistentEntityIdExtractor` that it can use to satisfy the `extractEntityId` and `extractShardId` requirements on `ClusterSharding.start`. With that in place, plus the functionality for `entityProps` and `entityName`, we can fully meet the needs for `ClusterSharding.start` in an abstract manner that will work for all of our aggregate subclasses.

Proper passivation of sharded entities

Back in the *The PersistentEntity abstract class* section, in `Chapter 4`, *Making History with Event Sourcing*, we added a feature to our persistent entities that allowed them to be passivated out of memory after a period of inactivity. If we don't do something like this, then we run the risk of hitting memory issues if we have too many entity actors currently in memory. To implement this process, we scheduled a `ReceiveTimeout` on the entity actor. Then, in the command-handling code, if we get the `ReceiveTimeout`, the actor will simply stop itself.

This seemed to work well enough but there is a small problem with it. If the actor receives another message while it is stopping itself, that message will be completely lost. It would be nice to avoid this corner case if possible. Thankfully, the Cluster Sharding system allows us to gracefully stop our entity actors without the risk of losing messages; we just need to make a few minor code changes to make this happen.

With Cluster Sharding, passivation is a two-part process. The entity that needs to stop will first send a passivate message to its parent shard actor. In that message, you will indicate the final stop message that the parent will send back to the entity when it can be safely stopped. Following this flow allows the parent shard to be aware of the fact that a particular entity instance is stopping and it can buffer any incoming messages to that entity until that stop is fully completed. Then, if there are any buffered messages that came in while the stop was happening, the shard can spin that entity back up and deliver these messages back to it, avoiding any message loss.

To get this system working in the bookstore code, we just need to make a few minor changes in the `standardCommandHandling` functionality within our `PersistentActor` abstract class. We need to change the handling for the `ReceiveTimeout` message to deliver a `Passivate` message to its parent shard. We also need to add handling for our custom stop message to complete the passivation process. Those changes are as follows:

```
case ReceiveTimeout =>
  context.parent ! Passivate(stopMessage = StopEntity)

case StopEntity =>
  context stop self
```

In this code, we are using our own custom stop message called `StopEntity`, which is defined as follows:

```
case object StopEntity
```

With this code in place, we will now get the benefits of a graceful two-part passivation process without any message loss during the stopping of the entity actor.

Cluster Sharding related homework

With the new changes in place, we can set about making the modifications to our actors and commands to work with those changes. As usual, I have already done this for you for the inventory-management and sales-order-processing modules, which is under the – `incomplete` bookstore code distribution for this chapter. Your work will involve modifying the user-management and credit-processing modules to work with Cluster Sharding.

Currently, those modules won't compile and you will need to make code additions to get them to function again. These code changes should focus on the following things:

- Removal of the ID-constructor arguments on the entity classes
- Updating the `entityProps` method to meet the new definition from aggregate
- Updating any commands to extend from `EntityCommand` and to satisfy the requirements from that trait

If you stick to these guidelines, you should not have any trouble getting these modules working again. As always, you can consult with my changes in the complete bookstore code for this chapter if you get stuck.

Using Cluster Singleton in the bookstore application

In `Chapter 5`, *Separating Concerns with CQRS*, we implemented the CQRS pattern using events from our event sourced entities to build out separate read models. To accomplish this, we set up `ViewBuilder` components built on top of Akka's persistence query functionality. These `ViewBuilder` components had live streams in events for a certain entity type, projecting them into Elasticsearch to build out the read model for that entity.

The system we built there certainly worked well to achieve our goal of separate read and write models, but it has a hidden problem that becomes more apparent when you have a multi-node system. If you run the `ViewBuilder` component for a particular entity on more than one server at a time, each one will process the save event stream and try and project the same events into Elasticsearch. This will lead to a lot of errors in the logs as each event can be projected into Elasticsearch only once, thanks to our version-enforcement logic. It seems fruitless and a waste of CPU cycles, so we need a solution to avoid this problem.

Besides the `ViewBuilder` components, we will have a similar issue with the event-listening code between the sales-order-processing module and the inventory-management module that handles inventory allocation. If this code is firing in multiple server nodes at the same time, we will run into issues as it will try and allocate inventory from the same order multiple times, causing too much inventory to be drawn down. This is another issue that we need a solution for.

Within Akka Clustering, there is a pattern called Cluster Singleton that should be a good fit for our problems with the `ViewBuilder` components and inventory allocation process. This pattern allows you to indicate that an individual component should only be running on one cluster node at any point in time. A solution like this should be perfect for what we want to do with our ViewBuilders and the inventory allocation process.

Now, we need to be careful if we choose to use the Cluster Singleton pattern as it comes with some drawbacks. For one, it can certainly create a bottleneck if you have a high volume of calls going through the singleton that needs a fast response time or throughput. For us, this won't be a problem as our code is just listening to events and reacting to them accordingly. If it gets behind, then our read models or order statuses are a little behind too, but that's not the end of the world.

Another potential issue is that you can't depend on this singleton component to be available nonstop. If the node that the singleton was running on dies, it will take a few seconds for this to be recognized and have that singleton be migrated to a different node. This means that you may have gaps where the component is completely unavailable. Again, this will not be an issue for us as these components don't need 100% uptime. Users don't call these components directly, so there is no direct user impact if they are down. The only impact, which is indirect, is that there will be a lag with the event processing, but this should be resolved pretty quickly once the component restarts on another node.

This definitely seems like a sound choice for our `ViewBuilder` components and the inventory allocation process. Over the next few sections, we will get an understanding of how to use the Cluster Singleton pattern. Then, we will take that knowledge and apply it to refactors for those application components and get them to work correctly within our clustered application.

Using the Cluster Singleton pattern

In order to use the Cluster Singleton pattern, you will first need to include the following dependency in your sbt build file:

```
"com.typesafe.akka" %% "akka-cluster-tools" % akkaVersion
```

Once you have that dependency in place, you can start using this pattern within your code. If you want to start an actor in your system to run as a singleton in the cluster, then you need to start an instance of `ClusterSingletonManager` to wrap and manage your singleton actor. This `ClusterSingletonManager` can be started on every node in your cluster, and is responsible to ensure that your single instance is always running, and running only in a single node. To start up a manager to run your singleton, you can use the following code:

```
system.actorOf(
  ClusterSingletonManager.props(
    singletonProps = Props[MySingleton],
    terminationMessage = PoisonPill,
    settings = ClusterSingletonManagerSettings(system)),
  name = "mySingleton")
```

Inside of `ClusterSingletonManager.props`, you need to specify the actual `Props` for the singleton actor to create via the `singletonProps` input. You will also have to specify a `terminationMessage` which is to be sent to the actor if it's being stopped by the singleton manager. Here, I'm using a regular `PosionPill`, with the implication being that I don't have any custom stop behavior in this actor to do things, such as closing resources/connections. If I have to do that, then I may use a custom class for the `terminationMessage` instead that is handled inside of that actor to perform the custom stop logic.

The `ActorRef` returned from that `actorOf` call will be the `ClusterSingletonManager` itself, and not the child actor that you are running as a singleton. If you want access to that actor so you can send messages to it, you will need to use a `ClusterSingletonProxy` to do so. The code to get a proxy for our singleton actor is seen as follows:

```
val proxy = system.actorOf(
  ClusterSingletonProxy.props(
    singletonManagerPath = "/user/mySingleton",
    settings = ClusterSingletonProxySettings(system)),
  name = "mySingletonProxy")
```

With that proxy in hand, you can now route messages to the singleton instance no matter where it is in the cluster. The proxy is also smart enough to realize that the singleton instance is moved and reacts accordingly.

Implementing Cluster Singleton for ViewBuilders

The first component that we need to refactor to use the Cluster Singleton pattern is the ViewBuilders in the bookstore application. Nothing about the actual view-building code inside of those actors needs to change at all. The only thing that needs to change is how we start up those actors, making sure to wrap them in a `ClusterSingletonManager` at the time of creation.

The work to start up our view-building components is done in individual Bootstrap classes, like `InventoryBoot`, for each module. In order to facilitate starting up an actor as a singleton, I have added a new method to the Bootstrap trait, which is as follows:

```
def startSingleton(system:ActorSystem, props:Props,
managerName:String,
terminationMessage:Any = PoisonPill):ActorRef = {

  system.actorOf(
   ClusterSingletonManager.props(
    singletonProps = props,
    terminationMessage = terminationMessage,
    settings = ClusterSingletonManagerSettings(system)),
    managerName)
}
```

This new method leverages the singleton starting process, which is discussed in the previous section. The method allows you to pass in the `Props` of the underlying singleton actor to be managed by a parent `ClusterSingletonManager`. It also allows you to pass in a custom termination message, defaulting to `PoisonPill` if you don't explicitly supply one. The method returns the reference to the manager actor, but it can easily return the proxy to the singleton actor instead with very little additional code. As we don't communicate directly with our singleton components, because they feed off of persistent events, I felt that part was not necessary to mention.

Armed with this new method, we can now start up our view-building components as singletons. I already did this for every module in the -incomplete and -complete code distributions as it wasn't very interesting homework and was very simple to do. An example of starting up the `BookViewBuilder` in `InventoryBoot` is as follows:

```
startSingleton(system, BookViewBuilder.props,  BookViewBuilder.Name)
```

Simple but effective! We can run this code in every node that is running the inventory-management module and know that only one actual instance will be started and running in the cluster.

Cluster Singleton homework

The second piece of the application that we need to refactor to use Cluster Singleton is the inventory allocation process. We need to take the event-listening code out of InventoryClerk and SalesAssociate and move that code into separate actor components that can then be started as singletons. I've already done this for InventoryClerk, leaving the SalesAssociate part to you as homework.

To take the code out of InventoryClerk, I created a new actor called InventoryAllocationEventListener, which is contained in InventoryClerk.scala. Let's take a look at how this new actor is set up, starting with the declaration and the event-listening code:

```scala
class InventoryAllocationEventListener(clerk:ActorRef)
extends BookstoreActor{
  import InventoryClerk._
  import context.dispatcher

  val projection =
  ResumableProjection("inventory-allocation", context.system)
  implicit val mater = ActorMaterializer()
  val journal = PersistenceQuery(context.system).
  readJournalFor[CassandraReadJournal]    (CassandraReadJournal.Identifier)
  projection.fetchLatestOffset.foreach{ o =>
    journal.
    eventsByTag("ordercreated", o.getOrElse(0L)).
    runForeach(e => self ! e)
  }
  . . .
}
```

This new component is your basic Akka actor; there's nothing special about how it's being declared. It accepts an ActorRef representing the InventoryClerk to route events to as a constructor argument. For this app, this will always be the local InventoryClerk to wherever this singleton event listener is running. As that may end up creating a hotspot for where these events are processed, if there is a large volume of events, for a real app, you may consider passing in a cluster-aware router group there instead. That will allow the events to be spread out across all InventoryClerk instances within the cluster.

Inside the constructor body, we will set up the event query and stream-handling code exactly as it was when it was inside of `InventoryClerk`. The code queries for events and then delivers them to itself for further processing in the receive-handling code, which is shown as follows:

```
def receive = {
  case EventEnvelope(offset, pid,
  seq, order:SalesOrderCreateInfo) =>

  clerk ! order
  projection.storeLatestOffset(offset)
}
```

Whenever this listener receives an `EventEnvelope` for a `SalesOrderCreateInfo`, it passes that `SalesOrderCreateInfo` along to the `InventoryClerk` for further handling. Then, it updates the projection offset to indicate that this particular event is handled.

With this new component created, all we need to do is to start it up as a singleton in `InventoryBoot` using the following code:

```
startSingleton(system,
InventoryAllocationEventListener.props(inventoryClerk),
InventoryAllocationEventListener.Name)
```

As your homework, you need to apply this same approach to the `SalesAssociate` and its inventory event-handling logic. As always, you can consult with the finished changes I made in the `-complete` code distribution if you get stuck.

Playing with the clustered bookstore application

Once you are happy with all of your refactoring work, you should play with the new clustered version of the bookstore application. I set up the config to enable a cluster with two seed nodes, in both the `-complete` and `-incomplete` code distributions. These two nodes will run clustering on local ports, `2553` and `2554`. Additionally, I added config to support having two separate HTTP port bindings, with the default being on `8080` and allowing it to be overridden by a system property. This will enable running multiple nodes locally to have a multi-node cluster.

Before getting started, you should clean up the existing state of the system and essentially start over again with what persistent data exists in the system. This will give you a clean start for this new clustered version of the application. To clean up the state in Cassandra, open up a cqlsh shell and run these following commands:

```
cqlsh> use akka;
cqlsh:akka> truncate table messages;
cqlsh:akka> use bookstore;
cqlsh:bookstore> truncate table projectionoffsets;
```

With the state in Cassandra all cleared out, you can now go into Elasticsearch and clear out the read-model data. You can do that by deleting the three indexes stored in there using httpie to do so. Run the following three commands to delete those indexes:

```
http DELETE :9200/user
http DELETE :9200/inventory
http DELETE :9200/order
```

With the system now fully cleared out, you can get the app built and started up. Start out by fully packaging the application using sbt and follow the same instructions from the *Building the example application* section in Chapter 1, *Building a Better Reactive App*. Once it's all packaged up, you can start up the first server node, which will use 2553 and 8080 for its two ports, by following the same instructions from the *Running the example application* section in Chapter 1, *Building a Better Reactive App*, using chapter8-server-complete or chapter8-server-incomplete as the archive name instead.

With the first node now running, you can start up the second node. This will be slightly different than starting the first node as we need to specify some overrides via system properties to get the second node on different ports. You can use the same command that you used to start the first node, just add the following to that command (after it) to pass in the appropriate system properties:

```
-Dbookstore.clusterPort=2554 -Dbookstore.httpPort=8081
```

With both nodes up and running, you can now start to play with the endpoints. Try creating multiple different users and seeing which shard ends up owning that user. When the request goes into a server that does not own it, you will see that the other node ends up processing the request. This is all happening as part of the Cluster Sharding strategy, which we implemented with our persistent entities.

Try making look up requests for the same entity using port 8080 first and then 8081 next. Doing this will guarantee that one of those requests might end up on the node that does not own the entity, and therefore it will pass it along to the other node. Also, be sure to make requests that will hit the read models, like looking up books by tag, to verify that our Cluster Singleton based view-building code is working as expected.

Summary

In this chapter, we learned how we can leverage both Akka Remoting and Akka Clustering to scale our applications out, adding more machines (and thus more CPU power) to do the work for us. Using Akka Clustering, and specifically Cluster Sharding and Cluster Singleton, we were able to close up a couple of loose ends in how our event sourcing and CQRS implementations would scale out. Our application now can be safely scaled out to meet its increased demand.

We're close to being done with the proposed refactors, but one big piece remains. We still have yet to fully break apart our monolith so that each module can be deployed independently. This will be the last step in the complete refactoring of the bookstore app, and something we will wrap up in the next chapter with the introduction of ConductR.

9
Managing Deployments with ConductR

As you start to scale out your applications using technologies such as clustering to gain horizontal scalability, you will solve one problem but you will end up creating another. You solve the problem of scalability and high availability by having multiple instances of services and applications running throughout your server nodes. But, in doing so, you create the new problem of having to deploy, manage, and monitor these applications and services across your multiple nodes. You will also need your loosely coupled HTTP-based services to be able to find each other, no matter where they are deployed across your cluster.

Lightbend's **ConductR** is a tool geared at solving these new problems that crop up when you are deploying your application components into an elastic cluster. It supports facilities to bundle, deploy, manage, and monitor your application services across a multinode and elastic cluster. It also has a simple API that allows services to locate each other throughout the cluster, no matter where they are and what local ports they are bound to.

In this chapter, we'll use ConductR to finalize the full separation of our service modules. This will be the final step in getting the application to run as a set of loosely coupled services, similar to what you see with a microservices architecture. We will also use ConductR to bundle and deploy our services to the cluster, simplifying the process of getting multiple instances of each service module running in the cluster. You can expect to learn the following topics in this chapter:

- Understanding what ConductR is and what it does
- How to install ConductR for development
- How to use ConductR via its CLI and via sbt

- How to deploy services via ConductR
- How to locate services with the ConductR API

An overview of ConductR

Before we jump into installing and using ConductR, it's important to get at least a basic understanding of what it is and what you can do with it. Armed with that knowledge, we can then start to leverage it to complete the process of separating our application components.

At a high level, ConductR is an application that allows you to deploy, manage, and locate application components across a set of server nodes. You can install ConductR on every server within your infrastructure that you will use to host your application bundles. You can also install a proxy, such as **HAProxy**, on these machines that ConductR will work with to give transparency to what services are running on what local ports. Communicating to services through a proxy also allows you to start/stop and upgrade individual modules without any service disruption, as long as there are other instances of that service available on other nodes that can be proxied to.

Within the ConductR lexicon, a set of application components that is deployed together in a single archive is referred to as a bundle. Each node in your ConductR environment can have multiple bundles deployed to it at the same time, with each one running in its own JVM. You can set the scale factor for each bundle, which will tell ConductR how many nodes to run the bundle on at once, allowing you to have separate scale requirements per bundle. Using the ConductR **command-line interface** (**CLI**), one can very easily manage their bundle deployments across any number of nodes with a few simple commands.

The ConductR process itself runs as an Akka Cluster across all of the server nodes that it is deployed on. Its primary responsibility is to react to bundle-related requests, such as load, start, stop, and so on, and take actions for them, such as starting or stopping a local JVM to run that bundle. Your components themselves do not run as part of this Akka Cluster. It is isolated to only run the ConductR process and manage the bundle deployments across your set of server nodes.

To better visualize how ConductR, the proxy, and bundles fit together within your set of server nodes, please refer to the following diagram:

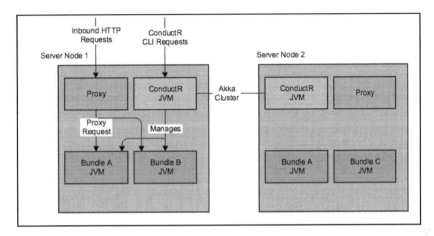

In this diagram, you can see that ConductR itself runs on each node in its own JVM, which is part of an Akka Cluster with the other ConductR JVMs across your server nodes. Each bundle then runs as a separate JVM with ConductR sitting in front and managing actions, such as load, run, and so on, on that bundle. The proxy is installed on every server node and handles proxying requests to the bundles over a known IP and port.

ConductR also comes with two primary APIs—the bundle API and the control API—both of which are available over HTTP/REST/JSON. The bundle API allows you to locate services from bundles throughout your cluster. This API also has a Java/Scala client that you can use in your application code when looking up services to consume. The control API is the backbone of deploying and managing your bundles into your ConductR environment. This API also has an sbt plugin built on top of it that we will use later in the chapter, when we are deploying our bundles to our local ConductR environment.

ConductR also has features to consolidate logging as well as monitoring. The consolidated logging feature is based on Elasticsearch and Kibana (two components from the ELK stack) and allows you to view logs from any server node, and any bundle on that node, in a single query-capable view. The monitoring feature is built on top of the Lightbend Monitoring suite of tools, and allows you to realize and react to issues within your ConductR environment.

Installing and setting up ConductR locally

If you want to use ConductR in your production environment, you will need to have a paid Lightbend subscription to do so. So, the scope of what we will do with ConductR in this chapter will be limited to how to install, set up, and use it locally for development purposes. There will be a few differences in how we use it locally versus how we will deploy it in production. The idea here is to give you a taste of what it can do, and if you have further interest in using it in production, you can pursue that path on your own.

The local development flavor of ConductR is referred to as the ConductR sandbox. It's a Docker image that allows you to simulate having a multiserver deployment, all on the comfy confines of your local computer. There are three main things that you will need to have installed locally in order to use the ConductR sandbox, which are as follows:

- Docker
- sbt
- conductr-cli

We already have Docker and sbt, so we really only need to install conductr-cli. We'll cover that, as well as anything else needed to get ConductR up and running, over the next few sections.

Installing the ConductR CLI sandbox

The ConductR CLI is a set of command-line utilities that you can use locally to interact with your ConductR sandbox installation. In order to install this tool, you will first need to make sure that you have Python 3 installed. If you don't already have Python 3 installed locally, then head over to one of the following links that matches your OS first, to get it installed:

- https://www.python.org/downloads/mac-osx/
- https://www.python.org/downloads/windows/

Once you have Python 3 working locally, then you will just need to use `pip3` to complete the installation of the CLI. The command to install the CLI is as follows:

```
sudo pip3 install conductr-cli
```

Setting up the ConductR sandbox

In order to use the ConductR sandbox, you will need to register for a Lightbend development account. If you hit the following link, for the sandbox documents, you will be taken to a screen where you can either log in or create a new account: `https://www.lightbend.com/product/conductr/developer`.

Once you have that done, you can start up Docker on your local machine. Once Docker is up and running, the next thing that we need to do is to make sure that we have enough memory allocated to Docker to support running the ConductR sandbox in it. How you do this will depend on what flavor of Docker you have installed. If you are running the native Docker app, then you can take the following steps to make sure you have enough memory:

1. Click the Docker whale icon in your system tray and select **Preferences** in the context menu that pops up.
2. In the **Memory** section, make sure that the slider there is set to at least **4 GB** of memory.
3. If you needed to make a change, click **Apply & Restart** to get Docker back up and running with the new memory setting.

If you are running Docker Toolkit, then go to the docker-machine terminal window that Docker is running in and execute the following command:

```
sandbox init
```

Executing this command will make any necessary tweaks to your docker-machine settings so you can properly run the ConductR sandbox within it.

Once you are sure you have enough memory in Docker, you're now ready to start up the ConductR sandbox. You can do that by executing the following command:

```
sandbox run <sandbox_version> --feature visualization --nr-of- containers 3
```

If you are running Docker Toolkit, you need to run that command from within the terminal window that your docker-machine is running in. If you are running the native Docker app, you can run that from any terminal window. In that command, you need to replace the `<sandbox_version>` part with the current version of the ConductR sandbox, which you can find on the ConductR Developer page that you were linked to earlier. It's also important that you added the `boot2docker` alias to your local `hosts` file per the Docker setup instructions from the first chapter. If for some reason you have not done that yet, go back and do that now, because without that, the inter-container communication needed for app in this chapter will not work.

After running that command, you should see the following output:

```
Starting ConductR nodes..
Starting container cond-0 exposing 127.0.0.1:9999..
49b9c30a36cfd3187a1b94ad87720a4f476813f1478ade580d7f1347596d6635
Starting container cond-1 exposing 127.0.0.1:9909..
d90ff8879b6d1025915d13930c63b97d9899895887b5d04fabd9d699bd48065a
Starting container cond-2 exposing 127.0.0.1:9919..
c6ca978eb25abf2a47cb0ae7dd5b51447b318d838631397c5d31fe13936a742a
```

This command will start up a three-node ConductR environment. It will also start the visualizer, which is a component that allows you to see a visualization of the current state, such as nodes or bundles, of your ConductR environment. If you want to see the current state of what's deployed into your ConductR environment, then you can run the following CLI command:

```
conduct info
```

Note that if you are running docker-machine instead of the native Docker app, you will need to run this command from a different terminal window than the one used to launch your docker-machine. If you run it in the same window, you will run into issues connecting to ConductR unless you pass an explicit ip argument to tell it where to find ConductR.

Once you successfully run that command, you should see the following output:

```
ID        NAME        #REP #STR #RUN
5821f26   eslite        3    0    1
7da0f07   visualizer 3     0    1
```

We'll cover more of what this output means in the next section. The basic implication here is that the visualizer is up and running on a single node in ConductR. Also of note is that the eslite bundle, which is used to consolidate logging, is up and running on a single node too.

Now that you've confirmed that the visualizer bundle is running, you can pull it up in your browser and see the current state of your ConductR environment. The URL to view the visualizer is contained as follows: http://boot2docker:<cond-0_port>

You will need to replace `<cond-0_port>` with the port that your `cond-0` ConductR node is using. This port is available in the output from the sandbox startup, which was `9999` in the example output shown earlier. So, for example, if your `cond-0` port was `9999`, then the visualizer URL will be `http://boot2docker:9999`.

When you pull up the visualizer, you should see something similar to the following image:

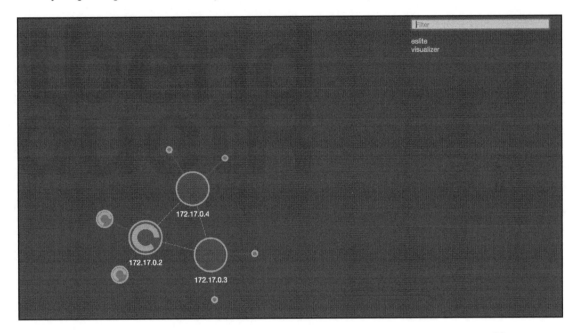

Each blue circle in the visualizer represents a node in your environment that is up and running. If that circle has an internal blue circular bar spinning around, then that means that at least one bundle is running on that node. The outer, green circles represent the bundles that are loaded into ConductR. A small circle without an internal bar spinning inside of it represents a bundle that is loaded on a node but not actively running on that node. A larger circle with an internal spinning bar represents a bundle that is actively running on that node.

If you want to see the names of the bundles, which don't show by default, then type something that matches part of one of the bundles into the filter field in the top right. This will change the view to show the bundle names for any matching bundles as well as shading out the bundles that don't match that input.

An image showing a filter being applied to the visualizer bundle is shown next:

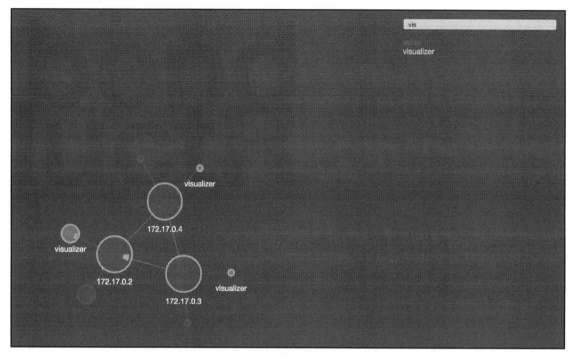

If you ever want to stop the sandbox and all of the nodes that it started up, then you can simply run the following command:

```
sandbox stop
```

Setting up sbt-conductr plugin

One additional component that you need to start developing locally against the ConductR sandbox is the sbt-conductr plugin. This plugin provides some commands to create bundles as well as commands to use the ConductR CLI to load and start bundles. You can either install this plugin in your global sbt plugin's file or you can add it to each project that needs it under project/plugins.sbt, which will be the approach for the bookstore components. The plugin to include for sbt-conductr is as follows:

```
addSbtPlugin("com.lightbend.conductr" % "sbt-conductr" % "2.1.7")
```

A quick note about the use of Docker in the sandbox

A big part of getting the ConductR sandbox up and running locally is using Docker to create the multiple ConductR node containers. One thing to be aware of with ConductR is that while we are using Docker here to get the sandbox up and running, Docker is not a requirement to use ConductR in production. All that a ConductR bundle should need to be able to run on a machine is the host OS's **Java Runtime Environment (JRE)**. Bundles themselves will contain all they need to run with the exception of the host's OS and the host's JRE. The bundles will start faster and use less system resources when used without Docker.

Docker can become relevant within your production ConductR environment if the bundle needs to start a program that does not run under the JVM. In a situation like this, Docker can come in handy to make sure that the host has those additional programs installed so that your bundle can use them.

To learn more about the decision of using Docker or not within your production ConductR setup, check out the following link: https://conductr.lightbend.com/docs/1.1.x/Bund leConfiguration#to-docker-or-not.

Using the ConductR CLI

The ConductR CLI will be your primary mechanism to interact with your ConductR environment. It will allow you do things such as see the status of your deployed bundles and the services within those bundles. It will also allow you to load, start, stop, and unload bundles into ConductR. You can use the CLI from a normal command window and within an sbt session via sbt-conductr.

To use the CLI, you will execute the conduct command and then give it an action to take as the next argument. Within this section, we'll go over all of the individual actions supported by the CLI and what they can do against your ConductR environment.

The next sections will deal with the most basic usage of each action. If you want to see more of what each action can do, then use the --help argument when running that action to see the full list of input arguments it supports.

Viewing the ConductR version information

If you want to see the version of ConductR that your setup is running, then you can use the `version` action, as follows:

```
conduct version
```

Running this action will produce the following output:

```
0.32
Supported API version(s): 1, 2
```

This output indicates that we are running ConductR version `0.32` and that this version supports the ConductR-API versions `1` and `2`.

Viewing the deployed bundle information

You can use the `info` action to view the status of the bundles deployed into ConductR. We used this command earlier to test whether or not our ConductR sandbox was up and running. The command we ran to do this was as follows:

```
conduct info
```

When you run this action, you will get an output table that looks like the following:

```
ID        NAME       #REP #STR #RUN
5821f26 eslite       3    0    1
7da0f07 visualizer 3    0    1
```

The output table contains the following columns:

- `ID`: This is the short-hash ID of a deployed bundle
- `NAME`: This is the name of a deployed bundle
- `#REP` This is the number of replications of a bundle across your nodes
- `#STR`: This is the number of instances of that bundle that are starting
- `#RUN`: This is the number of instances of that bundle that are running

The output here indicates that the visualizer bundle is replicated to all 3 nodes in our environment. It is currently being started on 0 of those nodes and is actively running on 1 node. When a bundle is deployed, it will be replicated to all of the active nodes, even though it won't be started on all of them. This is so that it can easily be started on one of those other nodes if need be, say if the node that it was running on goes down.

Viewing service information from your bundles

Every bundle can put out any number of different services. This includes things such as HTTP and TCP endpoints that other services can locate through the bundle API and consume. If you want to view what services are currently available for each bundle, then you can run the services action, as follows:

```
conduct services
```

Running this action will produce an output similar to the following:

```
SERVICE                      BUNDLE ID   BUNDLE NAME   STATUS
http://127.0.0.1:9200        5821f26     eslite        Running
http://:9200/elastic-search  5821f26     eslite        Running
http://:9999                 7da0f07     visualizer    Running
```

You will get one output row in this table for each service that is currently active in the ConductR environment. Using this information, I can see that the visualizer bundle is putting out an HTTP service on port 9999, which is the service that allows me to view the visualizer web view.

Viewing access-control lists for bundle services

When you declare services within your bundles, you have the ability to control their usage by other services via **access control lists** (**ACLs**). If you only want to allow bundle A to use bundle B's HTTP endpoint, then you can use an ACL to do this. This is not a feature we will be exploring in this chapter, but I wanted to mention this CLI command for purposes of complete coverage of all actions. To view the ACL information within your ConductR environment, run the following command:

```
conduct acl <service_type>
```

In this command, you need to replace <service_type> with the name of a service type, with http and tcp being the valid options. The output from running that command will show you any ACL-enforced restrictions you currently have setup for the services within your bundles, if you have any.

Loading a bundle into ConductR

The first step in getting a packaged bundle up and running is to load it into your ConductR environment. You can do so via the `load` action, as follows:

```
conduct load <full_path_to_bundle>
```

You must replace `<full_path_to_bundle>` with the full file system path on your local machine where the bundle to load is located. If you are running this in an sbt session, then you can type `conduct load` and hit the *Tab* key. This will autofill the path to the last bundle you built for that sbt project.

Running this action will produce an output similar to the following:

```
Loading bundle to ConductR...
Bundle f839d383f8d82965703e39e26b685de7 waiting to be installed
Bundle f839d383f8d82965703e39e26b685de7 installed
Bundle loaded.
Start bundle with: conduct run --ip 192.168.99.100 f839d38
Unload bundle with: conduct unload --ip 192.168.99.100 f839d38
Print ConductR info with: conduct info --ip 192.168.99.100
```

The output here lets me know that my bundle is loaded successfully. It also gives me the commands to either start or unload this bundle, which represents the two possible next actions to take.

Starting a bundle within ConductR

A loaded bundle is not yet running, so if you want to start it up, then you will need to use the `run` action, specifying the hash (short or long version) of the bundle that you want to run. An example of that action is as follows:

```
conduct run f839d38
```

Here, I'm using the short hash of a bundle previously loaded by you. The output for this action will look something like this:

```
Bundle run request sent.
Bundle f839d383f8d82965703e39e26b685de7 waiting to reach expected scale 1
Bundle f839d383f8d82965703e39e26b685de7 has scale 0, expected 1
Bundle f839d383f8d82965703e39e26b685de7 expected scale 1 is met
Stop bundle with: conduct stop --ip 192.168.99.100 f839d38
Print ConductR info with: conduct info --ip 192.168.99.100
```

There is an important argument to the `run` command, `--scale`, which dictates the number of running occurrences of the bundle that must be met across your set of nodes. If you leave this argument out, then you get a scale of 1 by default. This means that ConductR only needs to be running one instance of your bundle across all of the server nodes. As this is not really a highly-available model, you will more than likely be explicitly specifying a scale when using the `run` command. An example of setting the scale to 2 is shown as follows:

```
conduct run --scale 2 f839d38
```

Stopping a bundle within ConductR

If you ever want to stop a running bundle, perhaps to unload it and then load and run a new version, then you will use the `stop` action. This will stop the bundle from running, but will still leave it loaded in the individual nodes. At this point, you can unload it, which we will discuss next, or start it back up again. Stopping a bundle takes the hash, short or long, of the bundle you want to stop. An example of stopping a bundle is as follows:

```
conduct stop f839d38
```

Running the `stop` action will produce output similar to the following:

```
Bundle stop request sent.
Bundle f839d383f8d82965703e39e26b685de7 waiting to reach expected  scale 0
Bundle f839d383f8d82965703e39e26b685de7 expected scale 0 is met
Unload bundle with: conduct unload --ip 192.168.99.100 f839d38
Print ConductR info with: conduct info --ip 192.168.99.100
```

Removing a bundle from ConductR

If you want to remove a bundle, perhaps because you will be deploying a new version of it, then you first need to stop it via the `stop` action. You can't remove a bundle without stopping it first. Once you do that, you can remove it via the `unload` action. This action, again, takes the hash of the bundle that you want to remove. An example of using this action is shown as follows:

```
conduct unload f839d38
```

Running this action will produce the output that looks like this:

```
Bundle unload request sent.
Bundle f839d383f8d82965703e39e26b685de7 waiting to be uninstalled
Bundle f839d383f8d82965703e39e26b685de7 uninstalled
Print ConductR info with: conduct info --ip 192.168.99.100
```

At this point, the bundle is no longer present on any server node within ConductR. If you want to deploy a new code, you can build a new bundle for that module and then start the load-and-run process all over again.

Viewing bundle-related events in ConductR

When bundles are being loaded, run, stopped, and unloaded, various events will be generated detailing what's going on with that bundle during these actions. If you want to see these events for a particular bundle, perhaps to debug why a bundle didn't reach the desired scale within your cluster, then you can do so via the events action. This command will take the hash of the bundle you want to see the events for. An example of running this command will look like this:

```
conduct events f839d38
```

An example of the output for this command will look something like this:

```
TIME                EVENT                                DESC
15:16:32 conductr.loadExecutor.bundleWritten       Bundle written
15:16:34 conductr.loadExecutor.bundleWritten       Bundle written
15:16:36 conductr.loadExecutor.bundleWritten       Bundle written
15:16:50 conductr.scaleScheduler.scaleBundleRequested Scale bundle
requested: scale=1
15:16:55 conductr.scaleScheduler.scaleRescheduled   Scale rescheduled
15:16:55 conductr.scaleScheduler.scaleBundleRequested Scale bundle
requested: scale=1
```

Here, we can see that first the bundle was written to all three server nodes during the load phase. Then, we can see that the bundle was started with a scale request of 1. Using information like this will allow you to debug issues you run into when working with bundles within your environment. It can also be used as an audit log for the deploy-related actions for a particular bundle.

Viewing your bundle's logs

If you want to view the logs generated by your bundle, such as our Akka logs, then you can do so via the `logs` action. You can use this to check the logs after a deploy, to look for things such as errors or indications of success of the deployment. This command takes the bundle hash of the bundle that you want to view the logs for. You can run that action as follows:

```
conduct logs f839d38
```

The output you see from this action will be the Akka log output from your bundle as if you were tailing the logs from all of your nodes at the same time. This can be an invaluable tool during the deployment process to make sure everything is up and running smoothly.

Preparing your services for ConductR

Once you have a decent understanding of what ConductR can do and how you can interact with it via the CLI, it's time to start getting you code ready to deploy into a ConductR. There's not a ton of code changes you will need to make to build out ConductR bundles. You will only need to make a couple of additions to a regular sbt project and you are in business. I'll detail these changes over the next few sections and then we can dive into getting the bookstore application up and running on ConductR.

Bundling your components for deployment

If you want to deploy your application components into ConductR, then you will need to produce a bundle for them. One of the requirements for all bundles is that they contain a `bundle.conf` file. This file is essentially a manifest for your bundle, informing ConductR of the deployment requirements, such as memory, CPUs, and so on, as well as what services this bundle publishes.

When it comes to creating this necessary file, you have two choices. You can create this file by hand or you can leverage `sbt-conductr` and your sbt build file and have it created for you. We'll use the latter approach in this chapter as it's easier and fits well with us using sbt to package and deploy our bundles. As long as you add the `sbt-conductr` plugin to your projects, which was described earlier in this chapter, then you can use your sbt build file to describe what will go into your `bundle.conf`.

In order to leverage `sbt-conductr` to package your bundle and to generate your `bundle.conf`, you will first need to enable a native packager plugin in your project's sbt build file. You can do so by simply adding the following to your sbt build file:

```
lazy val root = (project in file(".")).
enablePlugins(JavaAppPackaging)
```

With the packaging properly set up, you can now start adding the bundle config-related keys into your sbt build file. The first few keys you can add using our inventory management module as an example are as follows:

```
normalizedName in Bundle := "inventory"

BundleKeys.system := "InventorySystem"
```

The `normalizedName` key dictates the human-readable name for your bundle that you will see in things such as CLI output as well as in the visualizer. The `BundleKeys.system` is used to represent a common name to associate multiple bundles together. Within a bundle that uses Akka Clustering, such as the bookstore app, you will use this to represent the clustered-actor system that the bundle will use. We will have access to this setting in our code when creating the actor system for each bundle, and it ensures that we have the same system name, as the cluster requires, for each JVM running that bundle. Your bundles don't need to use Akka Clustering, but if they do, you want to make sure they have the same actor-system name so they can communicate properly with each other. For our purposes, we will have a separate cluster per applic bundle that we will deploy.

ation bundle that we will deploy. When using Clustering with ConductR, you may be tempted to have one super cluster across all bundles. This may, however, prove shortsighted with the way that we use things such as Cluster Sharding and Cluster Singleton. With Cluster Sharding, for example, we don't want the JVMs running one bundle to end up being available shard hosts for entities from another bundle. With Cluster Singleton, when it starts, it will try and communicate with the singleton manager for each singleton across all available nodes to see if the singleton is already running or not. It won't get responses from all nodes, as some won't even be running the code that is trying to start the singleton, leading to issues for that bundle. For reasons like this, we will create separate clusters per bundle, giving us full isolation, including the actor system, for that bundle.

The next few keys you can set are referred to as scheduling parameters. These parameters describe what resources are needed by your application. ConductR then uses this information to figure out where in the set of nodes to deploy this bundle. An example of these keys is shown in the following code:

```
import ByteConversions._

javaOptions in Universal := Seq(
  "-J-Xmx128m",
  "-J-Xms128m"
)

BundleKeys.nrOfCpus := 0.1
BundleKeys.memory := 256.MiB
BundleKeys.diskSpace := 50.MB
```

The `javaOptions` key allows you to set what the minimum and maximum heap-memory footprint of this individual bundle is. The `BundleKeys.memory` is used to represent all resident memory needed, such as heap, code cache, the code itself, thread stacks, and so on, by the bundle. It is recommended that this setting be approximately twice the maximum heap size specified via the `-J-Xms` setting within `javaOptions`.

As each bundle is deployed to a server node, ConductR will keep track of what slice of the total server memory is needed by each bundle, which is represented by `BundleKeys.memory`. ConductR will then drop the total available memory of that server node down as each bundle is deployed. The total remaining available memory of each server node is then used by ConductR to determine which nodes can host a new bundle that is to be started.

The `BundleKeys.nrOfCpus` setting represents how much total CPU usage is required by this bundle. Again, as bundles are deployed, ConductR will keep track, on a per-server node basis, how much of the total available CPU is spoken for by running bundles. When the time to deploy and start a new bundle comes, ConductR will find nodes that still have enough available CPU headroom to handle this new bundle.

ConductR uses `BundleKeys.diskSpace` as an indicator of how much disk space is needed on the server node to handle the expanded bundle as well as any configuration it contains. Bundles can get big, as they will include all dependency jars, so ConductR needs to be sure that there is enough room available on a node before loading the bundle to it. This setting is the mechanism to communicate that information to ConductR.

If you want to set some start options for your application, such as environment variables to pass into the JVM or what main class to execute upon startup, then you can do so via the `BundleKeys.startCommand` setting. This setting is a `TaskKey[Seq[String]]`, so you can either append individual string elements into it via the `+=` operator, or append another `Seq` into it via the `++=` operator. If you wanted to, for example, add the name of the main class to run at startup, you would do this via `BundleKeys.startCommand` by adding the following to your sbt build file:

```
BundleKeys.startCommand += "-main
com.packt.masteringakka.bookstore.inventory.Main"
```

The last piece of bundle config that we will discuss here relates to informing ConductR of what services this bundle publishes. ConductR will then use this information to allocate ports for those services to use, making them available via environment variables. These environment variables are then used in the code that needs to bind to ports, such as HTTP and TCP, when figuring out what ports to actually bind to. Letting ConductR figure out ports for you avoids potential port conflicts if two bundles running on the same server node happen to want to use the same port for something. Each service will have a public facing service-port and then a local only bind-port. ConductR will then make sure the traffic to that service over the service-port is proxied to the bind-port so that the service receives its requests.

Service endpoints are added into an sbt key that is a `Map[String,Endpoint]`. The key to that `Map` represents the name of the service endpoint and the value is represented by the following structure: `Endpoint(bindProtocol, bindPort, services)`. An example of service declarations for one of our modules is as follows:

```
BundleKeys.endpoints := Map(
  "inventory-management" -> Endpoint("http", 0,
    Set(URI("http://:9000/inventory-management"))),
  "akka-remote" -> Endpoint("tcp")
)
```

The first service endpoint that's being declared here relates to the HTTP endpoint we need for our `inventory-management` API functionality. I'm indicating to that I have a named service called `inventory-management` that uses HTTP and wants to be proxied over port `9000` using the service name as the root path. So, the base URI to use this service is `http://<docker-machine-ip>:9000/inventory-management`.

You don't have to use the service name as the root path, substituting anything you want in there after the port if you so desire. We will be using that convention in the bookstore components—it seems a sensible choice when selecting the root path to namespace the remaining path under it.

In this example, I specify 0 here as the local bind port, which is also the default if not specified, as I don't care about what port it selects locally. By setting up this service, ConductR will make both, `INVENTORY_MANAGEMENT_BIND_IP` and `INVENTORY_MANAGEMENT_BIND_PORT`, environment variables available to my application code to use when actually setting up the HTTP server. We'll see this part in action later when we go over what kind of coding considerations we need when running in ConductR. Additionally, this service can now be looked up and consumed by other services running in ConductR via the service-location functionality within the bundle API.

The other service I'm declaring here is required for every bundle you deploy that wants to use Akka clustering. This `akka-remote` service is used when setting up our actor system's config to provide a unique port to use for Akka remoting, which is required for clustering. This prevents bundles running on the same host from trying to use the same port for remoting as long as you add this service to your bundle-config and start up your actor system in the manner described later.

There are plenty more bundle-config settings beyond what we showed here. These ones just represent some of the basics to get your bundles packaged by `sbt-conductr`. If you are interested in seeing the full set, then you can do so by clicking on the following link: `https://github.com/typesafehub/sbt-conductr#bundle-settings`.

Creating and deploying your bundle

With all of those settings in place within your sbt build file, you are now ready to create a bundle for your application code. To create a bundle, you will need to have an sbt session open for whatever project you are building the bundle for. Then, from within sbt, run the following command:

```
> bundle:dist
```

This will create a new ConductR bundle under the `target/bundle` folder of that project. From here, if you want to load that bundle into ConductR, you can run the following command from your sbt session:

```
> conduct load <HIT_TAB_KEY>
```

Hitting the *Tab* key there will bring up the full path to whatever bundle you most recently built for that project. If you hit *Enter* after that comes up, then you will see the output from the ConductR CLI indicating that your bundle is being loaded into your ConductR environment. Once that completes, grab the command from the output to run your bundle and plug it into your sbt prompt and hit *Enter* again. Now, your bundle will be up and running within your ConductR environment.

Code requirements for deployment into ConductR

In order for your bundles to work properly within the ConductR environment, you will need to make a few code changes. Thankfully, there's not a ton to do here, but you do need to do it or your bundles won't work properly. To start, we will need to pull in a new code dependency to our bundle projects. That dependency is as follows:

```
"com.typesafe.conductr" %% "akka24-conductr-bundle-lib" %
conductRLibVersion
```

At the time of writing, the `conductRLibVersion` that I used was 1.4.7. You should make sure that you use the most current version when using ConductR in your projects. The link for the main page for this library, where you can get the latest version information from, is as follows: `https://github.com/typesafehub/conductr-lib#typesafe-conductr-bundle-library`.

If you go to that page, you will notice that there are multiple flavors of this library, each one specialized for a specific usage of ConductR. The one we selected is specialized to work within the Akka 2.4.x series, which is what we are using for the bookstore app.

Armed with that library, we can start to discuss the kinds of code changes you will need to make in order for your code to work properly within ConductR. Those code changes are broken out over the following sections.

Signalling the application state

You need to let ConductR know when your application is fully up and running and ready to receive traffic. This prevents traffic from accidentally coming in, over the proxy, prior to you being ready to handle it. For our bookstore modules, this means that we have our actor system up and running and we have also properly set up our Akka HTTP server. Once you have everything set up properly, then you can signal back to ConductR that you are ready by adding the following call to your code:

```
implicit val cc = ConnectionContext()
StatusService.signalStartedOrExit()
```

The `ConnectionContext` created there is actually an implicit requirement of the `signalStartedOrExit` method from `StatusService`. In order to create it in the preceding way, you will need to have an implicit `ActorSystem` in scope. There is a lower-level way to create the `ConnectionContext` if you prefer to go down that route, which can be done as follows:

```
implicit val cc = ConnectionContext(httpExt, actorMaterializer)
```

Setting up your ActorSystem and HTTP server

There are a few considerations that you need to take into account within your code around setting up your `ActorSystem` and binding your Akka HTTP server to its port. Let's start by looking at the code that we use to create an `ActorSystem` when working in ConductR and using Akka clustering:

```
val config = Env.asConfig
val systemName =
  sys.env.getOrElse("BUNDLE_SYSTEM", "StandaloneSystem")
val systemVersion =
  sys.env.getOrElse("BUNDLE_SYSTEM_VERSION", "1")
implicit val system = ActorSystem(s"$systemName-$systemVersion",
config.withFallback(ConfigFactory.load()))
```

We start out here by establishing the base config for our system via a call to `Env.config`. This is a facility provided by the ConductR code library to create a base Akka config to run our system in a cluster. This includes setting the correct remoting port to use based on us adding an akka-remote service in our bundle config.

We will then read in some environment settings setup by ConductR that we will use when building the full name of our system. As discussed previously, we will need all the nodes from the same bundle to have the same `ActorSystem` name so that they can properly communicate with each other in a cluster. We can do this by reading the system name that we set up in our bundle config using a fallback in case we are running in standalone mode. We can also read in a system-version setting that defaults to one when not present, which we did not explicitly set in our bundle config. Combining name and version together gives us a unique `ActorSystem` name to use within the ConductR system. Additionally, incorporating a concept-like version into the name allows version-based isolation of systems that may be running the same components but different versions of those components.

With our system set up, we can now move on to binding our Akka HTTP server to its local IP and port. In order to do this, we will first add a little config to our `application.conf` to store the service IP and port to use for whatever service this bundle is hosting. Using `inventory-management` as an example, the config to add is as follows:

```
inventory-management{
  ip = "127.0.0.1"
  ip = ${?INVENTORY_MANAGEMENT_BIND_IP}
  port = 9000
```

```
    port = ${?INVENTORY_MANAGEMENT_BIND_PORT}
}
```

Here, we will set up a set of config, which will hold the IP and port that we need to bind to. We will give it default settings, `127.0.0.1` and `9000` respectively, in case we are running in standalone mode. Then, we will set up optional overrides that will be supplied by environment variables set by ConductR based on the service declared in our bundle config.

With that config in place, we can now safely start up our local Akka HTTP server without worrying about port conflicts and allow it to be properly proxied to by ConductR. The code to leverage that config and start up an Akka HTTP server is as follows:

```
val serviceConf =
  system.settings.config.getConfig("inventory-management")
val serverSource =
  Http().bind(interface = serviceConf.getString("ip"),
  port = serviceConf.getInt("port"))
```

Locating other services within the cluster

One of the benefits of ConductR is that it contains an API that allows you to locate and use the services published by one bundle in another bundle. This service can be running on any number of nodes within your ConductR environment, and can move around, and this API will still let you locate and then use it. For our purposes, in the bookstore app, we will use this API to complete the full separation of our services. We will use HTTP-based services when calling across app-context boundaries instead of making direct actor calls.

Before jumping into the Scala code for service location, it's important to first understand the core-bundle API that the Scala code is built on top of. Each ConductR node is running a service-locator service on a local port. The beginning part of the URL to perform service location will be available in each bundle's JVM with the environment variable, `SERVICE_LOCATOR`. Using this environment variable, one can perform an HTTP `GET` operation to find the location of any published bundle service within the environment. So, for example, if my `SERVICE_LOCATOR` has the value `http://172.17.0.5:9008/services`, then I can look up my `inventory-management` service with the following HTTP request:

```
GET http://172.17.0.5:9008/services/inventory-management
```

In that request, the last part of the URI path represents the name of the published bundle service that you want to look up. This is the same name that you will declare in your bundle config for the service that you want to publish. If the service can be successfully located, then an HTTP response similar to the following will be returned:

```
HTTP/1.1 307 Temporary Redirect
Location: http://127.0.0.1:9000/inventory-management
Cache-Control: max-age=60
```

This redirect-oriented response communicates the actual location of that service via the `Location` header. The response also instructs you on how long you can cache this location (in seconds) via the `Cache-Control` header.

This API is pretty simple, if you can invoke it directly via HTTP from your Scala code, but it's a bit low-level and missing some niceties. For the bookstore app, we will use the service-location facilities built into the Scala ConductR-bundle API that we added earlier as a dependency. This library has built-in location-cache handling and hides the details of having to first find the locator service itself before using it.

To use the locator API, you will first need to have a `ConnectionContext` and an instance of `CacheLike` handy to handle your location caching. Assuming that you had an implicit `ActorSystem` in scope, then you can build these two requirements as follows:

```
implicit val cc = ConnectionContext()
val cache = LocationCache()
```

With those two requirements in place, looking up the URI for our `inventory-management` service can be achieved with the following call:

```
val fut:Future[Option[java.net.URI]] =
 LocationService.lookup("inventory-management",
 URI("http://localhost:8080/"), cache)
```

If the service locator is able to find this service, then you will have a `Future` wrapping a `Some` for the root URI to that service. If the locator is not able to find the service, then the `Future` will wrap a `None` instead. Once you have this URI, you can start making calls to the endpoints under that root URI.

If you want to use service location within your actors, then you can mix in the `ImplicitConnectionContext` trait to provide that actor with an implicit `ConnectionContext`. It's also a good idea to pass in a shared `LocationCache` to your actors so that multiple instances of actors can share the same location-cache information. An example of the declaration of an actor that is ready to use service location is as follows:

```
class MyLocationUsingActor(cache:CacheLike)
extends Actor with ImplicitConnectionContext{

 . . .

}
```

Refactoring the bookstore for ConductR

With a basic knowledge of ConductR under our belts, it's time to start making changes to the bookstore app to allow it to run in ConductR. We will also use the features of ConductR, namely service location, to complete the full separation of our services. When done, we will have a more loosely coupled set of services representing our bookstore app versus the monolith we were using up until this point. The next sections will break down each of the major things we need to do to get the bookstore app running within ConductR.

Splitting apart the bookstore projects

Coming into this chapter, we allowed the different application modules to have dependencies on each other. We saw this in how the **sales-order-processing** module had dependencies on **inventory-management**, **user-management**, and **credit-processing**. By having dependencies on these other modules, the sales-order-handling code can make direct actor calls to actors within those modules using messages classes, which is also defined in the dependent modules. We also had a server project that depended on all module projects, tying them all together to produce our monolith via a multiproject sbt build. From a visual standpoint, the project dependencies look like this:

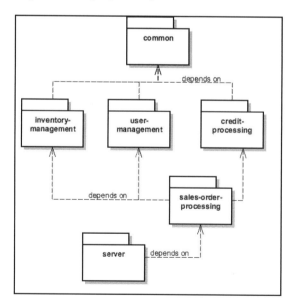

A big part of what we will do in this chapter is to separate the modules to the point that they can be deployed as isolated units. This means that **sales-order-processing** can no longer depend on **inventory-management**, **user-management**, or c**redit-processing**. In order for **sales-order-processing** to use functionality from those other modules, it will now need to use their respective HTTP APIs instead of direct actor calls, locating those services via ConductR's service-location functionality. Additionally, we will get rid of the server project and multiproject build setup as that was an artifact of deploying as a monolith and we won't be doing that anymore. The new module-relationship diagram of our system is as follows:

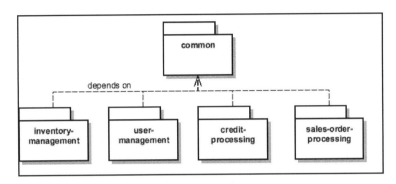

We'll keep the common project around as a dependency to all of the other modules. This is where we will keep our common abstractions that are used to build out our service's modules. With a microservices approach, you will want to strive for a share-nothing system, but sometimes you are better off with a common library such as this versus duplicating all of that code in every module. On the plus side, since each module will be deployed into its own JVM, each module can run a different version of the common project if necessary, opting into upgrades to that library when they are ready to do so.

Restructuring the projects like this will immediately break code in the **sales-order-processing** module. This code was dependent on classes in the other three services modules, so it won't compile once it can't see that code anymore. Fixing that code will be one of the two main focuses of the refactor work for this chapter, with the other being making all modules run properly in ConductR.

Common changes to support ConductR

As usual, I'll start by describing the common abstractions that were put in place for support of the ConductR concepts within this chapter. All the code that we'll discuss over the next few sections can be found in the `bookstore-app-complete` folder in the code distribution for `chapter9`. There will be no homework in this chapter, or the next one, so you only need to deal with code in the `-complete` code folder.

One thing to call out with the common project is that it now contains a `reference.conf` file containing the common configuration to use across all module projects. Earlier, we had a single `application.conf` contained in the server project, with each module possibly having a separate config file of its own, added into `application.conf` via an includes. All common config was contained in that single `application.conf` file. As we don't have the server project anymore, we will need a way to have common (overridable) config across all of the service-module projects. We'll be doing this via a `reference.conf` file now, which is contained in the common project.

The new Server class

Each module will now need to start up its own actor system and also start up its own Akka HTTP server, being sure to bind to the correct ports as indicated by ConductR. Each module will also need to be sure that it properly signals ConductR once it's up and running and ready for traffic. We will handle these concerns via a new version of the `Server` class, which was moved from the defunct server project into the common project.

Let's start by taking a look at the class definition for the `Server` class, which is seen as follows:

```
class Server(boot:Bootstrap, service:String){
    . . .
}
```

The new version of the `Server` class now has two constructor arguments that need to be supplied. The first is the `Bootstrap` class instance that will be used to boot up the actors and return the HTTP routes for whatever module is being started. The second is the name of the HTTP service that was setup in the bundle config for whatever module is being started up. We need this name to determine what HTTP IP and port to bind to per the contract of being a proper ConductR bundle.

The rest of the important changes in this class were previously discussed in the section *Code requirements for deployment into ConductR* of this chapter. The actor system is started up using a name that comes from the BUNDLE_SYSTEM and BUNDLE_SYSTEM_VERSION environment settings. It also leverages the service name to find the IP and port to bind to via Akka config settings injected by ConductR. Finally, after starting up the actor system and setting up the HTTP server, the code here signals to ConductR that the application is ready for traffic, making a call to StatusService.signalStartedOrExit().

The ServiceConsumer classes

Another big part of working within a ConductR environment is the ability to locate and then consume other services within the environment. As such, some common code was added to support performing-service location and service usage, which is contained in the ServiceConsumer trait. Let's start by taking a look at the definition for this trait as well as its companion and a support class:

```
case class ServiceLookupResult(
  name:String, uriOpt:Option[java.net.URI])

object ServiceConsumer{
  val GlobalCache = new LocationCache()
}

trait ServiceConsumer extends ApiResponseJsonProtocol
{ me:BookstoreActor =>

  implicit val httpMater = ActorMaterializer()
  val http = Http(context.system)
  . . .
}
```

The ServiceLookupResult class is used to represent the result of a service lookup. It's similar to an ActorIdentity result, in that, it contains the name of what was looked up and also an Option reflecting whether or nor the lookup was successful or not. But in this case, instead of ActorRef, the Option is for the URI of the looked up service, being a None if the service cannot be found.

The `ServiceConsumer` companion is used to define a global shared `LocationCache` that can be used for components that don't want to define a cache of their own. Part of the service-location API requires you to supply a cache to use to avoid always making HTTP calls to lookup-service locations. This shared cache allows you to share the cached locations of services across components if you have multiple components in the same bundle that use the same service.

The `ServiceConsumer` trait is set up as an extension of `ApiResponseJsonProtocol`. When invoking our services via their HTTP APIs, the response JSON will represent an `ApiResponse`. As such, we will need the JSON-format classes that can be used to properly parse these responses. Also, this trait has a self-type of `BookstoreActor` so that we can leverage actor-specific functionality inside this trait if necessary. This trait is set up with an implicit `Materializer` instance as well as a reference to the `HttpExt` extension class, both of which will be used when making HTTP calls to services.

With the basic definitions now covered, let's take a look at the method to look up a service within the ConductR environment. That method is as follows:

```
def lookupService(serviceName:String,
cache:CacheLike = ServiceConsumer.GlobalCache)
(implicit ec:ExecutionContext, cc:ConnectionContext) = {
  LocationService.
  lookup(serviceName, URI("http://localhost:8080/"), cache).
  map(opt => ServiceLookupResult(serviceName, opt)).
  andThen(lookupLogging(serviceName)
}
```

This method takes the name of the service to look up as well as the cache to use when performing that look up, defaulting to the globally defined cache from the companion if not explicitly supplied. It also has implicit requirements on both an `ExecutionContext` and a `ConnectionContext`. The `ExecutionContext` is required for the post-processing (the `map` and the `andThen` operations) calls on the `Future` returned from `LocationService.lookup`. The `ConnectionContext` is a requirement from the call to Akka's `LocationService.lookup`, so we need to make it available so that we can use that method.

Inside the body of `lookupService`, we will use the ConductR API call `LocationService.lookup` to get the URI of the service that we want to look up. We will then map over that result, producing a `ServiceLookupResult` that the caller can use to see whether or not the lookup was successful. We also add in some logging of the result so we can see what is happening as services are being looked up.

The `ServiceConsumer` also defined a method to use a looked up service. That method is as follows:

```
def executeHttpRequest[T:RootJsonFormat](request:HttpRequest) = {
  import context.dispatcher
  for{
    resp <- http.
    singleRequest(request).
    flatMap(successOnly(request))
    entity <- Unmarshal(resp.entity).to[ApiResponse[T]]
    if entity.response.isDefined
  } yield entity.response.get
}
```

This method is meant to invoke an endpoint and parse out the entity contained in the JSON response. The method is defined with a type `T` that represents the desired object that will be wrapped in the `ApiResponse`. It also requires an implicit `RootJsonFormat` for the type `T` to be available to properly parse that desired object out of the `ApiResponse`.

It takes the `HttpRequest` instance to execute and performs the following steps:

1. Executes the request using the `Future` based request-level API from Akka HTTP.
2. Checks that the response code was a success-level code (200 level), failing the `Future` if not.
3. Unmarshals the request entity into an `ApiResponse`.
4. Checks that the `ApiResponse` has a response value on it. This will fail the `Future` if that guard condition is not met.
5. Returns the object nested inside of the `ApiResponse`, which is of type `T`.

With these two methods (`lookupService` and `executeHttpRequest`) in place, we now have the framework in place to consume other services within our ConductR environment.

Turning the service modules into ConductR bundles

With the common code in place to work within ConductR, we can turn our focus to make modifications to the individual-service modules so that they can be deployed as bundles. Each service module will get the same treatment, which includes the following changes:

1. Adding an `application.conf` file to each service where we can set up the config for that bundle.
2. Modifying the sbt build file for each module to include bundle-config keys.
3. Adding a `Main` class to each project that will be used to start up that bundle.

Those three simple steps will allow us to bundle and deploy these modules into our ConductR environment. I'll break down these changes in more detail in the following sections.

Setting up an application.conf for each module

Previously, we had a single `application.conf` file across all application modules since we were deploying as a monolith. Now that we are breaking up the modules, each one will have its own config file where you can add additional config for that module and/or provide overrides from the standard config in the `reference.conf` project in the common project. There are two basic pieces of config that we will have present in each `application.conf` file. They are as follows:

- Config to hold the IP and port bindings provided by ConductR that the bundle is to use
- Config for the tag mappings for the Cassandra Akka Persistence plugin

Using the `inventory-management` module as an example, this is what those two pieces of config will look like for a given module:

```
inventory-management{
  ip = "127.0.0.1"
  ip = ${?INVENTORY_MANAGEMENT_BIND_IP}
  port = 9000
  port = ${?INVENTORY_MANAGEMENT_BIND_PORT}
}

cassandra-journal{
  tags = {
    book = 1
```

```
      bookcreated = 2
      . . .
    }
  }
```

The important piece of config here is the `inventory-management` section. This will match the name of the HTTP service that is declared for this bundle within our sbt build file. It sets default values for both IP and port bindings, and then accepts optional environment overrides when running within ConductR. This structure will be present in each `application.conf` file, with the service names changing to match the declared services from each bundle. This config is that used within our `Server` class to set up the correct IP and port for the Akka HTTP server that is started per bundle.

Adding bundle keys to our sbt build files

In order for our application-module projects to be built and deployed as ConductR bundles, we will need to make some additions to our sbt build files that describe what the bundle config will be for each module. The building of the bundles themselves is enabled by adding the `sbt-conductr` plugin to each individual module. With that plugin in place, we can then set about adding the necessary bundle-related keys to each module.

Using the `inventory-management` module again as an example, this is what the basic bundle config will look like in each sbt build file:

```
normalizedName in Bundle := "inventory"

BundleKeys.system := "InventorySystem"

javaOptions in Universal := Seq(
  "-J-Xmx128m",
  "-J-Xms128m"
)

BundleKeys.nrOfCpus := 0.1
BundleKeys.memory := 256.MiB
BundleKeys.diskSpace := 50.MB

BundleKeys.endpoints := Map(
  "akka-remote" -> Endpoint("tcp"),
  "inventory-management" -> Endpoint("http", 0,
  Set(URI("http://:9000/inventory-management")))
)

BundleKeys.startCommand += "-main
com.packt.masteringakka.bookstore.inventory.Main"lazy val root = (project
```

```
in
  file(".")).enablePlugins(JavaAppPackaging)
```

We covered the majority of what this config does in the section titled *Bundling your components for deployment*, so I won't go into too much detail about each setting here. There are a few things from that bundle config to highlight though, and they are as follows:

- As discussed earlier, each bundle has its own unique system name via `BundleKeys.system`
- Each bundle will always declare two services; one TCP service for Akka Remoting and one HTTP service for the routes in that bundle
- Each bundle will have its own main file, which will be invoked at startup via the `-main` switch supplied to `BundleKeys.startCommand`
- Each bundle will set up `JavaAppPackaging`, which is a prerequisite to using the `bundle:dist` command from `sbt-conductr`

Creating a main class to startup each bundle

The majority of the work to start up each bundle is contained in the common `Server` class and the `Bootstrap` class for each bundle. The `Bootstrap` class starts up all actors for that bundle and returns the routes to be incorporated into the Akka HTTP server for that bundle. The `Server` class uses the `Bootstrap` class to complete its work, mostly around adding the routes into the HTTP server. The `Server` class does a lot of the heavy lifting, but it needs two arguments—the `Bootstrap` class to use and the name of the HTTP service to bind—before it can do its work. That's where the bundle-specific main class comes into play.

Each bundle will have its own classes called `Main` that will have a `main` method entry point on it. This `Main` class will be responsible for starting up the `Server` instance for that bundle. An example of one of these simple classes, for `inventory-management`, is as follows:

```
object Main {
  def main(args:Array[String]):Unit = {
  new Server(new InventoryBoot(), "inventory-management")
  }
}
```

The `Main` class here is a singleton object so that it can be invoked as a main entry point. All it does is instantiate a `Server` instance, passing in the necessary constructor arguments to properly boot up the `inventory-management` bundle. The service name supplied there, which is `inventory-management`, will be used in the `Server` class to look up the correct config to use to bind the HTTP server IP and port. With this simple class in place, the `Server` and `Bootstrap` classes can now be hooked together to finish the work of starting up the bundle.

Refactoring the sales-order-processing module

With the basic ConductR bundle changes just described, the `user-management` and `credit-processing` modules can now be built out and deployed as ConductR bundles. The `inventory-management` module is almost there, just needing a small refactor around the handling of the inventory-allocation process, which we will cover after this section. None of theses three modules make cross-module service calls, so they won't need any refactoring around those kinds of calls. The `sales-order-processing` module is another story though. It uses all three of the other modules to perform its work, so it will need some changes in order to work as a standalone ConductR bundle. This module will also need changes around how it participates in the inventory-allocation process. We'll cover how to make this module work as a standalone ConductR bundle over the next few sections.

Refactoring the SalesOrderCreateValidator

As part of creating a new `SalesOrder` entity, we had a short-lived FSM actor that would do the work of validating some of the inputs to make sure we could continue with the creation of the entity. That class, called `SalesOrderCreateValidator`, was previously making direct actor calls to actors from the other three modules. It was dependent on being able to see the classes, such as message classes and fields-object classes, from those projects to do its work. Now that we have separated the modules so that none of them depend on each other, we will have to refactor this actor to instead make HTTP calls to the services it needs. It will use the ConductR service-location functionality via the new `ServiceConsumer` trait to find and then invoke these services, allowing it to serve the same function as before, albeit via a slightly different approach.

Let's start by taking a look at the new declaration for this actor, which is as follows:

```
private[order] class SalesOrderCreateValidator
extends BookstoreActor
with FSM[State, Data] with ImplicitConnectionContext
with ServiceConsumer with OrderJsonProtocol{
  . . .
}
```

There are three new mixins here that allow this actor to use other services within the environment. The first is ImplicitConnectionContext, which, as the name implies, gives us an implicit ConnectionContext instance, which is needed when performing our service lookups. The second is the ServiceConsumer trait, which allows us to perform service lookups and then make HTTP calls to those services. The last is OrderJsonProtocol, which is where we will define the spray-json formatting classes for any case classes that we use to map to and from JSON for those service calls.

Now, the first piece of functionality that needs rework is the process where this actor was looking up all of its dependencies. Earlier, this was a process of performing an actorSelection and then resolving that ActorSelection into an individual ActorRef. The process is similar here, except we will perform a service lookup instead of actorSelection, and we will hold onto java.net.URI instead of ActorRef. The updated functionality for the WaitingForRequest state, which performs the lookups, is as follows:

```
when(WaitingForRequest){
  case Event(request:CreateOrder, _) =>
  lookupService(InvMgmtName).pipeTo(self)
  lookupService(UserMgmtName).pipeTo(self)
  lookupService(CredProcName).pipeTo(self)
  goto(ResolvingDependencies)
  using UnresolvedDependencies(Inputs(sender(), request))
}
```

Here, we will perform three individual service lookups, piping the results from each resulting Future back to ourselves for further processing in the next state.

We will receive the results of those lookups in the UnresolvedDependencies state, where we will wait for all three to be resolved before continuing. The updated code for that state is as follows:

```
when(ResolvingDependencies, ResolveTimeout )(transform {
  case Event(ServiceLookupResult(name, uriOpt),
  data:UnresolvedDependencies) =>
  val newData = name match{
```

```
      case InvMgmtName => data.copy(inventoryUri = uriOpt)
      case UserMgmtName => data.copy(userUri = uriOpt)
      case CredProcName => data.copy(creditUri = uriOpt)
    }
    stay using newData
} using{
      case FSM.State(state, UnresolvedDependencies(inputs,
      Some(userUri), Some(inventoryUri),
      Some(creditUri)), _, _, _) =>

      findUserByEmail(userUri,
      inputs.request.userEmail).pipeTo(self)

      val expectedBooks =
      inputs.request.lineItems.map(_.bookId).toSet
      val bookFutures =
      expectedBooks.map(id => findBook(inventoryUri, id))
      bookFutures.foreach(_.pipeTo(self))
      goto(LookingUpEntities)
      using ResolvedDependencies(inputs,
      expectedBooks, None, Map.empty,
      inventoryUri, userUri, creditUri)
    })
```

This process is largely the same as before. We will wait for each lookup to complete with a properly resolved reference and add that reference to the go-forward state. We will then make some entity-lookup calls, pipe the results back to ourselves, and transition to waiting for those results. The big difference is that when making those entity-lookup calls, we are using a couple of new methods—findUserByEmail and findBook—to do so. These methods are where we are making the HTTP calls to those looked up services. The code for these two new methods is as follows:

```
def findUserByEmail(uri:java.net.URI,
email:String):Future[BookstoreUser] = {
  val requestUri = Uri(uri.toString).withPath(
  Uri.Path("/api") / "user" / email)
  executeHttpRequest[BookstoreUser](
  HttpRequest(HttpMethods.GET, requestUri))
}

def findBook(uri:java.net.URI, id:String):Future[Book] = {
  val requestUri = Uri(uri.toString).withPath(
  Uri.Path("/api") / "book" / id)
  executeHttpRequest[Book](
  HttpRequest(HttpMethods.GET, requestUri))
}
```

Each of these calls follows the same convention. Built out the full URI to the resource to be looked up and then use `executeHttpRequest` to perform the lookup. Note that the classes used to map the JSON to live in this project are defined in the `SalesOrder` companion. We no longer have references to the classes that are being returned from the other side of the call, so we simply map our own over here. This duplication is probably the only downside of separating the modules, but case classes are cheap and easy to create, and the benefit of module separation far outweighs this small downside. Also, when creating these classes, we will only need to map the fields that we care about, leaving out things that are returned in the JSON that we have no use for.

The logic to charge the credit card after looking up the books and `BookstoreUser` follows this same convention using a method called `chargeCreditCard` to perform the HTTP call over to the `credit-processing` module. We don't have HTTP routes for this module yet, so I had to add one to handle this call. It's not a very interesting code though, so it won't be shown here. Once the credit charge completes, the actor can finish its work as it did earlier, with no additional changes required.

Refactoring SalesOrderViewBuilder

`SalesOrderViewBuilder` is another class that needs a bit of refactoring work now that we don't have dependencies on other modules. This class will need to make HTTP calls to look up `Book` entities as part of building out the read-model representation of the orders, whereas earlier it was making direct actor calls. The first change involves the declaration of this class, which is as follows:

```
class SalesOrderViewBuilder
extends ViewBuilder[SalesOrderRM]
with SalesOrderReadModel
with OrderJsonProtocol with ServiceConsumer
with ImplicitConnectionContext{
  . . .
}
```

The difference here is that we added the same three mixins that we added to `SalesOrderCreateValidator`, which are `ImplicitConnectionContext`, `ServiceConsumer`, and `OrderJsonProtocol`. We add these mixins for the same reasons as with `SalesOrderCreateValidator`, which we now need to be able to look up and consume HTTP services from within the environment.

The next change to look at is how we are handling the book lookup within the processing of the events. The new code is as follows:

```
val bookLookup =
Flow[SalesOrderLineItemFO].
mapAsyncUnordered(4)(item => findBook(item.bookId )).
fold(Map.empty[String, Book]){
  case (books, Some(b)) => books ++ Map(b.id -> b)
  case (books, other) => books
}
```

The line that was changed is where we use `mapAsyncUnordered` to perform the book lookup. Before, it made a direct actor call via ask. Now, we will use a new method called `findBook` to perform that lookup and return a `Future[Book]`. The code for that new method is as follows:

```
def findBook(id:String):Future[Option[Book]] = {
  import context.dispatcher
  val fut =
  for{
    result <- lookupService("inventory-management")
    if result.uriOpt.isDefined
    requestUri =
    Uri(result.uriOpt.get.toString).
    withPath(Uri.Path("/api") / "book" / id)
    book <- executeHttpRequest[Book](
    HttpRequest(HttpMethods.GET, requestUri))
  } yield Some(book)
  fut.recover{
    case ex:Throwable =>
    log.error(ex, "Error loading book {}", id)
    None
  }
}
```

This method will start by looking up the `inventory-management` service to use for the lookup call. Note that even though we need to do this for every book that is to be looked up, we don't explicitly cache the resulting URI here, in this class. If we explicitly cached that here, and the service moved or becomes unavailable at that URI, we would run into all sorts of problems. Also, we already have a `LocationCache` in place to handle service caching and invalidation, so there is no need to do it here even though that call feels redundant.

If we get a URI back, we will proceed with the lookup call and wrap the result in an `Option` so we can properly represent the case where the lookup fails. We don't want a failed `Future` to fail the entire stream, so we massage failures into a `None` and let the downstream `fold` handle the optionality. Coding things this way makes this stream-based processing more resilient and unlikely to just stop as the result of a failed lookup.

Refactoring the inventory-allocation process

The last piece of work that we need to perform in the `sales-order-processing` module is to refactor how the inventory-allocation process works with the `inventory-management` module. Before, we had a reference to the event classes that drive the two-part allocation process. Now, we don't; so, we will need to make changes around that fact, allowing us to continue to handle these events going forward.

One of the benefits of us using protobuf is that all we need to read a serialized protobuf message is the IDL mappings that were used to create it. Using this IDL, we can create our own copy of the binding classes for the inventory events we need in this module. To make this work, I added a new `inventorydatamodel.proto` file in this project, under `src/main/proto`, with the following content:

```
package com.packt.masteringakka.bookstore.inventory;
option java_outer_classname = "Datamodel";
option optimize_for = SPEED;

message InventoryAllocated{
  required string orderId = 1;
  required int32 amount = 2;
  required string bookId = 3;
}

message InventoryBackordered{
  required string orderId = 1;
  required string bookId = 2;
}
```

The one strange thing to call out here is that the package name we use for the binding class uses inventory as the suffix instead of order. The Akka protobuf serializer that we use saves the full name of the class that was serialized so that it can be reconstituted later. If we want to be able to read those same events in another module, then the name of the binding classes needs to match what was originally saved. It's a small price to pay for the convenience of the built-in protobuf serializer, but I wanted to call it to your attention anyway.

With the binding classes generated to read in these two inventory events, we just need case-class representation for them and the code to map from data model to event model. The custom data model event adapter class we wrote also uses full class names to figure out what class to use when adapting the event. As such, we will need to mimic the structure created on the `inventory-management` side so that we have the right class names in place to perform the adaptation. The classes I created to map the data-model representations to can be found under the `.inventory` package within the `sales-order-processing` module, within the `Book.scala` file. The code for these classes as follows:

```
object Book{
  object Event{
    case class InventoryAllocated(orderId:String,
    bookId:String, amount:Int)
    object InventoryAllocated extends DatamodelReader{
      def fromDatamodel = {
        case ia:Datamodel.InventoryAllocated =>
        InventoryAllocated(ia.getOrderId(),
        ia.getBookId(), ia.getAmount())
      }
    }

    case class InventoryBackordered(orderId:String, bookId:String)
    object InventoryBackordered extends DatamodelReader{
      def fromDatamodel = {
        case ib:Datamodel.InventoryBackordered =>
        InventoryBackordered(ib.getOrderId(), ib.getBookId())
      }
    }
  }
}
```

This entire structure is needed, including the object nesting, in order to properly read the events that we saved on the inventory side of the system. Again, this is an effect of the convenience of the generic data-model adapter we created back in Chapter 4, *Making History with Event Sourcing*. If this methodology doesn't suit you, you don't have to follow the same convention that we did here. I just did it because it was simple and I don't really have a problem with having to mirror the class structure here a little in order to read in the events. It's a small price to pay for the simplicity of our adaptation layer and the flexibility we now get by separating our modules from each other.

One last thing that we need to do to make the inventory-allocation process work is to include the event-tag mappings needed from the inventory-management module in the application.conf file for this module. This is accomplished by adding the following config:

```
cassandra-journal{
  tags = {
    . . .
    inventoryallocated = 2
    inventorybackordered = 2
  }
}
```

When the Cassandra journal plugin queries for events by tag, it needs to know what tag column (tag1, tag2, or tag3) to use for whatever tag value is being queried for. This config lets the plugin figure that out, and we need to pull those mappings over from the `inventory-management` module into this config in order for our event listening to work properly. With all of this new code and config in place, the `OrderStatusEventListener` can now properly listen to and react to the inventory-allocation related events being produced within the `inventory-management` module.

Refactoring the inventory-management module

The `inventory-management` module is the other participant in the two-stage inventory-allocation process. Previously, we cheated a little in how this module listened to events from the `sales-order-processing` module even though it didn't have an explicit project reference to it. We created a trait within the `inventory-management` module called `SalesOrderCreateInfo`, which we then added to the `OrderCreated` event. This allows the inventory side of handling to see the event as `SalesOrderCreateInfo` at compile time with the actual class at runtime being `OrderCreated`. This only worked because we knew we were deploying as a monolith; so, at runtime, we had all of the classes across all of the modules in the same class loader. We don't have that benefit anymore, hence the need for a small refactor.

The refactor here will be the same as what we did with the inventory-allocation process on the `sales-order-processing` side of the system. We will pull in the protobuf mappings for the event from the `sales-order-processing` side that we care about (`OrderCreated`), generate the binding classes for it, and then also pull in the code to map from data model to event model. The protobuf definition that we will pull over into the `inventory-management` system, as `orderdatamodel.proto`, is as follows:

```
package com.packt.masteringakka.bookstore.order;
option java_outer_classname = "Datamodel";
option optimize_for = SPEED;

message SalesOrderLineItem{
  required string bookId = 2;
  required int32 quantity = 3;
}

message SalesOrder {
  required string id = 1;
  repeated SalesOrderLineItem lineItem = 4;
}
```

```
message OrderCreated{
   required SalesOrder order = 1;
}
```

One thing to note here is that we are only pulling in the fields that we are interested in using on this event and not the entire available set of fields. We can do this as long as we keep the numeric-field identifiers the same, which is a useful feature of protobuf.

With this file in place, we can generate the binding classes. After that, we can pull in the event-model classes and data-model adaptation code, which can be found under the `.order` package suffix, and we are in business. Lastly, we will just need to add the tag-mapping config for the `OrderCreated` event into the `application.conf` for this project. We will now have completely refactored the inventory-allocation process to work in a way where the two application modules involved are running in separate JVMs.

Building and deploying the bookstore bundles

At this point, we have all the necessary code changes in place to run the bookstore services within ConductR. Now, all we have to do is build and deploy the bundles using sbt and the ConductR CLI via `sbt-conductr`. The process will be the same for each module, so I will only describe it once—for `inventory-management`—and then you can repeat it across the other three modules. Before doing this however, we want to get the containers for Cassandra and Elasticsearch up and running. To do that, open up a terminal window to the root of the `bookstore-app-complete` folder from the `chapter9` code distribution and run the following command:

```
./launchDataStores.sh
```

Once you have those two containers up and running, you need to start up the ConductR sandbox so that we can deploy our bundles into it. As a reminder, the command to start up the sandbox is as follows:

```
sandbox run <sandbox_version> --nr-of-containers 3
```

Just be sure to replace `<sandbox_version>` with your version of the sandbox that you installed earlier in the section *Setting up the ConductR sandbox*. Here, when starting the sandbox, I've removed the visualization feature in order to save memory across the Docker environment. We'll be scaling our services by a factor of two, so we'll need all of the available memory we can get within our Docker environment.

With all of our containers up and running, we can start the process of building and deploying the bundles. First, we will need to get the common project packaged up and published to our local ivy repository. All of the other projects refer to this dependency, so we will need it in place in order to continue. Open up a terminal window in the common project within the `bookstore-app-complete` project for `chapter9`. When in there, open up an sbt session and run the following commands:

```
> clean
> compile
> publish-local
```

When that completes successfully, you should see an output indicating that it has copied the packaged up common library into your local ivy repository. Now, we can build and deploy the `inventory-management` module. Open up an sbt session in the root of the `inventory-management` project. From within that sbt session, run the following set of commands:

```
> clean
> compile
> bundle:dist
```

When the `bundle:dist` command finishes, you are now ready to load and run the bundle within ConductR. Staying within that sbt session, run the following command to load the bundle:

```
> conduct load <HIT_TAB_KEY>
```

Hitting the *Tab* key at the end will autofill the full path to the bundle that was built in the previous step. Hitting Enter after that will start the process of loading the bundle into the three ConductR nodes so that it can be started up. Once the loading completes, you can start up the bundle with the following command from within sbt:

```
> conduct run --scale 2 <bundle_short_hash>
```

You can get the short hash to plug into that command from the output of the previous step. Once you do this, the `inventory-management` bundle should be up and running in two of the three nodes. You can verify this by running the following command within your sbt session:

```
> conduct info
```

When that finishes, you should see a line in the output that looks like this:

```
ID         NAME     #REP #STR #RUN
7da0f07    inventory   3    0     2
```

Once you have verified that the `inventory-management` bundle is running in two nodes, you can test it via its HTTP API to really make sure things are running as desired. The best way to do this is to create a book and then look it up via its ID. To create a book, open up a terminal window in the `json` folder under the `bookstore-app-complete` folder for this chapter and run the following command:

```
http POST boot2docker:9000/inventory-management/api/book < book.json
```

When executing HTTP calls now, we will use the proxy (HAProxy) that ConductR has set up and let it figure out what node(s) to direct the traffic to. This level of indirection here makes it so that we don't need to know where any individual service is running in order to call it, as long as we know the proxy information that we set up for that service. If this command executes successfully, it should return the full JSON for the book that was created, including the value of the ID field. Grab that ID value (hang on to this for the next section too) and then run the following command:

```
http boot2docker:9000/inventory-management/api/book/<book_id>ss
```

This lookup request should return a JSON similar to what you saw as the result of the book-create request. The last thing to test is that our read model is being created properly. You can test that by performing a query by tag, which will hit our Elasticsearch read model. Execute the following command to test that out:

```
http boot2docker:9000/inventory-management/api/book tag==fiction
```

If the read model is being properly built, then this request should return at least one result, depending on how many books you created before. Look through the results and make sure that you see a record for the book that you just created. If you see it, then you are ready to move on to building and deploying the other modules.

Now we need to repeat the same set of steps we just did to build, bundle, and deploy the `inventory-management` module, but for the other three application modules. Run those same steps for each of the other three modules, in the following order, up to the point where you run `conduct info`:

1. `user-management`
2. `credit-processing`
3. `sales-order-processing`

With all four modules running in ConductR, running the `conduct info` command from within sbt should yield an output similar to the following:

```
ID        NAME      #REP #STR #RUN
d9df61b   user        3    0    2
```

```
d5acf03    credit      3    0    2
e1b90b1    inventory   3    0    2
72cc2ee    order       3    0    2
5821f26    eslite      3    0    1
```

This output lets me know that the four bundles are replicated to all three ConductR nodes and that each one is running on two of the three nodes. When you see output like this, you can move on to testing the functionality of the full set of services running in ConductR.

Testing the bookstore modules in ConductR

In the previous section, we created a new book entity as part of our testing to get the `inventory-management` module up and running. Our ultimate goal of testing things is to create a new `SalesOrder`, and having a book in the system with inventory on it is one of the preconditions to creating that `SalesOrder`. As the book does not yet have an inventory on it, we will need to add one before we can use that book in a `SalesOrder`. The command to add inventory to that book is as follows:

```
http PUT boot2docker:9000/inventory-
management/api/book/<book_id>/inventory/10
```

If you didn't save the book ID from earlier, then just run the lookup by tag query, shown in the previous section, to get the full Book JSON back, and grab the ID from there. Running this command will add the necessary inventory to the book so that we can create `SalesOrders` against it.

The other requirement to create a `SalesOrder` is to have a `BookstoreUser` in the system. You may already have `chris@masteringakka.com`, so you will want to check first and see if you need to create this user. You can do so by making the following request:

```
http boot2docker:9000/user- management/api/user/chris@masteringakka.com
```

If that request returns a `200` status with a `BookstoreUser` JSON response, then you are all set and won't need to create the `BookstoreUser`. If you get a `404` response, then you will need to create the `BookstoreUser`, which is written with the following command:

```
http POST boot2docker:9000/user-management/api/user < user.json
```

Now we are ready to move on to creating the `SalesOrder`. Still within the `json` folder, open up the `order.json` file and replace the `bookId` field value, which currently has a value of `PUT_YOUR_BOOK_ID_HERE`, with the ID of your newly created book from earlier. Then, you can initiate the creation of `SalesOrder` with the following command:

```
http POST boot2docker:9000/sales-order- processing/api/order < order.json
```

If this command executes successfully, then you should bring back the JSON representing the `SalesOrder` that was created, including the ID. A successful `SalesOrder` creation also indicates that the `credit-processing` module is working correctly, as that is a dependency to create a new `SalesOrder`.

The last thing we need to do now is to wait for the inventory allocation process to complete for this order. The first thing we can check for that is to go back and re-look up the book that we attached to this order. What you are looking for is that the `inventoryAmount` field in JSON for that book should drop from 10 to 9. This is the indication that the `inventory-management` module got the `OrderCreated` and has properly deducted the inventory from that book. Next, we can go and look up the newly created `SalesOrder` to see that the `status` field from the single line item has changed from `Unknown` to `Approved`. This is the indication that the `sales-order-processing` module got the `InventoryAllocated` event from the `inventory-management` module and updated its line-item status accordingly. To look up that `SalesOrder`, run the following command:

```
http boot2docker:9000/sales-order-processing/api/order/<order_id>
```

Once you see that the line-item status is updated properly, we can check whether the `SalesOrder` view is being built correctly or not. Run the following request that will hit the `SalesOrder` read model, verifying that it too has been properly updated with the information from the relevant events:

```
http <docker_machine_ip>:9000/sales-order-processing/api/order
bookTag==fiction
```

Take a look at the results there and find the newly created `SalesOrder`, by ID, and make sure that its line-item status is updated properly. Once you see that, then we're done verifying whether the bookstore services are running properly in ConductR or not.

Summary

This is the chapter where we really saw the fruit of all our previous work come together. Our main goal from the beginning had been to separate the application modules so that they were a set of loosely coupled, independent services. We had taken all the steps to facilitate this happening, but it was only with the introduction of ConductR that we were finally able to pull our service modules apart from each other and still have them work together regardless of where each one was deployed.

Throughout the content in this chapter, you learned what ConductR is, and how you can use it to deploy and manage your services across any number of nodes. You also learned how you can leverage the ConductR Scala API code to locate and then consume services throughout the ConductR managed set of nodes. With ConductR, we now have the complete Akka toolset in place to support the microservices architecture that will allow us to scale the bookstore app to meet our future needs.

The journey was a long one, but it's now at its conclusion. We did a lot to the bookstore app, taking it from something basic that wouldn't scale well all the way to a very flexible set of microservices. Throughout the chapters of this book, you've gotten a better understanding of the full set of tools that Akka has to offer and how you can leverage them to build loosely coupled services. With this new knowledge under your belt, you are now well on your way to mastering Akka!

10
Troubleshooting and Best Practices

It's been a long, and somewhat winding journey to get here, but now we've completed all of the refactoring goals that we set up back in Chapter 1, *Building a Better Reactive App*. At the beginning of our journey, we had an application that was an inflexible monolith, which was not likely to scale well. Now, we have a set of small, loosely coupled, independent service modules with a high scalability profile.

As part of our journey, you learned a bunch of new skills related to some of the newer offerings within the Akka platform. This was a guided journey that was purpose built to help you better master the entire Akka platform. You now know how to build scalable, reactive application components with things such as persistence, streams, Akka HTTP, and clustering.

With these skills under your belt, you are ready to employ them for yourself within your own apps and services. As such, it's always good to know the best practices for those tools and how to troubleshoot them if/when things go wrong. We'll be covering that kind of information within this chapter, as well as providing a quick retrospective of the changes we made to the initial bookstore application. In this chapter, you can expect to learn about the following topics:

- How our progressive refactoring solved the issues from Chapter 1, *Building a Better Reactive App*
- Troubleshooting and best practices to code Akka actors
- Troubleshooting and best practices for Akka HTTP
- Troubleshooting and best practices for Akka Clustering/Remoting

Refactoring retrospective

Throughout the previous chapters, we chipped away at the issues outlined in `Chapter 1`, *Building a Better Reactive App*, in an effort to build a more scalable and flexible set of application components. With each successive refactoring, which involved a new tool from the Akka platform, we helped improve the scalability profile of the bookstore app. The main goal was to end up with independent service components, which was finally achieved in `Chapter 9`, *Managing Deployments with ConductR*, with the introduction of ConductR. With our work now complete, it makes sense to go over what we did in each chapter, and how that contributed to the final set of components that we have now.

Coding better actors

The work we did in `Chapter 2`, *Simplifying Concurrent Programming with Actors*, wasn't directly related to solving scalability concerns, but it was important nonetheless. In this chapter, you learned how to identify poorly coded actors, ones that were too dependent on nested Futures and weren't fully leveraging the features of Akka.

Leveraging Akka's FSM feature, we coded a workflow-like set of state changes for the somewhat complex process of creating a new order. The resulting actor was easier to reason about and was a much better use of actors. By being more reliant on its mailbox instead of a bunch of nested Futures (that don't use the mailbox), the code for that actor will avoid some common pitfalls of mixing Futures and actors.

This chapter also introduced us to the concept of testing our actors. You learned the different levels of testing within the testing pyramid, and how each one is important in the total testing of the products you produce. You also learned how to use Akka's testing facilities, namely `TestKit`, `TestActorRef`, and `TestProbe`, to apply unit testing to our actors. Automated testing is extremely important in remaining agile and being able to continuously deliver new products and features to your users, hence the focus on it in this chapter.

Using Domain-driven design

In Chapter 3, *Curing Anemic Models with Domain-Driven Design*, you learned about the concept of **Domain-driven design** (**DDD**), and how it can help us design and build code more coupled to our business domain. Using DDD, we were able to build a richer model where the core-business entities themselves—Book, BookstoreUser, and so on—became more central to the code and the ubiquitous language used to discuss that code. The work done here was also a good precursor to the event sourcing work done in Chapter 4, *Making History with Event Sourcing*, as it got us thinking of business entities as the central point of our code.

Akka Persistence and event sourcing

Chapter 4, *Making History with Event Sourcing*, is really where the big refactoring effort began. In this chapter, we were able to clean up a bunch of issues identified in Chapter 1, *Building a Better Reactive App*. By switching to an event-sourced model, we got rid of our relational database and some of the problems we had in our usage of it. Instead of having poorly scaling, cross-domain transactions, such as decrementing inventory as part of an order, we ended up with a high-performance append-only means of persistence that was based on domain events instead of the current state of an entity.

Using these events, we were then able to follow a two-part action and reaction type approach to inventory allocation, which will scale better than the transaction approach used before. This in-memory event approach laid the groundwork to use persistent events, via Persistence Query, to perform side-effecting in the next chapter. Additionally, using protobuf as our serialization framework allows us to evolve the event model as necessary, by making backwards compatible changes to the IDL, and supports one module-reading event from another as long as it has the IDL. This will serve to allow us to completely separate the modules later on.

Lastly, PostgreSQL was a single point of failure in our system that we were able to eliminate by replacing it with Cassandra. Cassandra has high write performance, which fits our append-only event-sourced model very well. It is also highly available, being able to run in a masterless cluster where the data is replicated and follows a tunable consistency model. Cassandra is a great foundation to build on top of. It's a datastore that will truly scale along with the business.

Akka Persistence Query and CQRS

One of the nice things about a relational database is that it straddles the line between read and write concerns. It's a model that works well both for writing data to the backing store, and for reading that same data via rich query capabilities. When we switched over to event sourcing, we tilted ourselves over to a model that is more about writing than reading. By storing events instead of the current state of an entity, we lost the ability to query our entities to support bulk lookup-type calls. As such, building out a separate read model became a necessity for our application.

In Chapter 5, *Separating Concerns with CQRS*, we introduced the concept of **Command Query Responsibility Segregation** (**CQRS**), and how we will apply it to build out separate read models in Elasticsearch. The primary mechanism that we employed to build out the read models was to use Akka Persistence Query to listen to events from our persistent entities, by tag. Using those events, we were able to build out current state representations in Elasticsearch that we can then query against. Elasticsearch is also highly scalable, being clustered, replicated, and highly available, so it's a good compliment to Cassandra, which is handling our write model.

We also leveraged Persistence Query here to enhance our inventory allocation process. In Chapter 4, *Making History with Event Sourcing*, the events were in-memory, using Akka's event bus. That was a temporary solution as both sides of the system had to be up at all times together (which is not realistic) in order to work. Using Persistence Query, and resumable projections, we were able to build a robust system of using events to allocate inventory and mark order line items as approved or backordered.

Akka Streams

In Chapter 6, *Going with the Flow with Akka Streams*, you learned all about Akka Streams, and how it has its roots in the Reactive Streams initiative. Akka Streams allow us to build out back-pressure oriented, stream-based processes. This type of approach is great for avoiding issues such as out of memory problems due to reading in too much data or swamping slow downstream resources because they are having trouble keeping up with the flow of data.

The work we did in Chapter 6, *Going with the Flow with Akka Streams*, did not directly address an issue with the initial bookstore application, but it did fix some of the stuff we did with Persistence Query in Chapter 5, *Separating Concerns with CQRS*. In this chapter, we made better use of Akka Streams when processing the results of an event query via Persistence Query.

We also set up the stream handling to better respond to back-pressure, both when updating Elasticsearch, and when updating the offset value in our resumable projections. This will make our inventory allocation process more robust and less likely to run into issues when one of those downstream components, such as Elasticsearch or Cassandra, is having trouble keeping up with the data flow.

Akka HTTP

The main focus of `Chapter 7`, *REST Easy with Akka HTTP*, was updating our HTTP library usage from dispatch and unfiltered to Akka HTTP. Akka HTTP is a much more modern HTTP library that is part of the Akka platform. As Akka is the foundation of our application, having an HTTP library, which not only works well with it, but is actually part of it, is a big win. We will virtually eliminate the risk of one library evolving in such a way that it no longer plays well with the other. We will also do away with the scare that one library starts to bring in a transitive dependency that conflicts with the other library. Our usage of Akka and HTTP will continue to evolve together, which is not something we can say about dispatch and unfiltered.

Besides just library management, using Akka HTTP, which is built on top of Akka Streams, allows us to incorporate back-pressure into our usage of HTTP. On the inbound side, this means that we can build RESTful APIs that will support back-pressure signals from the downstream resources that handle the requests. On the outbound side, it means that we can make calls to things such as Elasticsearch in a back-pressure sensitive manner, which we did when we tied `Flow` to update the index for our `ViewBuilders` into the `Flow` that was processing our persistent events.

Akka Remoting and Akka Clustering

In `Chapter 4`, *Making History with Event Sourcing*, and `Chapter 5`, *Separating Concerns with CQRS*, we introduced components that won't work well in a multi-server deployment without some sort of coordination across the servers. In `Chapter 4`, *Making History with Event Sourcing*, this was our event-sourced persistent entities. As each individual entity instance was held in memory after it was recovered, until being passivated, we ran the risk of multiple-server nodes loading the same entity instance, each with a different state. We needed a way to make sure that each entity instance was only active in one server instance at a time, and all calls for that instance were directed to that server no matter where they initially started out. We achieved this using Akka's Cluster Sharding feature, with Akka now managing what `Shard` and `ShardRegion` each entity instance rolls up under.

In Chapter 5, *Separating Concerns with CQRS*, when we implemented our ViewBuilders, we introduced another component that won't work well in a multi-server environment. If these ViewBuilders started up in every node, then they would all be trying to process the same events against Elasticsearch at the same time, leading to issues. We need these components to always be running in a single node, even if the node that they were originally running in goes down. We are able to achieve this goal using the Cluster Singleton pattern within Akka, eliminating the potential issue of our ViewBuilders running in multiple nodes concurrently.

Separating the modules via ConductR

Up until Chapter 9, *Managing Deployments with ConductR*, even though we did a lot of refactoring work to support separating our modules, we were still building and running them all together as a monolith. If we were to split up the modules, we'd have the problem of a service from one module needing a service from another, and not knowing where to find it. We can try and solve this using Akka clustering features to look up and remotely send messages to actors that were deployed somewhere in the cluster. But this will require us to share code across the modules that were communicating together, creating the kind of coupling that we are trying to move away from. We wanted a solution based on calling other modules over HTTP, and ConductR allows us to do just that.

Using ConductR, we get a system to package and deploy our application modules over a set of server nodes. This certainly made it easy to deploy things in a highly available manner from an easy to use CLI via sbt. But, it also provided us with a way to locate services within the ConductR managed environment and then invoke them over HTTP. This was the last big hurdle in getting our services to run as independent, loosely-coupled modules, and ConductR enabled us to get over it.

Now, we have a set of application components that can evolve and scale independently from each other. We've removed single points of failure in our architecture, replacing them with highly available and highly scalable resources instead. We have a very solid foundation to build on, which consists of the following stack:

- Akka actors as the main component-building block
- Event sourcing via Akka Persistence/Cassandra for entities
- CQRS via Akka Persistence Query, Akka Streams, and Elasticsearch
- Akka HTTP to build and consume RESTful APIs
- Akka Clustering to manage entities and singleton components
- ConductR for deployment management and service location

Throughout this journey, we took a pretty grand tour through some of the newer features of the Akka platform. At this point, you're well on your way to mastering a lot more of what Akka has to offer. I'll arm you with a few more pointers over the next set of sections. Then, you are ready unleash this newfound knowledge on the world, building out your own scalable, reactive applications on top of Akka.

Troubleshooting and best practices for actors

Even though we are using some of the newer features of Akka, Akka actors themselves are still the core building block on our new stack. As such, it's important to know some of the most common **gotchas** when using actors, as well as some best practices. I'll use my experiences with Akka to present that information to you in this section in an effort to help you write good actors and avoid some common pitfalls in the process.

Avoid closing over mutable state with Futures

This one is sort of the cardinal sin of actors, and I'm sure it's been discussed a million times over on the Internet, but I'm including it anyway because it can cause all sorts of problems if not properly respected. You should never use or modify some sort of mutable state that is part of an actor within the body of any high-order function-based call on a `Future`, such as `map`, `flatMap`, `onComplete`, and so on. Consider the following example:

```
object UnsafeActor{
  def props = Props[UnsafeActor]
  case object GetCount
  case object UpdateCount
}

class UnsafeActor extends Actor{
  import UnsafeActor._
  import context.dispatcher
  import akka.pattern.pipe
  var count = 0

  def receive = {
    case GetCount =>
      sender() ! count

    case UpdateCount =>
      Future{0}.
```

```
    onComplete{
      case tr =>
        count = count + 1
    }

    sender() ! count
  }
}
```

In this actor, we will have code in the handling of `UpdateCount` that updates the mutable `count` variable from within the callback of a `Future`, which is not safe. As that `onComplete` will execute in a separate thread from the main dispatcher, it's possible that two threads are concurrently trying to update that `Int` at the same time, which can lead to inconsistent behavior. As incrementing the `Int` essentially reads the current value first and then adds one to it, it's possible that multiple threads read the same value at the same time. This makes it possible for both to add one to the same number, causing you to miss one of the increments.

When you close over a mutable state like this with a `Future`, you eliminate one of the best guarantees from an actor; in that, it will only ever process one message from its mailbox at a time. That guarantee allows you to update the `Int` from within the mailbox safely, never missing any increment operation. If you need to update some internal state after executing a `Future`, then you will need to send a message back to yourself to do so within the context of the mailbox, as shown in the following example:

```
case UpdateCount =>
Future{0}.
onComplete{
  case tr =>
    self ! FinishUpdate
}

sender() ! count

case FinishUpdate =>
count = count + 1
```

If you needed the increments to update the count after the `Future` completes, but before any other subsequent message is processed, then use a combination of stash and receive swapping, as follows:

```
case UpdateCount =>
 Future{0}.onComplete{
   case tr =>
   self ! FinishUpdate
```

```
}

context.become{
  case FinishUpdate =>
  count = count + 1
  unstashAll
  context.unbecome

  case other =>
  stash
}
sender() ! Count
```

In this version of the code, we will process an update and then switch into a receive that is waiting for the `FinishUpdate` message before allowing any other inbound messages to be processed. If we get anything else before the `FinishUpdate`, we will stash it. Once we get the `FinishUpdate` message, we can unstash any stashed messages that we couldn't handle previously before going back to the standard receive handling functionality. An approach like this ensures that we process the complete `UpdateCount`, including the `Future`-based message back to self, before processing the next message in the mailbox.

Avoiding closing over the sender

The advice to avoid closing over a mutable state goes double for the sender of the message, which is made available via the `sender()` method. A lot of times, people will perform work in an actor that involves a `Future` and when done, in a callback on the `Future`, try and send something back to the sender via `sender()`. The problem with this approach is that once in the callback for the `Future`, the actor has already moved onto the next message in the mailbox, if there is one, and has updated the mutable variable returned from calls to `sender()`. This means that you will either respond to the wrong sender, or more likely, respond to a dead letter if there is no current message being processed when you use `sender()` in your callback. Consider the following unsafe example:

```
def receive = {
  case _ =>
  import context.dispatcher
  Future{0}.
  onComplete{
    case tr =>
    sender() ! "foo"
  }
}
```

This code will not work as expected and will probably result in a lot of dead letters. If you want to safely send a message back to the correct sender, then there are two basic options. The first is to capture the sender in a variable before the callback on the Future, like this:

```
def receive = {
  case _ =>
  import context.dispatcher
  val originator = sender()
  Future{0}.
  onComplete{
    case tr =>
    originator ! "foo"
  }
}
```

Here, we grab the value of the current sender, before the Future kicks in, and assign it to a val that won't change from underneath us. Then, we will use that new val inside of the callback instead of using sender().

The other way is to use the pipe pattern, is as follows:

```
def receive = {
  case _ =>
  import context.dispatcher
  import akka.pattern.pipe
  Future{0}.
  map{ _ =>
    "foo"
  }.
  pipeTo(sender())
}
```

With this approach, we ensure that the correct sender is captured in the call to pipeTo, which executes in the current thread and before any callbacks happen on the Future. Under the hood, this captured sender is then made available after all of the callbacks have completed on the Future, ensuring that the response is routed back to the correct sender.

Minimize your use of ActorSelection

I always do my best to minimize the user of `ActorSelection` within my Akka projects. The reason is that it requires knowing the full path to the actor you want to communicate with to be embedded in the code that needs to use that actor. This can lead to lots of references to actor paths throughout your code if you are not careful, and since paths can change, you can end up with a lot of work tracking down and updating paths when they do.

Also, there is a cost associated with searching through the actor system to find matching actors for the path supplied to `ActorSelection`. This cost is proportional to the number of actor instances you have in your system, so frequent usage of `ActorSelection` against a system with a lot of actor instances in it can be a performance problem.

You can still use `ActorSelection` if you want to broadcast a message to a set of actors with a wildcarded path. You will also need it when using remoting to look up and invoke a remote actor. You should do your best to limit using it to these two cases.

So, how will you use one actor from another if you don't use `ActorSelection`? The best approach is to try and introduce an `ActorRef` to an actor instance that needs it. You can do this by supplying `ActorRef` to the constructor of the actor instance that wants to use it. You can also send that `ActorRef` to the actor instance that needs it via a message. These are the two most popular approaches to get two actors to work together without using `ActorSelection`.

Use tell instead of ask

The `ask` feature of Akka, which is represented by the `?` operator, is another feature that can be overused by developers. The problems with `ask`, to me, are twofold:

- It introduces the overhead of having to create a short-lived actor instance to receive the response from the actor being called to allow the Future to be completed.
- It will start you down the path of having a lot of mixing of actors and Futures, which is not a good practice as it can lead to issues such as closing over mutable state.

For me, the bigger issue there is the second one, as I feel heavy mixing of actors and Futures is a real anti-pattern. If you do perform a stateful request or response-style communication between your actors, then consider the following possible approaches instead of using `ask`:

- Use a short-lived actor and either `context.become` or FSM, as we did with the `SalesOrderCreateValidator` actor. In this approach, you can send a message via `tell` and then switch state to wait for the response back, holding onto the original sender so you can respond to them if necessary. You will still incur the actor creation overhead here, as with `ask`, but you won't run into problems with Futures.

- Forward messages back and forth, sending the full state back and forth between the actors as well so that when you receive the response back, you have enough information to complete the request. Forwarding here assures that you can hang onto the original sender when you get your response back. This approach avoids the overhead of creating short-lived actors, but is a little clunkier in that you may have to send a lot of state back and forth, which you can just keep internally when using short-lived actors.

Avoid creating a lot of top-level actors

A top-level actor is one whose parent is the root/user actor. Creating actor instances at this level is far more costly than creating actor instances that are nested further down the tree. You should try and use an approach where you have very few top-level actors that are nesting multiple levels of children underneath them. This type of structure creates a good, proper supervision tree, which those few top-level actors act as the top of the supervision tree for certain systems.

For example, each module in our application can have a top-level supervisor actor and any children, or grandchildren, will roll up under that supervisor. This will be a good way to build out a supervision tree and avoid having to create a lot of top-level actors.

Troubleshooting and best practices for Akka HTTP

When using Akka HTTP, there are a few best practices and a troubleshooting tip that I'd like to share with you. With the information in this section, you will be better equipped to employ Akka HTTP within your codebase.

Trouble with the tilde

Back in `Chapter 7`, *REST Easy with Akka HTTP*, when discussing the high-level Inbound HTTP API, we talked about composing routes together with the tile operator (~). At the end of the section titled *Composing directives together*, I gave a tip about forgetting to include the ~ and the effect it can have. Here, I'll provide a more concrete example of this problem and the symptom you will see when you encounter it. Consider the following set of routes that you set up to handle your inbound requests:

```
pathPrefix("book"){
   (get & path(Segment)){ id =>
     . . .
   }
   (post & entity(as[CatalogNewBook])){ req =>
     . . .
   }
}
```

The intention here was to set up two routes under the `"book"` root path-one to handle a GET request to lookup a book by ID, and the other, a POST request to create a new `Book` entity. With these routes setup, I start up my server and make the following HTTP request: `http :8080/book/abc-123`

When I make this request, instead of getting an `OK` (200 status code) response and some JSON, I get a `Not Found` (404 status code) error instead. Confused, I go back and look at my routes and see that I forgot to include the ~ between the two route definitions. By doing this, the GET route definition is ignored and only the POST is returned as the inner route of the `pathPrefix` root. It's a simple fix by just adding the ~ operator between the routes. This should be the first thing you look at when you run into issues where the routes you clearly see in the code are not being respected when you try and invoke them.

Building an inbound HTTP request log

Most of the application servers out there, such as Tomcat, Jetty, and JBoss, come with built-in HTTP request logging. This easily allows you to see what requests came into the system, how long they took to service, and what status code they returned. Information such as this can easily be mined to produce metrics about the HTTP requests your server is handling, things such as average request time and number of unsuccessful status codes. Akka HTTP doesn't come with this functionality out of the box, but it's pretty easy to add, and should be something you do if you decide to use it.

Let's start by defining the fields that will be represented in our log, and will be based on the **Common Log Format (CLF)** standard:

- IP address of the incoming TCP connection
- The RFC 1413 identity of the client, which will always be a hyphen, as we won't use this field
- The user ID of the caller
- The date and time the request was made
- The request information, including request method, path, query string, and the HTTP protocol used
- The status code of the response
- The response content length
- The time it took to service the request in milliseconds

The first seven fields there are from the CLF specification. The eighth field is extra, which is added by me, as I think it's a good piece of information to have so you can build metrics around average response times. Using the CLF will allow you to use a bunch of preexisting tools to mine these logs and produce analytics and charts from them.

With the format nailed down, we can start working on the code to make our access log work. All of the code that I'm about to show is in the `RequestLogExample.scala` file in the `samples` code folder for this chapter. The first thing in that code example to look at is a new directive that we will create to use in our routing tree to handle access logging, which is defined as follows:

```
def accessLogging(userId:String, log:LoggingAdapter):Directive0 = {
  extractClientIP.flatMap{ ip =>
    logRequestResult(
      LoggingMagnet(_ => requestTimeThenLog(ip, userId, log))
    )
  }
}
```

We know we need the caller's IP for the log line, so the first thing we will do in here is leverage the preexisting `extractCallerIP` directive to get us that information. Once we have the IP, we will use another preexisting directive called `logRequestResult`, which takes an instance of `LoggingMagnet`. `LoggingMagnet` needs an instance of a function of type `HttpRequest => (Any => Unit)`, which we will satisfy by calling a custom method called `requestTimeThenLog`, which is as follows:

```
def requestTimeThenLog(ip:RemoteAddress, userId:String,
log:LoggingAdapter):HttpRequest => (Any => Unit) = {
  val requestTime = System.currentTimeMillis()
  buildLogString(log, requestTime, ip, userId) _
}
```

Here, we will log the time before the request is completely executed so that we can gauge how much time elapses in servicing the call. Then, we will call another custom method called `buildLogString`, which will be invoked by Akka HTTP at the time of a request to give us the remaining information needed (`HttpRequest`, `HttpResponse`) to complete the log line. That method is as follows:

```
def buildLogString(loggingAdapter:LoggingAdapter,
requestTimestamp: Long, ip:RemoteAddress,
userId:String, level:Logging.LogLevel = Logging.InfoLevel)
(req: HttpRequest)(res: Any): Unit = {

  val elapsed = System.currentTimeMillis() - requestTimestamp
  val (status, contentLength) = res match {
    case RouteResult.Complete(resp) =>
    val length = resp.entity.contentLengthOption.getOrElse(0)
    (resp.status.intValue, length)
    case RouteResult.Rejected(reason) =>
    //Should't get here due to explicit handleRejections in tree
    //but need to handle anyway
    (0, 0)
  }

  val ipAddress =
  ip.toOption.map(_.getHostAddress()).getOrElse("0.0.0.0")
  val dateTime = ZonedDateTime.now().format(formatter)
  val path = req.uri.path
  val params =
  req.uri.queryString(Charset.defaultCharset()).
  map(q => s"?$q").getOrElse("")
  val proto = req.protocol.value

  val logLine = s"""$ipAddress - $userId [$dateTime]
"${req.method.name()} $path$params $proto" $status    $contentLength
$elapsed"""
  LogEntry(logLine, level).logTo(loggingAdapter)
}
```

Inside this method, we will build out the log line using the request and response information and then log that line to the `LoggingAdapter` that we specifically set up for the access log. With all of this code in place, we can use this new directive in the routing tree like this:

```
parameter('sessionToken.?){ tokenOpt =>
  identifyUser(tokenOpt){ userIdOpt =>
    accessLogging(userIdOpt.getOrElse("-"), accessLog){
      handleRejections(RejectionHandler.default){
        path("api" / "book" / Segment){ bookId =>
          complete(Book(bookId, "This is a test"))
        }
      }
    }
  }
}
```

In this sample route, the `identifyUser` directive will be something that is defined by you to take some input (I'm using a parameter called `sessionToken` here) and then identify the user for the call. Once we have that, we can apply the `accessLogging` directive into the routing tree. Note that I'm explicitly using `handleRejections` right under the `accessLogging` directive. I'm doing this so that any rejections from internal routes get properly transformed into `HttpResponse` instances before hitting the logging code. Doing this ensures that I have the right status code for a rejected request, and makes sure that the rejected requests are logged the same way as the ones that were accepted.

If you want to play with this access-logging sample, you can do so by opening an sbt session into the root of the `chapter10/samples` folder and running the following command:

> **runMain code.RequestLogExample**

This will start up the server and get it ready to receive requests. Once that's done, open another terminal window and tail the `access.log` file that is created inside of the `samples` folder. Lastly, issue the following request against the server: `http :8080/api/book/abc-123 sessionToken=def-456`

When that request executes, you should see the access-logging line appear in the window that is tailing `access.log`, verifying that our new access-logging code is working correctly. This example should serve as a decent guide on what you will need to do to get access logging working in your production code with Akka HTTP. There are some gaps to fill in for sure, such as identifying the caller, but it should be a decent starting point.

Building an outbound HTTP request log

If you're going to make a lot of outbound HTTP calls from your code, it's a good idea to log those calls, just like with the inbound HTTP calls we did in the previous section. We'll use an approach here, where we use the same log format as the inbound access log so that these logs can be mined in the same way. Let's start by taking a look at the signature of the method that will perform the actual logging after an outbound request completes:

```
def logCall[T](startTime:Long, userId:String,
request:Option[HttpRequest])
(result:(Try[HttpResponse], T)):(Try[HttpResponse], T) = {
  . . .
}
```

This method is set up to take in the initial start time of a request as well as the user ID of the person who is responsible for the outbound call being made. It also takes in an optional `HttpRequest` representing the call that was made. We will set this up as optional so that we can support a multi-call flow where we need to look up the original request based on the identifier tied to it, which we will see in a moment. The call also takes the result of host-pool based request, which is a `(Try[HttpResponse], T)`. This type will support using the host-level API and the flow-based variant of the request-level API. We'll add a helper method to get it to work with the connection-level API later.

Now, let's take a look at the code body inside that method, which is as follows:

```
val response = result._1
val elapsed = System.currentTimeMillis() - startTime
(request, response) match{
  case (Some(req), util.Success(resp)) =>
  val host = req.uri.authority.host
  val status = resp.status.intValue
  val contentLength =
  resp.entity.contentLengthOption.getOrElse(0)
  val dateTime = ZonedDateTime.now().format(formatter)
  val path = req.uri.path
  val params =
  req.uri.queryString(Charset.defaultCharset()).
  map(q => s"?$q").getOrElse("")
  val proto = req.protocol.value

  val logLine = s"""$host - $userId [$dateTime]    "${req.method.name()}
$path$params $proto" $status    $contentLength $elapsed"""
  externalCallLog.info(logLine)

  case (req, resp) =>
  //Error logging goes here
```

```
   . . .
}
result
```

The code here is similar to what we did with the inbound access log. We will take pieces of the request and response and use them to form the log line. That line is then logged using `LoggingAdapter`, which will be set up to log to a file called `externalcalls.log`.

An example of using this method to log a single external call with the request-level API is as follows:

```
val connPool = Http().superPool[Int]()
val time1 = System.currentTimeMillis()
val request = HttpRequest(HttpMethods.GET, "http://akka.io")

Source.single((request, 1)).via(connPool).
map(logCall(time1, "abc123", Some(request))).runWith(Sink.head)
```

In this example, we will get a reference to the request-level API's super pool using an `Int` as the request identifier. The code then makes a request through that pool and then adds a `map` stage to hook in the call to perform logging.

This same logging method will also work if you were sending multiple outbound requests, as shown in the following example:

```
val time2 = System.currentTimeMillis()
val request2 = HttpRequest(HttpMethods.GET,
"http://stackoverflow.com/users/2311148/cmbaxter")
val requests = Map(1 -> request, 2 -> request2)
Source(requests.toList.map(t => (t._2, t._1))).via(connPool).
map(r => logCall(time2, "abc123", requests.get(r._2))(r)).
runFold(Map.empty[Int, util.Try[HttpResponse]]){
  case(m, r) => m ++ Map(r._2 -> r._1)
  }
```

With this multi-request approach, we will store the requests in a `Map` so that we can pair them up with their responses for the purpose of logging. This allows us to call the logging method, getting the request for the response being processed by looking for it in the `Map`. This approach is the reason why the request parameter is optional on our logging method as, even though the request should be in the `Map`, it's not a guarantee.

You can also use this logging method when sending out requests via the connection-level API but adding a simple helper method to pass along the response information, which is not wrapped in a `Try`, to the `logCall` method. That helper method is as follows:

```
def logSimpleCall(startTime:Long, userId:String,
request:HttpRequest)(result:HttpResponse):HttpResponse = {
  logCall(startTime, userId, Some(request))((util.Success(result),    1))
  result
}
```

With this method in place, we can perform external call logging using the connection-level API, as follows:

```
val time3 = System.currentTimeMillis()
val conn = Http().outgoingConnection("stackoverflow.com")
Source.single(request2).via(conn).
map(logSimpleCall(time3, "abc123", request2)).
runWith(Sink.head)
```

Adding this helper method also allows you to log external calls when using the `Future` based variant of the request-level API. An example of that is as follows:

```
val time4 = System.currentTimeMillis()
Http().singleRequest(request2).
andThen{
  case util.Success(resp) =>
  logSimpleCall(time4, "abc123", request2)(resp)
}
```

This full set of examples, as well as the logging code, can be found in `ExternalCallLogExample.scala` within the `samples` project for this chapter. If you want to run this set of examples, you can open an sbt session into the root of the `samples` project and run the following command:

```
> runMain code.ExternalCallLogExample
```

When the program completes, you can open `externalcall.log`, which will be in the same directory where you ran the program. Inside that file, you should see the log lines produced from the five total calls made by this example program.

Like the access log example, this is by no means a finished product, but it's a decent starting point on how to get external call logging working within your code.

Troubleshooting and best practices for Akka Clustering/Akka Remoting

When using Akka's remoting or clustering features, there are a few things you should be aware of to avoid common issues. The following few sections will lay out some best practices and tips to use those two features.

Prefer using IP addresses over host names in config

If you are going to explicitly set up your cluster seed nodes, if not using ConductR, then you should use the IP addresses of your nodes in the config versus their host names. The same goes for looking up or deploying actors to a remote system via remoting. This advice goes double if you are in the cloud. The reason is that a blip or issue with DNS will cause the failure detector to think a node is not available when it clearly is still up and running. If the DNS problem persists, then the node will eventually get quarantined, and you will need to restart it even if the DNS issue clears.

Using IP addresses of your clustering or remoting config, instead of host names, you can take DNS out of the picture. Taking a step like this will help keep your cluster healthy even if there are transient DNS issues.

Configuring more than one seed node

Again, if you are not using ConductR and you are manually configuring your cluster, you should make sure you have more than one seed node configured. If you only configure one seed node, and that seed node happens to be down, no other nodes can join the cluster. By having at least two seed nodes, you mitigate the risk of a single seed node being down and the effect it can have on getting new nodes into the cluster.

Disassociated exceptions in the logs can be normal

When a node within your cluster goes down, even if it was a planned shutdown, the other nodes will start to log disassociated exceptions as their failure detectors start to kick in and see that node as unreachable. This is all pretty normal and not something to get too worried about as long as it's during a planned shutdown of a node. That node ID will eventually be quarantined, meaning that the other nodes will stop checking on it. When the node comes back up, it will have a new node ID and will join back into the cluster as normal.

The time to worry about disassociated exceptions is when they start to pile up in your nodes during a time when you were not shutting down a node. This means that a node has become unreachable for other reasons, such as long GC pauses maybe or network issues, and will potentially be quarantined if that unreachable state persists. So, don't ignore them completely, just be aware that they aren't always the harbinger of doom as long as you know you are stopping a node.

Further reading

With our journey now officially complete, I wanted to leave you with a few suggested reading items. Use these links to continue to expand your knowledge of what's out there within the Akka ecosystem. I wish you well in your future endeavors with Akka; it's truly been a pleasure working with you throughout this book.

Lagom

The Lightbend team recently released a new Java microservices framework called Lagom. This framework uses a lot of the same stack that we used in this book, namely Akka, Akka Persistence/event sourcing, CQRS, Akka Streams, and clustering and Cassandra, with ConductR also being supported. It's just a Java framework for now, but Scala support may be coming in the future. It's definitely a framework to keep an eye on for sure if you are into reactive microservices built on top of Akka:

- `http://www.lagomframework.com`

Akka Streams cookbook

This really is a great section from the Akka Streams documents. There are a ton of use cases in here to apply Akka Streams to solve real-world problems. I learned quite a bit by giving it a read, and I'm hoping you can as well:

- `http://doc.akka.io/docs/akka/current/scala/stream/stream-cookbook.html`

How to and common patterns

This is another great section from the Akka documents. In this section, you can find a lot of great patterns that people have developed as best practices to solve problems with Akka. You should read through all of the patterns here, and I'm willing to bet that you will find a couple that are of use to you:

- `http://doc.akka.io/docs/akka/current/scala/howto.html`

Akka Persistence schema evolution

If you're going to go all-in on Event Sourcing, then knowing how to handle schema evolution will be critical to your success. We covered this topic a bit in `Chapter 4`, *Making History with Event Sourcing*, but there are more patterns and techniques to learn on this important subject. It would be a good idea to read through Akka's documentation on the subject in more detail as it's far more thorough than what we discussed in this book:

- `http://doc.akka.io/docs/akka/current/scala/persistence-schema-evolution.html`

Other Akka books to consider reading

If you are interested in reading some more books about Akka, then there are two that I can suggest here for you. The first is *Reactive Design Patterns* by Roland Kuhn, with Brian Hanafee and Jamie Allen. This is a great book by Roland Kuhn, who was, up until recently, the CTO for Lightbend. It helps to lay out some great patterns that you can use with Akka to build out reactive applications. The other book is *Effective Akka* by Jamie Allen. This is not a long book, but it's packed with great tips and tricks on how to best make use of Akka actors. The links for those two books are as follows:

- https://www.manning.com/books/reactive-design-patterns
- http://shop.oreilly.com/product/6369228789.do

Domain-driven design by Eric Evans

If you are really into learning more about DDD, then you should check out the book of the same name by Eric Evans. This is really the gospel on DDD; an absolute must for anyone who wants to go deeply down that path:

- https://www.amazon.com/Domain-Driven-Design-Tackling-Complexity-Software/dp/321125215.

Martin Fowler on event sourcing

If you want to learn more of the hows and whys of event sourcing, then Martin Fowler is your guy. He provides a ton of information on where this pattern fits well and where it does not. I've provided a link to a post from his personal site, where he goes into great detail about event sourcing:

- http://martinfowler.com/eaaDev/EventSourcing.html

Summary

In this chapter, we did a quick summary of all the refactoring work we did throughout this book. It was a nice way to revisit our concerns from the first chapter, and how we alleviated them with features from the Akka toolkit.

We then discussed some tips and tricks for various parts of the Akka toolkit. We talked about the dangers of using Futures in actors and closing over mutable state. We also covered things like how to build out inbound and outbound HTTP logs for your Akka HTTP components, and some general best practices when using Akka Remoting and/or Akka Clustering.

We closed out the chapter with a discussion of some future reading materials to help expand on what we covered within this book. Hopefully this material will be useful to you as you continue your journey to master the complete Akka toolkit. Using all of your newfound knowledge, you should now be ready to start building your own scalable and reactive components on top of the complete Akka toolkit.

Index

44547613R00243

Made in the USA
Middletown, DE
10 June 2017